THE BEFORE AND THE AFTER

Before you start to read this book, take this moment to think about making a donation to punctum books, an independent non-profit press,

@ https://punctumbooks.com/support/

If you're reading the e-book, you can click on the image below to go directly to our donations site. Any amount, no matter the size, is appreciated and will help us to keep our ship of fools afloat. Contributions from dedicated readers will also help us to keep our commons open and to cultivate new work that can't find a welcoming port elsewhere. Our adventure is not possible without your support.

Vive la Open Access.

Fig. 1. Detail from Hieronymus Bosch, *Ship of Fools* (1490–1500)

THE BEFORE AND THE AFTER: CRITICAL ASYNCHRONY NOW. Copyright © 2024 by the editors and authors. This work carries a Creative Commons BY-NC-SA 4.0 International license, which means that you are free to copy and redistribute the material in any medium or format, and you may also remix, transform, and build upon the material, as long as you clearly attribute the work to the authors (but not in a way that suggests the author or punctum books endorses you and your work), you do not use this work for commercial gain in any form whatsoever, and that for any remixing and transformation, you distribute your rebuild under the same license. http://creativecommons.org/licenses/by-nc-sa/4.0/

First published in 2024 by Tangent, an imprint of punctum books, Earth, Milky Way.
https://punctumbooks.com

ISBN-13: 978-1-68571-198-6 (print)
ISBN-13: 978-1-68571-199-3 (ePDF)

DOI: 10.53288/0446.1.00

LCCN: 2024945618
Library of Congress Cataloging Data is available from the Library of Congress

Editing: SAJ and Eileen A. Fradenburg Joy
Book design: Hatim Eujayl
Cover design: Vincent W.J. van Gerven Oei

HIC SVNT MONSTRA

Sean Gurd & Mario Telò, eds.

The BEFORE and the AFTER

Critical Asynchrony Now

Contents

Introduction: Before · 13
Mario Telò

* * *

Part One: Spectralities

Irony, Philosophy, and Revolution: In the Beginning
Was the Concept (Socrates and Derrida) · 31
Paul Allen Miller

Late-Roman Post-Futures:
The Spectral Planets of Derrida and Gene Wolfe · 51
Ben Radcliffe

The Spectral Life of Friends: Derrida, Cicero, Atticus · 69
Francesca Martelli

Part Two: *An-arkhē*/Excess/(Un)Being

Thelyology: Apuleius's Morphologies of Damage · 91
David Youd

"A Lie about Origin": Plato's Archive Fever · 113
Karen Bassi

Feral Futures, or The Animal That Therefore I Am Not
(Less to Follow) · 135
Andres Matlock

"The Sun Is New Every Day" (Heraclitus D-K frg. B6):
Greek Ephemerality and Biopolitical Modernity · 163
Bruce Rosenstock

Part Three: Beyond Crisis, Beyond Time

Mourning Mourning: Sophocles, Derrida, and Delay · 195
Sarah Nooter

Steps in Time: Derrida's Impossible Hospitality and the
Apocalyptic Future of Cormac McCarthy's *The Road* · 215
Carol Dougherty

Blanchot, Derrida, and the Gimmick:
Writing Disaster in Euripides's *Bacchae* · 239
Mario Telò

The Future of the Past: Pericles, History,
and Athenian Democracy · 261
Ahuvia Kahane

Before and after Greece and Egypt
in the Eighteenth Century · 285
Daniel Orrells

* * *

After (News That Stays News) · 317
Sean Gurd

Bibliography · 325
Index · 369
Contributors · 373

Acknowledgments

The editors deeply thank the two anonymous readers and, especially, the formidable team at punctum books: Vincent W. J. van Gerven Oei for his vision and SAJ for their scrupulous copyediting.

INTRODUCTION

Before

Mario Telò

The archaeological motif of analysis is doubled by an
eschatological movement, as if analysis were the bearer of
extreme death and the last word, just as the archaeological
motif, in view of the originary, is turned toward birth.
— Jacques Derrida (1998b, 19–20)

Crisis
A singular moment heavy with delay.
— Adrian Parr (2020)

If we're worried, disoriented, and troubled today […] it's
because we've become accustomed to the here and now
perpetuating itself by excluding every possible elsewhere.
— Jean-Luc Nancy (2021, ix)

As Peter Szendy has observed, at the beginning of the pandemic, "it was as if we had woken up overnight in a completely different world. Wholly different but exactly the same." In his view, the event of the pandemic "appeared as the […] startling novelty of something that, after all, had already happened a long time ago" (Szendy 2021, 64). Brand new and as old as the world, the pandemic wreaked other paradoxes on time. The unexpected event almost immediately lost (or never fully revealed) its notional *punctum,* its punctual eventuality, turning into a sudden, exhausting routine, in spite of cyclical surges, peaks, and spikes. Rather than being *epi*-demic, the pandemic has been, from the very beginning, *en*-demic: it has imposed an immediate sense of stagnation, of entrapment in ongoing non-eventuality (Foucault 2001, 243, and see Szendy 2021). Pre-existing, chronic crises, both material and immaterial — consequences of the "ancestral catastrophes" of capitalism and racism — now press upon us as a diseased atmosphere.[1] Repurposing Jean Baudrillard's words from his 1989 essay *Anorexic Ruins,* one could say that our current predicament "is no longer a matter of crisis but [...] a catastrophe in slow motion," marked by "the horror and the charm of [an] ice age" (1989, 33–34).

In pandemic times, time becomes a painfully disorienting *pan-,* an all-encompassing expanse, while stark inequalities — the race-, gender-, and class-based hierarchies shaping the social — are aggravated (see esp. Brown 2020, Lorenzini 2021, Butler 2022, and Esposito 2022).[2] At the beginning of the pandemic, the non-privileged ones among us — those who are never fully in control of their time, who always experience time as alienated and alienating labor, that is, as a tangible symptom of their dispossession — were forced (even in academic institutions) to keep working, exposed to old and new technologies of exploitation, while, as Zadie Smith (2020, 20 and 25–26) put it in the context of the lockdown, more privileged people "suddenly confronted the perennial problem of artists: time, and what to do in it." In her intimate reflections on life during the pandemic, entitled *Intimations* — reflections also spurred by her reading of Marcus Aurelius's *Meditations* — she says to herself:

---

[1] Povinelli (2021, 2–3) defines "ancestral" as the "catastrophes" that "keep arriving out of the ground of colonialism and racism" and "ground environmental damage in the colonial sphere."

[2] As Povinelli (2021, 142) observes, "COVID-19 emerged from extractive capitalism. [...] It devastates the poor, Indigenous communities and communities of color because these communities embody the long arm of the ancestral catastrophe of racism and colonialism."

> Why did you make a fort in your living room? Well, it's something to do. Why dress the dog as a cat? It's something to do, isn't it? Fills the time. Out of an expanse of time, you carve a little area — that nobody asked you to carve — and you do "something" [...]. There really is only time, and there will always be too much of it. (Smith 2020, 20 and 25–26)

The present collection is a document of writing experiments that took place during the forced seclusion suddenly imposed by the pandemic. For people working in academia, the sense of stopped time, of unfillable time, of an imminent yet never-materializing end of time coincided with the experience of a chronic crisis turned into an institutionalized, perennial state of emergency — which the pandemic also seems to have quickly become.[3] The chapters we include here are responses to the no-time of this time of crisis. They reflect, in various fashions and from different angles, on (perennial) lateness and what we call the *beforeafter* — the name we give to literary instantiations, in antiquity and beyond, of the collapse and confusion of temporal registers. These chapters thus thematize lateness, achrony, the possibility of creative and destabilizing convergences, uncanny synergies, and intersections of anteriority and posteriority — as well as disjunctions of present, past, and future — by staging encounters between antiquity and contemporary critical theory. One way or another, almost all of the chapters collected here articulate the need, in this moment — which is not (yet) post-pandemic — for a renewed engagement with Jacques Derrida's "late" work, which responded to real or imagined, imminent and immanent disastrous events and forewarnings of (never-arriving) catastrophic ends of time.[4] The form of writing itself — with

---

3   This need not endorse Giorgio Agamben's irresponsible assimilation of the state of emergency brought on by the pandemic to a sanitary dictatorship: see Agamben (2021). For more sensible positions, see Toscano (2020), Lorenzini (2021), and Esposito (2022).
4   For example, Derrida's quite influential notion of autoimmunity is implicated with his response to the Cold War and September 11: see esp. Derrida (2003). Esposito (2022, 49–79) observes that the pandemic has

chapters that indulge in insistent *explication de texte*, accretive or looping modalities of argumentation, in late style itself, we might say — dramatizes the difficulty of filling apparently indivisible, immaterial time through the pleasure(-in-pain) of analysis ("division, destructuring").[5]

There is no question that the current political, ecological, and medical crisis has heightened and altered our sense of the overdetermined entanglements of "origin" and "lateness."[6] The fantasy of approaching the end of the world — or of regressing to a fantasized *arkhē*, the beginning before the beginning[7] — is countered by the chronicity of the crisis, neither a state of emergency nor an exception with a perceptible endpoint, but an endless dilation.[8] This time of crisis, dominated by the "arrival" (and prolonged stay) of the invisible Real of a virus, prompts us to re-theorize Derrida's *à venir*, even reparse it.[9] Stuck in the midst of an endless and agonizing stretch of no-time or temporal collapse, in the midst of crisis upon crisis, we may have an oppor-

---

heightened democracy's autoimmunitarian tendencies as theorized by Derrida (see esp. 2005a). The Cold War is also the at the center of Derrida's foundational article "No Apocalypse, Not Now" (1984b). On some of the implications of the very idea of "late" Derrida, see esp. Mitchell and Davidson (2007).

5   See Derrida (1998b, 27) on *analysis* as *"undoing, desedimenting, decomposing, deconstituting."*

6   Castrillón and Marchevsky (2021, 5) suggests that the pandemic causes "a progression into the past that undergirds a reaching into a future unknown and in doubt."

7   Colebrook (2020, 139) suggests that, in the current crisis, we might "shift from the post-apocalyptic, where the end of our world offers nothing more than desolation, to the apocalyptic — where the end of the world is the beginning of the earth."

8   Berlant (2020) suggests that "the fantasy of the emergency is messianic in that sense, wishing into being a fulfillment that produces a shift with no loss but a surprising better."

9   Derrida (1994c, 12) refers to deconstruction as "virology": see Fritsch (2020), and Telò (2022 and 2023b). The scholarship on the Derridean *à venir* — the formulation of which dates back to the 1980 essay "Of an Apocalyptic Tone Recently Adopted in Philosophy" (1984a, 33) — is vast: see, among others, Martinon (2007); Butler (2009, 301–5); Cheah (2009, 79–81); Rancière (2009); and Crockett (2018, 51–52).

tunity to re-orient the humanities away from temporal distinctions, partitions, and origins — whose perilous ideological charge is critiqued, through an emblematic example, by Daniel Orrells in his chapter in this volume. Could "these times" (as everyone suddenly seems to be saying) force us to rethink the relations between the "archaic" and the "belated," the "primitive" and the "decadent," and to reconceive the connections between periodization (a kind of literary-historical ordering) and poetic and prosaic form? As Jean-Luc Nancy puts it, "in Derrida the to come, the *à venir,* is always strictly opposed to the future, to *l'avenir,* that is, to the present-future that is projected, represented, given in advance as an aim and a possible occurrence" (Fabbri 2007, 431).[10] Whether applied to democracy, friendship, hospitality, or the archive, the notion of "the to come" opens a gap of ethical infinity in utopian or teleological fantasies (just as *à venir* iconically splits *avenir*), and it is distinctive of "the late Derrida."[11] This "lateness," of course, also defines the temporality of the *arkhē* as an origin, both ontological and nomological, whose phantasmic "again-ness," whose very impossibility, makes it (never) to come, a kind of negative *à venir.* In his chapter, David Youd explores aspects of these dynamics in relation to Apuleius's late style. Could the separable *a* in *a-venir* be understood not just as a prefix of motion (indicating a "toward") but also, at the same time, as a privative (the Greek alpha privative) and thus as a marker of movement toward a lack? How does the current crisis change the valence of the "future to come"?[12] What if instead of the unending approach or, alternately, a movement toward the end of the world and a return to the non-being before being, we are experiencing the "arrival" of achronicity, a

---

10 In a later intervention, Nancy said that the Derridean *à venir* "is not, and in not-being it exposes us to an absence or a void" (2020, 97).

11 For a critique of this phrase, which posits a phenomenological/ grammatological "before" and an ethical/political "after," see Hägglund (2008).

12 Westoby and Harris (2020, 554) observe that the pandemic has enhanced the possibility of "deconstructing community development for one yet-to-come."

sense of stuckness in a state of defective being (perhaps heightened by our curbed relationality and movement)?[13] Are we experiencing the end of life, the arrival of posthuman life, a heightened sense of never-being, or a hyper-lateness? In this book we invited contributors to engage with our political, ecological, and medical crisis as a breach in time or a collapse of time itself. The various articulations of lateness emerging from the Derridean "late" corpus, thought of not just as a philosophical but as a literary — and even lyrical — collection of texts, encourage us to enter into a broader interrogation of the ontological, ecological, and ethical implications of lateness in ancient, modern, and contemporary literature, as well as to rethink current notions of the archaic and futural, exploring imaginative possibilities for their blurring and defamiliarization.[14]

What does a "future" or "no future" reconceptualized as *a-venir* — with multiple meanings for *a* — look like? How should we revisit the idea of spectrality — as a convergence of ethics and temporality — at a time of paralysis, when the ghost cannot be separated from a virus? How can we reconceive the ethical lateness implicit in the idea of unconditional hospitality in a moment of sanctioned self-confinement? Can we find futural close-ness while closed in? What are the affects of "archive fever" in an atmosphere of suffocating, sealed-off presentness? Are there ways of pushing against or valorizing temporal sameness? Can attention to the feelings of lateness and temporal out-of-jointness generated by the practice of reading help us locate a positive experience of achronic sameness and, thus, a mode

---

13 In his last book, *The Fragile Skin of the World* (2021), Nancy seems to offer a somewhat negative reading of the Derridean *à venir* but one that does not reject the idea of the future: "the to-come [...] would be the pre-sence of the present, that which does not yet take place and which consequently is not [...] it is not, and in not being it exposes us to an absence, which will only give us a fugitive present in its approach and its coming about" (3).

14 Levinas (1976, 82) refers to Derrida's thought as "poetry." See Zhuo (2018).

of responding to chronic crisis — to a time when crisis seems to have become time tout court?

* * *

During lockdown, there was nothing for us (the book's editors and contributors) to do but *demeure* (Derrida 2000), to dwell in place, to linger, to experience not just endless waiting, but also a sense of continuous lateness, a spasmodic rushing to stock up (on groceries, books, TV shows, as well as time) accompanied by the feeling of having missed a deadline, of having come too late for the event.[15] The unsettling "presentism" — an oppressive feeling of suspension between "prehistorical catastrophe and anticipated extinction" (Toadvine 2018, 53)[16] — that has been inflicted by the pandemic is an experience of "no future," but also an experience without a past.[17] All manner of abandoned or forgotten modes and experiences seemed to rush in: personal memories, forms of contemplative existence that seemed oudated just weeks before, and not least of all a renewed reflection on the works of Derrida, who had begun to fade from some minds but came back, suddenly, with a renewed vividness. Maybe our questions about time and temporality in light of late Derrida are themselves anachronistic consequences of the distended moment in which we find ourselves.[18]

---

15 See Froment-Meurice (2007, 164): "The *demeure*, the dwelling place, is the place where you linger (in French *s'attarder*, containing *tard:* late) […] as if dying were nothing but this delay self-affecting time; in an instant, rather, which has no time to happen (to) itself and thus arrives; if death arrives only as if it had already taken place. […] The instant of your death is only the instant when you can say what the instant of death will have been — deferred, suspended, arrested." On the "frantic" temporalities imposed by the pandemic, see Halberstam (2020b).
16 Toadvine (2018, 53) also conceives of the present "as suspended between the geologically deep past and an indefinitely distant future."
17 Nancy (2021, 1) defines this "presentism" as "a time to come without past or future."
18 On anachronism and antiquity, see esp. Matzner (2016); Postclassicisms Collective (2020); Payne (2020); Umachandran and Rood (2020); and Telò (2020).

Why Derrida? The first and easiest answer is that the sense of an impending but never arriving end of times provoked by the pandemic provides us with a concrete, harrowing materialization of the impossibility of presence, even though the loss of the individual lives of loved ones — the primary futural hauntology of friendship, as Francesca Martelli discusses in her chapter in this volume — is, for Derrida, "nothing less than the end of *the* world" (2005b, 150).[19] The very sense of unfillable time — of an apparently material space of possibilities that remains abstract in its etymological sense, distant while never ceasing to envelop us — leads us to the paradoxical impression that "the present steps away from itself" or that "the present takes the place of a presence that never takes place" (Nancy 2021, 59). In a sense, the current times present us with the impossibility of death discussed by Maurice Blanchot, which was very influential for Derrida.[20] As Derrida might put it, dying is "an endless awaiting, which is interrupted by the arrival of an otherness, by death" (Hodge 2007, 114).[21] In the pandemic climate of ongoing waiting — for a resolution in and through death or a delusional return to ("normal") life — we cannot experience the ultimate event of death because we are wrapped in the ordinariness of the gerund *dying*. This dying brought on by the serial deaths of the pandemic makes death into a non-event, an iterative occurrence, an unremarkable routine that we are prevented from

---

19 Derrida (2005b, 140) also observes that the death of the other leaves the survivor "without world, without the ground of any world [...] in a world without world." See Toadvine (2018, 65). Derrida's position — his assimilation of the world to the (human) other — could be accused of anthropocentrism, but cf. his reference to the destruction of the world as the destruction of the *cosmos* in, e.g., *The Beast and the Sovereign* (Derrida 2011, 260)

20 On Derrida's relationship with Blanchot, see my chapter in this volume.

21 See Froment-Meurice (2007, 159): "That precise instant is the one when death comes, that is to say: it escapes us. Death only comes as it escapes us again; death slips aways, and this slipping away, this breakaway is 'my very death itself.' Death comes when 'instantaneously' it disappears. For death to come is to disappear. Death 'is' its own disappearance; its 'is' is without being."

dwelling on and, thus, intimately and publicly recognizing as "the absolute end of the one and only world" (Derrida 2005b, 140). Prevented by the virus (and the state) from mourning our lost loved ones — who were and still are our world[22] — we were just like Antigone in Derrida and Dufourmantelle's *Of Hospitality* (2000), discussed by Sarah Nooter in this volume.[23] The waiting caused by the pandemic is nothing but the condition of not at all being able to experience the catastrophe that has arrived, the event that has changed — palpably affected, violently touched — our lives, torturing us with its constitutive, "an-economic" incomprehensibility.[24] Waiting is a quintessential temporal and affective manifestation of repetition at a moment that seems to hinder productive cognitive repetition, that is, the epistemic reliance on a precedent, on an implicit or explicit comparison with the (previously) known.[25] As Derrida puts it, describing the waiting that the incomprehensibility of the event, the absolute unknown, like a guest, inevitably entails:

> The absolute *arrivant* must not be merely an invited guest […]. It must be someone whose unexpected, unforeseeable arrival, whose *visitation* […] is such an irruption that I'm not prepared to receive the person. […] Welcoming beyond my capacity to welcome means receiving precisely when I cannot receive, when the coming of the other overwhelms me, seems bigger than my house. […] In the arrival of the *arrivant*, it is the absolute other who falls on me. […] I was saying before that the saying of the event presupposed some sort of inevitable neutralization of the event by its iterability, that

---

22 In his famous article "No Apocalypse, Not Now" (1984b), Derrida remarked: "There is no common measure able to persuade me that a personal mourning is less grave than a nuclear war."
23 On Antigone and European states' COVID-related restrictions on burial rites, see Braunstein (2021).
24 On the "an-economic" quality of the event in Derrida, see Marder (2018).
25 Waiting is, in a sense, an expression of the "foundational negativity" that the intrinsically repetitious processes of education and knowledge disavow. See Edelman (2017).

> saying always harbors the possibility of resaying. A word is comprehensible only because it can be repeated. [...] The fact that, right away, from the very outset of saying or the first appearance of the event, there is iterability and return [...] means that the arrival of the *arrivant* — or the coming of the inaugural event — can only be greeted as a return, a coming back, a spectral *revenance*. (Derrida 2007a, 233)[26]

Waiting is the iterability that perverts and frustrates the very possibility of comprehensibility — but, as I discuss in my own chapter, it can also be conceptualized as an interruption of the normative cut of decision and decidability. In *Specters of Marx* (1994a, 142), Derrida famously observes:

> The time is out of joint. The world is going badly. It is worn but its wear no longer counts. Old age or youth — one no longer counts in that way. The world has more than one age. [...] We no longer realize the war, we no longer take account of it as a single age in the progress of history. Neither maturation, nor crisis, nor even agony. Something else. What is happening is happening to age itself, it strikes a blow at the teleological order of history. What is coming, in which the untimely appears, is happening to time but does not happen in time. [...] More than ever, for the future-to-come can announce itself as such and in its purity only on the basis of a *past end;* beyond, *if that's possible,* the last extremity. If that's possible, *if there is any* future, but how can one suspend such a question or deprive oneself of such a reserve without *concluding in advance,* without reducing in advance both the future and its chance? Without totalizing in advance?[27]

---

26 On the virus as the "visitation" of a "foreigner," an embodiment of unconditional hospitality, see Kamuf (2020).

27 For a reading of Derrida's reading of *Hamlet* in *Specters of Marx,* see Edelman (2011).

The waiting, the *dying* imposed by the pandemic, can be cast as an enervation of time itself, an undoing of its texture, of its notional organization, through a proliferation or thickening of threads. This dynamic is not simply a manifestation of the hauntology of time, of its intrinsic division by otherness, the ghosts, and spectral traces that Derrida theorizes in *Specters of Marx* to connect impossible presences: the origin with the *à venir*. Rather than an always-delayed event, what the current time seems to expose us to is, as I have said, the advent of a deprivation. The accented *a* of *à venir* seems to shift its morphological function: from the marker of the impossibility of a future present, of the gap that makes the future non-teleological, to the coming about of a mutilation (the alpha privative) — the mutilation of time itself. Time is indeed out-of-joint — its "joints," material and immaterial seams, are broken, disintegrated into an unboundedness. While we are disjointed — from our dear ones, from the community, and, to an extent, from our bodies as well — time exceeds itself and overwhelms the possibility of tasting its ghostly constituents, of smelling its hauntological aromas.[28] De-textured time is the counterpart of an anaesthetic mode of feeling (see Heyes 2020), or even an experience of unfeeling, of dis-affection.[29]

In *Specters of Marx*, Derrida makes a case for the "messianic" as the condition of the revolutionary. As he famously says, "the messianic, including its revolutionary forms (and the messianic is always revolutionary, it has to be), would be urgency, imminence but, irreducible paradox, a waiting without horizon of expectation" (1994a, 168). In this waiting, there is no expectation insofar as a "horizon of expectation" would compromise the notion of *à venir*, of a never-materialized future. Yet in these times — when we are confronted with the material negativity of

---

28 See Nancy (2021, 59): "The present steps away from itself […] the present takes the place of a presence that never takes place."
29 On unfeeling as a "reluctance to signify the appropriate expressions of affect that are socially legible as human" and on disaffection as "the unfeeling rupture that enables new structures of feeling to arise," see Yao (2021, esp. 6–7).

the pandemic—we seem to be confronted with a radical curtailing of messianicity (see Cheah 2016, ch. 6; Lai 2016; Glazier 2017; and Reinhart 2021),[30] with a closing off of the very horizon of a-waiting, that is, a closing off of a *projection toward* an object—yes, unknown, unknowable, never materialized, constantly deferred, but still notionally, imaginatively, conceptually "present" as a fantasy or a horizon of possibility.[31] The transitive verb a-wait etymologically contains a relation with an object (*ad-*), the intimation of a towardness. But it has now become more and more difficult to recognize this potential—projective and prospective—orientation behind the *a* in a-wait. With an ever-fading connection to the "original" *d* in *ad-*, we are increasingly tempted to see the simple *a*, a pure privative, as the object demanded by the compulsive transitivity of *await* in English. For Derrida, a "perhaps" is what defines the relation "to the coming of the event." In his words, "the event belongs to a perhaps that is in keeping not with the possible but with the impossible" (1994a, 54).[32] What happens to this "perhaps" at a time when one feels more than ever the sense that time "has […] run out" (Blanchot 1986, 34) but is also, simultaneously, an over-expanding hyperobject, both material and immaterial?[33]

---

30 For a critique of Derridean messianic politics, see Rancière (2009).
31 Castrillón and Marchevsky (2021, 5) observe that "this pandemic-induced enormous pause to life… may very well come to break open the closed, fateful, and guilt-laden box of the historicist's homogeneous empty time, allowing us a […] moment of disruption, rupture, discontinuity à la Benjamin."
32 As Cornell and Seely (2014, 7) put it, for Derrida, "it is by recognizing that both the symbolic and the narrative structures of history are fantasies that we might open ourselves to a future *beyond*—one that is indeed unknowable, but one that is *ours* to inherit."
33 See Hodge (2007, 91–92): "The time which has already run out, indicated by Blanchot, is akin to the time of living on, ghosting the time of past, present and future, but no longer delimited in relation to a natural or historical sequence of time and tense. It is this time that the complicated relation of mutual reading, also called friendship between Blanchot, Levinas, Derrida and their continuing points of reference: Aristotle, Augustine, Nietzsche; Hegel, Husserl, Heidegger, both intimates and renders the more paradoxical and aporetic."

While the pandemic has not stopped capitalistic extraction (it has, in fact, exacerbated it), it may allow us to glimpse the possibility of reimagining the borders of productivity and non-productivity, of interrupting the debilitating continuity of labor and work with moments of paralysis (see esp. Žižek 2020; see also Telò 2023a). In her discussion in this volume of the intersections of archaeology and psychoanalysis in Derrida's *Archive Fever,* Karen Bassi refers to "slow life" — in her formulation, "the condition in which the cumulative deaths of individual citizens signal the threatened survival of the species" or "the ordinary/everyday condition of living under the threat of collective annihilation." From a different perspective, the slowness of paralysis, while making us stuck (intermittently, imaginatively), loosens us, unties us from — or locates us "beyond" — the constriction of productivity, from the bounded organization of pre-pandemic life.[34] A mode of "crip temporality" (Samuels and Freeman 2021), chronic paralysis can amount to a deterritorialized space or a space of deterritorialization, that is, an unsheltered — and, thus, truly hospitable — space, the very space that Carol Dougherty discusses in her chapter in this volume. This may become an alternative space on the threshold between "beside" and "beyond," where we can test and inhabit — cognitively and ethically — the socially radical possibilities of achrony without ever fantasizing an (inevitably death-driven) *re-*turn, a *re-*storation, embracing, instead, a desire for the radical newness inherent to Hannah Arendt's notion of birth, which, in this volume, Bruce Rosenstock illustrates in relation to Heraclitus.

Speaking, in the time of the Cold War, of the apocalyptic danger of nuclear conflict — "a fabulously textual" event that "the growing multiplication of the discourse, indeed of the literature" has turned into a "non-event" — Derrida observed that "the nuclear age is not an epoch, it is the absolute *epokhē* [suspension]; it is not absolute knowledge and the end of history,

---

34 Once again, the "we/us" that I am positing here refers to those among us who have the privilege of spending time thinking and speculating instead of being dispossessed by a regime of unstoppable capitalistic productivity.

it is the *epokhē* of absolute knowledge" (1984b, 23). Embracing this *epokhē* — something similar to the revolutionary, inherently hauntological irony discussed by Paul Allen Miller in this volume — through the reading of *beforeafter* complexes in ancient literature and its receptions means valorizing and endorsing the interruptive power of literary discourse, and its tending toward the interruption of a world that is currently interrupted. Blanchot characterizes literature as "the being which protests against revelation" or as having "the defiance [characteristic] of what does not want to take place outside," the vocal and expressive force of "everything in the world that seems to perpetuate the refusal to come into the world" (Blanchot 1995, 330). As explored, through a Derridean Cicero or a Ciceronian Derrida, by Andres Matlock in this volume,[35] literature enables us to see human/animal, human/vegetal (re)connections and encounters, which may evoke novel, less toxic configurations of the *beforeafter* conflation brought into our lives by a virus birthed by extractive capitalism, by environmental violence, and by the persistent delusion of human primacy.[36] With its multiple agential entanglements (intersubjective and interobjective), literature may remind us of democracy's "entangled state," of the fact that the *à venir* of democracy relies not on "intertwinings of separate entities," but rather on "irreducible relations of responsibility," as Ahuvia Kahane observes in his chapter, connecting Thucydides's Pericles with Karen Barad's Derridean New Materialism (Barad 2010). Literature's "refusal to come into the world" may help us appreciate the benefits of "world reduction," of "a world [...] desaturated, opened up to possibilities of

---

35 According to Derrida (2005b, 55–56), "the world beyond humanity — animals, plants, and stones, oceans, atmospheres [...] — is the effective exteriority without which the very disposition of or to sense would not make [...] any sense."

36 Povinelli (2021, 142) aptly laments that "rather than seeing COVID-19 as a horrifying analytic of power's embodiment, as a devastating critique of late liberal capitalism — understanding this late liberal capitalism as the source of this horror we are experiencing — we are told to view the virus as our enemy."

reconfiguration excluded by the oppressive fullness of the 'actually existing' world," as suggested by Ben Radcliffe in his analysis, in this volume, of novelist Gene Wolfe's late-Roman postfutures through Derrida and Fredric Jameson. There is a sense in which the proliferation of meanings brought out by *logos* — in accordance with relentless exercises of Derridean *explication de texte* — can amount to a form of what Roberto Esposito identifies as affirmative biopower. As he puts it:

> At a time when human life appears to be threatened and overpowered by death, our common effort can only be that of "establishing" it again and again. What else, after all, is life if not this continuous "establishment," the capacity to create ever new meanings[?] (Esposito 2021, 87)

(Over-)analyzing the temporal out-of-jointness *of* and *in* ancient literature through case studies, localized instantiations of *before-after*, means to channel "the stubbornness of what remains when everything [seems to] vanish" (Blanchot 1995, 328).

* * *

In the first section ("Spectralities"), contributors explore future-past temporalities that emerge from the interrogation of Derrida's *Specters of Marx* (1994a) and *Politics of Friendship* (1997b) together with Plato, Cicero, or Gene Wolfe. Paul Allen Miller stages an encounter between the Socratic/Platonic "concept" and the out-of-joint ontology (or hauntology) that Derrida theorizes in *Specters*. Miller considers how the philosophical concept causes us to "find ourselves elsewhere, in an atopia," but also "out of time," placing us on the edge, making us sense, cognitively and affectively, that "revolution" (one of the possible interpretations of the future-to-come) is indistinguishable from the intrinsic spectrality of the past. Ben Radcliffe teases out the emancipatory potential of this futural spectrality in his analysis of Gene Wolfe's *Urth Cycle*. The return of the primitive envisioned as futural in Wolfe's novels and Derrida's reinterpretation of Marxism as a "desert-like" promise both articulate a Jamesonian "world reduction" that challenges capitalist accumulation. In her chapter, Francesca Martelli suggests that the temporal disjunctures produced by the editorial arrangement of Cicero's letters to his friend Atticus make us feel, in a time of crisis, the very spectrality of Derrida's ethics of friendship — its affective projection toward an "other" who resembles a future always divided from itself, never beginning or ending. In the second section, "*An-arkhē*/Excess/(Un)Being," lateness amounts to an excessive, an-archic temporality observable in texts that encompass aesthetics, eschatology, and biology. David Youd tracks the ways that Derrida's theory of the archive interfaces with theorizations of late style, where the late work of art, haunted by the specter of death, reveals in its formal blockage the limits of archival integration. Espousing "a certain interpretative microscopy," he suggests that this formal movement not only organizes the narrative structures of *The Golden Ass* more broadly, but "inflects also the more diminutive morphologies of Apuleius's style," repeatedly "perverting the transfiguring end into a late disclosure of damage." Equally reflecting on *Archive Fever*, Karen Bassi connects the eschatological origin myth that Socrates refers to as a "noble lie" in Plato's *Republic* with Derrida's discussion of Sigmund Freud's death drive, the principle that, for him, energizes yet threatens the archive. The outcome of this juxtaposition is a view of the death drive as the condition we are experiencing in the current pandemic: a "passing of time [...] relentlessly measured in death's approach," as Bassi writes, where death itself constitutes the *avenir* (in its various interpretive permutations). Andres Matlock tests the theoretical possibility of bridging the gap between being and becoming, using Cicero's discussion of vegetal life, in two of his philosophical works, as an illustration of the principle that "to be is to follow, to come already after the end." Drawing this principle from Derrida's discussion in *The Animal That Therefore I Am* (2008), Matlock makes us see how Cicero theorizes the overlap between what we can call floral lateness and time itself. Bruce Rosenstock's essay turns to the Greek reflection on ephemerality in order to respond to the crisis in what Tim Ingold (2015) calls "humanifying," a crisis that has acquired the unique power to upset the life-sustaining balance of earth and sun. By unpacking the significance of ephemerality in Greek poetic and philosophical sources, we gain an insight into the challenge to the future of the species that we have faced with growing urgency since the technological-industrial revolution inaugurated by the invention of the coal-run steam engine. In the third section, "Beyond Crisis, Beyond Time," models of late temporality that the current pandemic has forced us to revisit — suspension, waiting, imminence, distension, and return — are discussed through the Greco-Roman and Derridean thematics of mourning, disaster, solitude, democracy, and the issue of "origin" in intellectual history. Sarah Nooter brings together Sophocles's *Oedipus at Colonus,* Derrida's discussion of it in *Of Hospitality* (2000), and the experience of the COVID-19 pandemic to meditate upon the temporal/affective dimension of the current time and the use of the first-person plural in expressing the feel of suspended time, in conveying the temporal texture of impossible, forbidden, never-actualized mourning. Carol Dougherty explores the ramifications of the Sophoclean play and Derrida's unconditional hospitality in Cormac McCarthy's *The Road,* using this post-apocalyptic novel to theorize the possibility of a "peripatetic" *avenir*. In my chapter, I reflect on the impossible temporality of disaster through Blanchot's *The Writing of Disaster,* Derrida's *Demeure* (2000), and Euripides's *Bacchae,* reconceptualizing Derridean *a-venir* as a *jouissant* passivity. The passive and late affect that we feel in the "gimmicky" scene of old Cadmus and Tiresias in *Bacchae* encapsulates a form of resistance against the imposed frenzy of Dionysian intoxication, which is something like the manic impetus to make decisions and find solutions in the current crisis. In a chapter that circles back to Plato, Ahuvia Kahane theorizes the notion of a "return" to the future of antiquity. This return is a condition of lateness that allows us to assimilate Derrida's *avenir* to a kind of eternity. Regressing to the future of antiquity, as Kahane suggests we do through a rereading of Plato's *Republic* and Alan Badiou's *Plato,* may enable us to close the apparent gap between the late Derrida and recent returns to "realism." More importantly, it may point to ways of re-evaluating Greek democracy — something that survives and can be apprehended hauntologically, or through an eternal lateness — as a response to the crisis of our time. In the last chapter, Daniel Orrells explores the fraught dynamics of "before/after" in eighteenth-century attempts (by Winckelmann and Vico, among others) to define the relationship between Greek and Egyptian art. He revisits Derrida's discussion of the hieroglyphic to problematize — and warn us against — the (ab)uses of the idea of origin in resurging Western "neo-nationalist, neo-fascist, racializing" mythologizations of what we call antiquity, of the "before" that we fantasize as a reparative defence against crisis.

1

Irony, Philosophy, and Revolution: In the Beginning Was the Concept (Socrates and Derrida)

Paul Allen Miller

Philosophy begins in irony. It begins in our wonder at the moment when meaning estranges itself from itself, when what we thought we knew trembles before the force of its own implicit, unthought signification. The concept qua concept is always, necessarily, ironic in the moment of its articulation. It always means more than it says, more than what we meant to say, more than what we thought we intended when we began to speak. When Socrates asks what justice is, when he buttonholes us minding our own business in the *agora,* on the street, and says, "What do you mean by 'justice,' by 'courage,' by 'love,' by 'beauty,' by the 'good'?," he opens a space of difference (see Colebrook 2002, 104). Every example we give, every time we respond that justice is X or Y, we find that the concept by which we name and define our intention includes more than we know, that the other speaks within it, that the concept includes its own negation, its own "weight of the unthought" (Derrida 1995a, 52).

Plato's Socratic dialogues are littered with examples. "The just man is pious toward the gods." Does that mean he prosecutes his own father for wrongdoing, as in the *Euthyphro?* If so, then what exactly is piety? If not, then how is it just for a crime, in this case a brutal one, to go unpunished? "The just man helps his friends and harms his enemies," the traditional maxim of Greek ethics is cited in Book One of the *Republic* (332d).[1] But do we really mean what we say? Is it just to help one friend harm another if the latter is the enemy of the former? What about an enemy who wants to harm your friend's friend who nonetheless happens to be your enemy (it happens)? How do I justly and precisely determine who are my friends and who are my enemies, who is in my group (*philos*) and who is an other (*ekhthros*)?[2] "The just man is the man who pays what he owes" (*Republic* 331b–c). What do I owe to you? To the past? To the future? Is it even payable? If I borrowed your AK-47 to take care of some pesky squirrels, do I return it when I know you plan an assault on the Capitol? Does it depend on whom you plan to kill and why? Each new formulation finds its own negation, founders upon its own blind spots and exclusions, and in the process is changed. I discover that justice is not what I thought it was, but I also discover that I meant something more by justice than what I had thought initially. I discover that who I am and how I stand to the world must now be transformed if I am to give justice and the dialectic its due, if I am to be honest with myself and others about what I mean by justice, if I am to make a decision, take a stand in the world, and act according to that stance, which is only just (see Colebrook 2002, 34–35).

There is something profoundly Hegelian in this recounting of the Socratic journey of the concept, as each formulation discovers its own negation through the process of argument, application, and extension: transforming itself, negating its very negation in the course of reformulation (see Rush 2016). We think we know what we mean when we use these words — "justice," "beauty," "goodness" — but the *logos* ("language," "conversation,"

---

[1] For the text of Plato, I follow the edition of Burnet (1901–1907). Translations are mine, unless otherwise indicated.

[2] Benveniste (1969) had identified *philos* and *ekhthros,* often translated as "friend" and "enemy" as originally meaning something like, "member of the same group or body" and "someone external to the group." See also Nagy (1979).

"discourse") soon leads us to strange places and, often, to *aporia* itself. Yet this moment of perplexity, this moment of not having a clear way forward, a *poros,* is not the *telos* (end) of the journey, nor is it even the *arkhē* (beginning), which is why, in the end, Hegel is a profoundly unironic thinker: with his imperative to move toward an end, he works to put Socrates with all his capacity to discomfit us with his questions, his *atopia,* literally in his *topos* (place).

What I want to argue in these pages is that if we "do justice" to Socrates — not as the Athenian people did, which Hegel considered just and necessary (see Kofman 1989, 132, and Hegel 1971, 278) — but if we let him roam free, if we set no limit to the testing he does of us and our fellow citizens, then this Socratic impulse is both profoundly ironic and ultimately revolutionary: for this moment of irony is that in which new thought and new concepts can emerge, and this moment is a necessary, if not sufficient, cause of fundamental social change. There is, in fact, a reason Socrates was executed. The Socratic revolution does not necessarily require a vanguard, and it certainly does not aim at the creation of a party line that must be defended at all costs. Each of those gestures seeks to contain the initial moment of radical questioning, to convert Socratic *atopia* into a *topos* ("position"), to repurpose the initial impulse of radical criticism for the purpose not simply of achieving power (which may be necessary and requires a decision) but of maintaining it and enforcing it in the face of all counterclaims.

At the same time, true Socratic questioning can never be reduced to a philosophical quietism, a purely abstract undertaking that does not seek radically to remake both the individuals to whom it is addressed and their relations to governmental power. This is the entire gist of the *Alcibiades,* in which Socrates convinces Alcibiades, on the cusp of his majority, that he is not ready to lead the Athenian Assembly — something he takes as his right — because he neither knows what policies he should seek to enact, their basis in justice or the good, nor does he know himself sufficiently well to understand how to be able to seek and understand these concepts. Throughout the *Republic* and the *Seventh Letter,* Plato has Socrates argue that as our concepts of the good, of the just, of law, and of the state change, our actions must as well; that there is a reciprocal relationship between action and understanding, between city and soul (see Miller 2021b). As we come to know and change ourselves, and so to behave differently, we also interact with others differently. This is no trivial matter. There is no revolution without the recognition that the concepts, codes, and symbolic structures under which we live are contradictory, incoherent, or corrupt. If this were not the case, governments, organizations, and companies, across the ideological spectrum, would not work so hard to influence and, when possible, control what is taught, what is discussed, what is spoken, and by whom, to chart the journey of the *logos*. Karl Marx's apothegm, "Philosophers have hitherto only interpreted the world in various ways; the point is to change it" (1978, 145), may have much truth to it, but there is no changing the world if the ideas and concepts regulating our behavior remain unchanged. It may seem tautological, but we cannot change, if we do not change.

To make this case for the revolutionary potential of irony and the movement of the concept, I shall enlist the considerable help of Jacques Derrida. In particular, I will make use of his notion of "hauntology" as elaborated in *Specters of Marx* and related works from the eighties and nineties. Within this notion of hauntology, we find the simultaneous presence and absence of the past, an articulation of the way in which the play of *différance* in history, as the condition of possibility of meaning, and hence as a predicate for the articulation of the concept, is both rooted in history, a before-the-present, and makes possible a "future," understood as a world, a set of meanings, a way to organize and understand ourselves, *à-venir* ("to come"). In this reading, I will be following Clare Colebrook's acute observation that Derrida is himself a Socratic ironist (2002, 32), the biting fly who pesters us, demonstrating again and again that we do not know what we thought we knew, that our concepts are haunted by meanings, desires, and contingencies of fact that elude us, even as they open the possibility of our own remaking.

* * *

It is certainly not the case that Socrates was unimportant for Georg W.F. Hegel. As his lectures on the history of philosophy make clear, Socrates is critical for Hegel's project, but he is also, if not contained within his appropriate place, corrosive and dangerous. Socrates for Hegel represents the historical appearance of consciousness as self-consciousness, of the thinking subject as conscious of thinking and as therefore exterior to the community and its traditional notions of personal, familial, and political justice. When consciousness becomes conscious of itself, it no longer thinks in a linear way, in the fashion, for example, in which a computer reasons. It no longer applies a given set of rules and norms to extract consistent and appropriate conclusions. It comes instead to take that very process of application and extraction as the object of thought, it comes to question the formation of the concept, to reveal its unthought and ironic remainder. In this way, the rules and norms that govern the operations of thought cease to function as simple givens and become instead themselves the objects of thought, interrogation, and therefore criticism. In self-consciousness thought turns in on itself. Instead of judging whether a given act is just, we start to ask, "What is justice?" For Hegel this act of reflection is ultimately the institutional role of philosophy per se, as *Geist* charts its course from the rise of consciousness as the power of self-reflection to its culmination in the concrete universal of absolute spirit, in which communities, institutions, and the state become capable of reflecting on themselves, and a concrete rationality is elaborated within them. Within this narrative, Socrates stands as an external negation in relation to the progress of universal spirit, a necessary step in the journey of the concept. Hegel writes, "In Socrates, the subjectivity of thinking has become conscious in a more determined, more profound manner" (1971, 273). The Socratic subject's thinking, he contends, becomes the object of thought in a way that it was fundamentally not in Thales or Anaxagoras, but it is not yet self-conscious consciousness determining itself at the level of the universal. Important as Socrates's ironic questioning may be to the progress of universal spirit, it remains the activity of a troublesome individual who, in the end, must be eliminated and so sublimated, a literally vanishing mediator, that ultimately allows for the incorporation of the philosophical impulse within the *polis* and the state. This is the tragedy of the Hegelian Socrates (see Hegel 1971, 336–37).

Hegel's labor in these lectures on Socrates, then, is to surpass the exteriority of the Socratic dialectic, its status as the action of an individual, in favor of its "content," the ability of thought to reflect on and surpass itself. The true aim of what Socrates terms his maieutic, for Hegel, is not the destruction of false, incomplete, or unviable conceptions, what the former labels "wind eggs" in the *Theaetetus* (150a–151e), in favor of a nomadic journey of the concept whose end is not predetermined in its beginning. Rather, Hegel's Socratic midwife has a singular and specific function: the birthing, via deduction, of the universal (see Kofman 1989, 127). Philosophy, as in the *Phaedo*, becomes for Hegel an apprenticeship for the spirit's autonomy from the body (64a5–6), which comes to be seen as a supplement, a material irony, the assertion of an individual difference (1977, 288). When spirit is reconciled with the material from which it divides itself, Socratic irony will be reduced to the self-determining spirit of the universal through history. There will be a final adequation, a filling of the lack that produces solidity and rest (see Hegel 1971, 279–80, and Kofman 1989, 97 and 100–104). In this way, the concept can be tamed, domesticated: *aporia* becomes *poros* and ultimately *telos,* the individual and the deviant are integrated into the universal and the normative.

Aporia for Socrates and Derrida, however, is not a problem to be solved but rather the condition of possibility for a truly philosophical thought. It names the point of rupture where the concept recognizes its distinction from that which it contains and hence offers the possibility "to think differently" (see Gasché 2002, 106, 115, 188; Derrida 1986, 133, and 1994b, 21; and Lloyd 2018, 144). This last formula, of course, comes from the preface to volume two of Michel Foucault's *History of Sexuality*

(1984, 15). Foucault's late work is much influenced by the work of historian of philosophy Pierre Hadot. According to Hadot (2002), the primary practice from which all subsequent forms of self-formation in ancient philosophy derive is the Socratic *elenkhos,* the process of close questioning of the self and others that we sometimes vaguely refer to as the Socratic method. The goal of this practice, especially in the early Socratic dialogues, is not to reach a pre-determined truth. It is certainly not to build the conceptual apparatus necessary to justify where it is we have already determined to go (i.e., to find a way forward, a *poros*), but to produce a moment of genuine *aporia* or even destitution in which the concept itself brings us up short before ourselves, before our self-comforting conceits and ideological certitudes, and forces us, if we are genuine, to think differently (Hadot 2002; Foucault 2001; and Miller 2021a, ch. 3).

Irony in the work of philosophy then is not a simple trope, a rhetorical ornament that can be brushed aside in favor of the universal. It represents the materiality of the concept, the way in which it can never be fully subsumed within the universal, the way it always keeps producing more and other meanings. The act of thought is unrepeatable, and hence material and contingent, and that unrepeatability is on one level the limitation and negation of the concept. The act of thought, as opposed to the content of thought, is what leads to the moment of perplexity and dislocation, the crushing and exhilarating moment in which we realize that what we thought was true is not, in which what we thought we thought, in fact was something else. On another level, however, the unrepeatability of the act of thought is the guarantor of its truth, the guarantor that the concept is alive and not simply an entry in a data bank, the guarantor that our thoughts and actions are not mere repetitions of givens, applications of unchanging rubrics. The crushing and exhilarating moment in which the materiality and hence irony of our own thought is perceived is also the moment in which the thought of the present, haunted by the determinations of its past, becomes the possibility of a thought of the future, and hence of a self, a politics, and, yes, revolution to come.

In point of fact, the dislocation we experience at the hands of the concept is not simply logical and spatial. It is not simply a question of what is included within a given set, but there is also a phenomenology of the journey of the concept, a temporality of our experience of its appearance that breaks with a classical linear vision of time and that Derrida helps us understand. The movement of the concept presents not simply a succession of uniform instants without qualitative difference or reserves, but it also produces moments of negation, transformation, and decision, moments in which the now becomes internally divided and a distance that allows for judgement and differentiation emerges.

This simultaneous temporal and spatial movement of the concept precisely limns the politico-ontological significance of *différance,* in which the temporal and logical aspects of the movement of the concept are inextricably joined. As Derrida (1993a, 60) writes, "No *différance* without alterity, no alterity without singularity, no singularity without a here and now." Différance posits a movement of spacing in which meaning, the concept, the signified, is produced in a moment of self-differentiation between same and other, in which what is here and now is opened to a nonidentical future, in which our attempt to come to terms with the present necessarily opens a multiplicity of possible sequences (see Crépon 2008, 37, and Lewis 2008, 131). As the concept of justice moves through the world, whether in the figure of the Socratic questioner or the Hegelian *Geist,* it constantly confronts us with the fact that we say more than we mean and mean more than we say each time we try to determine what the scope of "justice" or any like concept is. And it is in this moment of realizing and recognizing the self-ironizing movement of the concept that we separate from what is given, and thus from ourselves. We experience the possibility of reflection, a folding of the self upon itself that produces a moment of nonidentity and aporia, that creates a reserve, which is also a space and time of potential action (see Derrida 1986, 132, and 1993a, 68).

In the moment of deconstructive *aporia,* we not only find ourselves elsewhere, in an *atopia,* but lifted up, momentarily, out of time's smooth linear flow. Time in the concept, as Hamlet says and as Derrida quotes in *Spectres de Marx,* is "out of joint." There is a kind of temporal disarticulation that happens in the moment of negation, when the concept recognizes the constitutive otherness already present within itself, when consciousness recognizes the voice of the other within that which tries to think the same:

> What happens in this anachrony? Perhaps "the time," time itself, justly and precisely, always as "our time," the epoch and world that exists between us, our own each day, the day of today, the present as our present. Above all when things are "not going well" between us, justly and precisely: when things "go poorly," when things don't work, when things turn out badly. But with the other, isn't this disjunction necessary, this lack of adjustment of the "not going well" in order that the good announce itself, or at least the just? Disjunction (being out of joint), is it not the very possibility of the other? How do we distinguish between these two lacks of adjustment, between the unjust and what opens the infinite asymmetry of the relation with the other, that is to say what opens the place for justice? Not for calculative and distributive justice. Not for the law, for the calculation of restitution, the economy of vengeance or punishment…. Not for calculable equality, therefore, for the symmetrical and synchronic compatibility or imputability of subjects and objects, not in order to render a justice that would limit itself to sanctioning, to restitution and rectification, but for justice as the incalculability of the gift and the singularity of the noneconomic ex-position to others. (Derrida 1993a, 48)

Philosophy, then, begins in irony, both logically and in the person of Socrates. It begins with the recognition of non-identity in the moment of the assertion of identity, in the recognition that what we call X may in fact be Y. It begins in the recognition that what we say to be "the just" may well be the unjust, or just not what we mean by "just." And this negation of the concept in the moment of its deployment creates a disjuncture in the fabric of time, in the unified succession of instances, that allows for the possibility of another justice, not only a more expansive version of the same concept of justice, one that incorporates its own determinate negation, but also a form of justice that can imagine an "other" that is not reducible to the rubric of the same, that is not calculable under any form of universal equivalent and hence cannot be reduced to exchange value. In this moment of temporal alterity, a kind of pause or *entretemps,* we can imagine a concept of the just that would actually allow us to do justice to the other as something other than an inverted reflection of the same (Derrida 1997b, 200). We can imagine a justice that promises not just equality before the law — giving to each what she is owed — but a new justice, a justice of infinite hospitality that would embrace the asymmetry of the other, even within ourselves, that would open ourselves to being changed by the other (Derrida 1997a, 13, 49, 79–80, 90–91, 102–6, 191–93, and 1996a, 28–29, 49).

If, on one level, our experience of time can be imagined as a pure succession of present moments, a perpetual now, on another, the concept lifts us up and out, or off to the side, of this succession and creates a moment of difference and deferral. I do not mean, and structurally cannot mean, when I reply to Socrates, that the justice of which we speak is only "just" in this instant or instance. I must, when I speak of justice, both refer to a series of actions and events in the past and a projected series *à venir* (yet to come), while also standing apart from and necessarily transcending any one of those actions and events, and thus always being different from them, being other than them, and thus never fully resolvable into a moment of reference or presence in which the concept is exhausted by what it points to or re-presents (R. Hill 2019, 275–76). The temporality of the concept is both what makes possible history qua history — an aconceptual history is, literally, unthinkable — and it is that which is never resolvable into the events that "history" would seek to name. History is not simply the succession of temporal instants, like the rotation of the planets or the shifts in tectonic plates, but the succession of self-conscious acts and struggles that make the past different from the future. Even the most materialist, economistic conceptions of history cannot do without the truth claims, the conceptual and organizational structures that give those struggles meaning, that differentiate them from any other momentary atmospheric disturbance. The irony of the concept creates a temporal reserve in the present that refers to the past and the future and yet must insist upon its difference from them and thus on the possibility of difference within the temporal field, an otherness yet to come, on the possibility of another world that stems from *atopia* and *aporia,* the possibility of what Derrida refers to as a messianicity without messianism (2002b, 69–70). There is a specter haunting Europe.

This specter Derrida names *hauntologie:*[3] the being of the present that contains both the ghosts of the past and the possibility of a future yet to come — a dislocated ontology, an ontology out of joint. He first explicitly formulates the term in *Spectres de Marx.* There, it names the structure of a present absence that moves through time, like the ghost of Hamlet's father. It is a phantom that defines the present by a past, one which is no longer fully realized and yet points to the possibility of a future (Derrida 1993a, 89). The specter haunting Europe in the *Communist Manifesto* to which Derrida's title gestures is the coming into consciousness, and thus into being, of the proletariat, a being that in 1848 does not yet fully exist (and whose fullness

---

3 The word is a homonym of *ontologie.* One could say it is "ontologie" with a "différance," but Derrida insists upon this *différance.* His project is not to give us the *logos* of being (*to on*), to return to a metaphysics of presence in which the concept is not always ironic, in which in the end, if only we work hard enough and police our language and that of others with sufficient rigor, the journey of the concept will come to rest, history will end, and we will finally know what we know: hence his emphasis on a present that is haunted by a past that in its difference from that present makes possible a future that is different from both, but never fully and finally self-present. Revolution in the Derridean sense is not a *telos* but an ongoing and interminable project (Derrida 2002b, 57–58 and 83–91).

we still await), a spectral presence, projecting the residuum of past struggles onto the possibility of a world *à-venir* (to come) (see Macherey 2008, 140–41). Hauntology is what makes the project of ontology—the delimitation of being into beings, in our thought and experience—through the concept both possible and interminable. It names a differential moment of space and time that opens into the future as both a coming difference and a return of the past, a revenant, that hollows out the solidity of the present.

The concept of "haunting" in Derrida first appears earlier in his work,[4] when he is in the process of coming to terms with the complex legacy of Paul de Man and his collaborationist writings from the 1940s, the ghost of deconstruction's past. I have covered this ground more extensively in "Ghosts in the Politics of Friendship" (2016). In the present context, let me just briefly note that in *Memoires for Paul de Man,* Derrida observes that for both Immanuel Kant and Martin Heidegger, the transcendental, the structure that makes possible the intelligibility of our experience—that is to say our experience of the concepts of pure understanding—presents itself under the figure of the specter, of a "presence without present of a present which, coming back, only *haunts*. The ghost, *le re-venant,* the survivor" (Derrida 1986, 64, my emphasis). This is very loaded language in the context of the Holocaust and its aftermath. There is a level on which the philosophical moves Derrida makes in this work are deliberately and consciously contaminated by the contingencies from which his conceptual apparatus arises and to which it must in the end refer. There are ghosts among us.

---

4   It is interesting to note that Sartre uses the word *hanter* in a very similar sense throughout *L'être et le néant,* which claims to offer an *"essai* d'ontologie *phénoménologique,"* to refer to the ways in which consciousness is "haunted" by its own past determinations and contingencies, which then both make possible and limit its future possibilities, *à venir*. For a sample of passages, see Sartre (1943, 51, 71, 126, 128–35, 140, 144, 147–48, 151, and 165). Whether Derrida is consciously reworking this Sartrean motif or unconsciously echoing the reading of his youth is difficult to determine.

In the isolation and constitution of a being, in the movement that realizes the identification of the ontic, there is always a moment in which the entity (the thing marked out by the ontic) is haunted by the other, by what must have come before it, either *a priori* or empirically, and therefore by what it must open itself out to as well, by the constitutive discourse of the other that identifies the entity, by the other as the negation of the same. For de Man, this discursive moment in the instant of its constitution, following Karl Wilhelm Friedrich Schlegel in his critique of Kant, is termed "irony," the moment in which an act of naming and identification is simultaneously an awareness of non-identity, the moment when, as Quintilian says in his definition of irony, the *intellectum* does not coincide with the *dictum* (6.2.15–16; see de Man 1983 and Rush 2016).[5]

It was this same turning of thought in on itself, this same eternal irony of the self-conscious subject, that Hegel, as the declared antagonist of Romantic irony and hence of Schlegel, tried both to account for and control in his lectures on Socrates, putting the gadfly in his place, sacrificing him to the demands of the community and the *polis* (see Kofman 1989, 116–18 and 139; cf. Colebrook 2002, 132–33, and Rush 2016, 158–61). For de Man when this discursive phenomenon is extended through time and becomes a narrative, irony is called "allegory." Derrida in his postmortem reading of de Man, thus, poses the following question to his dead friend, whose secrets he never knew, and to us: "Is it by chance that in the very steps by which he reopened the problem of allegory, Paul de Man convoked the ghost of Coleridge? […] Allegory speaks (through) the voice of the other, whence, the ghost-effect" (1986, 80). It will be this same figure of the specter, in turn, that some pages later Derrida uses to name de Man's willful "amnesia," his "guilty conscience" of a past that haunts the present like a "ghost" and that determines the paths possible for the future through its returning absence, through the insistent presence of what is not there (Derrida 1986, 122).

---

5 I refer to Butler's edition (1920–1922) of Quintillian's *Institutio Oratoria*. All translations are mine unless otherwise noted.

We are only haunted by those who are gone, and if any thinker were ever haunted by his past — a past that would refigure his writings of the present as a form of allegory, an ironic story of forgetting, of amnesia, and of the *re-venant à venir* — it was de Man, who became one of our most incisive theorists of irony in his aptly named "Rhetoric of Temporality."

Such ghostly hauntings, whether embodied in the crimes of de Man or in the struggles of the oppressed, never point just to the past. As Derrida observes in his 1984 memorial lecture for de Man, "My desire is to talk to you today about what is to come, about that future which, still to come, also comes to us from Paul de Man" (1986, 4). To speak of memory is always also to speak of what is "to come" (Derrida 1995a, 60). This is why the past must never be forgotten. We must fight against amnesia, we must engage in archaeology, we must read the ancient texts, because the structure of our future comes from them, or more profoundly, the "thought of memory thinks the future […] the experience of the coming of the future [*venue de l'à-venir*]" (Derrida 1986, 3), whether we "remember" it or not. Anyone who doubts this has not been paying attention to America's struggles with the history of slavery and systemic racism, to Europe's attempts to come to terms with its own racist and colonialist legacy, or to the entire history of the Israeli-Palestinian conflict. The past does not cease to haunt the future simply because it is ignored or forgotten.[6]

---

6   Derridian "hauntology" bears more than a passing resemblance to what Foucault in his lectures in the eighties referred to as a critical "ontology of the present." In these lectures on Socrates, Plato, and Kant, Foucault seeks to pinpoint what he calls a moment of emergence that is always poised between a future and a past in the possibility of a present. That moment of emergence, the radical possibility to think and act differently, in turn forces us to ask one of Foucault's most basic questions, "what is the ontology of the present, what is the nature of the moment in which we are constituting ourselves" (Foucault 2008, 22). It is a question whose answer can only be historical or genealogical in nature. There is a past that constitutes the present in its openness to the future. That is what the present is. It is haunted by a past projecting the specters of a future.

There is a specter haunting Europe (but surely not Europe alone), a past that a certain present must strive to forget in order to establish its hegemony, a moment of repression that inheres in the assertion of the unity of identity, a trauma whose violence mars the face of our reality with the traces of a past whose acknowledgement would tear open the smooth fabric of our existence.[7] Every moment of hegemony is haunted by what it seeks to repress: slavery, genocide, exploitation, abuse. If Walter Benjamin tells us that "there is no document of civilization which is not at the same time a document of barbarism" (1969, 256), Derrida draws the corollary that "there is no political power without control of the archive, if not of memory itself. Effective democratization is always measured by this essential criterion, participation and access to the archive, to its constitution and interpretation" (1995a, 15n1). Every moment of amnesia is, therefore, a moment of repression and thus simultaneously encodes the memory of its constitution in trauma and of repression, the constitution of its own archive, its own document of barbarism. "Let's move on," we are told. "We must not linger over a past that can't be changed." "Why bring that up? It only stokes hatred and division." But as Derrida reminds us in *Spectres de Marx,* "Hegemony always organizes repression and therefore the confirmation of a haunting. Haunting pertains to the structure of every hegemony" (1993a, 69). This haunting, this structure of hauntology, is where Marx meets Sigmund Freud in the moment of posing the Socratic question *ti estin,* "what is" justice, equality, hospitality, the state, etc. This locus of our ghosting is where the recognition of the irony of the con-

---

7 "As soon as there is the One, there is murder, wounding, trauma. *The One protects itself from the other.* It protects *itself* against the other, but in the movement of this jealous violence, it carries within itself, holding thus onto it, the alterity or the difference with itself (the difference of being with itself) that makes it One. The One differing from itself. The One like the Other. At the same time, simultaneously, but in one same disjointed time, the One forgets to recall itself to itself, it holds onto and effaces the archive of this injustice that it is. Of this violence that it does. *The One makes itself from violence.*" (Derrida 1995a, 124–25, emphasis original).

cept, in its deployment through time — when it is unflinchingly and rigorously embraced, when it is properly heard in all its dissonance, in its necessary negation — articulates the very possibility of revolution.

Derrida names this locus, which is transcendental in its structure and yet always empirical in its instantiation, in various ways in various texts. It is, I would contend, the structure named by the *khōra* in his text by the same name (1993b), and it is the structure to which he gestures in his discussions of a politics and a friendship to come in the *Politics of Friendship* (1994b) and *Adieux* (1997a). The *khōra* is first named in Plato's *Timaeus,* as a moment of absolute potentiality that exceeds every ontic instantiation and every concept of being itself. It designates a "place," that is *a-topos* (no place), a space of the "call for a thinking of the event *to come"* and hence "of the democracy *to come,* of the reason *to come"* (see Evans 2016, 156). Such a democracy and such a reason is never the fetishized form of a particular constitution, a particular mode of common understanding, let alone of what managers and administrators might call "data-driven decision making," but it takes the form of an injunction that democracy, justice, and reason can only ever be "to come," that any assertion of their finished form is a betrayal. It embodies a certain messianic promise of "a thought of the other and of an event to come" (Derrida 1993a, 267). As Derrida puts it, "It is perhaps simply the formality of a structural messianism, a messianism without religion, a messianicity, even, without messianism, an idea of justice […] and an idea of democracy" (1993a, 103).[8]

Ti estin? What is justice? What is democracy? These questions are inseparable from what these phenomena have in fact been, from what our experience of them has been, and from the necessary way in which their status as concepts transcends that past and points to a possibility as yet unrealized. Without the anchoring in the past, in the traces and memories that shape the future, those concepts are empty, without meaning or content. Without their transcendental structure, they are but the

---

8   Cf. Derrida (1986, 58, and 2002b, 78–79).

welter of the sensual manifold, without form or definition, without signification. The question of what is democracy must structurally look to the possibility of a democracy-to-come, a democracy that transcends the limitations of its past instantiations. Is it possible to think of a democratic state to come that is not bound to the arbitrary, that is not bound to specious ties of blood and soil, that is not predicated on exclusions that are themselves antithetical to a rigorous logic of what constitutes the *dēmos* and its ability to exercise *krateia* over itself? Is it possible to imagine a state in which equality before the law (*isonomia*) and freedom of speech (*isēgoria*) do not reduce each of our singularities to the status of a universal equivalent, to an identity of origin or being that is the denial of our status as autonomous citizens, a state in which we actually see the other as the other and hence as integral to our self-constitution? This is, in fact, the central question of the *Politics of Friendship* (Derrida 1994b, 128–29) and continues to be of interest to Derrida throughout this period. As he puts it in *Mal d'archive,* "Democracy remains to come: that is its essence in so far as it remains: not only will it remain indefinitely perfectible, thus always insufficient and future but, pertaining to the time of the promise, it will always remain, in each of its future times, to come, even when there is democracy, it never exists, it is never present, it remains the theme of a concept that is not presentable" (1995a, 339–40).

The concept, thus, contains within it, in its temporal and material nature, in its constitutive *différance,* the structural possibility of a revolution, of a new world-to-come incipient within the past, but only as a past that has been reconceputalized from the reserve of the present to envision a spectral future that will never be fully here, never be fully present. The formulation of concepts, as Gilles Deleuze and Félix Guattari (2005) observed, is the task of the philosopher, of the Socratic interlocutor, of the ironist and creator of fictions, to realize the concept in its dislocating difference, to speak the truth as a moment of strangeness and promise. As Derrida said in conversation with Elisabeth Roudinesco:

> I believe in the Revolution, that is to say in an interruption, in a radical caesura in the ordinary course of History. Besides, there does not exist any ethical responsibility, nor any decision worthy of the name that would not be, in essence, revolutionary, that would not be a rupture with a system of dominant norms. (2001, 38)

It is in this sense also that we must understand Derrida's declaration in *Spectres de Marx* that "deconstruction has never had any sense or interest, in my eyes at least, except as a radicalization of, that is to say as also *in the tradition* of, a certain Marxism, in a certain spirit of Marxism" (1993a, 51). Derridian deconstruction is a dialectical materialism that has no *telos,* a phenomenology of the concept that has neither origin nor end, but always is in permanent movement from an absent present to a world to come, toward a democracy and justice worthy of, and thus other than, the name. To this extent, it is also profoundly Socratic in its power, its scope, and its capacity to discomfit.

I want to linger over one last point in closing, and this is the most difficult of all: how does the revolution happen?[9] There are several responses worth considering here. First, even Marx himself does not explain the nature of revolution with any great specificity. It is a mistake to think, even from the most orthodox and traditional perspective, that there is a recipe. Revolution is not something that we simply go out and do. It is a process that takes place at different levels and speeds. Second, and this is a corrolary of the first, revolutions are not single points in time. We think of the American Revolution, the French Revolution, the Haitian Revolution, or the Russian Revolution, but when did these occur? Not in 1776, 1789, 1791, or 1917. I say this not only because their roots stretch well before the iconic moments of the signing of the US Declaration of Independence, the taking of the Bastille, the first slave revolts, or the storming of the Winter Palace, but also because it is far from clear when or if they

---

9   I owe Chris Breu a sincere debt of thanks for encouraging me to confront this last and most difficult challenge.

ended. The "self-evident" truths of the Declaration—human equality and the rights to life, liberty, and the pursuit of happiness—while still awaiting realization, were potent conceptual forces behind the Civil War, Reconstruction, Civil Rights, and ongoing battles for equality and liberation. In France, a Fifth Republic is still trying to realize the concepts denoted by Liberty, Equality, and Fraternity, or what might better be termed Solidarity. In Haiti, the struggles against racism, colonialism, and the effective continuation of enslavement by other means are as salient today as they have ever been. The Russian Revolution may have ended with the collapse of the Soviet Union, but the vision of a society of comrades working to build a world without exploitation, without imperialism, and where each is addressed according to their needs, still reverberates in struggles around the world. Third, and this is most important, the idea of revolution in Marx never referred to a punctual event. When in Marxist theory, we discuss the succession of modes of production and the cultural and intellectual apparatuses necessary to their functioning and self-replication, it is quite clear that feudalism did not succeed ancient slavery in a single paroxystic spasm, nor did capitalism emerge like Athena from the head of Zeus or even Adam Smith (see Jameson 1981, 95–197). The revolution will not only not be televised, as Gil Scott-Heron reminded us, it is in fact the very name for the processes of history, as human beings confront and try to understand their material and social world, face inevitable conflicts and contradictions, and seek to resolve them by changing that world.

From this perspective, the journey of the concept in its confrontation with its own unthought, with what escapes it, becomes an allegory for its own changing conditions of possibility and for the history produced by and encoded in those conditions (see Jameson 1981, 80 and 109–10). Each aporetic moment poses both the genealogical question of how have we arrived at this juncture and the speculative question of what is to come, *à-venir*. It demands an hauntology of the present that is both a call to action and a rethinking (and remaking) of our lives in common.

2

Late-Roman Post-Futures: The Spectral Planets of Derrida and Gene Wolfe

Ben Radcliffe

The world spirit is; but it is not a spirit.
— Theodor W. Adorno (1973, 304)

In the third chapter of *Specters of Marx,* Derrida sketches what he calls "a black picture on a blackboard," depicting the world in 1993. The picture is composed as a litany of disorders, numbered one through ten and discussed in short paragraphs; they include unemployment, homelessness, economic wars, the free market, foreign debt, the arms trade, nuclear weapons, inter-ethnic conflict, criminal cartels, and the shortcomings of international law. The darkness of this picture is very deliberate, amounting to a rebuke of the "euphoria of liberal-democratic capitalism" that accompanied the collapse of the Soviet Union and the apparent exorcism of the specter of communism. Derrida's bleak picture refutes the panegyrists of the New World Order on empirical grounds; but more to the point, it contests the concept of time that underlies the declaration that the end of the Cold War has marked "the end of history." The ten items in the blackboard picture do not belong to any "single age." They include "archaic" forms of ethnic hatred and the modern threat of nuclear holocaust. "Entire regiments of ghosts have returned, armies from every age" (Derrida 1994a, 94, 96–97, and 100). What darkens the picture is the inconsistency of time, as if the image of a world populated by so many anachronistic spirits should itself become spectral, barely discernible as black marks on a black background.

In this chapter I examine Derrida's *Specters of Marx* alongside philosophical and literary texts from the end of the Cold War, including Fredric Jameson's work on cognitive mapping, Jean-Luc Nancy's *The Sense of the World,* and Gene Wolfe's science-fiction tetralogy, *The Book of the New Sun*. Each of these efforts to picture the world—to render sensible an interconnected planetary reality—grapples with representing the anachronic condition of our globalized present, in which the archaic and the modern, the "armies of every age," must coexist in a single picture. I am interested in a paradox that Derrida's blackboard picture underscores: worlds depicted as dim or obscure seem to have some special value for him in clarifying the possibilities of political and ethical contestation adequate to the temporal incoherence of the planetary order. Derrida and Wolfe employ Greco-Roman antiquity as a particularly productive figure in this regard: the untimely image of the classical past serves as a prototype for the world-picture that each author attempts to construct, a picture that is at once comprehensive and obscure, totalizing and undecidable.

By "world-picture," I mean to invoke what Jameson called an "aesthetic of cognitive mapping."[1] The term designates practices of aesthetic sense-making by which individuals can render palpable and immediate their relation to the abstract totality of the world system. Alberto Toscano and Jeff Kinkle (2015) have recently revived the concept, interpreting a variety of media, including graphs of economic growth, geopolitical maps, landscapes, film, and television, as devices that can orient individuals—however partially and problematically—in relation to

---

1 Jameson defines the concept in "Postmodernism" (1984) and develops it in *The Geopolitical Aesthetic* (1992).

global capitalism. These materialist and affirmatively Marxian approaches form an unstable but productive pairing with Derrida's reevaluation of Marx's intellectual legacy. My goal is not to revisit the polemics that attended the publication of *Specters of Marx* or the charge that Derrida's work substitutes an aporetic negativity in place of the positivity of "committed" Marxian theory.[2] Rather, I assume that Derrida is committed, much like Jameson, to exploring the political and ethical question of how to orient oneself toward the "world-system" and toward the possibility of its eventual disruption.

Derrida's blackboard picture is so bleakly descriptive that it seems at first to project a realist anti-aesthetic, the verisimilitude of "just the facts." But Derrida insists precisely on the aesthetic overdetermination of his list, describing it not just as a "blackboard picture," but as a "tableau," "a ten-word telegram," the subtitles of a "freeze-frame image," and as "ten plagues." His depiction of the world is thus itself depicted as an aesthetic hybrid that might be regarded as a drawing, a painting, a film, a telegram, or a biblical narrative. The potential cognitive value of Derrida's picture is underscored by the didactic function of some of these media — a blackboard picture in a classroom, captions for a tableau, or subtitles in a film. This is not to suggest that this picture (or whatever it is) should be regarded as a definitive *solution* to the problem of cognitive mapping, of how to orient oneself within the confounding temporality of the New World Order. Rather, the picture opens up a range of possible orientations, ways of responding ethically to emerging patterns of globalized violence, governance, and technological acceleration.

The media-defying character of Derrida's picture invites comparisons with other genres that engage in fictive world-building. Derrida's concern with figuring the planetary — with sketching a planet in darkened outlines, in which the archaic and futuristic coexist under the sign of what he calls "techno-science or tele-technology" (1994a, 212) — resonates with elements of

---

2   See, e.g., Eagleton (1999) and other essays in the same volume, *Ghostly Demarcations;* see also Noys (2010).

contemporary science fiction, especially with the Dying Earth.[3] Stemming from the title of a 1950 collection of short stories by Jack Vance, "The Dying Earth" designates a sci-fi or science-fantasy subgenre set in distant futures in which the Earth faces terminal ecological and social decline, triggered, canonically, by the dimming of the sun.[4] This loss of vital energy configures the planet as a fevered archive of its past ages: relicts of futuristic technology coexist with archaic social relations — enslavement, feudalism, petty despotism — and in many instances with elements of fantasy and magic. The Dying Earth is situated after the future, not so much in a different time as in the undifferentiation of time. The premises of the genre channel the line of *Hamlet* repeated throughout *Specters of Marx* — "The time is out of joint" — as well as Derrida's characterization of the neoliberal present: "Neither maturation, nor crisis, nor even agony. Something else. What is happening is happening to age itself, it strikes a blow at the teleological order of history" (1994a, 96).

The "Dying Earth" text that resonates perhaps most closely with Derrida's world-picture in *Specters of Marx* is a tetralogy of novels written by Gene Wolfe in the early 1980s, the *Book of the New Sun*.[5] The novels blend elements of travel narrative, bildungsroman, political thriller, and war story within the conventional framework of the Dying Earth: the protagonist Severian recounts his journey, a decade before, from his childhood home in the decaying capital city of "The Commonwealth" through the nation's wild hinterlands, up to the frontier, and back home

---

3   Derrida refers infrequently to the sci-fi genre, despite his interests in technology, *tekhnē*, and fiction. In "Archive Fever" (1995b), after discussing the intersections between psychoanalysis and forms of communication technology (including the "mystic pad"), he wonders what might have happened if Freud and his collaborators had had access to computers and email: "I would have liked to devote my whole lecture to this retrospective science fiction" (17). For a Derridean reading of H.G. Well's *The Time Machine*, see Hollinger (1987).
4   For an overview of the Dying Earth genre, see K. Johnson (2016).
5   G. Wolfe (1994a, 1994b), originally published in 1980, 1981, 1982, and 1983. The sequel to the tetralogy (*The Urth of the New Sun*) was published in 1987, but I discuss the tetralogy as a single, separate work.

again. He gradually develops a more complete picture of the planetary situation and of his place in it, variously aided and confounded by spectral visions and temporal anomalies. Readers are partially synchronized with the narrator in this process of cognitive mapping, although the link is problematized by the unreliable and fragmented subjectivity of this protagonist. In any case, the narrative draws much of its energy from the gradual disclosure of information that gives readers a provisional, never-entirely secure sense of orientation in the world of the novels.

This process of sense-making is both stimulated and interrupted by a general confounding of temporal coordinates. The dim, impoverished planet is crisscrossed by time travelers from future utopias and amnesiac survivors from past epochs. Visions of apparently pristine landscapes are belied by the fact that "nature" in the tetralogy seems to comprise sedimented, recycled, or re-engineered remnants of earlier civilizations — parts of the planetary crust consist of fossilized wreckage.[6] This temporal disorientation is closely linked with genre: any given feature of the world, when first encountered, might belong to sci-fi, to historical fiction, or to fantasy, leading to a constant interplay between generic recognition and misrecognition. One soon gathers enough clues to infer, for instance, that the "castle" in which Severian was raised as an orphan is in fact the hollowed-out shell of a space-faring craft, abandoned during the collapse of the preceding civilization; that almost every reference to "ships" or "sailors" turns out to be a fossilized cultural memory of interstellar travel; and that a portrait, buried in a forgotten archive and depicting an "armored figure standing in a desolate landscape," is likely an image of a lunar astronaut from the twentieth century. But most of the names and common nouns in the novels are never clarified through this kind of

---

6   With this image, Wolfe vividly illustrates one of the contentions of Marxian ecology — "the immanence of social praxis to material nature" (Toscano 2018, 126); see also J.W. Moore (2015) and Allinson et al. (2021). See also Matlock in this volume on ferality as the mutually destabilizing entanglement of nature and culture.

recognition device; there are indications that words like "metal" and "horse" are only loose approximations for the things that they designate in the world of the novels. The referents of most words are left in ghostly superpositions of the paleolithic, the premodern, and the space-age.

Even as the novels guide readers through the steps of constructing a world-picture, the process reaches an internal limit, a point at which it becomes impossible to arrest the spectral indeterminacy of Wolfe's language. This is also the limit of the aesthetic as such, of the "picture" formed by the "mind's eye" of the reader. When it comes to anachrony, and to spectrality in general, as Derrida notes, it is not sufficient only to look — one has to speak with ghosts, relying on insensible words and silent letters (1994a, 11). Much as Derrida's famous *différance* differs from *différence* (1973), the name of the planet in Wolfe's tetralogy is "Urth," precisely the same sound as "our" Earth but admitting an inscrutable scriptural difference that disrupts any effort to form a clear world-picture of the planet. It may be an entirely different planet than ours, and the resemblances may be accidental, or it may represent Earth's distant future, "distant" meaning, according to one commentator's guess, at least a million years (Andre-Driussi 1994, s.v. "History of Urth").

In certain respects, however, the world-picture developed in the tetralogy forms a transparent allegory for Cold War geopolitics. The Commonwealth is locked in an intercontinental conflict with "Ascia," a totalitarian state that resembles Cold-War caricatures of the Eastern Bloc.[7] Wolfe's anti-communism is plain enough and was probably informed by his traumatic experiences in the Korean War. On the other hand, Wolfe is not a capitalist ideologue, and his tetralogy stresses the flimsiness of the ethical and political coordinates set by the novels' allegori-

---

7   G. Wolfe derived "Ascia" from Greek *askioi*, the "shadowless ones," inhabitants of equatorial regions who, in antiquity, were supposed to cast no shadow on the summer solstice (Andre-Driussi 1994, s.v. "Ascians"). Although the Ascians inhabit the northern hemisphere in the novels, the choice of the term seems to reflect a Cold-War era othering of the populations of the global south.

cal equivalent to the West. The Ascians' opponent in this post-futuristic Cold War is the Commonwealth, Severian's homeland, which exhibits in an exaggerated fashion many of the pathologies of late capitalism, especially of the American variety: heavily militarized and racially stratified, it is paralyzed by infighting among its ruling elite and resistant by design to political change. Severian is offered an opportunity to vanquish the communist Ascians and unite the planet under a revived Commonwealth,[8] but he refuses the offer and gradually recognizes that no extant or imaginable political order can resolve the impasses of the dying planet. Even as Severian maps for himself and for the reader the geopolitical contours of Urth, the world's temporal complexion — and its very capacity for a future — recedes into a state of obscurity.

By figuring the exhaustion of Urth's future, Wolfe's Cold War allegory anticipates the sense of temporal vertigo that Derrida would identify at the war's resolution, a decade after the publication of the *Book of the New Sun*. With the end of the Cold War, capitalism achieved a planetary ascendency that, far from clarifying the vectors of social progress, only deepened a sense of indirection and obsolescence, as conveyed in Derrida's blackboard picture. Perry Anderson (1992) observes that there is an element of truth in Francis Fukuyama's much-disputed claim that the disintegration of actually existing communism spelled the end of history, for it did indeed mark, at least in the present era, the closing of an operable outside to capitalism, an Archimedean point (real or imagined) toward which emancipatory movements could orient themselves and fix their place in the world. Writing in 1993 (the year in which Derrida delivered the lectures that became *Specters of Marx*), Jean-Luc Nancy (1997, 7) identified this movement by which global closure degrades the signifying and orienting capacity of the "world":

There is no longer any sense in a "sense of the world": the significations of each of these words, as well as the significa-

---

8   Typhon offers to make Severian autarch of Urth in Book III, chapter 26.

tion of their syntagma, is caught up in the circling back on themselves of all "occidental" significations, a circling back that coincides with a "becoming-worldwide" that no longer leaves any "outside" and consequently no longer leaves any "inside."

The process of "becoming-worldwide," of globalization, spans many centuries, but Nancy is clearly responding to the decisive acceleration of the process at the end of the twentieth century.[9] The "occidental" (the West, western philosophy, imperialism, and capitalism) achieved a kind of planetary dominion and thus closed in on itself, losing its external referents and constituting a world without boundary or definition, an obscure world. For Nancy, this is ultimately a promising development, because it means that the world no longer has sense as an extrinsic object of thought; it has to designate an immanent field of engagement, of transformation rather than interpretation. I will revisit this redemptive possibility in the conclusion.

* * *

The closure of the late-capitalist world illuminates one of the central figurations of anachrony in Wolfe's sci-fi world-building. As I discuss below, the "Commonwealth" of the novels invokes (and literally translates) the Roman *res publica* and draws pervasively on Greco-Roman vocabulary, social structures, and myths. For Wolfe, the classical world serves as the image of a world without an outside, a figure of temporal and spatial closure.[10] This image emerged already in antiquity: Roman imperial ideology

---

9 Nancy spells out this post-Cold War development in his discussion of labor, where he refers to "the global structuration of the world as the reticulated space of an essentially capitalist, globalist, and monopolist organization that is monopolizing the world" (1997, 101).
10 On the conceptual continuities between modern globalization and Roman imperialism, see Pitts and Versluys (2014) and Sommer (2014).

described its project as *imperium sine fine* ("rule without end"),[11] and Greek intellectuals living under Roman rule, like Polybius and Aristides, interpreted the extent of Roman *imperium* as the political actualization of the *oikoumenē*, the community of the inhabited world that had previously been only notional.[12] Of course, these claims reflect a certain world-picture promoted by Roman rulers and their adjuncts, not the world as it existed; the empire never controlled more than 4% of Earth's land surface. But for Wolfe, the Romanness of posthistorical Urth reflects this image of spatiotemporal closure: it is as if Rome, having outlasted its apparent *finis* in the fifth (or fifteenth?) century CE, has reemerged on the other end of history, transformed but distinctly and distressingly the same.

With closure comes obscurity. As we have seen, Urth is held in stasis by the accumulation of eons of temporal wreckage, such that every potential vector out of the planetary crisis is drawn into a circular impasse by an infinity of countervailing facts; the very possibility of a solution (or the future as such) is rendered obscure by the impression that everything has already been attempted and has failed. In constructing this scenario, Wolfe was probably influenced by an image of the later empire—ubiquitous in Roman historiography until only fifty years ago—as decadent, afflicted by a sense of cultural anxiety and indirection that accompanied the end of Roman expansion and its enclosure of the Mediterranean world.[13] Under such con-

---

11 The phrase is Vergil's (*Aeneid* 1.278); on the semantic development of *imperium* as a notionally unbounded territorial entity, see Richardson (1991) and on the uses of *oikoumenē* and *orbis terrarum* in imperial propaganda, see Geus (2016).
12 On Polybius's influential concept of world history and Roman *imperium*, see (for just one recent interpretation) Groves (2017), and on Aristides's speech *Eis Rhōmēn* and the concept of Mediterranean globality, see Sommer (2014).
13 The publication of Peter Brown's *The World of Late Antiquity* (1971) is usually taken as the watershed moment when the concept of late-antique "decadence" began to be decisively discredited, at least in academia; see Formisano and Fuhrer (2014) on the historiography of decadence and its continuing value in reception studies.

ditions, as Nancy suggests, the sense of the "world" is not simply given — there is too much circularity, too much closural regression; rather, as their efforts at world-picturing rebound off this ineluctable obscurity, subjects are left to engage in an interminable process of local, provisional sense-making.

This process figures prominently in the tetralogy's eccentric and variegated lexicon. One of the devices through which Wolfe imparts a sense of late-Roman obscurity to the world of the novels is his use (and invention) of dozens of Latin- and Greek-derived words and names: sampling from the beginning of the alphabet, these include "aureate," "atrox," "autarch," "autochthon," "avern," "baculus," "cacogen," "Caesidius," "caldarium," "Camoena," and "carnifex."[14] This accumulation of terms, drawn from every period of Greco-Roman antiquity, effectively totalizes the classical past, implying that it can be regarded synoptically as a closed field of cultural referents. Even so, following Wolfe's language requires a combination of research and guesswork — readers are effectively interpellated as translators of a translation, forced to pass through a field of obscure lexical fragments to comprehend references that are even more fundamentally obscure. The Appendix to the first book of the tetralogy is written in the voice of the fictive "translator" of the novels — who signs with the initials "G.W." but is not or is not simply "Gene Wolfe."[15] The translator, who claims to be an expert in "the study of the posthistoric world," has apparently obtained the protagonist's manuscript from the distant future and rendered it into English from "a tongue that has not yet achieved existence" (Wolfe 1994a, 211). They remark further that,

---

14 This is a small sample; in Andre-Driussi's *Lexicon Urthus* (an encyclopedia of distinctive terms in Wolfe's tetralogy) I count 37 Greek- and Latin-derived words and names starting with "A" alone.

15 Given G. Wolfe's arch editorial voice, one cannot rule out the possibility that "G.W." designates someone else, perhaps the notorious technician of philosophical time-travel who traced the end of history in the ruins of the present — Georg Wilhelm (Friedrich Hegel).

in many instances I have been forced to replace yet undiscovered concepts by their closest twentieth-century equivalents. Such words as peltast, androgyn, and exultant are substitutions of this kind, and are intended to be suggestive rather than definitive.

The classicizing translations, in other words, are meant to be "illustrative," allowing readers to apply a world-picture borrowed from Greco-Roman antiquity to illustrate or visualize a "posthistoric world" that exerts a stubborn aesthetic opacity.

And yet, the resemblance between Wolfe's Commonwealth and the classical past is uncannier than the translator's neat explanation might suggest. Like the Roman *res publica,* the Commonwealth is an agrarian slavery-based society dominated by a landowning elite, subject to a mixed constitution, constantly at war, and centered in a metropolis sustained by a vast hinterland. This is not a uniquely Roman situation, to be sure, but an array of smaller details strengthens the sense of spectral repetition. Are the translator's Greco-Roman glosses only dead letters linking two living historical periods? Derrida warns against precisely such an effort to distinguish, as Marx tried to distinguish in *The Eighteenth Brumaire,* between the genuine "spirit" of Rome that vitalizes new social formations (viz. the French Revolution of 1789) and the "specters" of Rome that haunt mechanical imitations of the past (the failed revolution of 1848):

> The great specter of the classical tradition (Rome) is convoked (this is the positive conjuration) so as to allow one to rise to the height of the historic tragedy, but already also so as to hide, in the illusion, the mediocre content of bourgeois ambition. […] It is at this point that Marx intends to distinguish between the spirit (*Geist*) of the revolution and its specter (*Gespenst*), as if the former did not already call up the latter, as if everything, and Marx all the same recognizes this himself, did not pass by way of differences within a fantastic as general as it is irreducible. (Derrida 1994a, 140)

By *une fantastique* ("fantastic"), Derrida evokes the matrix of fantasies through which we produce and distribute distinctions between appearance and reality, between the living spirit and the dead specter. Such distinctions give sense to the notion that a civilization lives, declines, and dies, and then becomes a (spectral) model for what follows it. This notion in turn predominates in contemporary classical reception studies, which tend to regard post-antique continuities with Greece and Rome as deliberate appropriations by which living societies purposefully adapt the non-living material of the classical past for their own uses.

The afterlives of antiquity at work in Wolfe's tetralogy do not fit this schema. On first inspection, the Commonwealth seems to evoke an image of antiquity that has a long history (arguably as old as the *Iliad*) and a great deal of cultural currency even today.[16] In the case of imperial Rome, it is the image of a world in decline, epigonic, and gradually succumbing to forces of cultural and political entropy (see Formisano and Fuhrer 2014). "Decline," in the sense that thinkers like Giambattista Vico or Oswald Spengler promoted, would be part of a trajectory in which a society flourishes, becomes decadent, collapses, and finds renewed vitality,[17] implying finite cycles that periodize historical change. What is happening to Wolfe's "posthistorical world" is not exactly decline, but more like interminable persistence, drawn out over eons, sublime durations that lack any meaningful measure or periodization except for the bare passage of years. It means endless sedimentation and compaction in a "natural" environment consisting of civilizational wreckage misrecognized as nature — an anthropocene eternity. In Wolfe's thought experiment, social configurations operate over geological timespans, and it becomes less meaningful to think of "Romanness" as a cultural model that can be appropriated

---

16 In the *Iliad,* the old counselor Nestor compares the current generation unfavorably to the heroes of old (1.259–73); a more systematic account of generational decline in early epic appears in Hesiod's myth of the races (*Works and Days* 109–201).

17 On the figure of decadence in modern historiography, see Morley (2004).

and adapted at will; it becomes, rather, like a low-energy, stable phase of the earth's climate, a million-year ice age of agrarian slavery punctuated by interglacial spells in which the future and modernity sometimes make brief showings.

The anachrony of Wolfe's late-Roman posthistory tests our intuitions about what it means to form a word-picture in the face of uncanny forms of continuity that, as Walter Benjamin puts it, "comprise the entire history of mankind in an enormous abridgment" (1969, 263). At several points in the tetralogy, Severian consults an anthology of myths and parables published centuries earlier, relating as embedded narratives the book's most recognizably classical content, including garbled versions of Theseus and the Minotaur and Romulus and Remus.[18] Both stories are shot through with anachrony, juxtaposing elements of premodern *Märchen* with hints of interplanetary travel that effectively perplex any effort to visualize the setting and scale of the narratives. The future has already happened, and, even when it happened, it followed tracks already set down during the first (classical) epoch of world-closure. "Already already": at a certain limit, Wolfe's anachrony amounts to what Nancy calls the "circling back on themselves of all 'occidental' significations," a tautological regression of sense that registers capitalism's planetary enclosure and its claim on the end of history (1997, 7).

* * *

In the face of this oppressive epigonic closure, there is a sense in which Wolfe's tetralogy is organized around the possibility of historical rupture. Urth's sun is dimming very gradually, and the planet has become colder and more impoverished, a situation that is widely recognized by characters in the novels and that becomes a spur for eschatological and utopian speculations. Fredric Jameson (2005, 267–80) developed a compelling interpretation of this kind of relation between cold, scarcity, and the

---

18 The narratives are entitled, "Tale of the Student and his Son" (2.17) and "Tale of the Boy Called Frog" (3.19).

utopian imagination in a 1975 essay on Ursula K. Le Guin's science fiction. Referring especially to Le Guin's *The Left Hand of Darkness,* which is set on an ice-age planet that lacks most forms of animal and plant life, and whose humanoid population lacks stable sex and gender dichotomies, Jameson (2005, 271) remarks that,

> Le Guin's experiment […] is based on a principle of systematic exclusion, a kind of surgical excision of empirical reality, something like a process of ontological attenuation in which the sheer teeming multiplicity of what exists, of what we call reality, is deliberately thinned and weeded out through an operation of radical abstraction and simplification which I will henceforth term "world reduction."

This passage is part of Jameson's larger argument that utopian imagination — the desire to envision a world radically different from the present one — is increasingly suppressed by "the massive commodity environment of late capitalism," the vast surplus of consumer goods that colonizes and weighs on the imagination (2005, 278–79).[19] By alleviating the weight of this "reality," world-reduction serves as a utopian sci-fi counterpart to the practices of cognitive mapping that Jameson theorized in *Postmodernism*. It advances a polemical world-picture in which individual or collective subjects have more room to maneuver, if only in thought, as they envision utopian futures.

As a literary technique, world reduction does not entail any straightforward reduction in descriptive detail: Le Guin's worlds, like Wolfe's, aim to immerse readers in a densely layered reality, in the mode of an anthropological encounter. What world reduction amounts to, rather, is the excision of precise features of our picture of reality as such, of any fully realized reality. A world reduced in this way is desaturated, opened up to possibilities of reconfiguration excluded by the oppressive

---

19 On Jameson's account of the endless present of late-capitalist consumerism, see Telò in this volume.

fullness of the "actually existing" world. The excised part, as it were, allows for movement in the structured whole of the world-picture, like the "empty square" that Deleuze (2004) identifies as the volatile, mobilizing element in structure. The principle "reduction" in Wolfe's tetralogy is effected by the slow death of the sun, which subtracts from the world-picture the sun's infinite excess of energy, the unconditional gift that underwrites the planet's metabolism and sustains a bass note of optimism about the possibility of the renewal of human life (see Bataille 1991). But in Wolfe's depiction, this unconditional renewal has morphed, through endless repetition, into a kind of futurelessness, or rather, as Derrida puts it, "a future that can always reproduce the present" (1992b, 27).[20] With the pending retraction of the sun's energetic gift, the posthistorical world faces the prospect of a radically different future, the unforeseeable "future-to-come." It is this prospect, rather than the image of planetary extinction *per se,* that gives the narrative its impetus. The end itself is probably still far off when the novels are set, but its approach colors every image of the world in the red light of the dying sun.

Some characters respond with dreams of social and political renewal, committing themselves to armed insurrection against the government of the Commonwealth. Their utopian aspirations are discredited over the course of the novels, and Severian follows a different trajectory, shaped by an almost-expressly Christian eschatology enriched by pervasive allusions to the Roman persecution of the early church. Depending on how one untangles the temporal structure of the narrative, Severian is, or will have been, or will be again, Urth's Messiah, destined to sacrifice himself on a mission — completed in the 1987 sequel to the tetralogy — to restore the sun. Wolfe's conservatism shows through here in his rejection of the possibility of immanent social renewal: redemption is achieved by a single individual who can mediate forces that transcend Urth and that hold the keys to its future. Even so, there is a certain resemblance between this variety of messianism and what Derrida

---

20 On the "future present" in Derrida and Blanchot, see Telò in this volume.

conceives in *Specters of Marx* as "the messianic without messianism," a "messianic opening to what is coming, that is, to the event that cannot be awaited as such, or recognized in advance" (1994a, 82). Wolfe's fugitive, aimless, but endlessly adaptive protagonist does not know how salvation will come, or from where, nor does he actively search for it or recognize it in advance. The world-picture that he forms in tandem with readers does not serve as a map for exercising effective agency but as a structure of experience, a kind of hospitality toward the future.[21]

Derrida's blackboard picture has a similar kind of cognitive value. Although it takes the form of a list, it is not simply a checklist of "urgent business" for left political activism. The value of the picture is that it is "bleak [...] almost black."[22] The monochrome uniformity of Derrida's bad news, its lack of colorful detail, the difficulty in "seeing" or discerning the significance of these ten figures of globalized disorder — all of these features effect a certain distancing from the empirical, what Jameson calls "ontological attenuation" in his discussion of world reduction. Derrida develops two interpretations of his world-picture. The first would call for renewed efforts to critique the empirical shortcomings of capitalist societies with respect to their own (enlightenment) ideals; Derrida's second, preferred interpretation (1994a, 108) stresses that,

> beyond the "facts," beyond the supposed "empirical evidence," beyond all that is inadequate to the ideal, it would be a question of putting into question again, in certain of its essential predicates, the very concept of the said ideal.

The ideals in question include "democracy," "human rights," and "liberty," among many others, all manifestly contradicted by the contents of the blackboard picture. The dimness of the picture,

---

21 On Derrida's concept of unconditional hospitality, see Dougherty in this volume.
22 Cf. Adorno's remark in *Aesthetic Theory* regarding the use of color in modern art: "radical art… is synonymous with dark art; its primary color is black" (1998, 39).

its accumulation of violence and insecurity, discloses an opacity in our ethical relation to the world system. One could attempt to change the picture's content to match the ideals, but the ideals — the vision — are shown to be inadequate tools for orienting oneself in the picture; this task has to call on other, submerged or marginalized resources of sense-making. In *Memoirs of the Blind,* Derrida claims that every drawing "has something to do with blindness" (1993d, 2), configuring blindness here not privatively, as *dis*-ability, but as the potency of the unseen, the rich array of mediations — thoughts, dreams, and memories — that facilitate and exceed the powers of sight. This is especially true of pictures that make a virtue of obscurity. Against neoliberal discourses that fetishize transparency and the limitless accumulation of information, the world-pictures in Derrida and Wolfe aim to render the present's empirical content obscure by conflating it with ancient pasts and imagined futures. Paradoxically, this anachronic obscurity clears zones of maneuver in which we might contest the unseen givens of our geopolitical vision and construct an infrastructure for orienting ourselves in the end of history.[23]

---

23 Derrida invokes the figures of blindness and invisibility at least twice in *Specters of Marx* (1994a): "This condition of possibility of the event is also its condition of impossibility, like this strange concept of messianism without content, of the messianic without messianism, that guides us here like the blind" (82), and "One must see, at first sight, what does not let itself be seen. And this is invisibility itself" (187).

3

The Spectral Life of Friends: Derrida, Cicero, Atticus

Francesca Martelli

In two, three or four words, is the friend the same or the other?
— Jacques Derrida (1997b, 4)

A guiding premise of *The Politics of Friendship* is that friendship is structured from the outset by the prospect that one friend will die before the other, and that the surviving friend will be left to bury, commemorate, and mourn the one who has died. But who or what do I mourn with the death of my friend? And how does my anticipated grief over their death structure the time of my life? Derrida surveys a number of treatises on friendship, the friend and, indeed, the enemy, in order to extrapolate the political implications of this fundamental insight: that friendship is lived in the future perfect, and looks towards a mutually implicating, yet asynchronous, future of death (for one friend) and privation (for the other).

The starting point for Derrida's tour through the discursive history of friendship is Cicero's *De amicitia* (*On Friendship*), which provides him with a negative foil for the inquiry that follows. For Derrida, Cicero's *On Friendship* effaces the alterity of the friend too far to approximate the model of friendship that he understands. But what of Cicero *as* a friend? What, in particular, of his friendship with Atticus, which hovers around the margins of *On Friendship,* both preceding it and succeeding it, as part of this treatise's own *à venir*? This, one of history's most famous friendships, is structured by the very same anticipation of death, mourning, and survival that provides the key to Derrida's formulation of friendship, but which Derrida denies to Cicero *qua* author of *On Friendship.* Recuperating this dimension of Cicero matters not because of the corrective that it issues to Derrida for failing to form a proper intimacy with this particular ancient author, but because it allows us to see how the discursive history of friendship that Derrida plots is already structured by the same dynamic that he locates in the temporality peculiar to friendship — or could be, if he would only recognize Cicero as a fellow friend. Cicero, the first author that Derrida treats in any depth in *The Politics of Friendship,* anticipates Derrida's view of friendship by some millennia, and thereby forms part of the discursive *à venir* that Derrida's own treatise on friendship materializes.

In this chapter, I make the case for a Cicero who speaks back to Derrida about friendship in Derrida's own terms. I will begin by looking at how *On Friendship* figures in Derrida's opening discussion of friendship — at how he sets up Cicero's idealizing view of the friend within this treatise as the main point of departure for his own view of friendship — before then considering whether his reading of the text tells the whole story, whether we might find in *On Friendship* a view of friendship that approximates more closely to what Derrida has in mind. And I will then turn to another Ciceronian testament to friendship, *Letters to Atticus,* a collection of letters addressed to Cicero's friend Atticus, to argue that this text answers even more closely to the view of friendship that Derrida is at pains to promote.[1] My discussion will touch on the resemblance that Derrida's view of the friend

---

1 I follow the Cambridge Classical Texts edition of Shackleton Bailey (1999). I do not follow Shackleton Bailey's numbering of the letters, but follow the order transmitted in the manuscripts. All translations are mine, unless otherwise noted.

shares with the ghosts of *Specters of Marx,* which haunt the present from both the past and the future of their asynchronous horizons.[2] And because *Letters to Atticus* is a (if not *the*) major source of what we know about a particular period of ancient history, as well as being a foundational text for the rediscovery of classical antiquity in the Renaissance, I will consider in passing how far the spectral temporality of the friendship that it discloses structures the history of the late Republic, as well as the relationship with antiquity that it opens up for Renaissance readers and their successors.

Derrida's *De Amicitia*

In his critique of Cicero's *On Friendship,* Derrida focuses his discussion on a passage in which Cicero looks to the exemplary friendships that history holds up for emulation, in order to argue that the ideal friend should appear as the *exemplar,* or mirror image, of the self:[3]

> For the man who keeps his eye on a true friend, keeps it, so to speak, on a model of himself [*verum etiam amicum qui intuetur, tamquam exemplar aliquod intuetur sui*]. For this reason, friends are together when they are separated, they are rich when they are poor, strong when they are weak, and — a thing even harder to explain — they live on after they have died (*mortui vivunt*), so great is the honor that follows them, so vivid the memory, so poignant the sorrow. That is why friends who have died are accounted happy, and those who survive are deemed worthy of praise [*ex quo illorum beata mors videtur, horum vita laudabilis*]. (23)[4]

Derrida (1997b, 4) highlights the ambiguity of Cicero's use of the term exemplar, meaning both original and copy, to show how it

---

2 In this, it revisits a question explored by P.A. Miller (2016).
3 This passage is quoted directly in Derrida (1997b, 5).
4 I follow the text of Falconer (1923).

reduces the alterity of the friend, making self and other collapse in one another:

> Cicero uses the word *exemplar,* which means portrait but also, as the *exemplum,* the duplicate, the reproduction, the copy as well as the original, the type, the model. The two meanings (the single original and the multipliable copy) cohabit here; they are — or seem to be — the same, and that is the whole story, the very condition of survival. Now, according to Cicero, his *exemplar* is projected or recognized in the true friend, it is his ideal double, his other self, the same as self but improved. Since we watch him looking at us, thus watching ourselves, because we see him keeping our image in his eyes — in truth in ours — survival is then hoped for, illuminated in advance, if not assured, for this Narcissus who dreams of immortality. Beyond death, the absolute future thus receives its ecstatic light, it appears only from within this narcissism and according to this logic of the same.

Derrida also highlights the limitations of the mode of futurity that such a model of friendship opens up beyond death: when the friend is viewed as the mirror-image of the self, their death (or mine) is compensated for by the survival of either one of us, who lives on simply to perpetuate the renown of the other in a form of self-extension that is as predictable as it is onanistic.[5] This narcissistic view, says Derrida, in fact spells the death of friendship. For what else is friendship if not a relation to someone who is *not* me and whose difference from me is a necessary and insurmountable condition for the friendship between us?

Turning away from Cicero to seek out discourses on friendship that stress not resemblance and reciprocity, but rather its asymmetries, Derrida lights on the seventh book of the *Eudemian Ethics,* where Aristotle's insistence on the idea that, in friendship, it is better to love than be loved, provides him

---

[5] See Derrida (1997b, 5) on the fantasies that some people harbor of friends delivering funeral speeches at their graves.

with the key to undoing the narcissism of Cicero's formulation of friendship.[6] For Aristotle, the act of loving in friendship, without the expectation of any return, takes precedence over everything else, and is nowhere better illustrated than in the love we feel for the friend who has died. As Derrida points out, this fundamentally recasts the relationship between friendship and death.[7] For this asymmetrical feeling generates a very different view of future time: no longer the future of predictable self-extension and renown, the future that the anticipated death of my friend brings is unknown and unknowable in advance because it comes to me from the other. The "anguished apprehension" of this moment plunges me "before mourning, into mourning" (1997b, 29). It opens the time of my life to theirs, and the same goes for my friend, who in turn bears my death and mourns my life in advance. According to this model, the chief reciprocity of friendship is a distinctly asymmetrical one insofar

---

[6] Aristotle, *Eudemian Ethics* 1239a35–b2: "Loving rather than being loved is the measure of friendship; being loved is a matter of the merits of the beloved. For evidence of this, consider whether a friend would prefer to know, or be known by, the person he loves, assuming that it is impossible to have both. To know, surely, as women do when they give up their children for adoption, like Andromache in Antiphon's tragedy. The desire to be known, indeed, something selfish, aimed at getting rather than giving, whereas one desires to know in order to give practical effect to one's love. That is why we praise people who go on loving those who are dead: for they know, but are not known." I refer to the Oxford Classical Texts edition of Rowe (2023). All translations are my own, unless otherwise stated. See Derrida (1997b, 8–12), for discussion of the connection that Aristotle draws in this passage between loving, knowledge, and the question of adoption that Antiphon's *Andromache* raises.

[7] Derrida (1997b, 29) says: "This *philia,* this *psukhê* between friends, survives. It cannot survive itself as act, but it can survive its object, it can love the inanimate. Consequently it springs forward from the threshold of this act, towards the possibility that the beloved might be dead. There is a first and irreducible dissymmetry here. But this same dissymetry separates itself, after a fashion, in an unpresentable topology; it folds, it turns inside out and doubles itself at the same time in the hypothesis of shared friendship, the friendship tranquilly described as reciprocal. I do not survive the friend, I cannot and must not survive him, except to the extent to which he already bears my death and inherits it as the last survivor."

as it lies in the extent to which we both anticipate mourning the death of the other, an event that only one of us will be allowed to experience. Or, as David Webb eloquently puts it, my friend and I are "implicated in the structure of each other's finitude without sharing a common horizon" (2003, 122), each one haunted by the possibility of the other's death.

Atticus's *De Amicitia*

This, in summary fashion, is how Derrida sets up the view of friendship that Cicero expounds in his own treatise on friendship, only to discard it in favor of an alternative view. Yet while his analysis may offer a fair enough assessment of what Cicero's *On Friendship* has to say explicitly about friendship, there is a gap between what the dialogue says and what it does — a gap that poses one of its most challenging hermeneutic puzzles for readers. This dialogue is set a generation before Cicero was born, and portrays a conversation between Gaius Laelius and his two sons-in-law, a few days after the death of Laelius's great friend, Scipio Aemilianus in 129 BCE; Laelius offers his views about friendship, inspired by the memory of his recently deceased friend. But the treatise as a whole is dedicated by Cicero to his close friend Atticus. Composed in 44 BCE, the year before Cicero died, when, as he points out, he and Atticus were both old men, it demands to be read in the context of their own lifelong friendship. And this produces an unmistakable disjunction between what Laelius says about the exemplary friend as an idealized second self, as demonstrated by the friendship between himself and Scipio — two public figures of the same senatorial class — and the status of Atticus himself, the dedicatee of the treatise, a man who had chosen not to pursue a life of public office at Rome, and who could not, therefore, offer Cicero the kind of idealized specular double that a Scipio could offer Laelius, or vice versa.[8] While the disparity between Cicero

---

8   See Habinek (1990, 179–81), on how the disparity between Cicero and Atticus, with regard to their respective social positions, is a necessary

and Atticus is never explicitly addressed in the dialogue, it is alluded to early on in an anecdote about a friendship that turned sour between Publius Sulpicius, a cousin of Atticus's, and Quintus Pompeius Rufus, during the factional fallout of the Social Wars.[9] The violent death of Sulpicius at the hands of the Sullan partisans of his friend-turned-enemy is thought to have been the chief event that motivated Atticus's withdrawal from politics and removal to Athens, where he spent the next 20 years of his life, thus earning himself the cognomen Atticus. Mentioned briefly at the start of *On Friendship,* the anecdote reminds the reader of the career choice that set Atticus apart from the likes of Laelius and Scipio, even if Cicero never spells out its consequences for his friend in as many words.

Nevertheless, the consequences of Atticus's decision to retreat from public life are felt throughout *On Friendship,* in the mismatch that is generated between what the dialogue says about friendship (as a relationship between peers), and what it is (or what it does) as a tribute to Cicero's unequal friend. This mis-

---

predicate for the frankness of their exchanges — and for the intimacy of their friendship, since equality of rank may engender competition. This insight is borne out by the different tone (and content) of Cicero's letters to Atticus, as compared with the letters to many of his senatorial friends in the *Ad Familiares,* although within that social rank there are also shades of difference. Habinek (1990, 176–78) productively contrasts Cicero's strained letters to Appius in *To Friends* 3 with the frankness of young Caelius's letters to Cicero in *To Friends* 8. Cicero's tendency to confide in Atticus on matters as disparate and personal as his unorthodox desire to erect a shrine to his dead daughter in book 12 and his financial straits in book 16 of the collection) is a measure of the intimacy, and disparity (as far as social position goes), of their friendship.

9 Cicero, *On Friendship* 2: "You, Atticus, were much in the company of Publius Sulpicius, and on that account are more likely to remember what great amazement, or rather dismay, there was among the people when Sulpicius, while plebeian tribune, separated himself in deadly hatred from the man who was then consul, Quintus Pompeius, with whom he had lived on the most intimate and affectionate terms [*quocum coniunctissime et amantissime vixerat*]." I refer to the Oxford Classical Text edition of Powell (2006). All translations are mine, unless otherwise noted. See P.A. Miller (2015, 189–90), for discussion of the significance of this anecdote for the relationships that the dialogue invokes.

match is openly flagged for readers in the dedication of the treatise to Atticus, when Cicero, having spent some time explaining why Laelius is the ideal mouthpiece for a dialogue on friendship, tells Atticus that he will recognize himself in Laelius's account:

> But as in that book I wrote as one old man to another old man on the subject of old age, so now in this book I have written as a most affectionate friend to a friend on the subject of friendship [*sed ut tum ad senem senex de senectute, sic hoc libro ad amicum amicissimus scripsi de amicitia*]. In the former work the speaker was Cato, whom scarcely any in his day exceeded in age and none surpassed in wisdom; in the present treatise the speaker on friendship will be Laelius, a wise man (for he was so appraised), and a man who was distinguished by a glorious friendship [*et amicitiae gloria excellens*]. Please put me out of your mind for a little while and believe that Laelius himself is talking. Gaius Fannius and Quintus Mucius Scaevola have come to their father-in-law's house just after the death of Africanus. The conversation is begun by them and reply is made by Laelius, whose entire discourse is on friendship, and as you read it, you will recognize in it a portrait of yourself [*respondet Laelius, cuius tota disputatio est de amicitia quam legens te ipse cognosces*]. (*On Friendship* 4–5)

There are, as Paul Allen Miller points out, a number of different ways of parsing the relational terms of the comparison drawn in the closing lines of this passage (2015, 183–84):[10] either Atticus will recognize himself as Scipio, the object of Laelius's discourse on friendship; or he will recognize himself as Laelius, in which case Laelius's comments about Scipio represent Cicero's projection of what Atticus thinks about Cicero. Or Atticus will quite literally come to know himself in the course of reading the dialogue, because of the ways in which it helps to exterior-

---

10 P.A. Miller (2015, 183–84) describes the involutions of this passage as "worthy of Derrida himself."

ize his subject position in the mirror of all the figures that the dialogue holds up as exemplary friends. The problem, as Eleanor Leach (1993, 17–18) highlights, is that none of these exemplars — neither Laelius nor Scipio nor the generalized *exemplum* of friendship that together they and others combine to construct — amounts to a model of friendship that fits Atticus's mold, precisely because of the emphasis on public service that characterizes all of these exemplary friends.

This realization comes to the fore in the eulogy of Scipio that Laelius delivers near the start of the dialogue, which is particularly striking when read in light of Derrida's comments about the funeral orations that friends deliver at the graves of the dead, because of its marked resemblance to a funeral speech.[11] The terms of this eulogy make it hard to see it as part of Cicero's tribute to Atticus's friendship. It makes far more sense, perhaps, to imagine it as Cicero's fantasy about the kind of speech that Atticus might deliver at his funeral — along the lines of the narcissistic fantasy that Derrida describes (1997b, 5). But even then, Atticus would not be the obvious person to deliver this speech because his own removal from the public sphere means that he is not equipped to perpetuate this kind of renown through his own living example. So, however we attempt to map Cicero and Atticus onto this exemplary pair of friends, a fundamental mis-

---

11 Cicero, *On Friendship* 11: "But who would say things had not gone wonderfully well with him [Scipio]? For unless he had wished to live forever — a wish he was very far from entertaining — what was there, proper for a human being to wish for, that he did not attain. The exalted expectation that his country conceived of him in his childhood, he at a bound, through incredible merit, more than realized in his youth. Though he never sought the consulship, he was elected consul twice — the first time before he was of legal age, the second time at a period seasonable for him, but almost too late for the safety of the commonwealth. And he overthrew the two cities that were the deadliest foes of our empire and thereby put an end not only to existing wars, but to future wars as well. Why need I speak of his most affable manners, of his devotion to his mother, of his generosity to his sisters, of his kindness to his relatives, of his strict integrity to all men. These things are well-known to you both. Moreover, how dear he was to the State was indicated by the grief displayed at his funeral."

match keeps recurring, as the parity of status between Laelius and Scipio serves to underscore the disparity that characterizes Cicero's friendship with Atticus. And the dialectical movement that this mismatch generates between the content and the frame of the dialogue means that an alternative view of friendship, embodied by Cicero and Atticus, and marked by the kind of alterity that characterizes Derrida's preferred version, hovers around the edges of the exemplary friendship that the dialogue explicitly celebrates throughout.

What that alternative model of friendship is, however, is barely sketched out for us within *On Friendship,* where it appears only very faintly as a kind of hologram around the canonical friendship that Laelius and Scipio represent. It will take another text transmitted within the Ciceronian corpus, the *Letters to Atticus,* to flesh out the details of what this alternative view of friendship looks like. This letter collection appears (from the testimony of Cornelius Nepos, Atticus's personal friend and biographer) to have been compiled in the interval that falls between the death of Cicero in 43 BCE and the death of Atticus some eleven years later, in a sixteen-book format that sounds very much like the collection that was transmitted.[12] Nepos's biography provides important testimony of Atticus being the friend who survives — surviving the proscriptions that ended Cicero's life, and reaching an accommodation with Octavian and the others who enabled him to live in peace until he died of natural causes in 32 BCE (Nepos, *Atticus* 19–22); a vindication, perhaps, of the choice he made early on in his career to remove himself from the dangers of the political arena. The fact

---

12 Nepos, *Atticus* 16 (text of Rolfe 1929): "[T]hough Marcus Cicero, loved him above all men, so that not even his brother Quintus was dearer or more closely united to him [*quamquam eum praecipue dilexit Cicero, ut ne frater quidem ei Quintus carior fuerit aut familiarior*]. In testimony of this fact (besides the books in which Cicero mentions him, and which have been published to the world), there are sixteen books of letters, written to Atticus, which extend from his consulship to his latter days [*ei rei sunt indicio praeter eos libros, in quibus de eo facit mentionem, qui in vulgus sunt editi, sedecim volumina epistularum, ab consulatu eius usque ad extremum tempus ad Atticum missarum*]."

of his survival invites us to view the sixteen-book letter collection that seems to have been compiled between Cicero's death and his own as a product of that process of surviving: Atticus's tribute to his dead friend, and part of his own work of mourning for him, although whoever actually compiled the collection remains unknown and unknowable.

As a testament to the friendship between the two men, the collection of *Letters to Atticus* is one that squarely displays the alterity of that friendship in part because of the way in which it limits itself exclusively to Cicero's side of the correspondence. Toward the end of *The Politics of Friendship,* in the context of discussing the absolute singularity of the friend and the friend's resistance to being generalized, Derrida (1997b, 294) cites the words of Maurice Blanchot (1971, 328–29) to this effect:[13]

> Friendship, this relation without dependence, without episode, into which, however, the utter simplicity of life enters, implies the recognition of a common strangeness which does not allow us to speak of our friends, but only to speak to them, not to make of them a theme of conversations (or articles), but the movement of understanding in which speaking to us, they reserve, even in the greatest familiarity, an infinite distance, this fundamental separation from out of which that which separates becomes relation.

In emphasizing Cicero's side of the correspondence, *Letters to Atticus* supplements *On Friendship*'s discourse about friendship with a portrait of their friendship that shows Cicero's abiding need, over decades, to speak to his friend in letters that offer a view of their friendship that is very far from the version idealized in *On Friendship*. The epistolary medium of the portrait that the *Letters to Atticus* offers raises up the letter as the perfect vehicle for both communicating and enshrining that movement

---

13 On the relationship between Blanchot and Derrida, see Telò in this volume.

of understanding across distance (and difference) of which Blanchot here speaks.

The Politics of Friendship in *Letters to Atticus* 1

In the latter part of this chapter, I will argue that the collection of letters addressed to Atticus, haunted as it is by our advance knowledge that Cicero will die before Atticus and that Atticus will be left to mourn his friend, displays the spectral temporal dynamic that Derrida identifies as a basic premise of friendship in its very organization. My guiding question is: why does the collection begin as it does with the sequence of letters that we find in *Letters to Atticus* 1, when Cicero's close friendship with Atticus predated this letter sequence by several decades? The book as a whole is a chronologically and thematically mixed bag, unevenly covering a period of nine years from 68–60 BCE, without following chronological order, and stands apart from the other books in the collection as a result of this. But one of the book's most striking points of coherence comes from the way in which it echoes or anticipates themes and preoccupations from the very end of Cicero's life. Cicero's late philosophical dialogues, for example, were written long after these letters were composed, but precede their publication in the collection, haunting the letters in this letter book from both the past and the future.

One dialogue that looms particularly large over this book is none other than *On Friendship* itself, which was composed in 44 BCE, the year before Cicero died, and, as noted above, reflects, albeit obliquely, on his lifelong friendship with Atticus in retrospect. Here in the opening book of their published correspondence we encounter two letters that proffer the most direct comment that we have in the Ciceronian corpus on the value that Cicero places on his friendship with Atticus, in terms that seem designed to complement or supplement the views on friendship set out in *On Friendship,* which was written some 15 years later.

Letter to Atticus 1.17 is a reply that Cicero writes to a letter that he has received from Atticus, defending himself in response to a recent falling out with Cicero's brother Quintus, to whom Atticus's sister was married, which seems to have been occasioned by Atticus's refusal to accompany Quintus to Asia, where the latter had been appointed to a provincial posting. Cicero writes to Atticus to tell him how little he needs to justify his actions as far as their own friendship goes, and makes a point of emphasizing how he has never felt the intimacy, or indeed, the parity, of their friendship challenged by the choice that Atticus made not to pursue public office (1.17.5):

> I am perfectly aware of your large-minded indifference to personal profit, and I have never felt any difference between us except in the modes of life we have chosen [*neque ego inter me atque te quicquam interesse umquam duxi praeter voluntatem institutae vitae*]. What may be called ambition has led me to seek political advancement, while another and entirely justifiable way of thinking has led you to an honorable independence [*quod me ambitio quaedam ad honorum studium, te autem alia minime reprehendenda ratio ad honestum otium duxit*]. In the things that really matter — uprightness, integrity, conscientiousness, sense of obligation — I put you second neither to myself nor to any other man [*vera quidem laude probitatis, diligentiae, religionis neque me tibi neque quemquam antepono, amoris vero erga me*], while as to affection towards me, leaving aside my brother and my own home circle, I give you first prize. I've seen with my own eyes and very thoroughly noted your anxieties and your joys in the ups and downs of my career [*vidi enim, vidi penitusque perspexi in meis variis temporibus et sollicitudines et laetitias tuas*]. Your congratulation has often given me pleasure in success and your comfort consoled my apprehensions [*fuit mihi saepe et laudis nostrae gratulatio tua iucunda et timoris consolatio grata*] […]. In short, whether working or resting, in business or in leisure, in professional or domestic affairs, in public life or private, I cannot for any length of time do without your affectionate advice and the delight of your con-

versation [*non privatae carere diutius tuo suavissimo atque amantissimo consilio ac sermone possunt*].

In all things that matter, says Cicero, we are the same, and he offers a rationale for their different career choices that makes these appear as equal alternatives, rather than the unequal paths that they really were — his insistence on their personal equality a desperate attempt to compensate for the patent disparity that comes from his own pursuit of life in the public eye. Never mind the fact that, as Thomas Habinek (1990) points out, that disparity may be the basis on which the candor of Cicero's friendship with Atticus is premised — a candor that displays itself in Cicero's reliance on Atticus for everything, from cultural goods (as provided by his library) to financial loans and advice.[14] At first sight this letter (along with its successor, 1.18), seems to supplement the treatise *On Friendship* by underscoring, despite Cicero's protestations to the contrary, the unequal status between the two friends, and all the differentials that entail from that fundamental point of disparity.[15] But when we read this letter

---

14 Cicero's reliance on Atticus for financial help, in particular, may strike modern readers as evidence of an instrumentalizing view of his friend, one that is starkly incompatible with his position in *On Ends* 2.84–85 (text of Madvig 1876), where he denounces the utilitarian view of friendship espoused by Epicureans, but see Martelli (2024) on how Cicero's position on friendship at this point in *On Ends* is challenged by the portrait of his relationships with friends in the *Letters to his Friends*. According to the model of friendship that Derrida prefers, however, dependence may be seen as a symptom of that very alterity between friends that he prizes. Cicero's reliance on Atticus for financial and other favors may be seen to manifest the Derridean ideal of friendship, rather than being something that undermines it. It is impossible, for example, to imagine him leaning on a senatorial figure such as Appius Claudius Pulcher (his addressee in book 3 of *Letters to his Friends*) for the kind of financial help he asks of Atticus. As ever, the candor of true friendship is based on alterity or disparity.

15 This point is made openly in the following letter (*To Atticus* 1.18), where Cicero, in the course of telling Atticus that as long as he is away from Rome he has no true friend to talk to, draws a distinction between his true friend (Atticus), and the *ambitiosae* [...] *fucosaeque amicitiae* that dominate his life in the public eye: "My worldly, meretricious friendships

THE SPECTRAL LIFE OF FRIENDS

with the benefit of hindsight, the further point that it raises is that Atticus's career choice may have been the right one. It was certainly the choice that ensured his survival. This possibility hovers over *On Friendship,* which was written at a time when Cicero had good cause to weigh Atticus's career choice favorably against his own, without ever being broached directly. This letter, haunted as it is not only by the future event of Cicero's death but by Atticus's survival too, fills out the details of Cicero's unequal friendship with Atticus, which *On Friendship* leaves screamingly unmentioned, and shows how far that disparity could be recalibrated in different circumstances. In a climate in which political engagement and political retreat meant death or survival respectively, the disparity that entails from these alternative career choices could be radically overturned.

On Friendship looms large over this letter and its successor, haunting them both from the past and from the future, in the same way that these two letters, when published, will haunt *On Friendship,* laying bare all that its idealized view of exemplary friendship occludes. But in addition to the thematic resonance that we find between these letters on friendship and the theme of one of his later dialogues, there are also situational details that anticipate or remind us of this moment of philosophical activity late in Cicero's life. One narrative thread that runs through

---

> make a fine show in public, but at home they are barren things [*nam illae ambitiosae nostrae fucosaeque amicitiae sunt in quodam splendore forensi, fructum domesticum non habent*]. My house is crammed of a morning. I go down to the Forum surrounded by droves of friends, but in all the multitude I cannot find one with whom I can pass an unguarded joke or fetch a private sigh [*itaque, cum bene completa domus est tempore matutino, cum ad forum stipati gregibus amicorum descendimus, reperire ex magna turba neminem possumus, quocum aut iocari libere aut suspirare familiariter possimus*]." The true friend appears from this passage to be the unequal one, a sentiment that Derrida would approve, as he would also endorse Cicero's distinction between the singular true friend and the many people who bear the name of friend without living up to it. The refrain, attributed to Aristotle, that recurs throughout the *Politics of Friendship,* "O friends! There is no friend!," provides Derrida with a spur to reformulate again and again the question that friendship raises about the extent to which true friends can exist in the plural.

a number of letters in the book concerns Cicero's purchase, through Atticus, of various statues designed to decorate his villa at Tusculum, and turn it into a venue fit for the cultural aspirations he harbors for the place (*Letters to Atticus* 1.4.2):

> I'm pleased with what you have to say about the Hermathena. It's an appropriate ornament for my Academy, since Hermes is the common emblem of all gymnasia and Minerva special to that one [*est ornamentum Academiae proprium meae, quod et Hermes commune omnium et Minerva singulare est insigne eius gymnasii*].

This is the first occasion that we hear of Cicero describing his Academy as such, in ways that make us look forward to that later point in Cicero's life when he would undertake his most intensive phase of philosophical activity in this location. In *Letters to Atticus* 1.10, this moment is explicitly evoked, when Cicero mentions a library of books in Atticus's possession that he wants to purchase from him alongside the statues to be what he describes as a *subsidium*, or relief, for his old age.[16]

Cicero's mention of *this* Academy turns our minds to its model in Athens, where Cicero joined Atticus in 79, eleven years before their correspondence begins, at a formative stage of the former's education. This place receives a haunting description at the outset of Book 5 of *On Ends*, Cicero's dialogue on the chief goals of the three main philosophical schools; he wrote Book 5 in 45 BCE, at least in part at that villa at Tusculum, but it is set in 79 BCE, when he and Atticus were both in Athens. The inter-

---

16 *To Atticus* 1.10.3: "Yes, I'd be grateful if you would ship when you most conveniently can my statues and Heracles herms and anything else you come across that would be suitable for the place — you know what it's like — especially for the palaestra and the gymnasium. That's where I'm sitting and writing now, so my thoughts naturally turn to it. Please also get me some bas-reliefs which I can lay in the stucco of the small entrance hall and two figured puteals. Mind you don't promise your library to anyone, however ardent a suitor you find. I'm saving up all my small change to buy it as a prop for my old age [*nam ego omnes meas vindemiolas eo reservo, ut illud subsidium senectuti parem*]."

locutors involved in this dialogue are Cicero, Atticus (who is not yet called Atticus at this point), Cicero's brother Quintus, his cousin Lucius, and Marcus Piso, who becomes the mouthpiece for the Antiochean system that unfolds in the rest of the book. It begins by describing their walk to the Academy in the middle of the day, which they find predictably deserted (*On the Ends* 5.1):

> Once, Brutus, I'd been listening to Antiochus, as I was in the habit of doing, with Marcus Piso in that building which they call the School of Ptolemy; with us were my brother, Quintus, and T. Pomponius [Atticus] and Lucius Cicero, whom I loved as a brother but who was actually my first cousin. We decided to take our afternoon stroll to the Academy, mainly because this place would be empty of any crowd at that time of day [*constituimus inter nos ut ambulationem postmeridianam conficeremus in Academia, maxime quod is locus ab omni turba id temporis vacuus esset*]. And so we all met at the chosen time at Piso's place. From there, in various conversations, we covered the 6 stades from the Dipylon gate. When we reached the Academy's walkway, which is justifiably famous, we found solitude there as we'd hoped [*cum autem venissemus in Academiae non sine causa nobilitata spatia, solitudo erat ea, quam volueramus*].

This description gives way to a series of meditations on the power of place to summon up for the living the images of the dead who have once inhabited those places: for Piso, the Academy calls to mind Plato, who seems to appear before his very eyes; for Cicero, it is Carneades that the place evokes; and so on (*On Ends* 5.2–4).

This dialogue is haunted by the past, but it is also haunted by the future. Cicero teases Atticus at one point saying (*On the Ends* 5.4): "As for our friend Pomponius, I believe he's joking! And no doubt he's a licensed wit, for he has so taken root in Athens, that he's almost an Athenian. In fact, I expect he'll get the surname Atticus (*ita enim se Athenis collocavit, ut sit paene unus ex Atticis, ut id etiam cognomen videatur habiturus*)!" These games in the frame of the dialogue with the past and future of Cicero's interlocutors find a thematic point in the content of Book 5's argument, which, as Andres Matlock (2020, 49–105, and 2021) has emphasized, draws its conclusions about the chief goals of the various philosophical schools from the boundaries that delimit a human lifetime. It is, therefore, striking that this thoroughly spectral late dialogue should be recalled and anticipated in *Letters to Atticus* 1, the earliest dated letter of which (5) opens by recounting the death of Cicero's cousin, Lucius, one of the interlocutors of *On Ends* 5.[17] This letter, the earliest in the correspondence, recalls the death of a cousin, whose youthful self of eleven years earlier Cicero will immortalize in one of the dialogues of 45 BCE, when he was on the verge of death himself. Like many of the letters in this book, it is haunted by the past and by the future, by past realities and by the future fictional versions of those realities that Cicero constructs in his late dialogues and in other ways too (such as the way in which he decorates his villa).

* * *

There is an unmistakable spectrality to Derrida's conception of friendship, that suggests itself in its resonance with what he has to say in *Specters of Marx* about the unique temporality of ghosts. The ontological or hauntological peculiarity of the ghost derives from the way in which it, without existing in the present,

---

17 *Letters to Atticus* 1.5.1: "Knowing me as well as you do, you can appreciate better than most how deeply my cousin Lucius's death has grieved me, and what a loss it means to me both in public and in private life [*quantum dolorem acceperim et quanto fructu sim privatus et forensi et domestico Luci fratris nostri morte, in primis pro nostra consuetudine tu existimare potes*]. All the pleasure that one human being's kindness and charm can give another I had from him [*nam mihi omnia, quae iucunda ex humanitate alterius et moribus homini accidere possunt, ex illo accidebant*]. So I do not doubt that you too are sorry; for you will feel my distress, and you yourself have lost a family connection and a friend, one who possessed every good quality and disposition to serve others, and who loved you both of his own accord and from hearing me speak of you."

acts on the present from both the past and the future, its virtual agency an effect of its paradoxical ability to return to the present from the past. Throughout *The Politics of Friendship,* Derrida uses the language of ghosts and of haunting to imply that the ghost's peculiar relation to what-is-not-yet as well as to what-is-no-longer is similar to the friend's,[18] since mourning a friend is not just something that happens after the event, but rather haunts the friendship as a future possibility from that friendship's inception.

The letters in *Letters to Atticus* are haunted by the prospect of Cicero's death, and by the fall of the Republic that coincides with that event, as well as by Atticus's survival. In the new proto-Imperial era that Atticus will live to see (but which Cicero will not), the specter of the Republic will haunt the monarchy that replaces it, both in the constitutional traces that it leaves behind as empty signs (in the consulship and senate, for example), and as a political ideal that refuses to die for some time. Much like the specter of Communism, which haunts the neoliberal world order that the fall of the Berlin Wall was widely acclaimed to have ushered in, the ghost of the Republic haunts the Roman Empire, the emergence of which was likewise hailed as an end of history and accompanied by a very similar triumphalist rhetoric. The publication of *Letters to Atticus* after Cicero's death, and therefore at some point within the imperial period, can only have served the interests of this haunting: in perpetuating the memory of the Republic through letters exchanged between two of the most intimate friends, the collection addressed imperial readers as friends of the Republic. They (and we) read Cicero's messages of concern and despair for the Republic over Atticus's shoulder, and find themselves (ourselves) addressed as Cicero's

---

18 P.A. Miller (2016) draws attention to the way in which *Specters of Marx,* in its published format, is haunted by the friendships that Derrida had lost since delivering this work in person some twenty years earlier. See also P.A. Miller (2016, 116–21) on the significance that the hauntological currency of friendship holds for the idea of a "democracy to come" in *Specters of Marx* and *The Politics of Friendship.* See also Miller's and Radcliffe's chapters in this volume.

beloved friend (and therefore, implicitly, a friend of the Republic whose imminent collapse he mourns) in a different historical age. The space that the letters are called upon to bridge, in the name of friendship, when collected and published at this later point in time is one of different political systems and different historical periods. Indeed, the publication of *Letters to Atticus* may help to articulate this historical shift for imperial readers, who can only have read the collection with a sense of how far the political losses that Cicero anticipated had materialized. As later readers who read these letters in Atticus's stead, we begin by inhabiting the differential dimension of friendship that both Derrida and Blanchot stress, but are drawn into ascribing to this dimension at least a certain degree of sameness.

The attachments that these letters engender would be reactivated at a later historical moment when Petrarch rediscovered the collection in the Renaissance. Kathy Eden (2012) credits this moment with generating the rediscovery not just of the (many) historical details that this particular text laid bare, but of a familiar mode of communication, one that Petrarch and his successors read, admired, and strove to emulate in their own communications with friends. Petrarch's twenty-four volume *Epistulae ad Familiares* (*Letters to Friends*) replicates not Cicero's *Ad Familiares* (which was only discovered after Petrarch's death and named after his own letter collection)[19] but the familiar epistolary style of Cicero's letters to Atticus, which then influenced the letter-writing of subsequent generations. Among the *Ad Familiares* are the letters that Petrarch composed to ancient authors, including Cicero, which demonstrate the attachment that this newly discovered mode of epistolary intimacy could generate toward those authors from the ancient past who bequeathed it

---

19 See Hinds (2005, 53), on the hypothesis that Cicero's *Letters to Friends* was named *after* Petrarch's letter collection (which was itself influenced by — another — Ciceronian letter collection), and the involutions that this example of "reverse-chronological influence" represents. When put in dialogue with *The Politics of Friendship,* we might note how these reversals are worthy of Derrida himself.

on later authors like him.[20] *The Letters to Atticus* gave Petrarch an idiom for communicating across the barrier of distance and difference to his contemporaries as well as to his virtual "friends" from the ancient past.[21] In a medium well-suited to the spectral structure of friendship, they enable Cicero to return from the past to the present, as one friend to another, again and again across time.

---

20 Güthenke (2020, 55): "Petrarch's emphasis on 'intimacy' as a mode of approaching the classical past is a trope that reaches through the early modern well into the modern period. It shaped literary and intellectual language across Europe and continues to shape our affective habits as scholars, extending down even into the hermeneutical traditions of the twentieth century."

21 That Petrarch's letters to Cicero should be marked by the disappointment that he feels upon encountering the version of this ancient author that the *Letters to Atticus* had revealed to him is itself a position that replicates the positions that Cicero takes up in relation to Atticus time and again in his letters to him. Yet this too is part of friendship's alterity, as P.A. Miller (2016), reading Derrida (2005a), underscores.

4

Thelyology: Apuleius's Morphologies of Damage

David Youd

In *Archive Fever,* Jacques Derrida calls attention to the ways that techniques of archival inscription inevitably codetermine the meaning of archived materials, belatedly constituting the recorded event at the very moment of recording. The archive, we recall — the *arkheion,* the house of the *arkhōn,* the site of record-keeping — depends upon its "con-signation": consigning to a hypomnesic substrate and *"gathering together signs"* (Derrida 1996c, 3). By thus coordinating "a single corpus, in a system or a synchrony in which all the elements articulate the unity of an ideal configuration," the *arkhōn* secures the grounds of its nomological *arkhē* through its authority over the ontological one (two orders of "order": jussive and sequential). Yet if the *arkhē* ("originary presence") it seeks to record is not only irredeemably lost but, as Derrida (1996c) suggests, at least in part, an *effect* of the apparatus of inscription, the "trouble" that disorders the archive proves no less than a radical evil: absolute heterogeneity, the "secret" of which is "there can be no archive, by definition" (100) which accordingly poses a threat to the very "possibility of consignation" (4). This *mal d'archive,* the archive's constitutive lack which it itself constantly produces, thus inflames both the feverish desire to archive what is forever lost (what the archive is forever losing) and the anarchiving *jouissance* of destroying without a trace.

Derrida's recognition of the integral role of technical form to ontological possibility — of mimetic form to content — bears far-reaching implications for reading. Symptomatic reading, for one, insofar as psychoanalysis, "in its archive fever, always attempts to return to the live origin of that which the archive loses while keeping it in a multiplicity of places" (Derrida 1996c, 92). The analytic fantasy of reducing the multiplicity of symptoms through the revelation of the repressed cause, its detective plot of uncovering the aetiological *arkhē* and thereby smoothing out the signifying fabric of the text, itself depends upon a signal repression: the epistemic damage arising from the signifier itself. In its conceit that technical prosthesis is merely a "secondary and accessory exteriority," classical psychoanalysis hides from itself the more fundamental repression that the recording prosthesis in its primacy creates. In truth, any text, discourse, or semiotic institution is "not only haunted by this or that ghost" (Derrida 1996c, 87), but by *spectrality itself*: by that which is forever lost because never recorded, eluding registration because precluded by the register. What haunts the archive is more than just this or that document suppressed, unpublished, yet to be elaborated, subject to philological reinterpretation, pending subsequent papyrological finds or archaeological digs; it is that which is altogether alien to archival inscription.

As Derrida attentively shows, of course, Sigmund Freud himself invoked this ghost of aneconomy in his late turn to trauma in 1920 — an endeavor to account for those unaccountable losses within the economy of pleasure, to domiciliate what lies before, behind, and *beyond* the pleasure principle. Under the heading of death drive, he gives name to that which destroys "without a name, without the least symptom, without even an ash" (Derrida 1996c, 101). But not without *exception;* except, that is to say, when this aggressive force "disguises itself [...] tints itself, makes itself up or paints itself (*gefärbt ist*) in some erotic color" (Derrida 1996c, 11). Paradigmatic for Freud on this point are those sado-masochistic economies that alloy desire and destruction, while Derrida points up the metaphorics of painting that color Freud's account and link the death drive to depiction: "as inheritance, it leaves only its erotic simulacrum, its pseudonym in painting" (11). Never represented directly, it appears even so as representation's perverted form. To be sure, *every* attempt at reproduction harbors the specter of its negation inasmuch as the recording prosthesis (the sign, the letter, movable type) follows the same "logic of repetition" as the destructive drive (11–12), and this is the general thrust of Derrida's argument. Of particular interest, however, are those specific forms of aneconomy on display in moments of prolonged speech and vexed temporalization, the "apparently useless expenditure of paper, ink, and typographic printing" (12) that give archival body to pure loss.[1] Thus, where the Freudian death drive manifested in the form of compulsive repetitions, temporal distortions, and destructive negativity, Derrida has it infect the very constitution of *Archive Fever* by dis-ordering his exposition through a series of anticipations and delays ("exergue," "preamble," "foreword"), supplying his theses only belatedly as a "recapitulation" of what "has insinuated itself *already and in advance*" (81), and displacing to a final "postscript" (with its supplemental thesis) his central thesis of a supplement that records only ruin.

This "late" development in the psychoanalytic corpus, in which its patriarch turned his back on the consignation of his own theoretical archive by entertaining an evil completely foreign to its founding principles, interfaces with Theodor Adorno and Edward Said's theorizations of late style: the tendency of the artist, in the twilight of life, to turn away from resolution and closure and introduce instead "intransigence, difficulty, and unresolved contradiction" (Said 2006, 7). Concerning "the relationship between bodily condition and aesthetic style" (Said 2006, 3), late style describes the disintegrating force of death,

---

[1] "The time Freud consecrates to this long voyage in a field of excavations also says something of a *jouissance*. He would like it to be interminable, he prolongs it under the pretext of pedagogy or rhetoric" (Derrida 1996c, 93).

when life's close reveals its basic fragmentation rather than any essential wholeness. In such works, the supplement that was supposed to redeem the whole is perverted into a revelation of irreparable damage, remorphologizing the corpus as mere *disjecta membra*. Though pertaining *sensu stricto* to the work of the expiring artist, then, late style could stand more generally for any archival technique that allows the ghost of radical finitude finally to appear, if only as negation and aesthetic blockage.[2] Relinquishing the position of *arkhōn,* in other words, the late author abandons the project of consignation, plying their prosthetic pen now only to abort unification, to summon the specter of disintegration, to expose the corrupting malady at the heart of their corpus. In this perverted libidinal economy, where the rupture born of impending death is invested with desire and anticipated in the work of art, the shattering revelation of loss comes as a rapture; it comes, like *la petite mort,* with an ineffable *jouissance* (see Telò 2020, 77).

* * *

Such an economy, I would like to suggest, conditions both the narrative form and the more granular aesthetic texture of Apuleius's *Metamorphoses*.[3] Long described as "late" or "baroque," both in terms of its style and its place in the corpus of Latin literature, the novel is informed by its persistent obstruction of the transformations it relates.[4] Prominently, the final book, which purports retroactively to transform and determine the meaning of the entire work in conformity with the Isiac cult, has installed an unbridgeable gap instead, dividing interpreters

---

[2] Communicating itself, "like a cipher, only through the blank spaces from which it has disengaged itself" (Adorno 2002, 566).
[3] For the text of Apuleius, I follow the edition of Zimmerman (2012). All translations are mine, unless otherwise noted.
[4] See, e.g., W.S. Smith (2001, 436): "The often bizarre and baroque style of Apuleius who often seems bent on leaving his readers baffled by wrapping up his point inside a unique combination of poetic, colloquial, archaic, and invented words."

and bedeviling every effort to subsume the novel's meaning into a unitary whole.⁵ This is both the thesis and, in part, the product of John Winkler's pioneering reading (1985): the end of the work, far from supplying the unity and closure that interpreters have looked for, instead throws unity into question and Lucius into disgrace.

Yet a similar frustration of the transfiguring end inflects the more diminutive morphologies of Apuleius's novelistic style. As the prologue informs us, the novel will concern the "figures [*figuras*] and fortunes of men turned into other images [*imagines*] and restored back into themselves [*in se rursum… refectas*]" (1.1). When the work has scarcely announced its theme, however, the promised restoration of figures is formally subverted in the series of transformed but unrestored *figuras* (namely "word forms") that appear in the very next sentence: *Hymett__os__ Attic__a__ et Isthm__os__ Ephyrae__a__ et Taenar__os__ Spartiatic__a__* ("[My origins lie in] Attic Hymettos and Ephyrean Isthmos and Spartan Taenaros").⁶ Each of these ostensibly masculine nouns — for nowhere else are *Hymettos* or *Isthmos* attested as feminine, and *Taenaros* only rarely — must be belatedly reparsed as feminine with the arrival of each modifier's unassimilable termination (*os… a*).⁷ Voiced in the dissonance of these forms is not the confirmation of masculine identity, but precisely its negation; the author or the book — who speaks is unclear — thus pens *in parvo* the aporetic impasse that actuates the larger work, figured here as a micrological problem of morphology and gender, of a *before* and an

---

5   Compare Mal-Maeder's suggestion that the novel as we have it may owe to an accident in the manuscript tradition which left it "tronquée de sa fin burlesque (la même que dans l'Onos)" — its end quite literally broken off (2001, 15; cf. 422n3).

6   Because much of my argument revolves around verbal play with Apuleian morphologies and the component parts of word forms, I have, by way of clarification, underscored, in certain words and phrases, the specific morphemes and letters that are germane to the point under contention.

7   This regendering is discussed in Tilg (2007, 179); cf. Finkelpearl (2014, 466).

after that do not agree.[8] What such minuscule yet unmistakable fissures demand is a certain interpretive microscopy: a mode of close reading verging on "too close" that could adequately attend to the superfine detail (see D.A. Miller 2021). What they reveal, as we shall see, is the transformation of the archival prosthesis, and most spectacularly the Apuleian signifier, from an archontic technology of the self into the means of its undoing.

* * *

To examine the novel's perversion of the end into a late disclosure of damage, we could hardly do better than the macabre tale of Thelyphron, that "incomputably clever and unimaginably grisly autobiography" (Winkler 1985, 114) related at the end of book 2. The story can be sketched briefly as follows: traveling through Thessaly, the heartland of ancient witchcraft, the young Thelyphron runs out of funds and takes a job as a night watch, keeping vigil over a corpse against the nocturnal depredations of witches. The youth is informed that the shapeshifting hexes will adopt the forms of animals or cast a deep sleep on him to despoil the body. Worse: whatever parts of the corpse are found missing the following day must be repaid by his own pound of flesh. After the bereaved widow dutifully notes the condition of her late husband's body, she locks Thelyphron in for the night. He succeeds initially at warding off a witch in the form of an intrusive weasel, but soon succumbs to slumber: "so dead asleep that not even Apollo could tell myself and the corpse apart" (2.25). Waking in a cold sweat, he rushes to check the cadaver for damage — yet to his surprise and ours, the body remains unscathed. Prematurely relieved, Thelyphron receives his payment and thanks, but, when he inadvertently implies the widow is accustomed to bumping off husbands, he also receives a drubbing from the furious domestics: "cuffed on the ears, mangled and mutilated like Pentheus or Orpheus, I was turned out of the house" (2.26). Once

---

8   On the prologue, see, e.g., Winkler (1985, 180–203); Harrison (1990); and Kahane and Laird (2001).

again, however, Thelyphron emerges remarkably unharmed. Yet when the funeral procession sets out, the young widow of the deceased is dramatically accused of having poisoned her late husband to run off with his estate and her adulterous lover. To substantiate the allegation, an Egyptian priest named Zatchlas is produced to reanimate the corpse and recover his damning testimony. This is the critical juncture. Sitting up on his bed, the resuscitated cadaver affirms the charges of adultery and murder. As proof of his trustworthiness, he offers to disclose what no one else could know, namely that in the course of the previous night witches had cast a soporific spell on the hired watch, but, unbeknownst to the witches and, until this moment, ourselves, both custodian and corpse bear the same name: Thelyphron. Intoning this name (clearly, in this tale, one to conjure with), the witches fortuitously ensorcel not the dead but the merely "dead asleep" to his feet, amputating his ears and nose through a hole in the wall and concealing their theft by means of wax substitutes. As the reanimated corpse falls silent, all eyes turn to the living Thelyphron. In horror, he tugs at his nose: it follows; he pulls at his ears: they fall away. Mutilated and humiliated, he withdraws in shame through the cackling crowd.

The story belongs to a series of inset narratives in the first three books of Apuleius's *Metamorphoses* in which a young man's journey through Thessaly is interrupted by a fateful encounter with magic, precluding a return home and ending in a form of living death. Positively mortified by the disgrace of his bodily disfigurement, Thelyphron forsakes his ancestral *Lar* (2.30) and instead leads a larval existence in "*La*rissa" (2.21): the crossroads of Thessaly. In a sense Thelyphron himself, whose story begins *Pupillus ego* and ends in surrogation, becomes in his exile the *pupulus* (puppet) customarily suspended at the crossroads as effigies of the living during the *Compitalia*—the festival of the *Lares*. As a matter of fact, it is on the eve of the *Risus,* the festival of laughter where Lucius too will be put out of countenance, that the ungracious host Byrrhena badgers Thelyphron into "retracing" the tale with his "usual urbanity" (*more tuae urbanitatis* […] *remetire,* 2.20), while his audience's peals of laughter (both in the tale and at the banquet) leave Thelyphron the renewed object of derision. Origin and destination, *before* and *after,* thus give way to ruminative rehearsal and repetition of the traumatic episode.⁹

Like other inset stories, the "disquieting quality" or "strange and romantic" effect (Mayrhofer 1975, 80, 69) of Thelyphron's tale has been attributed in part to its disruption of linear causality, its "absence of a natural and normally logical sequence of events" (Perry 1949, 40).¹⁰ In fact, the modern scholarly interpretation of the episode can be said to begin with Perry's source-critical analysis designating it a "somewhat awkward compound [...] of three entirely different stories" (Perry 1929, 231), based on his detection of its abrupt dislocations in narrative motivation. The mutilation we are led to expect as a result of the Shylockian contract is unexpectedly withheld when, on the following morning, the corpse betrays no discernible damage. Instead, Thelyphron's verbal gaffe occasions the beating that arrives as a "substitute for" (Perry 1929, 233), or a "device for postponing" (Mayrhofer 1975, 79), the expected *dénouement*.¹¹ So, too, the abrupt transformations of genre. Part of the narrative's eerie effect thus owes to its continually shifting horizon of expectations: we find ourselves now in a witch story, now in a comedy of manners with the familiar trauma of the unwitting *faux pas,* now in an adultery tale with a necromantic cast. At each of these junctures, the anticipated outcome, the narrative *avenir* approached in a linear trajectory, is abruptly renounced, producing the disjointed tale's interpretative unruliness: the frustrated unification characteristic of late style.

Not unlike its discontinuous causality, the tale's temporality is conspicuously out of joint. Perhaps the most prominent narra-

---

9   For the resignification of the *à venir* as "the 'arrival' of a-chronicity, a sense of stuckness in a state of defective being," see Telò's "Before," in this volume. For artistic lateness as a form of "self-imposed exile," see also Said (2006, 8 and 16).
10 Similarly, Shumate (1999, 114) observes that "several lapses in logic and expectation [...] give this tale as well as others an unsettling quality."
11 That is, mutilation at the behest of the angry widow for his failure to protect the corpse.

tological feature of the story is the way the scene of Thelyphron's mutilation is itself cut from the narrative and only analeptically restored at the very end, reproducing the trauma in the unfolding of the text. The wax replacements for Thelyphron's nose and ears thus in some measure double for the piece of narrative grafted onto the end of the story, both artfully concealed before finally revealed (cf., e.g., Mal-Maeder 2001, 420). The prosthesis is already textual, a point insinuated in the proviso that, should Thelyphron not return as an *integrum corpus* ("intact body/text") at the end of his watch, he must furnish a restitution for whatever parts have been "excerpted or abridged" (2.22), while the witches' handiwork, whose verisimilitude fools even Thelyphron himself, bears an uncanny affinity to his own spellbinding art in narrating his tale.[12]

* * *

In what follows, I attempt to shift the locus of deconstructive reading from the story's larger narratological structures to its smaller morphologies of bodies, words, and syntax. If Thelyphron's deformity scars both his body and his tale, it leaves a mark more minutely on the morphemes and signifiers with which his corpus is composed. The multiplying wounds that score the textual surface, however, amount to more than so many symptomatic expressions of the repressed scene that the narrative will finally reveal, as though through proper analysis we could reconstruct the story's, if not Thelyphron's, underlying unity. Instead, they evince a diffuse rapture, a compulsive repetition of the fundamental rupture that leaves Thelyphron bereft of bodily integrity. More, the tale's narratological resistance to unitary interpretation is mapped onto the specter of castration — as the damage to that signifier *par excellence* — formally embedding, not unlike the "castration desire" Mario Telò has recently ascribed to the Jocasta of Euripides's *Phoenissae,* a yearning for

---

[12] On "the relation between the mimetic and the prosthetic" in Thelyphron's tale, see most recently Boxall (2020, 1 and 14–16).

"a loss not of the anatomical penis, but of the Lacanian, symbolic phallus" (2020, 83n114).

Pupillus ego: these are the curious words with which Thelyphron embarks on his tale ("As a young man," I 2.21). As we have seen, the doubly diminutive epithet evokes the *pupulus* ("puppet") from which it derives (*pupillus* < *pupulus* < *pupa*); to the keen eye, however, it suggests also the ocular *pupilla* ("pupil") so-named for the doll-like reflection of the self there on view.[13] This eye-catching equation of the speaking I and spectatorial eye finds corroboration first in the *spectaculum Olympicum* ("the spectacle of the Olympic games") for which he sets out, and more directly when, with an eye to securing the position of night watch, Thelyphron affirms his watchful vigilance with the boast that "you see here a man sleepless and made of iron, surely more observant than Lynceus or Argus himself: *for I'm all eye* [*oculeum totum*]" (2.23). To be sure, this vaunt of an iron will will prove purely ironic when, Argus-like, he swiftly succumbs to slumber. In retrospect, however, his profession to *be* "all eye" imparts to the programmatic *pupillus ego* a conspicuous marker of the tale's unsettling specularity, since the collocation condenses in its grammatical equation of the "self" and the "pupil/puppet" the constitutive misrecognitions that both drive and confound the autobiography, where Thelyphron mistakes the integral image of the other (an *alter ego*) for the integrity of the self (cf. Winkler 1985, 114–15).[14] By inscribing this determinant misprision in a problem of syntactical identity, Thelyphron fixes the reader's gaze from the outset on the significance of the double — and on the double that is the signifier.[15]

---

13   For comparable play on the various senses of the Greek equivalent *korē* (maiden, doll, pupil of the eye), see Telò (2020, 61–63).
14   If the tale admits of interpretation as Thelyphron's "mirror stage," then, it images not (only) the dependence of the ego's unification on the "prop" furnished by the specular *imago*, but the specter of fragmentation that returns in images of bodily dismemberment, "disjointed limbs," and so on (Lacan 1977, 6).
15   On the pupil and eye as crucial "indices" in the second-century semiotics of masculinity, "reflect[ing] on its surface the disturbances of the soul's depth," see Gleason (1990, 410–11).

The hermeneutic imperative to look closely, however, presaged by the inaugural *pupillus ego,* is augured also by the troubling auspices — the *fuscis avibus* ("dark birds") — under which Thelyphron claims to have reached Larissa (2.21). This vaguely inauspicious sign soon takes on concrete significance when the prospective watch is warned he must "keep attentive vigil with steadfast, unblinking eyes" since, among other things, the witches who prey upon the dead habitually "assume the guise of birds" (2.22). Thus advised, the vigilant reader might detect an ominous note in the introduction of the widow in mourning, discerning in her *fusca veste* ("dark cloak," 2.23) a murky portent of something more sinister inasmuch as *fusca veste* disguises within its morphemes the baleful *fuscis avibus* with which the narrative set out. Clothed in this troubled *divisio verborum* and invested in this facsimile of lexical forms is a covert insinuation that the portentous *mulier* may bear a shrouded affinity to those *sagae mulieres* (lit. "portentous" or "soothsaying women," 2.21) who don avian forms: an insinuation shortly borne out when the adulterous widow who preys upon her husband's estate is uncloaked as but a mirror image of the "libidinous" witches (2.22) who prey upon his corpse. The clandestine, adulterous double, then, that casts a pall over the house and produces its uncanny atmosphere — *unheimlich* because sheltering within itself the threat from outside — is prefigured first in the metamorphosing *figurae* of her shadowy garb.[16]

Such foreshadowing provides but the first tokens of what will prove the tale's central repression, the scene of trauma cut from the signifying fabric and resurfacing in the signifiers onto which it is displaced. Indeed, this dislocation of damage onto anticipatory premonitions and late recapitulations is itself announced beforehand in the crier's warning to the prospective watch. For only belatedly, after enumerating the sundry artifices by which the *versipelles* ("shapeshifting," lit. "skin-changing") witches will contrive to plunder the corpse, does he note the severe penalty

---

16 The chamber where she attends her husband's corpse is itself *umbrosum* ("full of shade," 2.23).

to be exacted in the event of a botched job, a chilling omen that Thelyphron will eventually pay through the nose (2.22):

> Ah yes, and — what I had almost omitted to mention [*quod paene praeterieram*] — if he does not restore an intact corpse [*integrum corpus... restituerit*], he will be compelled to restore every mangled or diminished part with a piece cut from his own face [*sarcire compellitur*].

In this highly suggestive addendum, the disfigurement underwriting the compulsory restoration of the *integrum corpus* in the harsh terms of the contract is presented in miniature by the final *sarcire compellitur,* where *sarcire* (to restore, mend) conjures up the indemnified *sarc-* (Gr. "flesh"; cf. *sarkizō:* "to flay") and *com<u>pell</u>itur* ("com-pelt"), an image of monstrous recomposition. Any chance the job might prove no skin off Thelyphron's nose is foreclosed by this late disclosure; plainly both witch and watch will change their skin (i.e., *pellis*). Perhaps most compellingly, however, by rhetorically casting this appended warning as a near *praeteritio* (*quod paene praeterieram*) — as a belated recompense for what in hindsight becomes a virtual omission — the warning itself formally anticipates the late and mutilating restitution it describes: a retroactive revelation of damage.

Corpus, of course, is a commonplace synecdoche for the *membrum virile,* a *totum pro parte* ("whole for the part") which refers, *in malam partem,* to the part of the man that embodies his man*hood*. Thelyphron's story has been read as another allegorization of the Isis and Osiris myth where Isis, as we recall, gathers together the dismembered body parts of her consort Osiris — all except the phallus which must be replaced with a wooden prosthesis (see Tatum 1969, 495; Lateiner 2001, 325; and, apropos of the end of the novel, Winkler 1985, 178). In this mythical act of consignation, or "gathering together of signs," it is the phallic supplement that affords the illusion of wholeness to a fundamentally riven body. The consignation of the Thelyphronic archive, by contrast, revolves around the sign of a *lack* first signaled by his name (Gr. "female-minded") whose more than nominal significance is clinched in the bilingual pun that reactivates its Greek signification (see esp. Frangoulidis 2002; 2008, 101n198; and Ingenkamp 1972).[17] For when, after hearing the dreadful terms of the night watch, he declares *animum meum conmasculo* ("I manned up my mind/spirit," 2.23), he coyly alludes to his name's unmanly drift while effectively turning the word *animum* into a masculine double of himself: an uncanny specter — literally his "spirit" — in the text that will suffer the ghastly disfiguration in his place.

Thelyphron begins his spell as watchman by singing to himself in an effort to "soothe his spirit" (*animum meum permulcebam cantationibus,* 2.25), an equanimity he struggles to maintain when a furtive *mustela* (a "weasel" or "ferret") steals into the room. Although he was warned to keep a "sharp eye" (*acies,* 2.22) out for witches, this penetrating gaze is soon turned back on him by the bristly intruder:

> A weasel fixed itself opposite me and transfixed me with its piercing [*acerrimum*] gaze, such that this tiny little animal [*tantillula animalis*], with its inordinate confidence, unsettled my spirit [*turbarit animum*].[18]

The fear of penetration here is barely suppressed. The sharpness of the "piercing" gaze resurfaces in the biting dentals of the alliterative Latin co<u>ns</u>titit op<u>t</u>utumque acerrimum in me de<u>st</u>ituit. But the confrontation between witch and watch is figuratively rendered as a contrast between the *animalis* of the one and the unnerved *animum* of the other: while the doubly diminutive *tantillula <u>anima</u>lis* paradoxically stretches out and enlarges the weasel's feminine *anima,* the truncation of Thelyphron's animus is formally inscribed in the verbal contraction of *turba(ve)rit*

---

17 Cf. Margaret Doody (1996, 119): "Certainly, masculinity is under threat in this tale, comically castrated."

18 The *Thesaurus Linguae Latinae* glosses this singular use of *optutum* [...] *destituit* as = *defigere:* "to drive into, fix." For an obscene pun with *acer* as both penetrating discernment and sexual penetration, compare Martial, *Epigrams* 5.51.10.

animum, where the syncope excising the temporal marker (*-ve-*) aesthetically prefigures Thelyphron's own syncope, and stands in for the excision of the moment of trauma.

Unmanned, the mousy watch summons the courage to expel the *mustela,* affecting a spirited machismo to regain his poise and reassert his manful *vis*:

> Shoo! [*Quin abis?*] vile beast, and sequester yourself with males like yourselves [*ad tui similes masculos*] before you experience my strength [*vim... experiaris*]. Shoo! [*Quin abis?*].[19]

While textual critics have routinely rejected the reading *masculos,* preferring either the alternate *musculos* ("to rodents like you") or more intrusive emendations,[20] the equivocal weasel-word aptly conveys Thelyphron's (castration) anxieties about the cocksure weasel and, at the same time, recalls the well-known belief in antiquity that the weasel conceived by taking the *semen masculi* into its mouth (see, e.g., Bettini 2011, 37). The vociferous "go find males like yourself!" thus registers his recognition of what such a *mustela* might wish to ferret out, and encloses an impassioned plea to leave his manhood intact.[21] A plea, moreover, redoubled at the level of its form: for, by bookending the utterance, the epanaleptic *Quin abis?* effectively forms a perimeter around it, while the terminal cadence of *experiaris* (‒ u u ‒ x), the so-called *heroica clausula* proscribed by classical rhetoricians for its epic affectation, brings the exclamation to a dramatic, mock-heroic close, endowing it with the same *vis* ("potency") with which he threatens the *mustela.*[22]

---

19 My translation of this quotation is adapted from Hanson (1996).
20 See Mal-Maeder (2001, 343): "*Musculus* est une injure dans la bouche de Thélyphron: la belette n'est pas une souris, elles chasse les souris."
21 Even taken as an error, a sort of *lapsus amanuensis,* the manuscript's *masculos* records the specter of castration that haunts the episode.
22 "*Gravitas autem atque vis illius clausulae augetur, ubi metrum ‒ u u ‒ ~ unius verbi tenore exprimitur,* veluti II 25 *experiaris*" (Schober 1904, 13).

In his attempt at claustration, however, Thelyphron appears to produce the very castration he meant to ward off. The weasel is "banished" (*exterminatur*) — but so is his own *animus*, as if in exorcizing the witch's weaselly double he had expelled his own spirit: I lay "so inanimate [*inanimis*] and in need of another watchman [*indigens alio custode*] I almost wasn't there [*paene ibi non eram*]" (2.25).[23] Of course, the watch who needs "another watchman" brings to mind Juvenal's famous tag, "but who will watch the watchmen themselves?" (*sed quis custodiet ipsos / custodes;* Juvenal, *Satires* 6.347–48[24]) — and that passage's themes of adultery and (pseudo)castration. But it is his loss of consciousness, conveyed by the privative modifier *in-animis,* that finally marks the long awaited deprivation of "female-spirited" Thelyphron's feebly masculinized *animus.* The adjective, strikingly, is an Apuleian neologism, elsewhere invariably formed *inanimus, -a, -um.* By way of this anomalous form, whereby the regular and regularly gendered *inanimus* is supplanted with the epicene *inanimis,* Apuleius quite literally deprives Thelyphron's "spirit" of its masculine inflection.[25] At the proper moment of its occurrence in linear time, then, the repressed scene of bodily disfigurement, by now so long anticipated and foretokened, manifests only spectrally as the dis-figuration of Thelyphron's *animus.*[26]

* * *

---

23 The elision marring *paene, paen-* ("almost") having stood in a paronomastic relation to the nearly homophonous *pēn-* ("penis") since Plautus (cf. *Truculentus* 518), provides another intimation that the penal damages may prove penile. I refer to the Lindsay (1905) edition.
24 I reference the Clausen (1992) edition. Translation mine.
25 The weasel's "removal" (*ex-terminatur*) from the room thus foreshadows the removal of the *animus*'s gendered "termination" (an observation for which I thank Tommaso Bernardini). Compare Attis's famous grammatical castration in Catullus 63 (on which, see Skinner 1993), or the fabulous pun (*fabulus/fabula*) earlier in the *Metamorphoses:* "having feasted only on stories" (*cenatus solis fabulis,* 1.26), where "stories" (*fabulis,* from *fabula*) evokes the expected but withheld "beans" (also *fabulis,* from *fabulus*). See also the Mynors (1958) edition of Catallus.
26 For other gendered play on *animus/a* in Apuleius's *Metamorphoses,* see, e.g., 6.26, 7.6, and 8.11.

If the excised trauma is cast as a form of castration, displaced onto the morphological damage of the signifier, the tale's supplementary finale that purports to afford it restitution is given symbolic body in advance through a ubiquitous tropology of erection. Could it be without significance, after all, that what presently rouses Thelyphron from his deathly slumber, in a fetish-like displacement of the phallus, is the "crowing of the cock" (2.26)?[27] Or, yet again, after the second unexpected trauma when, in a travesty of Pentheus's transvestism and dismemberment, Thelyphron is torn apart and booted from the house (*distrahere* [...] *discindere* [...] *in modum superbi iuvenis Aonii* [...] *laceratus atque discerptus*, 2.26) — when, that is, the battered Thelyphron attempts to "rouse" his flaccid spirit (*refovens animum*), with all the erotic ardor entailed in such a "warm caress" (< *foveo*), that what arises is the apparition of the "stiff," as though a hypostasis of the *animus* he sought to revive: "behold! now duly mourned, the dead man appeared [*processerat mortuus*] — carried by a funeral procession" (2.27).[28] Thelyphron, indeed, will later nod to the fact that the corpse who will supply the missing piece of the truth in his own self-knowledge comes as a compensatory double for his loss, first when his self-examination before the throng of onlookers (*praesentium denotor*, 2.30) reprises the widow's earlier examination of her husband's remains before a corresponding crowd (*praesentium* [...] *praenotante*, 2.24), and finally when, with a wink, he figuratively transforms the grave of his missing organ, "covered" by a "linen" pall (*linteolo* [...] *obtexi*, 2.30), into a cryptic effigy of the corpse likewise "covered with linens" (*linteis coopertum*, 2.24).

---

27 What the euphemism *cristatae cohortis* ("crested cohort") covers up by way of substitution, of course, is the *gallus* ("cock") — thus introducing, by the same token, the specter of the *Gallus* (self-castrated priest of Cybele). On *gallus/Gallus*, cf. Tougher (2020, 142n78). On the ancient metaphorics of the rooster, symbolizing "love and war, life and death, and consequently ephebe and cock," see, e.g., Csapo (1993); for *cristatus* alone as an obscene reference to the penis, see Adams (1982, 98).

28 Cf. Murgatroyd (2004, 495): "the rather odd expression *processerat mortuus* for the carrying out of the dead man conjures up a picture of him in motion himself."

In a chain of deferrals, in fact, and with an endless play of substitutions that (un)ground our tenuous knowledge, the corpse is implicated as a double of the narrator from the very instant of his conjuration. Upon bringing the funeral cortège to a halt, the uncle of the departed purports, with a conspiratorial air, to have "long since" contracted the services of the priest Zatchlas to help expose the conspiracy of the widow, who has allegedly poisoned her husband "to gratify her lover and steal the inheritance" (2.27).[29] Both Zatchlas and his necromancy, then, are purely supplementary. He conjures the dead to expose the widow's *coniuratio* and thereby exorcise her ghost; yet this conjuration is itself not without its adjuvants since, in service of his priestly art, he invokes the "increases of the august Sun" (*incrementa Solis augusti,* 2.28), the Sun "august" because bestowing "augmentation."[30] With this dramatic *mise-en-scène,* he "arouses" (*adrexit*) the spectators' desire for a marvel, a marvel that soon appears when, under the spell of the thaumaturge, the carcass convulses back to life: "now the chest is raised with swelling [*tumore... extolli*], now veins throb with life, now the body is filled with spirit [*spiritu corpus impleri*]" as the cadaver "rises up" (*adsurgit*) on the couch (2.29).

As the revenant begins to speak, however, the distinction between the two Thelyphrons begins to collapse. For like the cadaver erect on his *torum* ("bier," 2.27) — the overdetermined site of emasculation inasmuch as it was also the *torum* ("marital bed," 2.29) on which his cuckolding took place — our Thelyphron narrates the tale at Byrrhena's banquet while recumbent on his own *torum* ("sympotic couch"). It was on this couch, indeed, that he himself had adopted the hyper-virile pose of the orator, as rigid as the corpse he will soon ventriloquize (2.21)[31]:

---

29 Translation by Hanson (1996).
30 See Mal-Maeder (2001, 375): "Un jeu de mot redondant avec *incrementa* (*augustus < augere*)."
31 Translation by Hanson (1996).

And so Thelyphron piled the coverlets in a heap [*aggeratis in cumulum stragulis*] and propped [*effultus*] himself on his elbow, sitting half upright [*suberectusque*] on the couch [*torum*]. He extended [*porrigit*] his right arm, shaping his fingers to resemble an orator's: having bent his two lowest fingers in, he stretched the others out at long range [*eminus porrigens*] and poised his thumb to strike, gently rising [*subrigens*] as he began.

The notably prolix description extends like the erect posture it describes: its turgid distension and fetishistic fixation on rigidity and erection (-*rectus, -rigit, -rigens,* and -*rigens*) might duly be suspected of attempting to compensate for a certain lack.[32] In fact, the repeated refrain of rigidity in the preamble to the tale is so emphatic that various editors have leveled charges of interpolation, while recent critics have defended the manuscripts' profusion.[33] The cumulative force of this rhetorical *accumulatio* is, after all, already imaged by the *cumulum* (heap, but figuratively indicating a rhetorical surplus or excess), namely the pile of coverlets that serves to "bolster" (*effultus*) Thelyphron's semierect posture and thus, from the outset, to rest erection on its incumbent narrative support. Yet like the prosthetic appendages that Thelyphron ends his story by *removing,* Thelyphron's phallic gesture proves but a prop for the self-unmanning story he proceeds to tell, donning the phallus solely in order to doff it.

Pressed to spell out the circumstances of his death, the reanimated cadaver promptly affirms the charges of adultery and murder; yet in the contretemps that erupts over his suspect *fidem* ("trustworthiness," 2.29),[34] he substantiates his allegation

---

32 In the preceding pages, Lucius had remonstrated to Photis in a bawdy double entendre that he feared lest his *nervus* ("bowstring," a euphemism for the penis) should burst "with an excess of rigidity" (*rigoris nimietate rumpatur,* 2.16). For the thumb as a phallic symbol in this gesture, see Corbeill (1997, 7).

33 Leo and Helm strike out *porrigens,* while Price emends *subrigens* to *subridens.*

34 Some in Thelyphron's audience impugn it, while others clamor, in an evident transposition of the cadaver's own premature death and

of his bride's *in*fidelity by returning to the scene not of his own trauma, but of Thelyphron's. What the revenant tenders as "evidence of unadulterated truth" (*intemeratae veritatis documenta*, 2.30) — the "unadulterated" truth, that is, that would incriminate his widow of adultery — is not the "secrets of his death" (*mortis* [...] *arcana*, 2.29) which he was conjured to relate, but the uncanny secret that haunts the story and divides the Thelyphronic archive: namely that the *corpus* and the *custos* bear the selfsame name. As the former informs us, it was by this token that the witches, chanting the name "Thelyphron," enchant not the corpse but his homonymous double back to life. "Rising up [...] like a lifeless specter" (*exsurgit* [...] *in exanimis umbrae modum*, 2.29) — in actuality like the lifeless corpse who only moments ago "rose up" (*adsurgit*) under the spell of Zatchlas and who even now speaks — the Thelyphron only "dead asleep" trudges with "sluggish joints and frigid members" (*hebetes artus et membra frigida*, 2.30) to the hole in the wall — the *foramen* ("hole") itself a stopgap for the *foribus* ("doors," 2.30) diligently locked — through which he offers his appendages, first his nose and finally his ears, over to the butchery of the witches. The living Thelyphron's unwitting mutilation at the hands of the witches and their *artis magicae* (2.30) thus repeats and, at least in the corpse's forensic account, stands in for the ravages inflicted by the dead one's widow with her *malis artibus* (2.29).[35] The veracity of the cadaver's account of his emasculating cuckoldry is thus implicitly authenticated through its archival inscription on the face of the other, in the grisly wounds the witch received "as a substitute for myself" (*vicariam pro me*, 2.30).[36]

At this decisive juncture, the tale's noted dichotomy between male and female magical agency — where the patri-archal,

---

late resurrection, for the vivisepulture of the widow (*viventem* [...] *sepeliendam*).

35 As Mal-Maeder (2001, 385) observes, the cadaver's disclosure "does not constitute a direct proof of [the widow's] culpability."
36 As Ingenkamp (1972) documents, the amputation of ears and nose was a traditional punishment for adultery in antiquity. Thelyphron's wounds thus seem to condense both the emasculation of adultery and the penalty it incurs.

philosophico-religious (i.e., *sagus*) agency preserves archival integrity (and narrative continuity) by filling in the gaps in our knowledge introduced by the *sagae mulieres*—finally breaks down. For if the mordacious witches plunder the mortuary to pilfer its morsels (*ora mortuorum* [...] *de-morsicant*), if they leverage their necromancy to lift the necrotic tissues that will serve as *artis magicae supplementa* (supplements for their magical art, 2.21), it is through the narrative supplement of the lifeless corpse, revived by the male priest Zatchlas, that Thelyphron makes this revelation, while the wax prostheses fashioned by the witches and now pulled away in horror render the story complete only by revealing the face imagined whole to be the site of gaping wounds. The virtuosic mastery displayed by the narrator at this dizzying moment is total, but directed entirely at a self-effacing denial of totality and mastery. All along, in fact, and right under our noses, Thelyphron had mocked himself for his lack of sagacity, his lack, as it were, of a good nose (*nares*): "knows he not [*ig-noras*]," he has a bystander say, "that he's in Thessaly?" (2.21). Unable to smell trouble, he sniffs at all the warning signs: *ineptias* [...] *mihi narras* ("oh, you're narrating nonsense," 2.23). When at last, in another instance of gender trouble in Apuleian morphologies, he has his doppelgänger sardonically dub him *sagacissimus* (most *keen-scented*, 2.30), Thelyphron playfully twists the appellation *sagus* into an association with the *sagae mulieres;* and when, with excoriating sarcasm, he flays himself with the epithet *ig-narus* (witless, but, following Isidorus, *sine naribus*),[37] he anticipates and inflicts upon himself at the level of the signifier the nasectomy to follow (2.30). Not unlike the magical *supplementa* his excised extremities become, then, Thelyphron translates the prosthetic *nares,* already filling in for a lack, into the parergonal supplements of his own narrative art, remorphologizing himself first as *ig-narus* and finally, in a queer sort of colophon, as physically bereft of nose and ears: the symbolic seats of perception.

---

37 Isidorus, *Origins* 10.142: *olfecisse enim veteres scisse dicebant.* See the Lindsay (1985) edition of Isidore.

Thelyphron thus links his own *ars* as a charming raconteur with that of the *cantatrices anus* whose ravages coincide with the gaps in his account and whose artful restorations Thelyphron himself at length restores.[38] Bringing his bodily double back to life at the same narrative moment and in the same thaumaturgical manner as the witches resurrect his own slumbering bones, he brings into the representational economy that which should wholly escape all representation: the *mal d'archive,* a harbinger of radical finitude and incurable loss. Holding the place of that corruption that leaves the archive forever separated from the origin it would (re)store, the *anus* become, in their effacement of the *arkhē,* a cipher for that *arc-anus* (secret) which bedevils the archive and effaces its completion.[39] Yet rather than simply reinvesting this figure of diabolical destruction in a theodicy of the self or compensating for the *lacunae* in his account(s) by way of a discursive representative, Thelyphron allies himself with it, pressing the prostheses into service to uncover the voids they were designed to cover up. His deft deconstruction of the masculine *ego* as archontic transforms the revelation of the *arcana* into a disclosure of a fundamental lack. Surrendering the supplements that were supposed to make whole in preference of the empty hole, he exchanges the archontic position for that of the *anus,* or — how else to render it? — that of the *arkhos.*[40]

Thelyphron's bewitching tale of the day he forever lost face can thus be read as a dramatization of the lateness of Apuleius's novelistic style. In the very act of debasing himself, he transmutes his drossy lack of sense — his *caput mortuum* — into a dazzling exploration of identity's limits and undoing. By mapping the tale's formal blockage of archival restitution onto a troubled masculinity, first heralded by his name and subsequently archived in the epicene *inanimis,* his textual corpus embodies a critique of patriarchal, religio-philosophical *phronesis,* substi-

---

38 Thelyphron was in fact the first to tranquilize his *animus* by *cantationibus* ("songs" or "incantations," 2.25).
39 On the archive's "radical destruction," see Derrida (1996c, 12–13).
40 On this meaning of *arkhos* (anus), see Agamben (2019, 52–53); cf. Telò (2020, 252–53).

tuting for the erectile, linear trajectory towards a *telos*, a cyclical enjoyment that circles around a rupture figured as *thelus* ("feminine"): the *thely*ology dis-ordering Thelyphron's *logos*. Critics have noted the plain if unavowed delight he takes in his narrative self-effacement: "though he is annoyed at the bad manners of those who laugh at his deformity, Thelyphron is pleased to tell the story" (Mayrhofer 1975, 75). Likewise, Carine Ferradou argues that he and his listeners share a certain *plaisir*, with the danger posed by the narrative "entirely mastered" (2003, 353–54). Yet is the peril so easily contained? Is Thelyphron's story not about the very unravelling of mastery and entirety, about the failure of patriarchal sovereignty to order the archive? All the same, even as Thelyphron renounces the imagined wholeness of the archontic position, it is not without perverse enjoyment. In this narrative "act of autosadism" (Winkler 1985, 113), the lure of masochistic submission — first to the *instantia* and *adiuratio* of the *domina* Byrrhena (2.20) and then to Zatchlas's threats of literal torture of his *membra* ("limbs" or "members," 2.29) — incites the tale and drives it forward.[41] The protracted withholding of the *dénouement*, repeatedly postponing the climax in a sort of narrative "tease and denial" or textual edging, leads only to an end that unveils beneath the narrative repression a more fundamental loss: to the hole in the wall through which Thelyphron at last gives himself over to dissolution.[42] By thus replaying the traumatic scene with endless variations, indelibly engraved in the prosthesis of his language, Thelyphron rewrites the fantasy of an appendage that would lend archival and autobiographical completion by revealing, at bottom, the rapture of its loss: an anarchivic *jouissance*.

---

[41] Both Byrrhena and Zatchlas cut imposing figures "of the first rank" (*primatem feminam*, 2.19; *propheta primarius*, 2.28), while both Thelyphrons speak only after some show of resistance (*commotus*, 2.20; *commotior*, 2.29).

[42] Cf. Telò (2020, 240): "The rapture of the broken, suspended face […] the pleasure-in-pain of an attempted exit from oneself."

5

"A Lie about Origin": Plato's Archive Fever

Karen Bassi

In Book 3 of Plato's *Republic,* Socrates argues for the value of what he calls a *gennaion pseudos* ("noble lie," 414b–d) or more literally, a lie or falsehood about origin or descent.[1] This lie is told in support of the idea that there are to be three classes of citizens in *Kallipolis* (the beautiful city), two that guard the city and its constitution and one that produces what the city needs. The "lie" that supports this socially stratified city is presented in the form of a hierarchy of metals as assigned to each of the different classes of citizens — gold, silver, iron, and brass (414e–415c).[2]

---

1 See Williams (2013, 370), on the meaning of *pseudos* as "lie," or the less motivated "falsehood." See also, Andrew (1989). Schofield (2007, 138) discusses the meaning of *gennaios* (noble). For the text of Plato's *Republic,* I follow the edition of Burnet (1901–1907, vol. 4). All translations are mine, unless otherwise indicated.
2 Cf. the myth of the metallic ages in Hesiod, *Works and Days* 110–58. Unlike Hesiod's account, in which each succeeding race of men comes into being and then dies out, Socrates's lie tells of succeeding generations who must be made to believe that their metallic ancestors were in some original dream-like state while they were actually being formed and fashioned under the earth. Most (1997, 115) convincingly argues that the metallic ages in Hesiod are less hierarchical than they are comparative: "Hesiod's point in describing [the] first two races must be not that we are or were

Socrates argues that if the people believed this lie "[it] would have a good effect, making them more inclined to care for the state and for one another" (415c–d). It is further described as "a contrivance for one of those falsehoods that come into being in case of need [...,] some lie about descent" (414b–c). In this chapter, I argue that Socrates's lie has what Jacques Derrida in *Archive Fever* calls "archontic power;" like the archive under Derrida's description, the lie "gathers the functions of unification, of identification, of classification" (1996c, 2). At issue is the epistemological conundrum introduced by a lie whose repetition puts these functions to work in order to justify a future truth. I take this process of justification to be a constituent feature of Derrida's archive fever. Brought on and sustained by the death drive in Derrida's account, as discussed below, this fever is a chronic condition of Western philosophy.

The "truth" of Socrates's *gennaion pseudos* ("noble lie") is an effect of repeating what we would now call a national myth whose principal variables are numerical, social, intellectual, ethical, and ecological. Each of these variables in Plato's scheme is judged and tested by a particular criterion, namely, the (male) citizen's fear of death. At the beginning of Book 3 of the *Republic,* Socrates asserts that the *arkhontes te kai phulakes* ("city's leaders or guardians") must "hear from childhood [...] sayings that will make them least susceptible to fearing death" (386a–b; cf. 413c).[3] This fear defines the future, qualified in political and social terms, as a stand-off between possibility (in the form of a mortal threat) and certainty (human mortality). Presented in its negative register as opposed to its prudent or defensive deployment, the fear of death is simultaneously invoked and assuaged in the lie's repetition from generation to generation; Glaucon locates its effect on *alloi anthrōpoi hoi husteron* ("men of the

---

or should be similar to them, but rather the very fact that they are so different from us."

3   For arguments against the common understanding that the myth of the metals attests to Plato's belief in a natural inequality among humans, see Hall (1967) and Andrew (1989).

future," 415d). The lie thus infers a co-dependency between the survival of the *anthrōpoi* ("human species") and the maintenance of a hierarchical — if flexible — class structure.[4] The fear of death is the point of intersection, the "origin," of the horizontal and vertical axes that map this co-dependency.

If the presence of gold in the lie is the material standard against which the value of the lesser metals is measured, the absence of the fear of death is the ethical standard against which civil society is ordered.[5] In both cases, intrinsic value is unsurprisingly assigned to what is rare and difficult to attain.[6] But how are we to understand the implied or metaphorical link between mineralogical and eschatological values? For those of us living in the Anthropocene, Socrates's account measures the survival of the human species in what Kathryn Yusoff (2013) calls "geologic time," beginning with the emergence of the metallic men from under the earth (414d) and extending to an indefinite future.[7] This measurement is articulated in the number of words for earth in the account, together with near homonymic words that refer to begetting or offspring. The earth (414c) is the mother of the metal men who are earthborn (414c). Addressing these earthborn men, Socrates explains that "the god mingled gold into the generation [*en tēi genesei*] of those of you who are fit to rule" and that "since you are all kin to one another [*sungeneis*] you will, for the most part, produce offspring [*gennōte*] after your kinds" (415a). Here apostrophe and polyptoton combine to interpellate Socrates's interlocutors and, by extension, Plato's future readers into the truth of the lie, encouraged by the

---

4 Socrates states that the metals can be "intermixed" and admits what we would call class mobility (415c).
5 Men who are mingled with gold are "the most honored" (*timiōtatoi*, 415a).
6 Fear in general is a recurring desideratum in Socrates's discussion of what the guardians must guard against, as at 413c. My contention is that the fear of death is its ultimate form.
7 Yusoff (2013, 781): "[T]he Anthropocene defines a new temporality for the human as a being situated in geologic time." I am grateful to Mario Telò for recommending Yusoff's work to me. See Telò (2023b).

prospect that we and our offspring may have some gold in us.[8] Apostrophe — addressed to both the living and the dead — is a key trope in this chapter. In the texts discussed, apostrophe — addressing both those who have died and those who are not-yet-born — situates the reader in a present suspended between these existential indices of before and after (before one is born and after one has died).[9] It should be acknowledged too that the myth of the metal men is also hyperbolic, making its truth value subject to what might be called rhetorical saturation or overkill.

The prospect mentioned above is embedded in a subterranean economy in which value is apportioned "under the earth" and is then inherited as an indelible marker of human survival. This economy melds mineral and biological processes and is epitomized, as we have seen, in the assertion that men are earthborn (*gēgenoi,* 414c). Dependent on an always fertile mother earth (*gē*) or, in more recent terms, on the inexhaustible extraction of the earth's mineral resources, the lie works to alleviate the fear of death by positing the presence of an inorganic and renewable source of human life; mortal mothers are passed over. But this tentative consolation is compromised by the fact that, beginning with the Homeric poems, "under the earth" is also the traditional and terrifying domain of dead humans.[10] If Socrates's lie is one of those sayings that are intended to "make the guardians least susceptible to fearing death" (386a–b), in other words, its subterranean milieu only provokes that fear through omission.

---

8   See Althusser (1971). This prospect anticipates on a symbolic level the condition of living under capitalism, on which see Yusoff (2013).
9   B. Johnson (1986, 29) asks: "Is there any *inherent* connection between figurative language and questions of life and death [...]?" Her article answers this question in the affirmative in a study of apostrophe in lyric poetry from Baudelaire to Adrienne Rich, with a focus on poems about abortion. I believe that apostrophe also makes this inherent connection in ancient Greek prose genres, where it both invokes and refuses lyric's efforts at immortalization.
10 Hades is "lord of those beneath the earth" (*anax enerōn, Iliad* 20.61–65).

In the Athenian context, autochthony or birth from "under the earth" constitutes a nativist claim to exceptionalism and is commonly understood as a feature of democratic ideology.[11] As such, it is often credited in legendary accounts of military victory, such as Erechtheus's defeat of Eumolpus or the defeat of the Persians at Marathon.[12] It may be that autochthony is "part of the patriotic consciousness of the Athenians" (Rosivach 1987, 304). In more concrete terms, however, it is called up when the city and its citizens are at risk of annihilation. This helps explain why the earthborn men in Socrates's lie are said to be provided first of all with weapons and military equipment (*hopla kai hē allē skeuē,* 414e). When Glaucon tells Socrates not to be afraid to tell the lie (*kai mē phobou,* 414c) his admonition is both cautionary and proleptic. It introduces the difficulty of overcoming fear and it anticipates the fabricated oracle with which Socrates brings the lie to an end: according to this oracle, the city will be utterly destroyed (*tēn polin diaphtharēnai,* 415c) if ever an iron or copper man becomes its guardian. Here the fear of telling the lie (because it may not be believed) is overcome only to introduce the fear of the city's destruction (because the lie may be believed), where the city is metonymy for its citizens. In short, "earthborn" is a defense against annihilation. In spite of producing the consoling effect of projecting human existence into an indefinite future, however, accounts of human origins lead inevitably to death's door.

These remarks are preliminary to situating Socrates's lie about origin in a circuit of "before and after" readings that takes Derrida's *Archive Fever* as its origin or point of departure. This circuit includes *Archive Fever* as a reading of Yosef Hayim Yerushalmi's *Freud's Moses* and both works as readings of Sigmund Freud's revisionist history of the origin of Judaism in *Moses and Monotheism.* I take "reading" in this context to be a

---

11 Rosivach (1987, 297) notes that *autokhthōn* can be a synonym of *gēgenēs,* citing Plato, *Sophist* 247c with 248c.
12 See Rosivach (1987, 303–4) and the sources cited there, including Plato's *Menexenus* 239a–b.

form of repetition as well as one of the meanings of "impression" in Derrida's subtitle.[13] As suggested above, moreover, apostrophe is a governing trope in this circuit. Thus, in the form of an apologia, Derrida (1996c, 4) addresses his readers at the beginning of *Archive Fever*:

> I dream now of having the time to submit for your discussion more than one thesis, three at least. This time will never be given to me [*Ce temps ne me sera jamais donné*]. Above all, I will never have the right [*je n'aurai jamais le droit*] to take your time so as to impose upon you, back to back, these three + *n* essays. Submitted to the test of your discussion, these theses will therefore remain, for the moment [*pour le moment*], hypotheses.[14]

In this guarded address to an indeterminate "you," Derrida's dream of having time is answered by its denial (*ne* [...] *jamais*), declared to be unjustifiable (*je n'aurai jamais le droit*), and finally given up "for the moment" (*pour le moment*). Apostrophe is the pretext for naming and repeating "time" as the elusive medium of theses that will remain hypotheses. As discussed in more detail below, the trope is also an unsettling harbinger of what Derrida calls "the future to come" (*à venir*).

Within this circuitous reading, Socrates's account of the metal men exerts a centripetal force, not because it is the oldest text but because, as described above, it epitomizes a conceptual link between origin stories, their repetition, and a confrontation with death.[15] In *Archive Fever*, this link is forged in Derrida's

---

[13] The subtitle *A Freudian Impression* (*une impression freudienne*) was added after the lecture was delivered under another title. Referring to Freud's archive, Derrida speaks of "the printed and the printing of impression" (1996c, 16; cf. 18).

[14] The French is taken from Derrida (1995a).

[15] See Weber (2011, 4), on reading and relative chronology, or what he calls "reversability": "Freud can be read as coming 'after' those who read him, and not only Derrida." Weber notes that the same can be said of Socrates and Plato.

sustained attention to the death drive, famously if tentatively described by Freud in *Beyond the Pleasure Principle* as "an urge in organic life to restore an earlier state of things" (Freud 1955a, 47), or, in Jean Laplanche's succinct phrase, a movement "from the vital to the inanimate" (Laplanche 1976, 107). This movement is manifested in the repetition of past traumatic events, first exemplified for Freud in the experiences of soldiers in World War I.[16] The drive, in other words, is a response to the threat of annihilation which is eased — paradoxically — by the prospect of returning to a pre-organic state. In Derrida's reading of Freud (1996c, 11), the archive presents a similar paradox:

> [If] there is no archive without consignation in an *external place* which assures the possibility of memorization, of repetition, of reproduction, or of reimpression, then we must also consider that repetition itself, the logic of repetition compulsion, remains, according to Freud, indissociable from the death drive. […] The archive always works, and *a priori,* against itself.

Claiming to preserve the past, the archive attests to its (the past's) disappearance or destruction; it "works against itself." As the principal symptom of the death drive, repetition is the formal expression of this "working against;" in the pursuit of mastery over the past, repetition ossifies it into a singular set of prior events (a history). Human origin stories — epitomized here by Socrates's account of the men of metal — work against themselves in a similar way; told to be repeated, they ease the fear of annihilation by positing an earlier state of (pre-)existence. In each case, repetition confounds the relative chronology of "before and after" in order to assert that humanity has a future.

---

16 The designation "First World War," of course, only came into existence after 1945 when "Second World War" was coined and is thus a singular example of the conundrum of "before and after."

Archive Fever is itself a return to and a repetition of an earlier state of things; it is a late work in which Derrida (1996c, 88 and 91) frequently refers to his own earlier works ("I tried to discuss this elsewhere"; "as I tried to show"). More generally, *Archive Fever* is a study of the unconscious as counterhistory, that is, as an archive that ignores the historical presumption of a strict linear chronology in pursuit of some future truth. The argument outlines the ways in which the archive resists what Vered Lev Kenaan calls "the logic of chronology" (2019, 11). To illustrate this resistance to linearity, Derrida defines *archive fever* in a barrage of near synonyms: it is "a compulsive, repetitive, and nostalgic desire for the archive, an irrepressible desire to return to the origin, a homesickness, a nostalgia for the return to the most archaic place of absolute commencement" (1996c, 91). As this (repetitive) definition demonstrates, *Archive Fever* is both a study and a product of the death drive as Freud describes it. It is a response to human trauma (the history of the Jews) enacted in repeated returns to an originary datum (a text, a place, an event, an impression, etc.).

In thinking about Socrates's lie as a symptom of this fever, my discussion is loosely structured around three related approaches to the human past — archaeology, epistemology, and eschatology — in which the last, that is, the idea of an afterlife, is a recurring if sometimes latent motif. This motif is perhaps most evident in Derrida's frequent invocation in *Archive Fever* of a paternal genealogy going back to Moses and including the dead fathers and grandfathers of Freud, Derrida, and Yerushalmi — but notably not their mothers or grandmothers.[17] Derrida even conflates this paternal genealogy with autobiography when he says that when speaking of Yerushalmi he is really speaking of himself (1996c, 88). Guided by the tension between origin and repetition in *Archive Fever*, the question posed in this chapter is, "What is the archival status of Socrates's originary lie?" The myth of the metallic men focuses our attention on the predic-

---

17 See Aiello (2016, 132), quoting Felman (2014, 63): "In the case of both Freud and Derrida, the archive seems to have erased the women."

tive capability of origin stories or, put the other way around, on how such stories are retrospectively defined by that capability. Destined to be repeated as the truth among future generations of fathers and sons, the lie epitomizes Derrida's observation in *Archive Fever* that the Greek word *arkhē* "names at once a *commencement* and a *commandment*" (1996c, 1).

That Socrates's lie about origin is archival first of all in its relation to the death drive is formally expressed in the hesitation with which Socrates justifies the lie and Freud justifies the drive: Socrates asks how he can find the courage to propose such a lie (*hopoia tolma,* 414e); Freud repeatedly refers to the death drive as speculation (1955a, 295).[18] Similarly, Derrida says that "nothing should be sure" in *Archive Fever* and that "'archive' is only a notion" (1996c, 28 and 36).[19] These shared hesitations are more than rhetorical.[20] They imply that both Western philosophy and psychoanalysis risk being dead on arrival, the victims of internal doubt and external suppression. Subject to hesitation and disbelief but expected to be repeated from generation to generation, Socrates's lie about origin shares this risk and also reflects on our own recent predicament. In a pandemic whose beginning and end are respectively unknowable and unpredictable, when the passing of time is relentlessly measured in death's approach (*à venir*), when we are living in a so-called "post-truth" world, and when the prevalence of systemic racism and anti-Semitism has been exposed, the lie about origin examines the conditions under which the past justifies the future (l'*avenir*). It tests, in Derrida's phrase, the *"truth of delusion"* (1996c, 86).

---

18 See McNulty (2017). See also Laplanche (1976, 106), on Freud's "profoundly baffling" description of the death drive.
19 Derrida draws attention to Freud's hesitation in invoking the death drive in *Civilization and Its Discontents* (Freud 1955b, 7–8). When Derrida asks, in Freud's name, "Does this merit printing?" he is, of course, asking whether *Archive Fever* merits printing. In *Archive Fever* Derrida (1996c, 48) evokes "the essential modality of the *perhaps*" while discussing Yerushalmi's "Monologue with Freud" (Yerushalmi 1991, 81–100). Perhaps hesitation is the most prevalent form of repetition.
20 It is relevant too that Yerushalmi begins *Freud's Moses* with a list of things that the book is not intended to do (1991, xvii–xviii).

Derrida begins *Archive Fever* by refusing to begin at the beginning: "Let us not begin at the beginning [*Ne commençons pas au commencement*]" (1995a, 1, and 1996c, 1).[21] He then begins with an etymology, that is, with the most predictable and conventional kind of beginning. In Derrida's succinct definition, as noted above, *arkhē* "names at once the *commencement* and the *commandment*."[22] The archive is constituted in the temporal priority (the *commencement*) and sanctioned justification (the *commandment*) assigned to this gathering. But how are these temporal and defensive mechanisms related? Does the choice of a beginning — a point of origin — presume a justification, whether expressed in national myths, narrative histories, literary plots, philosophical proofs, or museum collections? And in what sense is this presumption also a form of violence, as Derrida's refusal to begin at the beginning suggests?

As noted at the beginning of this chapter, Plato begins Book 3 of the *Republic* with Socrates's admonition that the city's leaders must "hear from childhood [...] sayings that will make them least susceptible to fearing death" (386a–b).[23] The admonition comprises the span of a human life — from the cradle to the grave — in which "before and after" are the temporal markers of political and ethical regimens. In Derrida's terms again, the admonition names both a *commencement* (from childhood) and a *commandment*: the sorts of tales or sayings (*muthoi*) that invoke the "terrors of the underworld" must be tightly controlled. Illustrated by examples from Homer, such poetry, Socrates tells Adeimantus, will weaken the guardians' courage and should be wiped out (*exaleiphō*, 386c) in Kallipolis.[24] In

---

21 On Derrida's engagement with beginnings, see Rollins (2020, 1–24).
22 Derrida (1996c, 1).
23 Throughout Book 3, Socrates repeatedly speaks of the kinds of behaviors that citizens should either accept or reject from childhood.
24 The first meaning of *exaleiphō* in Liddell–Scott–Jones is "to plaster or wash over" as in Herodotus, *Histories* 7.69. I refer to Wilson's (2015) edition of the *Histories*. See Euripides's *Iphigenia in Tauris* 698, where Orestes says that his house will not be childless and "wiped out" if Pylades marries Iphigenia. See Kearns's (2023) edition.

fact, the more poetic (*poiētika*) such tales are, the more harmful they are to "boys and men who are destined to be free and to be more afraid of slavery than of death" (387b). This examination of proscribed poetry then leads to examples of lies (391d) about the words and deeds of heroes and gods that are *tois ge akouousin blabera* ("harmful to those who hear them" 391e). Such lies are measured against political and ethical criteria and have the effect of weakening the hearer's *autarkes* ("self-sufficiency," 387d) and *sōphrosunē* ("self-control," 389d–e, 390a, and *passim*). As Socrates will argue at length later in the dialogue, this sort of pseudo-poetry is particularly dangerous when spoken in the first person, that is, wholly through mimesis or imitation (393d–94d). For such imitations, if "continued from youth and throughout life, become habitual and instinctive [*eis ēthē te kai phusin kathistantai*] in body, speech, and thought" (395d). The fact that the Platonic dialogue is "wholly" mimetic ironizes this indictment in the process of querying its relevance to prose works whose interlocutors are formerly living humans (i.e., not characters from myth or legend). According to Socrates, poets and other craftsmen who produce *kakias eikosi* ("likenesses of evil") must be censored as a defense against evil accumulating in the souls of those who spend time with such likenesses (401b–c). Socrates's hesitant defense of the lie about origin is part of this ethical regimen beginning *euthus ek paidōn* ("earliest childhood," 401d) and subject to habit-forming or repetitive imitations.

In *Beyond the Pleasure Principle,* Freud explicitly rejects the notion that an "imitative instinct" can explain the repetition compulsion that belongs to the death drive: "It emerges from this discussion that there is no need to assume the existence of a special imitative instinct [*Nachahmungstrieges*] in order to provide a motive for play" (1955a, 17). As William N. West (1999) notes, Freud's unnamed target in this passage is Aristotle who — in contrast to Plato — asserts in the *Poetics* that imitation is natural (*sumphuton*) in humans from childhood, that they learn their earliest lessons through imitation, and that they feel pleasure (*to khairein*) in things imitated.²⁵ Predicated on an extended sense of ontological security, Aristotle sums up this process as "learning and inferring what each thing is" or, more succinctly, that "this is that" (*hoti houtos ekeinos*, 1448b). This educative effect explains why humans take pleasure in seeing imitations of painful things, like corpses. West concludes that "Freud's dismissal of mimesis opens the door for his theory of the death drive to explain this kind of repetition" (1999, 140). But Freud's dismissal also admits an analogy between mimesis and the repetition compulsion in the act of rejecting it. In repressing an originary text and its author (Aristotle's *Poetics*), he elevates the pleasure of mastery by relinquishing the compulsion to repeat.²⁶ The result is that Aristotle's *Poetics* — and by extension Plato's *Republic* — haunts *Beyond the Pleasure Principle* in the tension between imitation and repetition as innate or instinctual vehicles of "the pleasure of unpleasure" (Laplanche 1976, 103). Readers may recognize in this formulation too Derrida's punning "hauntology," which Martin Hägglund describes as marking "a relation to what is no longer or not yet" (2008, 47).

If Freud's dismissal of Aristotle's "imitative instinct" opens the door to the death drive, it does so in exposing the sources of this haunting. Or, more to the point, it does so in revealing the ways in which Aristotle's account of imitation tests Freud's account of repetition, and vice versa. The implied analogy between them is predicated on deferral "as a fundamental property of both," as West (1999, 154) notes. At the same time, Freud's

---

25 For the text of Aristotle's *Poetics*, I follow the edition of Lucas (1968). All translations mine, unless otherwise indicated.
26 West speaks of Freud "imitating Aristotle but suppressing his name [...] trying not to imitate him" (1999, 140). Following the quotation above, Freud comments, "We may add the reminder that the dramatic and imitative art of adults, which differs from the behaviour of children in being directed towards the spectator, does not however spare the latter the most painful impressions, e.g., in tragedy, and yet can be felt by him as highly enjoyable." Freud goes on to note that these cases "bear no witness to the operation of tendencies beyond the pleasure-principle" (1955a, 17), i.e., to the death drive. The reference to a tragic spectator brings us back again to the *Poetics* without naming it. See Telò (2020).

hesitant return to the place of origin, that is, to Aristotle's *Poetics,* is an expression of his own singular death drive; it speaks to the founder's efforts to master the terms of psychoanalysis. It also demonstrates how hesitation, as the temporal dimension of indecision, stretches out the time between an original (traumatic) event and its repetition, or between a before and an after. As noted above, hesitation forges a rhetorical link between Socrates's lie, Freud's death drive, and Derrida's archive. More generally, hesitation specifies the aporia intrinsic to a "belief in the future," where the phrase connotes both a future belief (the lie, for example) and that there will be a future (*l'avenir*).[27] According to Derrida (1996c, 78):

> If repetition is [...] inscribed at the heart of the future to come [*à venir*], one must also import there, *in the same stroke,* the death drive, the violence of forgetting, *superrepression* (suppression and repression), the anarchive, in short, the possibility of putting to death the very thing, whatever its name, which *carries the law in its tradition.*

This relationship between repetition and superrepression describes how the *Poetics* haunts *Beyond the Pleasure Principle* in psychoanalytic terms, including the proposition that both texts carry "the law in its tradition." Expressed in Freud's dismissal of Aristotle's imitative instinct, this haunting heralds a future to come (*à venir*), understood as the temporal mode of indecision between repeating and forgetting. It names a mode of expectant hesitation in confronting the "unknowable to come" (Rollins 2020, 31).

As noted above, insofar as Plato's *Republic* is the source or target of Aristotle's disinterest in "the deceptive qualities of mimesis," it is included in this anarchivic archive (West 1999, 145). For Plato, imitation can lead to "habitual and instinctive" behaviors that are either good or bad depending on the original source of the imitation; the former are unified and disciplined

---

27 See Rollins (2020, 33–34) on Derrida's "aporetic ethics."

while the latter are manifold and varied (*to pantodapas morphas tōn metabolōn ekhein,* 397c). Here "varied" refers to the formal aspects of musical harmony and rhythm but is closely aligned with ethical structures or with what might be called ethical volatility in a city in which the ideal is that "each person does only one thing" (*hekastos hen prattei,* 397e). These varied or manifold imitations — the bad sort — are of greatest interest to Socrates when they are "imitations of a life" (*biou mimēmata,* 400a).

In addition to threatening to "wipe out" these dangerous and deceptive "imitations of a life" in Kallipolis (386c), Socrates advises Homer and the other poets not to be angry if a line is drawn through the offending passages (*diagraphō,* 387b; cf. *aphaireō* "to take away," 387c; *exaireō* "to take out," 387e). Here the repetition of traumatic events — a defining feature of epic poetry in its form and content — is repeatedly interrupted by arguments against its cumulative effects. I refer here too to the *Republic*'s citational style, that is, its selective extraction of illustrative passages from the Homeric poems. The threat to draw a line through offensive passages illustrates by way of a refusal Derrida's assertion that "repetition is [...] *inscribed* at the heart of the future to come [*à venir*]" (1996c, 78, my emphasis), and that "one must also import [into the future to come], *in the same stroke,* the death drive." This future to come takes the form of a palimpsest, where the metaphor comprises an "original" text together with its various iterations or repetitions. Within this anarchival archive, imitations and lies are singular forms of repetition in which the compulsion to repeat is repeatedly checked by hesitancy. Given the lie *qua* lie, it is not surprising that this hesitancy arises in confronting the truth and, more immediately, in confronting death. Death, the object of existential fear, is the final test of truth. In summing up his account of harmful lies — beginning with those that instill the fear of death — Socrates asserts that "a high value must be placed upon truth" (389b). But he then pivots to conclude that while a *pseudos* may be useless to gods, it can be "useful as a form of medicine" for humans (*pharmakon,* cf. 382d), with the proviso that such lies may only be told by the rulers "for the benefit of the city" (389b).[28] Socrates admits at this point that the account so far is "sketched in outline and not with precision" (*en tupōi, mē di' akribeias,* 414a). It is, in other words, under threat of being "wiped out" or of having "a line drawn through it." This threat — another iteration of the threat of annihilation — hovers over the sections of the dialogue that present and defend the lie.

Following his defense of truth-telling, Socrates concludes that "men are unwillingly deprived of true opinions" (413a). In order to avoid being so deprived, would-be rulers must be "tested much more carefully than men do gold in the fire" (*basanizontas polu mallon ē khruson en puri,* 413e). In a version of what Leslie Kurke (1995) calls "the language of metals," the metaphor of testing gold anticipates in retrospect the lie about origin. On the one hand, testing gold as the means of ascertaining the truth endorses the lie about those most precious rulers who have "gold mingled in their generation" (*khruson en tēi genesei,* 415a). Such rulers, it is implied, are wedded to the truth. But on the other hand the truth of the metaphor itself is challenged by its (the metaphor's) implicit inclusion in the lie. This paradox, bookmarked by retrospection and hesitation in asserting what is true, frames the lie's trajectory toward Derrida's future to come (*à venir*).

A similar paradox attends Derrida's reading of Yerushalmi's *Freud's Moses* in *Archive Fever.* Yerushalmi's final chapter, titled in something of an oxymoron, "Monologue with Freud," takes the form of an apostrophic address to Freud. Derrida (1995a, 95, and 1996c, 59) states that while this chapter is "the most fictive, [it] is certainly not the least true" (*Mais le dernier chapitre, le plus fictive, n'est certainement pas le moins vrai*). Here the trope of litotes — or a hesitant version of that hesitant trope — reveals the epistemological and explanatory limits of speaking to a formerly living (i.e., historical but now spectral) human. Apostrophes

---

28 On "pharmacological lying" in the *Republic,* see Carl Page (1991, 18): "In speaking of drugs, Socrates implies that pharmacological lying is the judicious use of a poison, the poison of deceit. […] If it is a good drug, a good lie will be purged with the illness it removes (to the extent that the illness is correctable)."

to dead humans are, of course, standard features of European literature beginning with the Homeric epics. If Yerushalmi's oft-repeated apostrophes to Freud ("Dear, esteemed professor Freud," etc.) constitute, as Derrida later remarks, "an uncommon and perhaps unprecedented scene in the history of psychoanalysis" (1996c, 30) — and if the "Monologue" is at the same time the "most fictive [and] certainly not the least true" chapter of Yerushalmi's study — it is also an ironic inversion, perhaps even a parody, of psychoanalysis as a process of getting at some truth about the past by talking to a (living) analyst.

Addressing Freud and invoking the psychoanalytic concept of "deferred obedience," says Derrida, Yerushalmi "painfully, laboriously justifies himself" to the founder (1996c, 61). It is perhaps more accurate to say, however, that Yerushalmi (1991) labors to justify himself to his readers. At times, he even speaks for Freud or as if he were Freud.[29] In other words, he prefigures Derrida's confession, mentioned above, that when speaking of Yerushalmi he is really speaking of himself. So too, we might say that when speaking of Freud Yerushalmi is really speaking of himself. What necessitates these repeated acts of identification as self-justification? We are reminded here too of Freud's self-justifying dismissal of Aristotle's imitative instinct. Are such acts somehow inherent in the archive? A key heuristic in *Archive Fever* is a distinction between the history of psychoanalysis and the work of psychoanalysis, each of which has its own distinct if related archive. According to Derrida (1996c, 64, and 1995a, 108; my emphasis):

---

29 Yerushalmi (1991, 99): "I carry within me a pent-up feeling, an intuition, that you yourself implied something more, something that you felt deeply but would never dare to say. I will take the risk of saying it. I think that in your innermost heart you believed that psychoanalysis is itself a further, if not final metamorphosed extension of Judaism, divested of its illusory religious forms but retaining its essential monotheistic characteristics, at least as you understood and described them. In short, I think you believed that just as you are a godless Jew, psychoanalysis is a godless Judaism. But I don't think you intended us to know this."

> Now Yerushalmi knows very well that Freud's intention is to analyze, across the apparent absence of memory and of archive, all kinds of symptoms, signs, figures, metaphors, and metonymies that attest, at least virtually, an archival documentation where the "ordinary historian" identifies none. […] Only the texts of this archive [the unconscious] are not readable to the paths of "ordinary history" and this is the very relevance [*l'intérêt*] of psychoanalysis, *if it has one.*

I note again Derrida's hesitancy, here, in affirming the very relevance of psychoanalysis. These remarks pertain to the last paragraphs of Yerushalmi's book, in which the scholar of historical Judaism poses the question to Freud of whether psychoanalysis is a "Jewish science." "That we shall know," he says, "if it is at all knowable, only when much future work has been done" (quoted by Derrida 1995a, 70). The living Freud had addressed this question, but not sufficiently, according to Yerushalmi: "I only want to know whether you ultimately came to believe it to be so" (1991, 100). And he promises not to reveal Freud's answer to anyone, in effect to erase it. The inference in the "Monologue" is that Yerushalmi expects the dead Freud to answer in the affirmative, in spite of the fact that his previous chapters chronicle the living Freud's insistence that, as a science, psychoanalysis must be universal. This universalism may be highly contested but, as Arnold D. Richards puts it, science was Freud's "bulwark against anti-Semitism" (2014, 1001).[30] In the context of *Archive Fever,* the more general point is that the promise of "future work" is forestalled in a question that the dead "father" of psychoanalysis cannot answer and in the ambivalence that the question itself reveals. As exemplified by this question, moreover, the source of Derrida's hesitation about the relevance of psychoanalysis ("if it has one") is rooted in an implied correlation between traditional "science" and "ordinary history." Both are inadequate to putting in order and assigning value to "all [the] kinds of symptoms" that make up the archive of psychoanalysis in practice. The rele-

---

30 Cf. Yerushalmi (1991, 97–100).

vance of psychoanalysis, in other words, is evident in the lacuna introduced by Yerushalmi's question as expressed in the phrase "if it is at all knowable."

Addressing the relationship between ordinary history and psychoanalysis, Joan Scott (2018, 98) finds a "distinction between reality and truth" in Freud's writing. For Freud, she says:

> [F]inding "truth" meant looking beyond the self-justification offered by actors, not in order to impugn their motives or discredit their aims, but to uncover the desires and anxieties they contained, the collective representations they appealed to, in order to better understand how those psychic processes — those of the people in the past as well as of their historians — enabled and informed what has come to count as history.

The test case for this conclusion is Freud's revision of Jewish history in *Moses and Monotheism*. The "psychic processes" that, in Scott's terms, enable and inform this history are summarized by Freud (1955c, 94):

> From [the time I wrote *Totem and Taboo* (1912)] I have never doubted that religious phenomena are to be understood only on the model of the neurotic symptoms of the individual, which are so familiar to us, as a return of long forgotten important happenings in the primeval history of the human family, that they owe their obsessive character to that very origin and therefore derive their effect on mankind from the historical truth that they contain.

In this formulation, "historical truth," as Scott suggests, is manifested in the obsessive return to a long-forgotten originary event. Interestingly, the historian Yerushalmi confesses to "a tangle of unconscious motives" in writing *Freud's Moses,* motives which he stresses are counterbalanced by his "conscious" intentions (1991, xv). Here "ordinary history" vies with psychoanalysis, epitomized in the conflict between the "unconscious motives" and "conscious intentions" of the historian. This conflict is arguably the source of Derrida's conclusion that Yerushalmi proves in the "Monologue" what he is attempting to disprove, namely, Freud's account of repressed trauma and guilt. Manifested in a spectral continuum that includes both the formerly living and the now dead Freud, the apostrophic "Monologue" — says Derrida — affirms "the future to come" (*à venir*). Implicitly drawing on the anachronic potential of a postscript as something "written after," he continues, "This postscript of sorts retrospectively determines what precedes it" (Derrida 1996c, 39). Derrida calls it a "postscript of sorts" because Yerushalmi does not refer to his final chapter as a postscript; as noted above, the title is "Monologue with Freud." But this fact only raises the question of a relationship between this postscript "of sorts" and the actual (titled as such) postscript of *Archive Fever*.

In this "Postscript," Derrida turns to Freud's 1907 *Delusion and Dream in Jensen's Gradiva* in which Freud discusses Wilhelm Jensen's 1903 novella, subtitled *A Pompeian Fancy*.[31] As Daniel Orrells notes, "Freud was developing theories of psychoanalysis at a historical moment when classical archaeology had asserted a confident self-image both inside and outside the academy" (2010, 159). The novella tells the story of Norbert Hanold, a young German archaeologist who, after seeing an ancient bas relief depicting a young girl whom he calls Gradiva, dreams about her, and then travels to Pompeii where he seems to see her walking in the city on the day of its destruction in 79 CE. But this of course is a delusion; she is in fact a "living German girl" named Zoe Bertgang, who turns out to be Norbert's forgotten childhood friend and would-be lover. According to Freud, "The peculiar unconscious content of [Norbert's] dream, the amorous longing for the once-known Zoe, is transformed into the manifest-content of the destruction of Pompeii and the loss of Gradiva" (2014, 174). For him, this story of dreams, delusions, and repressed childhood attachments illustrates and justifies in advance the work of psychoanalysis.

---

31 See Armstrong (2006, 11–25).

In Freud's analysis and Derrida's postscript, archaeology is a topographical metaphor for psychic life in which a traumatic past is uncovered in the process of learning the truth about the patient's present condition. In the novella, says Freud, "The burial of Pompeii, this disappearance, with the preservation of the past, offers a striking resemblance to […] repression" (1907, 162). At the center of this psychoanalytic narrative about the push and pull between the disappearance and the preservation of the past is an iconic artifact: the ancient bas relief. This object is the one element that, in another moment of hesitation, Freud finds it difficult to account for in the narrative. How to explain the physical resemblance of the two women, the one who is presumed to have died in Pompeii in 79 CE and the other living woman whom Norbert has presumably not seen since childhood? In hindsight, the ancient relief is an instance — says Orrells — of "the copy coming before the original" where this temporal anomaly is significantly figured in the image of a formerly living human (2010, 166). In Derrida's terms, it is the agent of Harold's archive fever.

The aetiological account of Socrates's metallic men seems to me to be very close to what Orrells calls Freud's "dream of archaeology." The latter comprises an always unfulfilled "desire for origins" as expressed, says Freud, in Norbert's first dream: "This was the wish, comprehensible to every archaeologist, to have been an eye-witness of that catastrophe of 79" (2014, 235). An eye-witness, we might reply, but not a victim. In Freudian terms, the story of the ancient bas relief validates a scientific process of discovering and alleviating past trauma. In Platonic terms, the lie about the metallic men validates a process of discovering and justifying social and political relations. In both, the truth about the past is measured in the interplay of originals and copies where the original is an ever-receding illusion or dream, and where the threat (or promise) of collective annihilation is its lingering after-effect. We can include in this dreamscape Derrida's unfulfilled dream of having time in *Archive Fever,* a dream motivated by the fear that time will "never be given" (*Ce temps ne me sera jamais donné*). In the end, archive fever is a symptom of human precarity, of hoping that the past justifies some consoling truth about the future to come and — in the form of "an irrepressible desire to return to the origin" — of wondering whether death is worth waiting for.

This state of wondering, both in the lifetime of an individual and in the survival of the species, is perhaps the cruelest expression of what Lauren Berlant, in a brilliant formulation, calls "cruel optimism" (2011). According to Berlant, this optimism emerged in response to "good life fantasies" in Europe and the United States after WWII, that is, in response to post-war capitalist fantasies (2011, 2). Beyond this historical framing, however, cruel optimism is founded on the expectation — borne of varying degrees of privilege — that we will live another day, or on what Berlant calls "living on."[32] The cruelest forms of optimism comprise the mythological, theological, and psychological discourses that confront and wrestle with the limits of and threats to living on, that is, with death's approach. With reference to Barbara Johnson's article, mentioned above, Berlant locates cruel optimism in the trope of apostrophe which she describes as the formal trace of a "convenient absence" (2011, 25).[33] Under this description, absence is convenient from the point of view of a reader for whom the (absent) addressee is some other "you" or, in absolute terms, someone who has died or has not yet been born. But convenience is only a temporary diversion. More cruelly and in the throes of archive fever, apostrophe feeds the hope of a "you" that lives on. This is the hope — or perhaps it is a resignation — that both justifies and denies the truth of Socrates's lie about origin, and predicts its hesitant defense against the fear of death and the threat of annihilation.

---

[32] Berlant's framing is both historical and genre-based; she focuses on more recent genres in contrast to what she calls "older realist genres" (2011, 6).
[33] Berlant (2011, 25) refers to B. Johnson (1986).

6

Feral Futures, or The Animal That Therefore I Am Not (Less to Follow)

Andres Matlock

The genesis of time, according to Derrida's Biblical reflections in "The Animal That Therefore I Am (More to Follow)," arises from a conflation of "being" and "following." The inversion of priority between God's creation and its naming jumpstarts a temporality that is always already a *contretemps* (Derrida 2008, 17):

> God lets Ish [*sic*][1] call the other living beings all on his own […] these animals that are older and younger than him, these living things that came into the world before him but were

---

1 Guenther (2009) discusses Derrida's (mis)reading of *ha'adam* and *Ish* for sexual difference. Derrida's late turn to animal studies remains controversial, especially in light of the claim in his 1997 address that the arguments he has been making "for a long time" in a "deconstructive style" have always been "dedicated to the question of the living and the living animal. For me that has always been the most important and decisive question. I have addressed it a thousand times, either indirectly or obliquely, by means of readings of *all* the philosophers I have taken an interest in" (2008, 34). For critical evaluations of this sweeping retrospective claim and his contributions to post-humanism, cf. Derrida (1996b) and see, e.g., Calarco (2004); Bruns (2008); Wolfe (2010, esp. 3–144); Guerlac (2012); Kaufman (2013); Boisseron (2015); and Derrida (2020).

135

named after him. [...] In both cases, man is in both senses of
the word *after* the animal. He follows him.

The dual sense of "to follow"—to come later or after, and to
pursue as a hunter pursues—defines human time in relation to
the animal in terms of lateness, anachrony, and other forms of
retrospective "out-of-jointness." In the myth of his text, Derrida
deconstructs the anthropocentrism of time's origin by examining the shame he feels when he is confronted, naked, in his
bathroom, by his cat. This event also possesses a specific temporality—or rather an atemporality—unfolding "within that
time frame [*depuis ce temps*] [...] 'since time,' that is to say, since
a time when there was not yet time, when time hadn't elapsed,
if that is possible, before the verdict, the reckoning, or the fall"
(Derrida 2008, 21–22). This preapocalyptic *depuis ce temps* (time
frame), which Derrida inhabits with his cat, in his bathroom, is
deferral in itself—what the title of the text refers to endlessly
as "more to follow." Through this suspension of priority, Derrida repeatedly asks the question, "Who am I (following)?" in
order to widen, sharpen, and redraw the differences that render impossible abstractions like "the animal," "the human," or
"the living." The animals in Derrida's bestiary are all Chimeras:
hybrid yet irreducible, inhabiting language, but not subjected
to it, marked by division, however multiplex and mutual. These
Chimerical beasts rise up from the text to put to shame simple
identities and superficial taxonomies.

From this deferral of priority, Derrida shows little interest
in returning his beasts to time. The Chimera exists, by Derrida's devising, *depuis ce temps*—freed, at least for the time
being, from the shame of following or the threat of being followed. Derrida is unconcerned, at least for the moment, with
how we might conceive a time *of* the Chimera—in the sense
of an evolutionary time, a becoming-Chimerical or a Chimeri-

cal becoming.² In order to "restart the clock,"³ I follow Derrida's deconstruction of the human/animal into the thicket of vegetation that, in post-Aristotelian biology, stands both at and just beside the origins of life. Porphyry, quoting from Theophrastus, who, in turn, is drawing on Aristotle's doctrine on the parts of the organism, articulates the idea clearly that only animals and humans possess the same *arkhai* ("beginnings" or "first parts"), such as "skin, flesh, and the constituent fluids of animate beings," but all living things, including plants, share a set of *stoikheia* ("first elements").⁴ From these different starting points, Porphyry argues that humans live with animals or, better, animals live within humans. This common, visceral origin is why, for Porphyry, we should not eat them — this is also why, for Derrida, we feel shame in front of them. Vegetal life, on the other hand, occupies somehow a more elemental, yet, at the same time, dis-

---

2   A notion of evolution is almost entirely absent from the four lengthy addresses collected in Derrida (2008), but see the brief discussion of Immanuel Kant's engagement with evolution as part of an "anthropologism of the 'I think'" (96–102). Similarly, despite widespread awareness already in the late 1990s, Derrida does not mention "global warming" or the degradation of global ecologies, but see how he situates his argument in the development of industrial animal farming (23–29; see also note 5).

3   See Derrida (2008, 24, my emphasis): "For about two centuries, intensely and by means of an alarming rate of acceleration, *for we no longer even have a clock or chronological measure of it,* we, we who call ourselves men or humans, we who recognize ourselves in that name, have been involved in an unprecedented transformation." In the twenty-plus years since Derrida spoke these words, awareness of the chronologies of the Anthropocene has made such a mindset impossible; see Hatley (2012) on the "virtue of temporal discernment."

4   Porphyry, *On Abstinence* 3.25 (Theophrastus, fragment 531): "And thus, too we hold that all humans are akin [*sungeneis*] to one another, and not only to one another but to all animals as well. For their bodies developed from the same beginnings [*arkhas*]; but by 'beginnings' I do not mean first elements [*stoikheia*] — for they are found in plants also — but such matter as skin, flesh, and the constituent fluids of animate beings." I refer to the Bouffartigue and Patillon (1992) edition of Porphyry and the Fortenbaugh et al. (1992) edition of Theophrastus. Cf. Aristotle, *Parts of Animals* 646a. I refer to the Pierre (1956) edition of *Parts of Animals*. See Brink (1956) and Crowley (2008) on these Aristotelian categories.

placed position at the foundation of this biological regime. For Porphyry, to think about plants requires us to confront a form of life that is simultaneously encompassed within and categorically alien to our animal origins. Importantly, as well, Porphyry's categorization by origins leaves in suspense a distinction of ends, deferring closure for the developmental trajectories envisioned in the difference between *stoikheia* and *arkhai*.

In ancient natural taxonomy, therefore, plants create a rich ground on which to consider difference in kind and changes in time that are not reducible to degree or linear succession. By examining a series of vegetal entanglements in agricultural texts by Cicero, Theophrastus, and Columella, I argue that attending to plant-life produces a conflation between "to be" and "to be transformed" that parallels Derrida's elision of "to be" and "to follow." While Derrida's deconstruction of the relationship between animal and human responds to the question "who am I (following)?," the procedure applied to plant-life asks, "when am I (transformed)?" — that is, when do I exist? When am I no longer? To pursue the parallel further, Derrida's Chimera enters what I call a "feral" future. I borrow this term from current trends in ecology because it seeks to name, as Derrida did, the supplementality of nature and culture. Beyond Derrida's encounter with the genesis of this supplement, the feral future haunts its end, appearing in the traces of mutualisms, both constructive and destructive, that develop between animals (humans included) and plants.[5] Viewed from this future, the feral changes that are just coming into focus in the ecology and philosophy of the Anthropocene have never been ancillary to, but are rather constitutive of life's dis/continuity.

---

5   Much current work on ferality comes from the "hard" side of ecology; see Gering et al. (2019) for the state of the field in evolutionary science. Tsing et al. (2021) apply the idea to a wider discourse on global capitalism and post-modernity, particularly through the feral effects of human "infrastructures." Halberstam (2020a, esp. 77–111) introduces an "epistemology of the *ferox*" as a "wilding of queerness," although, as I discuss below, this only partly overlaps with the sense I intend.

In the philosophical imagination, then, plants offer a distinct origin point for life. As the brief example from Porphyry demonstrates, however, a thinking of a distinct *end* of plants tends to be postponed or obscured. Instead, the regularity of growth, decay, and regeneration that humans observe in plants provides a sense of consistency and cyclicality, which can readily be mapped onto and provide the model for the developmental processes of other (especially animal) organisms. In the final book of Cicero's *On Ends,* the speaker Piso invokes this elemental, vegetal principle to argue that, just as all forms of life possess a common life-cycle, they must also all share an orientation toward a natural *telos.* This lengthy, skeptical dialogue challenges the correspondences that, in Hellenistic philosophy, conjoin the beginnings of life with each school's ethical *summa bona.*[6] So, Cicero's construction of Piso's argument is not disinterested. But he puts into his character's mouth an elaborate defense of natural teleology that draws from Peripatetic and Stoic sources — although, as always with Cicero's philosophy, the precise origins of the argument are much debated:[7]

> Plants also have a development and progress to maturity [*educatio quaedam et perfectio*] that is not unlike [*non dissimilis*] that of animals; hence we speak of a vine as living and dying, or of a tree as young or old, in the prime of life or decrepit; consequently it is not incongruous [*non est alienum*] to suppose that with them as with animals certain things are suited [*apta*] and certain other things foreign [*aliena*] to their nature; and that their growth and nurture is tended by a foster mother [*cultrix*], the science and art of agriculture, which trims and prunes, straightens, raises and props [*amputet, erigat, extollat, adminiculet*], enabling them to advance to the goal that nature prescribes, till the vines

---

6   This is the so-called "cradle argument," on which see Brunschwig (1986). For Cicero's skeptical strategies in *On Ends,* see Brittain (2016).

7   For source-critical approaches, see esp. Gill (2016) and Inwood (2016).

themselves, could they speak, would acknowledge this to be their proper mode of treatment and care.[8]

Piso lays claim to an analogy between plant and animal life-cycles, observing that, as for animals, "we speak of a vine as living and dying, or of a tree as young or old, in the prime of life or decrepit." According to his argument, these perceptual and lexical similarities are evidence for a shared principle of development governing all life: the pursuit of things that are "suited" to the individual's nature and the avoidance of foreign or adverse things. It is perfectly natural, says Piso, to name and apply the same categories of growth, maturation, and senescence to plants because, in turn, animals derive their own transformations from this common biological orientation.

Yet such an analogousness between the development of plants and animals relies perhaps more on a logic of dissimilarity than this initial explanation allows. In its search for things *apta* ("suited") and avoidance of things *aliena* ("foreign"), the plant retains its non-identity with animal life, despite or, in a sense, because of Piso's assertion of identity. The *educatio* [...] *et perfectio* ("development [...] and progress to maturity") of plants is only ever *non dissimilis* ("*not* unlike") that of animals, while their common orientation — the source of their purported similarities — follows upon this as a *non est alienum* ("*not* incongruous" step). This pile-up of negation suggests the possibility that the very things that plants seek to avoid as foreign to their nature could be contained within the commonality imposed by Piso's comparison. To render a *perfectio* ("totality") of plant-life as an object of comparison, Piso's analogy requires a gap between his logical category of "foreign" and the categorical content of what is, in fact, alien or hostile to plant-life. The analogy must be drawn not because plants and animals are so similar, but because, in the end, they may not be.

---

8   Cicero, *On Ends* 5.39; passage continues below. The text of Cicero's *On Ends* is Madvig (1876) and translations are adapted from Rackham (1931).

The logical coercion underlying Piso's claim is elaborated as he works his way up to the capabilities associated exclusively with humanity in Aristotelian science. By calling on agriculture as the *cultrix* ("foster mother") of plant-life, Piso contributes to his argument, against the Stoics, that the "perfection" of any life involves techniques and tools external to the innate faculties of the individual. But how similar, really, is a plant that is tended by a farmer to a sick man who visits a doctor, or a student who attends lectures by a philosopher? To confirm his analogy, Piso must grant (temporarily) power of speech to the plant — a point I will return to in a moment. Yet, even prior to this point, Piso's argument elides a tension between "nature" and "culture," influenced, especially in the context of Peripatetic philosophy, by the difference between plants grown spontaneously and those grown under cultivation. In *On the Causes of Plants,* Theophrastus demonstrates how malleable the *phusis* ("nature") of plant-life is, asking, "Are we to study the nature of a plant in those that grow spontaneously [*tēn phusin ek tōn automatōn*] or in those growing under various forms of cultivation [*ek tōn kata tas ergasias*], and which of the two kinds of growth is natural?"[9] Unable to define "natural" simply in terms of spontaneous growth, Theophrastus admits that there is, in the very least, agreement that "Nature always sets out to achieve what is best." But to this he adds that "what proceeds from cultivation does this too." And so, the expected division of nature and culture into "spontaneous" and "cultivated" breaks down quickly into different paths to achieving the natural goal of "what is best" — that is, according to Theophrastus, regularity and consistency in reproduction. In fact, the spontaneous growth of seeds is just as liable to produce a *atopon* […] *kai hōsper para phusin* ("strange and almost unnatural result") as is misapplied "cultivation." Conversely, the arts of agriculture work by supplying a plant with "what it happens to lack, such as food of the right kind," thereby reproducing the "natural" conditions of "the

---

9 Theophrastus, *On the Causes of Plants* 1.16.10–12; text and translation from Einarson and Link (1976).

regions appropriate to a given plant." Theophrastean nature is cultivated, and culture is naturalized in order to reinforce the orderly and consistent reproduction of life.

To return to Piso's argument, the vine, since it first entered the text, already existed in logico-philosophical and agricultural context that has changed its nature. Not to say that it has become more or less "natural" in the primary sense considered by Theophrastus, but it has been categorized and cultivated to accommodate a different, yet still natural, *telos*. This cultivated — or perhaps "cultured" vine — endowed with a "naturalness" that has nothing to do with its nature slips in and out of its place on the *scala naturae*. In the same breath, Piso denies speech to plants and argues that "the vines themselves, could they speak, would acknowledge this (i.e., viticulture) to be their proper mode of treatment and care" (Cicero, *On Ends* 5.39). The space between the silence and (imposed) speech of the plants again discloses the dissimilarity or non-relation at work within the analogy. This slipperiness continues as Piso moves to consider a particularly sensitive topic in Greek thought about plants — whether they possess sensation and mobility:[10]

> But suppose the vine receives the gift of sensation, bestowing on it some degree of appetition and power of movement; then what do you think it will do? Will it not endeavor to provide for itself the benefits which it previously obtained by the aid of the vinedresser? But do you see how it will further protect its sensory faculties and all their appetitive instincts, and any additional organs it may have developed? Thus with the properties that it always possessed it will combine those subsequently added to it, and it will not have the same end as the cultivator who tended it [*nec eundem finem habebit quem cultor eius habebat*], but will desire to live in accordance with that nature which it has subsequently acquired. (Cicero, *On Ends* 5.40)

---

10   A central *locus* for this issue is Plato, *Timaeus* 76e–77c; see Wilberding (2014). I refer to the Burnett (1968) edition of Plato's works.

Like his comment about plant-speech, this positive claim for a shared *finis* is premised on the vine's apparent lack of sensation, appetition, and movement, yet momentarily endows it with these (animal) capabilities in order, again, to demonstrate a continuity of natural orientation up and down the Great Chain of Being. The cultivated vine, granted the ability to perceive, desire, and move like an animal, progresses upwards, first securing for itself the benefits that it had previously received externally from the vinedresser, before developing its own abilities to "protect its sensory faculties" and to pursue its "appetitive instincts" into the world. Like a modern capabilities-approach to environmental ethics, Piso invites us to imagine that the differences between plant and animal life are only a matter of degree: provided with those abilities they lack, plants will turn out to be "just like us."[11]

The end of this argument, therefore, seeks to cultivate and categorize the vine for the purpose of establishing its nature according to human ideas and material needs. Accompanying this end, however, the latent instability that we have also been tracing — the *non dissimilis* on which Piso's argument relies — returns in his remark: "Thus with the properties that it always possessed it will combine those subsequently added to it, *and it will not have the same end* as the cultivator who tended it." As it turns out, the vine is no longer a vine — nor is it even a sum of its capabilities. Combining the vine's "natural" orientation with the tools of the vinedresser has produced a new *finis,* which is not reducible to the prior configuration of either component, but is determined by their interaction and the vine's own sensation and movement through the world. This vine-that-is-no-longer will live according to an entirely new "nature which it has subsequently acquired." On the one hand,

---

11 Indeed, the next step in Piso's argument imagines that the vine, endowed with self-determination, will "naturally" *choose* to become first an animal, then a human ("By gradual stages, it will arrive at the highest point — total integrity of body and a mature exercise of reason," *On Ends* 5.40). Cf. Nussbaum's influential formulation of a "capabilities" approach to social justice (see esp. 2011); for an ecological application, see, e.g., Kortetmäki (2017).

this conclusion does little to disturb Piso's essential claim that all living things, regardless of capabilities or status on the *scala naturae,* possess an end that is determined by their particular "natural" orientation, which, as Theophrastus emphasizes, may be cultivated as well as spontaneous. On the other hand, this remark amounts to an admission of the differences in kind that separate plants and animals and the changes in kind that plants undergo and create in their environments through the processes of cultivation. These are the non-relational elements of vegetal life that Piso's argument otherwise silences or drowns out. The vine, of course, could never actually be heard in the text. Yet, echoing in this silence and amplified by the ecological effects of two thousand years of agriculture, Piso's assertion that the vine "will not have the same end as the cultivator who tended it" rings like a denouncement from out of the future: perhaps the differences between plants and humans are not simply a matter of degree. And, furthermore, perhaps humans are not in control of the transformations wrought by agriculture.

Reading Piso's argument from this perspective puts it into dialogue with recent eco-critical interest in agriculture as a fraught anthropological inheritance. Timothy Morton has argued that the Neolithic revolutions in sedentism provide a deep history for modern, capitalist industries and their resulting geo-physical effects referred to as the "Anthropocene" (Morton 2012).[12] The structure of this deep history follows what Morton refers to as an "Oedipal loop," which passes from human activities, such as farming, to a belated recognition of the full ecological effect of these activities. Like Oedipus's delayed realization of the outcome of his — or more accurately his father Laius's — attempts to cheat fate, humanity meets itself again in the uncanny forces unleashed by its own manipulation of earth's vegetal life. Morton's purpose is to explain why a concept like "human-caused

---

12 See Morton (2012); this attention to deep history is not widely shared among scholars who tend to use the term "Anthropocene" to refer exclusively to the geological impact of human actions in the postindustrial age. On the terminology, see, e.g., Haraway (2015) and Tsing (2015), esp. 19–22.

climate change" is so difficult to grasp. In his analysis, the "causation" implied in global warming operates through the intentional and unintentional dynamics that we also see in the myth, where Oedipus, through his characteristic combination of tenacity and ignorance, hope and horror, is equally responsible and unresponsible for his fate. For Morton, the connection between myth and crisis is not coincidental. Agriculture's Oedipal loop, he argues, and the technologies through which it operates are embedded in the philosophy of past societies, such as the Greeks and Romans, who have informed our own cultural contexts for viewing and interacting with the non-human world. The embeddedness of agriculture in technical and social thought is especially apparent in a widespread metaphysics of presence that privileges some things as "more real" or "more natural" when they are in contact with human needs and activities.[13]

Piso's vine-that-is-no-longer demonstrates *in nuce* the Oedipal dynamics of agriculture that Morton describes. Through human cultivation, the plant has become what it always was already: a shapeshifter, a mutant, a *monstrum*,[14] which, endowed with the tools and techniques of the vinedresser now applies them with self-determination, defending its sensation and

---

13 See Morton (2012, 16–17, my emphasis): "Ecological awareness requires us to realize the truth of Oedipus, the primal myth of the agricultural age — the age we still live in, the age that is responsible for much global warming, the age that established the template for the rest of global warming. Established it, because it reifies Earth into slabs of abstract space, ready for filling and ploughing. *Established it, insofar as it attempted to impose consistency upon a fundamentally inconsistent reality. The agricultural age is responsible for the metaphysics of presence.* An ecological age must necessarily be a post-agricultural age, which means that an ecological age must push against thousands of years of human history." A complementary attempt to think around the "metaphysics of presence" can be found in Meillassoux's work on ancestrality (2008, esp. 13–18).

14 On plants (especially hybridized ones) as portents or, more generally, "wonders" in Latin literature, cf., Virgil, *Georgics* 2.69–82, which describes a range of possible to impossible tree grafts, and the debate about these influential lines from, e.g., Thomas (1988), Lowe (2010), and Gowers (2011). See Mynors's (1969) edition of Vergil's works.

organs, created by its cultivated nature, yet unintentionally liberated from a human-imposed goal. What happens when the vinedresser meets his creation on the other side, at the uncanny crossroads, of the vine's transformation? How will the vinedresser respond when the plant, now fully endowed with speech, asks him: When was I transformed? How did I become who I am? When will I be no longer?

To push this eco-critical perspective further, and to see how we might expand on Morton's observation about the embeddedness of agricultural technologies in ancient philosophy, I turn to consider some of the particular methods of cultivation and "naturalization" that Cicero and Theophrastus describe. These techniques, I will go on to argue, both produce and are shaped in our historical understanding by the feral future, as they reveal the entanglement of intention and its unintended consequences for ecological development. Yet, by focusing less on agriculture's past, as Morton does, and more on a deconstruction of its future, I suggest a different, more mutually dynamic way to conceptualize the relationship between human action and natural reaction.

Certainly, both Cicero and Theophrastus demonstrate how agricultural practices enact a metaphysics of presence. According to Piso's argument, the vinedresser "trims and prunes, straightens, raises and props" — methods that combine extrinsic violence with paternalistic care. As Piso stresses, the intended purpose of these human actions is always to enable the vine "to advance to the goal that nature prescribes" — picking up on the Peripatetic argument for a determinative teleology that always tends towards what is best, what is most consistent, and so what is most natural. In this vein, Theophrastus's works are more explicitly and extensively concerned with techniques of naturalization. In one such passage from *Enquiry into Plants,* he relates the wisdom of local approaches for attaining productive growth in fruit trees:

If a tree does not bear fruit but inclines to a leafy growth, they split that part of the stem which is underground and insert a stone corresponding to the crack thus made, and then, they say, it will bear. [...] Into the almond tree they drive an iron peg, and, having thus made a hole, insert in its place a peg of oak-wood and bury it in the earth.[15]

Theophrastus then records that the practitioners of these techniques refer to them as *kolazein* ("punishing") the tree in order to restrain its *hubrizon* ("luxuriance"). As Ann Michelini has shown, *hubris* ("hybris") is a common descriptor of exuberant growth in plant-life, especially when it is not under cultivation.[16] Conversely, hybris also often carries its vegetal connotations when applied to human arrogance and excess. This deep connection — not quite a metaphor, not quite an etiology — between a moral concept and the characteristics of vegetal growth seems ultimately to derive (*pace* Piso!) from a perceived lack of natural limits in plants such as those imposed on animals by aging.

Whether we start from plant-growth itself or humanity's attempts to regulate it, Theophrastus's pairing of *hubris* with the marked verb, *kolazein,* demonstrates the depth of correspondence between agriculture and philosophy that Morton observes. In the Platonic dialogues, *kolasis* ("punishment") refers to a reformative process whereby a wrong-doer is not only "straightened" with respect to his own fault, but, perhaps more importantly for Greek political sensibilities, is restored

---

15 Theophrastus, *Enquiry into Plants* 2.7.6–7; text is Wimmer (1854) and translation adapted from Hort (1916).
16 Michelini (1978) examines instances, such as this passage from Theophrastus, where a plant is described as "hybristic" because it grows beyond its ability to reproduce itself (also described as going "wood-mad," *hulomanein*), as well as poetic images of hybris itself "flowering" like a plant (e.g., Aeschylus, *Persians* 821–22 and Sophocles, fragment 786). On the connection between the two, Michelini says, "The figure of indefinite expansion applies very nicely to plant growth. [...] Since a tree reaches no *telos* at maturity (*hēbē*) as higher animals do, its eventual size and rate of growth will, in the absence of outside restraint, be limited largely by the availability of *trophē*. Plant growth is a good metaphor for what one may call the hybristic process, an uncontrolled extension or expansion that may lead to disaster" (41–42). See Radt's (1977) edition of Sophocles's fragments, and Page's edition (1969) of Aeschylus's works.

to his proper place within the civic order.[17] Aristotle, in turn, distinguishes *kolasis* from a more atavistic *timōria* ("revenge"): whereas revenge is taken "in the interest of him who inflicts it," punishment is meted out "in the interest of the sufferer."[18] This distinction is further heightened by the Stoics, for whom a desire for "revenge" was the central component of anger — that most destructive and seductive emotion — but *kolasis* offers a response to individual or collective harm that is categorically free from anger.[19]

When Theophrastus employs this language with respect to plants, then, he is invoking both a reformative, passionless response to a perceived fault and the intended benefit that such reformation promises not just for the individual, but for a whole network of relations. As Danielle Allen reads this passage in her history of Athenian penal practices, "Removal of a problem within the tree, a problem of *hubris*, improved the entire tree. It is *because* the horticulturist needs to improve a tree that is out of order or hubristic that the process can be described as *kolasis* or a form of punishment" (Allen 2000, 70). This discursive interchangeability coercively reinforces an enacted correspondence between a system of human ethics and the development of non-human life. Theophrastus's plant punishments record in explicit terms the violence that humans visit upon plants — vio-

---

17 See, e.g., Plato, *Gorgias* 476d [Socrates]: "The one who punishes 'rightly' punishes justly?" (*ho de orthōs kolazōn dikaiōs kolazei*; text is Dodds 1959). Platonic usage often stresses the distinction between *kolasis* as a function of the *polis* and the forms of retribution that belong to the familial sphere; see, further, *Euthyphro* 5b and 8b, *Protagoras* 323d–326d, and *Gorgias* 476a–491e. See Burnett's (1968) editions of *Euthyphro* and *Protagoras*.
18 Aristotle, *Rhetoric* 1369b12–14. Text is Kassel (1976). Cf. the archaeology of "torture" and "punishment" by Foucault (1977, esp. 73–103); for the social history of the ancient Greek distinction, see esp. Hunter (1992) and Allen (2000).
19 For the Stoics, see *Stoicorum Veterum Fragmenta* ("Fragments of the Old Stoics") 2.1003, where *kolasis* is described as a "setting straight" (*epanorthōsis*), and 3.395–98, where Chrysippus defines anger as "a desire for revenge on the person who appears to have wronged us undeservedly." See Arnim's (1986) edition of the *Fragments*. For a recent discussion of the wider Hellenistic context, see Armstrong and McOsker (2020), esp. 21–88.

lence taken without anger and in the interest, so the agricultural thinker believes, of the plant itself — with the intention of remaking them according to the material needs and ethical expectations of human society. Nature itself appears as a "correctional facility," a prison or clinic. A tree that has been "punished" or "corrected" may grow on an artificially bifurcated stem or be pierced permanently by a peg made of foreign material. But agricultural thought configures these physical alterations as a process of naturalization, transforming plants to achieve a higher, straightened, more orderly state.

We are rounding the bend on Morton's Oedipal loop. Yet, viewed from a more "feral" perspective, Theophrastus's punishments suggest another way to traverse this cycle. Typically, we use this word to refer to a specific individual or group, like a cat, a herd of pigs, or a type of weed. Previously habituated to life alongside humans by means of domestication, transplantation, or simple proximity, these feral animals or plants have since "re-wilded," somehow "returning" to or recovering for themselves a non-habituated state. Moreover, we (as humans) tend to speak about and act towards feral entities in ways that reflect and deflect our sense of culpability, using the feral to indulge our own fantasies of return. Summoning rhetoric eerily familiar from Theophrastus's "punishers," we assert that, to save or rehabilitate an ecosystem, we must eradicate "invasive" species. We devise elaborate, often government-sponsored schemes that seek to bring feral populations "under control," thereby removing a threat to "native" species, restoring ecological efficiencies (especially as they relate to human food production), and cleansing bio-contaminants from formerly "pristine" wilderness.[20]

In the 2021 *Feral Atlas: The More-Than-Human Anthropocene,* however, anthropologist Anna Tsing, along with a group of biologists and artists, argues that our sense of the feral needs to be expanded to encompass global environmental trends in

---

20 See, e.g., Finch (2015) for a critical history of reactions to the spread of feral kudzu in the American south.

many, diversely human-affected ecosystems.²¹ Ferality, in this project's understanding, is "a situation in which an entity, nurtured and transformed by a human-made project, assumes a trajectory *beyond* human control" (my emphasis). This expanded definition resonates profoundly with Piso's vine that "does not have the same end as the cultivator who tended it." This ancient figure of thought stands in the deep historical background of the feral developments that the Atlas explores: fields of heavily treated soybean crops choked with herbicide-resistant Amaranth weeds, novel parasites carried in the wooden pallets of global commerce appearing in North America tree farms, and aquacultured ponds of water hyacinth in South India, which reproduce only genetic clones.²² Despite the dystopic feel of these feral mutations, the authors of the Atlas remind us that "There is nothing bad about lack of human control per se." In fact, they write, "Humans could not survive without feral activity; it's what allows plants and animals to continue to survive human insults" (Tsing et al. 2021). With this claim for the ecological significance of feral developments, the authors emphasize the often devastating effects of human activity, but they also acknowledge the dynamics that respond to, limit, and, finally, transform human agency.

Being feral, in this sense, is far from a "re-wilding" or the rebirth of an unadulterated animal or plant nature.²³ Yet it is also

---

21 That is to say, most ecosystems: conservative estimates of the amount of earth's habitable land that has been directly modified by human activity stand at greater than 50% and the rate is increasing. See Hooke et al. (2012).
22 These examples are drawn from field reports collected in *Feral Atlas* by Rachel Cypher, Marissa Weiss, and Iftekhar Iqbal in Tsing, Deger, Saxena, and Zhou (2021).
23 This sense is closer to what Halberstam (2020a, esp. 77–86) means by feral "wildness" as a potentially eroticized indifference to human attachments. Halberstam maps the *ferox* onto a queer epistemology — a "desire for wildness that […] cannot be found in the catalogs of sexual identity produced by Freud or by Kraft-Ebing and Havelock Ellis before him, and […] stands apart from the tidy homo/hetero binary we have used to explain and understand the organization of bodies at the turn of the last century." On this sense of queer ferality, see also Telò in this volume.

not simply the outcome of human force, an unchanging imprint of extrinsic violence. Rather, it is a manifestation of what lies beyond these poles. In other words, the feral is supplemental to Morton's Oedipal loop between intended human action and unintentional natural reaction. Because they are supplementary, feral traits and shifts bear deep ambivalence to the relationship between nature and culture to which they are inseparably joined. As Derrida (1976, 235) demonstrated regarding Jean-Jacques Rousseau's supplementation of speech and writing with gesture, the existence of feral developments belies any true origin or fixedness in the human relation to the natural world.[24] The continuous potential for and even necessity of feral changes within populations and ecosystems implies that there is no set order for this loop, which can be reversed, tied into a knot, or severed altogether to be joined in new configurations. Instead, as "a surplus, an overabundance [...] a frivolous futility" (Derrida 1980, 101), what is feral appears both as the specter of an unbridgeable polarity, even animosity, between nature and culture and, equally, as the vital substance that actualizes and joins these terms.

This haunting logic of the supplement is evident through two etymologies which reach the English word "feral" through Latin. On the one hand, there are the adjectives *ferus* or *ferox*, which come from the same root as the Greek noun, *thēr*, meaning a "wild beast" or a "monster." It is from this root that the modern English word properly descends. On the other hand, there is the wide family of words related to the verb *ferre*, "to bear or carry," and especially the adjective, *ferax*, which means "fruit-

---

24 See Derrida (1976), 235: "Gesture is here an adjunct of speech, but this adjunct is not a supplementing by artifice, it is a re-course to a more natural, more expressive, more immediate sign. It is the more universal the less it depends on conventions. But if gesture supposes a distance and a spacing, a milieu of visibility, it ceases being effective when the excess of distance or mediation interrupts visibility: then speech supplements gesture. Everything in language is substitute, and this concept of substitute precedes the opposition of nature and culture: the supplement can equally well be natural (gesture) as artificial (speech)."

ful, fertile, or bountiful."[25] We can see the interplay of these two word families in the opening of Varro's *On Agriculture*, where the speakers Stolo and Scrofa are discussing how to determine if previously uncultivated soil will be suited to cultivation: quoting from an authority, Diophanes of Bithynia, Stolo suggests that perhaps the best way is to look at whether the *fera* ("wild vegetation") growing in it "bears fertilely [*feracia*] the products that should be born naturally from it" (Varro *On Agriculture*, 1.9.7; text of Varro is Goetz 1929). Varro's circular logic demonstrates a promiscuity of sound and sense which also informs our modern understanding. It is not simply that there is a unifying tension between wildness and fertility. More importantly, this conflation lays bare the developmental dynamics — the movement "beyond" nature and culture — that are at stake in imagining the feral future.

We can trace this movement of the feral supplement further by noting where it converges with the speculative inquiry pursued by Freud "beyond" the pleasure principle.[26] In Freud's attempts to name and diagnose this same supplementality, a *Unbehagen* (discontent) characterizes the disjuncture, *Natur* and *Kultur,* belonging to both and neither category properly. As Eric Santner (2022, 188–89) explains, "a certain *stasis* or 'civil strife' already plagues the pleasure principle at work in the homeostatic imperatives governing life and […] human culture emerges out of that 'static.'" Read in this direction, the discontent of (human) civilization is a residue or "encystance" (Santner 2022, 205) of a disorder that already disturbs life in its "simpler" forms. Yet, Santner continues, "this relation can at least appear to move in reverse order, that is, that a gap haunting the constitution of human societies […] introduces a fateful disorder into natural life, renders it self-destructive, 'over-heated.'" So, does

---

25 These words are traceable to distinct PIE roots via Greek cognates: *thēr* and *pheromai;* see Walde and Hofmann (1938, 483–485) for *ferre*; and 487–488 for *ferus*.
26 Canonically, this inquiry begins with *Beyond the Pleasure Principle* and culminates in *Civilization and its Discontents*. On Freud's thought in this period broadly, see, e.g., Laplanche (1976, 103–24) and Gay (1988, 403–553).

Freudian discontent originate in *Natur* or in *Kultur*? Does feral activity begin with "us" or "them"? And, regardless of where it begins, where will it end? Derrida contends in his own venture into Freud's "beyond" that "from whichever *end* one takes this structure [...] it is death. *At the end,* and this death is not opposable, does not differ" (1987, 284–85).²⁷ Freud's tentative distinction between pleasure and death collapses irretrievably into the maw of Thanatos. As another face of this unequivocal structure, the feral supplement as both *ferox* and *ferax* appears as the strangest gift: never truly "given," but uncannily offered, extended in the forbearance — the unpayable debt — that the Anthropocene manifests as natural history. If ferality, like Freud's discontent, is constitutive of life's dis/continuity, our relation to it is conditioned both by the more-than-human labor necessary to sustain the remainders of life through time, and by the concomitant urge to get rid of that remainder once and for all.

For Freud, then, the so-called death drive arises not from any true antinomy, but from the very conservative tendencies of an organism toward self-preservation.²⁸ Similarly, to return to Piso's speech in *On Ends,* just before introducing the feral vine, he claims, as another piece of evidence for his teleological view, an instinct toward self-preservation that is shared between humans and the creatures he refers to as *ferae* ("beasts"), quoting the archaic poet Pacuvius:

> Yet what is there that is more obvious than the fact that every organism loves itself very much indeed? For who or how many among us are there for whom, when death approaches, does not "blood retreat and faces grow pale with fear and fright"? Although perhaps here there is a fault — to be so strongly frightened at the dissolution of nature [*dissolutionem naturae*]. [...] But as much as some people do this to the point of censure, so much must it be understood that these excessive cases would not have occurred unless there was a

---

27 Cf. the extended treatment of Freud in Derrida (2020, 241–59).
28 On the death drive, see also Bassi's and Youd's chapters in this collection.

certain natural measure. [...] For often even in young children who don't think about these things at all, if sometimes in play we threaten to let them fall from some height, they are deeply afraid. Pacuvius says that even "beasts [*ferae*] who lack the stratagem of taking forethought," when the fear of death rises inside them, "bristle with horror" [*horrescunt*]. (Cicero, *On Ends*, 5.31)

Piso stresses a distinction between "a certain natural measure" of concern for self-preservation, which is shared across mature humans, children, and *ferae*, and an excessive anxiety about death, as the loss of life's good things or a fear of pain. Unlike these conditioned responses, which are proscribed by both Epicureanism and Stoicism, even *ferae* respond strongly to a rudimentary, necessary fear of death. In Pacuvius's phrase an inchoative verb, *horrescunt*, describes the inevitability of the response, which occurs even though beasts lack any "stratagem of taking forethought" that would allow them to conceptualize their own demise rationally. The source of this response seems to be an instinctual conflation of the dissolution of one's own particular nature with *dissolutio naturae* ("the final demise of nature itself"). Yet Piso also indicates that our perception of this double death is structured and reinforced by repetition from infancy, as when a child misconstrues a game of "don't drop the baby" as a mortal threat.[29] So, as in Freud, Piso's "instinct" for self-preservation is, in fact, part of the psychological patterning or acculturation that we inherit from those *ferae* that came before us and that we, as *ferae*, pass on to our own offspring. In accordance with this inheritance, Freud insists, the repetitive tendencies of the Ego-instinct "assure that the organism shall follow its own path to death, and [...] ward off any possible ways of returning to inorganic existence other than those which are immanent in

---

29 Cf. Derrida's discussion of Freud's game of *fort/da* with his grandson, e.g., "And I would say [...] that the logic of Beyond, of the word 'Beyond' (*Jenseits* in general) is the logic of the *fort/da*. [...] The death drive is there, in the pleasure principle, setting the *fort/da* in motion" (2020, 254).

the organism itself" (1920, 47). At the limit of Freud's and of Piso's thought, is the idea that the self-preservative drive of all *ferae*, as both individuals and an inter-generational collective of feral life, is a manifestation of "the organism's wish to die only in its own fashion" (47).

And yet, what is feral, as we have seen from our first example of Piso's vine, is not only "beastly" in this sense of satisfying a repetitive death drive. Rather, a feral trajectory implies a change of type — the emergence of a new goal that is not shared by determining forces or constituent parts. Likewise, according to the "speculative" Freud of *Beyond the Pleasure Principle*,[30] there are organisms within the organism that escape the pressure of development. Reproductive "germ-cells," Freud suggests, retain "the original structure of living matter" and so lack the accretions of complex life forms. As the remainders of life, they separate themselves from an organism and establish an independent existence beyond them: "These germ-cells, therefore, work against the death of the living substance and succeed in winning for it what we can only regard as potential immortality, though that may mean no more than a lengthening of the road to death" (Freud 1920, 47–48). As Derrida stresses, and Freud's heavy-handed qualifiers ("potential," "may mean no more") make clear,[31] we should not see the germ-cell as the result or agent of a truly antipodal drive, restoring a realm of "pleasure" to its own proper limits. Germ-cells, in Freud's view, must derive from a larger organism, which has all the repetitive compulsions that

---

30 Freud repeatedly insists that his "findings" in this text are "unsatisfying" and "speculative": e.g., (1955a, 26): "What follows is speculation, often far-fetched speculation, which the reader will consider or dismiss according to his individual predilection." Derrida (1987, 274–78; cf. 2020, 221–22) reads this overabundance of speculation as indicative of the work's conceptual drive for non-oppositional thought that mirrors the non-opposability of the death drive. But cf. Damasio (2019, esp. 44–70) for a contemporary account of the interplay between homeostasis and the evolutionary impulse of the simplest organisms.

31 This passage is further complicated in biographical readings of *Beyond the Pleasure Principle* that relate it to Freud's grief for his daughter, Sophie; see esp. E. Jones (1957, 40–41); cf. Derrida (2020, 255–59).

are the hallmark of increasingly complex biological development. They are conditioned by the histories of *Unbehagen* like every other life-form. Yet their structure retains the simplicity and minimal differentiation necessary for novel life. Indeed, it is the germ-cell's double form that Freud identifies as key to their function, which is "only made possible, if it coalesces with another cell similar to itself and yet differing from it." The recombinative potential of gametes, the similarity-in-difference between male and female is, for Freud, the only possible source of creation. How, then, should we view inter- or trans-species reproductive entanglements found in feral ecosystems?

Although wedded to a mammalian notion of reproduction, Freudian Eros presents itself as a potentially post-agricultural, even post-human conception of fertility because it frees generation from causal origin. This dynamic is also reflected in the use of the adjective *ferax* in Columella, another agricultural writer who, like Theophrastus, discusses techniques of tree discipline:

> Sometimes, too, when the fig trees begin to bear leaves, it is beneficial to cut off the uppermost tops of the fig-tree with a very sharp knife; the trees will then become stronger and more fertile (*firmiores arbores et feraciores fiunt*). It will always be beneficial, as soon as the fig-tree begins to put forth leaves, to dilute ochre with lees of oil and pour it over the roots together with human ordure: this makes the fruit more abundant and the "stuffing" of the fig more attractive in appearance and fuller (*ea res efficit uberiorem fructum et fartum fici speciosius et plenius*).[32]

Columella recommends that force be exerted on the fig tree by pruning the upper branches "with a very sharp knife," and altering the chemical make-up of the plant's soil through artificial fertilizer, which mixes the waste of human industry and digestion with a naturally occurring clay. Yet the *fartum* ("stuffing")

---

32 Columella, *On Trees*, 21.2. Text is Lundström (1897) and translation is adapted from Forster and Heffner (1968).

of the fig's fruit is transformed from the inside out, gaining in density and richness.³³ This intensification of fertility is communicated in the text by the sound patterning of initial *"f"*s and a string of comparatives: the trees become *firmiores et feraciores* ("stronger and more prolific") and the "stuffing" becomes *speciosius et plenius* ("more attractive and fuller"). These internal dynamics are related to the arborist's external action, but not directly caused by them. In the same way that Freud envisions the germ-cell's conditioning by but independence from the death drive, the fig's fertility requires a more dynamic process of generation than simple cause and effect.

In this instance, the fertile relationship between tree and farmer is haunted by yet another interspecies entanglement. While absent from Columella's human-oriented discussion, other ancient writers, including Aristotle, Theophrastus, and Pliny, describe the process of "caprification," a symbiosis found in many edible fig varieties and their primary pollinators: highly specialized species of wasps.³⁴ These tiny wasps — some nearly invisible to the human eye — lay their larvae inside the fig's fruit, which is, in fact, the plant's reproductive organ, bearing male and/or female flowers inside its enclosed segments. For fig varieties that are dioecious, wasp larvae are most often laid within fruit bearing exclusively male flowers, the shape of which seems to be adapted to suit this need. But the female wasps who utilize these nest-sites also visit female-bearing trees, fertilizing their fruit with the pollen they have gathered from the male trees. It is this highly variable and still poorly understood inter-

---

33 *Fars* is a rare word, found primarily in agricultural and culinary contexts (e.g., Varro, *On Agriculture* 3.8 or Pliny the Elder, *Natural History* 28.117, edition of Jones 1963), but it comes from the verb *farcio* "to stuff," which is used with a violent sexual meaning in Catullus 28.13, where a master abuses his slaves by "stuffing them" with his uncircumcised penis (*verpa*): see Richlin (1992, 149).

34 On "caprification," see Aristotle, *History of Animals* 5.26 (edition of Peck 1970); Theophrastus *Enquiry into Plants* 2.8.1.–3, and *On the Causes of Plants* 2.9.5.–14; and Pliny, *Natural History* 15.21 (edition of Rackham 1945).

species relation, which long predates human involvement, that ultimately reproduces most fig trees.[35] In this case, then, the relationship between fig and wasp, physically hidden from human practitioners and logically excised from Columella's account, looms just beyond the fertilizing actions that are his focus. Expanding our view from Freud's mammalian view of reproduction, we can see that "the gift" of fertility is never given but is instead the result of a shared labor that sustains the remainder of life, a surplus of pleasure that is produced by and reproduces across a whole ecosystem.

What emerges from this model of the feral as both beastly and fertile, and through this juxtaposition to the Freudian drives, is an understanding of the relationship between animals and plants that is mutually dynamic, even evolutionary. The interactions that bring about feral changes are generative without being causal, teleological (eschatological?) but not determined, and ecological instead of intentional. Like Freudian *Unbehagen,* the feral both limits and enables the dis/continuity of life through time. In a theory of feral change, humans are not isolated observers of a natural process, nor are they the unrivaled architects of nature's transformation. Rather, humans are actors and catalysts even as our interests and abilities to shape nature only work from within the ecological, especially vegetal, forces that constrain and transform them in turn. This view encourages us to imagine the future through the ways we ourselves inhabit and are inhabited by feral trajectories. We will not share the same ends as the vines, but our future stands in a relation *non alienum.* To return to Cicero, I offer through him a sketch of what the feral future might look like.

In Cicero's dialogue, *On Old Age,* the main speaker Cato contrasts two archetypal figures of Roman culture as they relate to the future: the father and the farmer. According to Cato's paternal model, the father creates in his son an identity of traits, character, and goals, through which the son may realize the poten-

---

35 For the ancient understanding, see Thanos (1994); for a contemporary explanation, see Mars, Trad, and Gaaliche (2017).

tial of the past from the future. This relationship of paternity is exemplified by Scipio Aemilianus, soon to be the famous "hero" of the Third Punic War, and his many renowned ancestors. Addressing Scipio emphatically toward the end of his speech, Cato explains the aim that is shared by all those participants in Rome's paternal future:

> No one will ever convince me, Scipio, that your father Paulus, or your two grandfathers Paulus and Africanus, or the many other outstanding men, whom it is not necessary to enumerate, would have attempted so many things which would matter to the memory of posterity [*ad posteritatem memoriam pertinerent*], unless they perceived in their mind that posterity would matter to them [*posteritatem ad ipsos pertinere*]. (Cicero, *On Old Age,* 82; text is Powell 1988)

Drawing Scipio's attention to both his biological and adoptive lineages — the Pauli and the Scipiones — Cato articulates the motivation of these father-figures and "the many other outstanding men" of the Republican past in whose shared legacy he now urges Scipio to take part. For these glory seekers, the pursuit of "things that would matter to the memory of posterity" will ensure that this legacy extends also to their own lives. The repeated use of the verb *pertinere* underscores both the relevance of the actions that qualify these men for memorialization and the faithful maintenance of their legacy carried out by future avatars.

Working alongside paternity in *On Old Age,* however, we find a contrasting relation to the future, which relies not on the father's replication of himself but rather on the care for other forms of life after the model of the farmer. In his account of the sensual pleasures that are still available to old men, Cato selects for special attention "the Roman farmers in the Sabine field, my neighbors and friends, who are hardly ever absent when there is important work to be done, such as sowing, harvesting, or storing up the crops." Considering the unfailing attention of these elderly farmers, he muses:

> Although this is hardly surprising for those plantings [which they know will matter to them] — for no one is so old that he does not think he can live another year — even still, they lavish the same care on those that they know will never matter directly to them at all [*sciunt nihil ad se omnino pertinere*]: *He plants trees to benefit another age* [*alteri saeculo*] as our [Caecilius] Statius says in his "Young Comrades." (Cicero, *On Old Age*, 24–25)

The traditional wisdom of the farmer, "He plants trees to benefit another age," offers a strong sense of the *alteri saeculo* (future as alterity) that is differentiated explicitly from the continuous replication of paternity. In contrast to Cato's depiction of those who act in order to maintain their relevance to posterity and the relevance of posterity to them — a relation indicated with the verb *pertinere* — farmers care even for plantings which "they know will never matter [*pertinere*] directly to them at all."[36] Through this commitment to engaged indifference, the farmer views himself only as a caretaker for another's future, even given his certain knowledge that his actions will not pertain to himself *in any way*.[37]

In Cato's farmer, therefore, Cicero locates a mode of futurity that is based not on paternal continuity or Roman glory,[38] but in the development of other, especially vegetal, forms of life. The

---

36 This second use of *pertinere* recalls the Lucretian "symmetry argument" — the idea that, just as nothing "mattered to us" before birth, so nothing will matter to us after death: cf. Lucretius, *On the Nature of Things* 3.830–42; see, e.g., J. Warren (2001).

37 Cicero's interest in this relation of engaged indifference echoes Levinas's idea of the "fecundity of the future"; see esp. (1979, 267–68): "Fecundity encloses a duality of the Identical. It does not denote all that I can grasp — my possibilities; it denotes my future, which is not a future of the same — not a new avatar: not a history and events that can occur to a residue of identity, an identity holding on by a thread, an I that would ensure the continuity of the avatars. And yet it is my adventure still, and consequently my future in a very new sense, despite the discontinuity." See Oliver (2001) and Lin (2013).

38 On the relationship between the two, see esp. Habinek (2000).

feral vine reappears as the counterpoint to this farmer, as the conduit through which *he,* in turn, is transformed from out of the future, no longer himself:

> The vine which by nature is crestfallen and, unless it is propped up, is carried to the earth, will raise itself by its hand-like [*quasi manibus*] tendrils and embrace whatever supports it has. And, as it is twining its way with its meandering and twisting course [*quam serpentem multiplici lapsu et erratico*], the skill of the farmers, by trimming with a knife, will check it so that its shoots do not become woody [*silvescat*], and it does not spread out all its parts too far. (Cicero, *On Old Age,* 52)

It is hard to tell where the vine ends and the farmer begins: the vine's tendrils are *quasi manibus* ("like hands"), which become an impersonal "skill of the farmers" that trims back the wandering shoots with a knife. In this expression of human care as a violent manipulation of the vine's "crestfallen" nature, we recognize again agriculture's Oedipal loop. Yet, haunting this repetitive cycle, the beastly fertility of the vine has already changed itself, as it becomes other plant and animal forms of life, now "meandering" like a *serpentem* ("serpent") and now becoming "woody" like a *silvescat* ("tree"), testing always to see the contours and limits of itself, which is not itself, as it threatens to spread out "all its parts too far." Too far for it? Or too far for us? What Cicero offers as a way of relating to the future through human-centered care and cultivation, we can inhabit as our own feral future, shaped by the unintended effects of human violence and a history of vegetal transformation. By willingly, even pleasurably entering into this future, the farmer has also become feral, asking along with the vine, "when am I transformed?"

7

"The Sun Is New Every Day" (Heraclitus D-K frg. B6): Greek Ephemerality and Biopolitical Modernity

Bruce Rosenstock

The anthropologist Timothy Ingold in his *Life of Lines* has recently taken up the thirteenth-century theologian Ramon Llull's thesis that all nominal terms are rooted in verbal terms,[1] and that therefore the Latin noun *homo* must correspond to a verbal form that did not survive. Llull offers a neologism to capture this lost verb, *homoficare*. Thus Llull writes: *homo est animal homificans*, "The Human is the humanifying animal." Ingold (2015, 118) argues that humanifying should not be construed as added on to an animal substrate, but rather that humanifying is the undoing of the animal as noun and its remaking into a new verbal form of life, the species life of *Homo sapiens*:

> In comparison to the animal, in whose horizon there is no past or future, only an ever-evolving now, the movement of human life is temporally stretched. Out in front is the "not

---

[1] "D-K" in the title refers to the edition of Diels and Kranz (1958), which I follow for the fragments of both Heraclitus and Parmenides.

yet" of aspiration, bringing up the rear the "already there" of prehension. At once not yet and already, humans — we might say — are constitutionally ahead of themselves. Whereas other creatures must be what they are in order to do what they do, for humans it is the other way around. They must do what they do to be what they are. Flying does not make a bird, but speaking makes us human. It is not that humans are becoming rather than being; rather, their becoming is continually overtaking their being. This, I suggest, is what Llull had in mind when he spoke of man as a humanifying animal.

Ingold is here claiming that whereas other animal species are, as it were, activities congealed into substances and thus do not have *tenses* but only a "now," the humanifying species is never a substance but an activity stretched across time where "becoming is continually overcoming being." Ingold furthermore identifies humanifying with speaking. What it means to humanify, to act in such a way that the species *being* of *Homo sapiens* is overtaken by species becoming, is to relate to time in and through speaking. Speaking undoes and recreates human being. Ingold would argue that humanifying, once it emerges as a life form of the *Homo sapiens* species, does not evolve in the way that other species evolve, through the natural selection of individuals with inheritable traits that provide greater success at adapting to environmental pressures. Humanifying alters itself through the manipulation of symbols. Rather than passing selected alterations of the species-defining genomic code to offspring, humanifying transmits to the next generation symbolic representations of learned adaptive behaviors. Or, this is how it has been until the biopolitical present, when we now face the possibility of technologically altering our genome. How this technological capability to alter the human genome changes the way of life of the humanifying animal will be a central question of this essay. In thinking through this question, I return to the resources of Greek poetry and philosophy. In Greek poetry and philosophy, the humanifying animal speaks about itself, questioning the fundamental relationship between *logos* (speaking) and *chronos* (time). In this essay I will set the technological alteration of the human genome within the context of an exploration of the Greek self-questioning of the humanifying animal. In particular, I will focus on one particular Greek word, *ephēmeros* ("ephemeral"), as a key to understanding how Greek poetic and philosophic self-questioning reveals the temporal structure of humanifying that has prevailed until modernity.

Ephemerality, I will argue, poses a problem that is the driving motor of humanifying. To be ephemeral is to always be overcome by *becoming,* but not in some vague or abstract relation to time. Rather, humanifying's ephemerality is a relation to a certain fixed place (the solid ground of the earth upon which humans stand and walk) and a certain movement (the rising and setting of the sun). In other words, ephemerality captures humanifying's dialectic of being and becoming in its earthly embodiment. Ephemerality sets the conditions of the essential problem that humanifying seeks to solve: how to join being and becoming in such a way that a *mortal* and *earthly* life is judged to be a *life worth living.* Apart from the experience of ephemerality, *Homo sapiens* would not be a species that humanifies. In Aeschylus's *Prometheus Bound,*[2] Prometheus seeks to raise humanity (through the gift of fire and the *tekhnai* it makes possible) above its condition of ephemerality in order that human life becomes worth living. But Prometheus, despite his love for humanity, never expresses a desire to undo the condition of human ephemerality altogether. But today, biotechnology holds the promise of eliminating the condition of ephemerality altogether, making aging and death no longer the destiny of those humans who have access to the power of these biomedical advances. But the end of ephemerality threatens to also end humanifying as well. In the biopolitical regime of modernity, *life worth living* is no longer an individual life but living as such. Living as such is judged (by the sovereign power of the state) to be worthy of *making more life,* of having its "biopower" pro-

---

2 I follow the text of D. Page (1972).

tected and enhanced, perhaps even *immortalized*. Michel Foucault (2001, 241) distinguishes sovereign power's shift from its earlier form (as a right over individuals) to its biopolitical form (as a right over life itself): "The right of sovereignty was the right to take life or let live. And then this new right is established: the right to make live and to let die."

My essay turns to the Greek reflection on ephemerality in order to respond to this volume's call to think about the present-day crisis in what Ingold calls "humanifying," a crisis that troubles the very relationship of our species to its future. The Promethean gift of technology threatens the foundation of humanifying, the condition of ephemerality. While I will focus on the challenge posed by genome-altering biotechnology, this challenge is just one among several that technology today poses. Through technology, humanifying has acquired the unique power to upset the life-sustaining balance of earth and sun, the photosynthesis-based ecosystem within which all organisms flourish. As Mario Telò writes in "Before," the introduction to this volume, "What if instead of the unending approach or, alternately, a movement toward the end of the world, a return to the non-being before being, we are experiencing the 'arrival' of a-chronicity, a sense of stuckness in a state of defective being (perhaps heightened by our curbed relationality and movement)?" I will argue that by unpacking the significance of ephemerality in Greek poetic and philosophical sources we can gain an insight into the challenge to the future of the species that we have faced with growing urgency since the technological-industrial revolution inaugurated by the invention of the coal-run steam engine.

My reflections on technology's threat to the experience of ephemerality are indebted to Hannah Arendt's analysis of the three activities (or life forms) that constitute the structure of humanifying in *The Human Condition:* labor, work, and action. Without using the term "ephemerality," Arendt captures the experience of ephemerality when she speaks about "the futility of mortal life and the fleeting character of human time" (1998, 8). She relates this experience to the condition of being earthbound: "The most radical change in the human condition we can imagine would be an emigration of men from the earth to some other planet" (1998, 10). The experience of "the fleeting character of human time" is the experience of the sun's movement from the vantage of an earth dweller, the experience of the day. The temporal and spatial conditions set by the experience of ephemerality do not constrain the human species to certain fixed patterns of behavior, but call forth self-transforming activities, what Ingold had called "humanifying." At the base of these activities is labor, the activity that takes place within the domestic space of a family, from birth to marriage and reproduction, old age and death. Work is the activity whose products "bestow a measure of permanence and durability upon the futility of mortal life" (1998, 8). Finally, Arendt explains that action is what humans do in "founding and preserving political bodies" within which they find the possibility of "remembrance," of having their names passed on as participants in the life of the city (1998, 9). Although labor is foundational to all other activities in a very overt way (no work or action can take place if the species is not reproduced), labor reveals an aspect of the human condition that it passes on to work and action, an aspect that Arendt calls "natality." All human activities, all humanifying in other words, is a response to and a nurturing of "the new beginning inherent in birth" (1998, 9).

Natality is much more than biological birth, however, because human birth is already entwined with humanifying as the "overcoming of being by becoming," an overcoming that marks the difference between *Homo sapiens* and other animal species. Humanifying is not the replication of a product, where the "whatness" or being of the thing produced would define becoming, but the inauguration of a new way to humanify. Arendt writes: "We are all the same, that is, human, in such a way that nobody is ever the same as anyone else who ever lived, lives, or will live" (1998, 8). Natality means that newness is inseparable from humanifying. It also means that *plurality* is inseparable from humanifying. Arendt argues that the verse in the Hebrew Bible that shifts between calling the *adam* (human) a "him" and also a "them" (Genesis 1:27) holds the key to the essential plurality of the human, as over against the creation story in Genesis 2 where the second human, the female, is only added later. What Arendt wants to claim on the basis of Genesis 1:27 in contrast to Genesis 2 is that the focus upon the individual's relation to their death (she mentions Paul's focus on individual sin and salvation) leads to a concealment rather than revelation of natality—in fact, it constitutes a denial of natality.[3] Only a focus upon birth as newness that erupts from within a plurality of different humans (minimally understood to be a man and a woman) allows humanifying to express its authentic character of *becoming overtaking being*. But here is the deepest problem that the experience of ephemerality poses to humanifying: death is the focus of ephemerality, not birth. Each new human is born on a certain day, but the experience of the day as such, ephemerality, is determined not by one's birth day but by the day of one's death. Aside from his gift of fire and the *tekhnai* it makes possible, Prometheus lifted humanity beyond its enslavement to the condition of ephemerality by taking from humans the knowledge of the day of their death (*Prometheus Bound* 250).

Arendt is of course aware that the condition of ephemerality had been essentially understood in antiquity not only as an earth-bound condition, but as condition defined by humanity's relationship to death. But the argument of *The Human Condition* as well as of *On Revolution* (1990) is that the response to ephemerality in modernity (humanifying, in other words) shifts away from being defined in relation to the day of *death* to being defined in relation to the day of *birth*. With this change,

---

3   She also draws attention to Augustine: "Especially interesting in this respect is Augustine (*On the City of God* 12. 21) , who not only ignores Genesis 1:27 altogether but sees the difference between man and animal in that man was created *unum ac singulum,* whereas all animals were ordered 'to come into being several at once' (*plura simul iussit exsistere*). To Augustine, the creation story offers a welcome opportunity to stress the species character of animal life as distinguished from the singularity of human existence" (Arendt 1998, 8).

it is no longer *blind hope* that is necessary to make human life worth living, but faith that the future is not determined by the past (the power of natality to begin something new). Only with the American Revolution does natality come into focus as the basis of the inauguration of a new action within a plurality of humans — the constitution of a new body politic — without relying upon what Arendt calls an "absolute," a legitimating power that is different from the power of natality itself. But the political revelation of natality as a principle in the American Revolution also exposes natality as something to be used. In other words, natality becomes subject to technological work: birth becomes the object of a clinical-technological investigation (how to lower the infant mortality rate, for example). This is the theme that Foucault pursues in his studies of the rise of biopolitics in the nineteenth century. Arendt herself is aware of the danger that work poses to natality. She discusses how the death of the individual human being, so basic to the problem posed by ephemerality, seems in the modern era to be no longer pressing; life as such holds its immortality within itself. Human existence on the face of the earth, Arendt writes, if we take a distant view of it from the "Archimedian point" where the earth can be moved by a large enough lever, "would appear not as activities of any kind but as processes, so that, as a scientist recently put it, modern motorization would appear like a process of biological mutation in which human bodies gradually begin to be covered by shells of steel. For the watcher from the universe, this mutation would be no more or less mysterious than the mutation which now goes on before our eyes in those small living organisms which we fought with antibiotics and which mysteriously have developed new strains to resist us" (1998, 322–23). Although Arendt only mentions the "mutation" of the automobile-driving human "covered by shells of steel,"[4] her words, without intending to do so, portend the possibility of an attempt to technolo-

---

[4] For a discussion of how Arendt's categories of work, labor, and action can be used to understand the technological alteration of the world in the Anthropocene, see Hyvönen (2020).

gize the genome, to "mutate" into a life-form that manages its own mutations.

Arendt's reflections on the transformation of the human condition in modernity draw heavily from her engagement with the thinking of Martin Heidegger. In discussing the Greek concepts of birth, death, and the earth in the Parmenides seminar, Heidegger declares: "For the Greeks, death is not a 'biological' process, any more than birth is. Birth and death take their essence from the realm of disclosiveness and concealment. Even the earth receives its essence from this same realm" (1992, 60). Ephemerality discloses the earth as the space where the day measures one's life, with two days defining the finitude of one's life, the day of birth and the day of death. But the Greek experience of ephemerality, as we will see, seems to disclose death and conceal birth. Heidegger argued that in modernity death is not experienced in its disclosive power. *Dasein,* Heidegger's phenomenology of modern humanity, expounds its loss of the Greek experience of ephemerality. He argued that in modernity death is not experienced in its fully disclosive power, the power that grants to *Dasein* its Promethean character. Heidegger hoped for a return to the Greek "morning" when the consciousness of death and ephemerality defined the conditions of human existence, and awakened a new attempt to rise beyond the illusory comforts of irrational hope. Arendt did not want a return to the Greek experience of ephemerality and death, but rather believed that a shift of focus to the disclosive power of birth, of newness and plurality, might yield a wholly new possibility of earthly existence, the possibility that all the activities of humanifying might together nurture natality rather than expose it and use it as the basis for making more life.

Arendt did not undertake an analysis of why Heidegger sought to recover the Greek experience of ephemerality by way of *Dasein*'s relationship to death rather than, as she would argue, grounding the human response to ephemerality in the power of birth to open a space for the newness of action by a plurality of humans, where action is understood to be the creation of a political order in which the power of birth — the power to begin — is protected against the technologized instrumentalization of life. But in a work that has much to say about how modernity has altered our experience of life's ephemerality, the philosopher Edith Wyschogrod (1990) has offered an explanation of Heidegger's focus on death in his recuperation of Greek ephemerality. She explains that, for Heidegger, *Dasein*'s "authentic" relationship to the radical "my-ness" of human death opens *Dasein* up to become receptive to the Being of the world, that is, to the world's presence as other than a collection of objects to be technologically re-worked into a "'standing reserve' of energy destined for a future use" (1990, 179). Death shatters the immersion of *Dasein* in *das Man* (the They) and, by radically singularizing *Dasein,* it then places *Dasein* into the world again. Wyschogrod's point is that Heidegger's focus is on *Dasein*'s relation to the presencing of the world and its things, but the *human* other "is for Heidegger the one with whom I share the world: my relation to the other never bypasses the world, rather it passes through the circuit of the world" (1990, 166). Wyschogrod shows how even such a social phenomenon as language only comes into its truth, according to Heidegger, when it reveals the Being of the world, with the poet's act of naming, allowing the named things to escape the oblivion of their everydayness. But for Wyschogrod, language with its power to name is primordially a social phenomenon and, far from poetic naming having priority over all other linguistic acts, "only the language which names the near ones — the language of kinship structure — names in the required manner" (Wyschogrod 1990, 198). Or, as she later puts it, "Against Heidegger's view I argue that language is primordially this calling forth of the other into community. This is attested in the universality of kinship structure" (1990, 208). Wyschogrod therefore explains Heidegger's focus upon death as part and parcel of his devaluation of human kinship, the institution whose focus is *natality*. To be sure, Heidegger gave pride of place to the historico-metaphysical significance of Greek and German *peoplehood,* but, much like Hegel before him, kinship for Heidegger was situated outside the realm of history. Indeed, apparently in agreement with Heraclitus's apothegm that "War is the father and king of all" (Diels-Kranz 1958, B53), the truest form of kinship for Heidegger seemed to be the brotherhood of those who, in battle, are willing to lay down their lives for the historical destiny of the German people. After quoting the conclusion of the 1933–1934 Hölderlin seminar where Heidegger says that "the camaraderie of the soldiers at the front [in World War I] [...] lies solely therein that before all else the proximity of death as a sacrifice placed them all before the same nothingness," the Heidegger scholar James Phillips comments: "The authentic Being-toward-death that, in 1927 [in *Sein und Zeit*], is named the concealed grounding of the historicality of *Dasein* is identified seven years later with the experience of the trenches" (2005, 70). Heidegger sought to bring modern *Dasein* back to the Greek experience of ephemerality in order to prepare German peoplehood for their historical confrontation with the Heraclitean "father and king of all."

Even though Arendt turned to natality rather than "Being toward death" as her preferred response to the experience of ephemerality, she did share in some measure Heidegger's devaluation of kinship, consigning it to the realm of the domestic and labor, the space of the woman, the child, and the enslaved person in Greek antiquity. Therefore, she was unable to understand that the assault on natality in the totalitarian reduction of the human to mere life began with an assault on kinship. As Wyschogrod points out, the concentration camp and the Gulag rely upon the "enforced destruction of kinship," replacing the proper name given to one by one's parents with a number or some other imposed designation. I will return in the conclusion of the essay to the way that bioengineering is an assault upon natality by way of kinship, and how this functions in the manner of what Derrida would call an "autoimmune disorder": in the attempt to "purify" the human genome, the very strategy used against so-called "subhuman" populations (and historically deployed against enslaved people[5]) — the destruction of kinship — is turned against those who wield the bio-technological power.

Arendt believed that natality's power, if it were to be freed from the death-focus that defines the experience of ephemerality, could revolutionize the human condition. But instead, the modern focus on birth has endangered humanifying as never before, exposing life to the manipulation of new genetic technologies. It is as if Prometheus *unbound* sought to *immortalize* ephemeral humans rather than only deprive them of the knowledge of the day of their death. What can be done to redirect the problem of ephemerality away from death and towards the newness and plurality that is the power of natality concealed with the three activities of humanifying? If we as a species are going to respond to the technological challenges of modernity, we need another political revolution in which the power of natality is revealed, protected, and nurtured. We need to reveal the authentic power of natality so that the experience of ephemerality, an ineluctable experience, no longer drives all the activities of humanifying toward the overcoming of the day of death and "the fleeting character of human time." The rest of this essay explores the Greek poetic and philosophical reflections about ephemerality in order to uncover the traces of natality that may lie beneath the surface, concealed by the *forgetfulness of birth's promise*. At the end of the essay I will offer some reflections about what lies behind this forgetfulness, both in its ancient and modern forms, and what may hold the power to reawaken us from this amnesia. In these final reflections I return once more to the theme of kinship.

Let us begin by reconsidering the context within which the Greek problematic of ephemerality is revealed, the relationship between speaking and time that constitutes Ingold's "humanifying." We saw that Ingold appealed to Llull for the insight that in the development of language, verbs take precedence over nouns. But Plato had much earlier in the *Cratylus* expressed this insight,

---

5 See the classic work on the topic of kinlessness and slavery by Patterson (1985).

and he himself attributed it to Heraclitus. Plato suggests that Heraclitus's theory that "all things move and nothing remains still" could be evidenced by the verbal nature of the names for the gods (402a).[6] Heraclitus himself, as Heidegger has argued in numerous texts, often used word play not only to reveal the dynamic tension subtending the apparent stability of objects in the world, but also to restore our words, and therefore our lives, to their original attunement with the deeper *logos* of the world. If we wished to follow Heidegger's lead and turn to Heraclitus for evidence of how human *logos* both bears the trace of the verbal nature of the world's *logos* and is the medium in which what Ingold calls "humanifying" comes to speak (about) itself, we might begin with any number of Heraclitus's sayings, but I have chosen the one I quote in the title to this essay. It reads, *ho hēlios neos eph' hēmerēi estin* ("The sun is new every day"). It is within this apparently simple apothegm that, I believe, the whole problematic of the experience of ephemerality is revealed, from the forgetfulness of birth to the fleeting character of human time.

We could restate Ingold's claim about humanifying by saying that animal life "in whose horizon there is no past or future" is lived within the horizon of the Heraclitean sun, a horizon of movement that repeats itself as the same *eph' hēmerēi*, "every day"; the humanifying animal, by contrast, lives not just within the horizon of a single day but rather within the horizon of a multiplicity of days. Indeed, Hesiod titled his poem about the activities that comprise human life, *Erga kai hēmerai* (*Works and Days*). Heraclitus is not primarily making an astronomical observation about the sun; he is, rather, reflecting upon the significance of *hēmera* ("day") as the name for the measure of human life. If the sun were itself a living being, as it is possible Heraclitus believed it was, then it would be like an immortal animal, born every day without a memory of its prior existence. Its relation to *logos* ("language") would also be that of a

---

6 For a discussion of the Heraclitean names of the gods, see Rosenstock (1992). For the text of Plato's *Cratylus,* I am following the edition of Duke, Hicken, Nicoll, Robison, and Strachan (1995).

mute animal. It would not be able to articulate the Heraclitean *logos*, since it would not know itself to be born new every day. Only beings with memory would grasp that every day the sun is a *neos hēlios*, a "new sun" or possibly a "young sun," another meaning of *neos*. The Heraclitean *logos* gathers together, as Heidegger would say, the phenomenality of the sun's appearing; it lets it shine forth in a truth that the sun itself would not grasp.

Heraclitus's statement implies that the sun lives its whole life in a single day, from youth at daybreak to middle age at noon, and old age at sunset. The sun is not only "new" or "young" *eph' hēmerēi*, every day, but, if it is indeed born anew every day, the sun would also be quintessentially *ephēmeros*, a "creature of a day," doomed to die every day. Unlike humanifying animals, however, the sun can neither name itself nor describe itself as *ephēmeros*. It neither recalls a world before its birth nor expects anything beyond its death. Therefore, no day, from the sun's perspective, is different from another. Only the humanifying animal can think of its life as *ephēmeros*, which, as Hermann Fränkel (1946, 131) argued in a now classic article, acquired the significance in early Greek literature of "subject to the changing day, variable." Fränkel argues that when *ephēmeros* has this significance, the day is literally *epi* ("upon") us in the sense that we are "at the mercy of" the variable nature of the days of our lives. And one day, any day, death will be "upon" us. That fact is the only one that never varies from one day to the next. Ephemerality is the temporal horizon of a mortal animal that gathers itself into relation with a variable day and an invariable day. Although the invariable day seems to put all variability into question (life always ends in the same way), it is not necessary that the day of one's death defines one's entire relation to the days of one's life. In the Heraclitus fragment, the sun is new (young) "every day" but it is not at the mercy of the changing day because every day is the complete horizon of its being. It is immortally new. Aristotle makes this point explicit when he somewhat flatfootedly adds to his Heraclitean quotation that the sun is "always continuously [*sunechōs*] new" (*Meteorology* B 2.335a13).[7] Heraclitus's *logos* thus awakens the reader to the meaning of ephemerality as a *human* condition determined by the movement of the sun, sharing both the sun's daily newness and the sameness that marks its ineluctable terminal moment. Heraclitus's *logos* holds a paradoxicality that provokes the listener to search for some pattern or rhythm in the apparent variability of her days, perhaps one that could give all her days the shape of a single day, of a life from the morning of infancy, afternoon of maturity, and evening of old age. In other words, the sun's ephemerality (a whole lifetime transpiring in a single day) can provide a model for how a human being can transform the sheer variability of human ephemerality into a complete life that is not consumed by the sameness of its last day. But how can a human life be new every day? How can the *newness* of each day become the basis for the *completeness* of all the days of one's life? These are the questions that the revelation of natality requires us to answer. I believe that the Heraclitean *logos* raises but does not answer these questions.

The Heraclitus fragment takes us to the heart of the problem posed by ephemerality, how to make one's life worth living every new day. The sun is a negative model because every new day is the same day. Every day, for the sun itself, is lived with neither memory of past days nor anticipation of future ones. To understand that the sun provides a negative model for a complete life is to understand the riddle of the Sphinx. To know that human life unfolds in the shape of a single day is to know how to walk the variable path of a human life, in full awareness that with every day the path may alter for good or evil, perhaps even making it seem as if it were better not to have been born. Arendt, at the end of *On Revolution,* quotes the lines spoken by the Chorus in *Oedipus at Colonus,* cursing the condition of ephemerality: "Not to be born prevails over all meaning uttered by words; by far the second-best for life, once it has appeared, is to go as

---

7 I follow the edition of Lee (1952). Translation mine.

swiftly as possible whence it came" (1990, 281).[8] After quoting this passage, Arendt rejects its finality and argues that Theseus in the play offers a solution that enables young and old "to bear life's burden." "It was the *polis*," Arendt says, "the space of men's free deeds and living words, which could endow life with splendor — *ton bion lampron poieisthai*" (1990, 281). If it is truly the *polis* in which natality is revealed as that which "endows life with splendor" (Arendt is referencing lines 1143–44), I would interpret this to mean the human plurality as such, and not some particular governmental institution. But let me draw what Arendt says back to Heraclitus and the sun. Natality *makes* life shine. If life negates itself as swiftly as possible, if it lives under the *logos* that "not to be born prevails over all meaning uttered by words" (in the Greek, the last phrase in Arendt's rendering is only one word, *logon*), then every day is transformed into night. As we will see, this is the life of the shades in Hades. The only hope to battle ephemerality is to awaken from the dominion of the night, to *choose life*, to *choose birth*. But of all things, one's birth is the least under one's control. What does it mean, then, to choose birth? Is not the technologization of the genome the quintessential expression of such choosing? Since we were led down the path of these reflections by a quotation from *Oedipus at Colonus*, let me pursue some answers by turning to *Oedipus the King*. And in the final paragraph of the essay I will gesture towards another formulation of an answer.

Sophocles in *Oedipus Rex* presents a day in the life of a figure whose relationship to his birth made it impossible for him to share in the gifts of natality, newness, and plurality. Oedipus presents the negative model for the human solution to ephemerality. One might go so far as to say that Oedipus embodies, in the day we witness as well as in his life until that point, the negative model of the day of the sun. Oedipus, who solved the riddle of the Sphinx and therefore understood how one day, the day of

---

8   The translation (by Arendt herself) is of line 1225; the edition I follow for Sophocles's works is Lloyd-Jones and Wilson (1990). On this passage of *Oedipus at Colonus*, see Bassi's chapter in this volume.

the sun, could be a metaphor for a whole human life, mistook the model that the sun provides for that wholeness. He took the sun as a model for making his life into a whole circle, evading time's linearity and its end which for Oedipus was connected with a destiny that negated the worth of being born.[9] Tiresias tells Oedipus that "this day shall give you birth and destroy you" (438). Although we may not initially read this line as likening Oedipus to the sun, the fact is that Oedipus will no longer see a "new sun" after this day has "destroyed" him. Furthermore, once Oedipus blinds himself to the sun, for the remainder of his life he will see only the truth revealed in the one day of his life on which he truly imitated the day of the sun, from dawn-birth to night-death. Oedipus's day will thereafter "give birth and destroy" him at once, by showing him as one whose birth negates the worth of being born by violating the very conditions that make birth possible. Condemned to negate his birth every day in his self-imposed blindness to the sun's rebirth every day, the gods will ultimately negate Oedipus's death, rendering it invisible to mortal eyes.

Oedipus is the negative model for how to solve the problem of ephemerality. Neither birth nor death is supposed to be negated as a human solution to the problem of ephemerality (how to shape a life worth living out of the variability of day). Ephemerality defines the condition of life on earth for humans; the negation of that condition means the annihilation of that life. That is why Oedipus had to remove himself from both the domestic space of reproduction and the political space of human togetherness, or plurality. Oedipus's life in blindness not only negates birth and death, as if each day repeats — just as does each new day of the sun, the day that "will give you birth and destroy you" — Oedipus also negates plurality. Indeed, the entire play revolves around Oedipus's attempt to solve the problem that he implies cannot be solved: "It could never happen that one is equal to the many" (845). Oedipus has already equated himself

---

9 For the classic exposition of the circularity of the life of Oedipus and the tyrant more generally, see Vernant (1990).

with the all of the city in its pain: "Your pain touches one taken separately and no other, but my soul grieves for the city and myself and you all together" (62–64). Tiresias has said Oedipus's woes "shall equate you with yourself and your children" (425). The newness of birth — unequateable with any other birth, each child unique — and the plurality of our shared habitation of the earth — providing space for the newness of action — are inextricably bound together. There can be no greater demonstration that the attempt to master natality — the newness of each birth and the plurality to which each birth adds its newness — will end in the destruction of natality.

But how, then, should ephemerality be overcome, if we hope to avoid the destruction of natality? One possible solution is provided in the poetry of Pindar. In a way, it is the inverse of the Oedipus model. Rather than compressing life into one day that gives birth to and destroys the individual, Pindaric poetry compresses life into a single day that gives birth to and *immortalizes* the individual. What is probably the most famous use of the adjective *ephēmeros* in Greek literature appears in Pindar's *Pythian Odes* 8.95–96, where the poet writes: "Beings of a day [*epameroi*]. What is a someone, what is a no one? Man is the dream of a shade. But when the radiance given by Zeus comes, there is at hand the shining light of men, and the life-force [*aiōn*] gives sweet pleasure [*meilikhos*]."[10] In this passage, human ephemerality is not about the struggle to survive until the end of the day, but it rather characterizes human existence in the absence of the "life-force" that only the "radiance of Zeus" can provide. This life-force, *aiōn,* is what Aristotle defines as "the completedness (*telos*) that circumscribes the time of the life of each thing and which by its own nature nothing can exceed" (*On the Heavens* 279a25; edition of Guthrie 1939). For an ephemeral being like the human, its *aiōn* is achieved on the day that gives completion to its whole life. For Pindar, this is the day of athletic victory. The glory of that victory does not negate ephemerality but allows one day to be the day on which the sun sheds its

---

10 The translation is taken from Nagy (2000, 110).

brilliance upon the wholeness of life. Of course, the sun itself, and not even Zeus himself, can accomplish this *aiōn* — creating brilliance without the contribution of the activity that is central to humanifying, speaking. The day of victory shines beyond that single day because it becomes the matter of a song. Apart from that single day of glory, Pindar views the remainder of human life as if it were lived in a condition of quasi-anonymity where being "a someone" and "a no one" are indistinguishable. Pindar compares this anonymity to the kind of existence that is possessed by the shades in Hades. In a striking metaphor, he declares that ephemeral humans lead their lives as the dream of a shade, as if one's present life were nothing more substantial than the dreamlike memory of one's posthumous shade. As beings of a day, we exist in posthumous anonymity, not quite but nearly as if we had never been born. But on one day in our life, if the radiance of Zeus shines upon us, the dreamlike anonymity of our existence can be transfigured into a reality with the full sweetness of the life force.

In a close reading of the ode in which these lines appear, Gregory Nagy (2000) argues that when the athletic victor is thus transfigured by Zeus's radiance, the athlete also is seen by the shades of his ancestors who become witnesses to his glory. In their prophetic or mantic dream, they see forward in time to the glory of their descendant. Pindar uses the verb *theaomai* for this special form of mantic seeing. In this piece Nagy points out that Pindar himself claims to be able to "see clearly" the glory that irradiates the present moment in just the same way that the ancestral shade can see the future glory of his descendant. Pindar himself is a mantic seer who both testifies to and vouchsafes the immortality of that which he sees through the words of his poem. Past, present, and future are thus intertwined in this single day of victory as it comes to expression in the poem. The poet Pindar therefore uses the adjective *ephēmeros* with a double connotation: humans are "beings of a day" in the sense that their whole lives, mostly led anonymously, can be compressed into the insubstantial dream of a shade, but they are also "beings of a day" in the sense that in a single day one's *aiōn* can be fully realized. One day's achievement can grant them immortal glory in a radiant light that stretches across time and comes to fulfillment in the "winged words" of the poet-seer. Here is how Nagy (2000, 111) puts it:

> I suggest that the shade of the dead person is literally dreaming — that is, realizing through its dreams — the living person. In other words, the occasion of victory in a mortal's day-to-day lifetime is that singular moment when the dark insubstantiality of an ancestor's shade is translated, through its dreams, into the shining life-force of the victor in full possession of victory, radiant with the brightness of Zeus. It is as if we the living were the realization of the dreams dreamt by our dead ancestors.

If Nagy is right, then Pindar is giving poetic expression to the philosophical perspective of Parmenides about the nature of human ephemerality. Parmenides, although he never uses the word *ephēmeros,* opens his poem by recounting a journey to the "gates of night and day" (B 1.11), and the section of his poem called the "way of seeming" condemns the naming (substantializing) of the "flaming *aithēr* of the sun" and the "thick heavy shape of dark night" as constituting the essential error of mortal humans (B 8.53–61). If Pindar is saying that our lives are dreams of shades that only become real with the achievement of athletic glory immortalized in song, then both he and Parmenides seem to agree that our ephemeral lives are an illusion, that the passage of time marked by night and day is not real, and that the only truth is what never changes, what neither comes into being nor passes away, "that singular moment when the dark insubstantiality of an ancestor's shade is translated" into the "shining life-force" of Being.

Have we really found a solution to the problem of ephemerality that does not negate birth and destroy natality? Both Pindar and Parmenides deny the reality of birth, equating life rather with a kind of death-in-life. Perhaps we should better say that Pindar and Parmenides represent the attempt to transcend

181

ephemerality as one's earthbound condition and, somehow, dwell entirely in the realm of *logos*. In both cases, in different ways, Being threatens to overtake Becoming. We need a different way to solve the problem of ephemerality, one that respects the need to allow Becoming to overtake Being if humanifying is to remain an imperfective activity and not congeal into a perfective, aoristic state. This imperfectivity is what the newness of natality promises.

I would like to offer some speculative thoughts about the background for the Greek denial of birth that we have noted explicitly in Sophocles's Oedipus plays, in Pindar, and in Parmenides. This speculation will take me back to natality and the modern technological threat to natality that is posed by the manipulation of the human genome. But before turning to these concluding thoughts, I have two more texts to examine.

In what is certainly the funniest use of the adjective in Greek literature, in Aristophanes's *Clouds,* Socrates, who is hanging from a basket above the stage, addresses Strepsiades below him, saying, "Oh being of a day [*O 'phēmere*]." When Strepsiades asks him what he is doing in the basket, Socrates says "I am walking in the air and contemplating the sun" (226–27).[11] To be ephemeral, it is clear, is to be earthbound and therefore incapable of "mixing one's subtle mind with the kindred air" (229–30)." To lift oneself away from the earth is to remove oneself not only from the gross materiality of the earth, but also, if only one could rise to the height of the clouds, to remove oneself from the darkness that falls upon the earth when the sun departs behind cloud cover. To seek to escape the conditions of earthbound ephemerality is to seek to overcome one's biological constraints as an earthbound creature. Socrates imagines that the ephemeral life of Strepsiades is no different from the life of the gnat whose leaping capacities are the subject of his students in the Thinkery. From the perspective of Socrates, birth and death are only biological processes. If we recall what Arendt said about the perspective of the technologist-engineer looking upon the earth from an

---

11 I follow the text of Henderson (1998). Translations are mine.

"Archimedian point," we could say that, in modernity, humans have internalized Socrates's distanced "observational" position in relation to the ephemera of earthly existence, and, also like Socrates, we have also lost our faith that heaven is the abode of the gods. We "walk upon the air and turn our thoughts to the sun" (1503). There is no difference between earth and heaven as far as human life is concerned. We look with contempt upon our ephemerality, the mortal condition that makes natality possible, because we see ourselves from a humanly-made observational perspective that sets us apart from our earthly habitation and its limitations. Adam McKay's 2021 film *Don't Look Up* brilliantly parodies both our general obliviousness to what technology has done to threaten our earth-bound condition and also the blind hopes that biotechnology has engendered in the superrich that they may, as it were, "walk upon the air" and ship out towards other suns. And, just as Aristophanes warned, if our *logoi* become completely disconnected from the earth and the day that measures life's finite span, neither birth (one's parents) nor plurality (the just city) will be safe against the violence that lies within the humanifying animal's speech. Speech that is disconnected from ephemerality will not reveal humanifying, but rather manipulate it as the raw material of a speech-making *tekhnē*. It is quite likely that, as Plato's *Apology* reports, the historical Socrates judged the Aristophanic parody to be the total inversion of his relationship to life's ephemerality. For Socrates, the *tekhnē* associated with human speech, if such a *tekhnē* exists, would necessarily be the *tekhnē* that transforms ephemeral life into a life worth living.

An entirely different perspective on ephemerality than we have so far encountered is presented in Aeschylus's *Prometheus Bound,* the single Greek text with the most occurrences of the word (3).[12] The play offers an aetiology of ephemerality, the condition of being earth dwellers whose temporal horizon from birth to death is measured by the daily movement of the sun through the sky. Ephemerality is presented as the individualiza-

---

12   In my approach to *Prometheus Bound,* I owe a debt to Loney (2021).

tion and mitigation of an originally *collective* death sentence. Zeus distributed honors to the gods who allied themselves with him against the Titans, but he planned to eliminate humans and establish a new mortal race in their place. Prometheus took pity upon humans and freed them from their underground existence "like gust-blown ants in the sunless recesses of caves" (452–53), lacking speech and reason (443–45). They lived out their lives "like shapes in dreams, doing everything in confusion and without purpose" (449–50). Recalling what humans were like, the Chorus refers to them as *ephēmeroi* ("the ephemeral ones," 255). What kept humans in this condition, if they were in fact capable of acquiring speech, thought, and all the arts that Prometheus ultimately provided to them? The answer to this question is not entirely clear, but we do know one further thing about them that perhaps holds the key to their failure to climb out from their cave: humans foreknew the day of their death. Actually, Prometheus simply says that, out of pity for them, he put an end to "mortals [*thnētoi*] foreseeing their destiny [*moron prosderkesthai*]." Their cave-dwelling lives were, in fact, indistinguishable from the existence of the shades in Hades. Why should they climb out of their cave if the one thing they knew was that they were doomed to return to the cave no matter what they did above the ground? Prometheus therefore gave them, as the "cure for the disease" of foreknowing their destiny, "blind hopes." We see a paradigmatic case of a mortal human with ignorant hopes in the figure of Io. She appears on the scene in a state of unspeakable suffering, transformed into a cow that is forever driven by a stinging gadfly, a punishment inflicted by a jealous Hera who seeks to thwart and avenge Zeus's infidelity with her, as he had raped Io. Any mortal in Io's condition, were she deprived of hope, would choose immediate death rather than live another day. Indeed, when Prometheus seems to have shattered her hopes for an eventual end to her suffering, Io says "What gain is there to me in living? What don't I throw myself from this rocky cliff? […] It is better to die once and for all than to live one's days in suffering" (747–51). Prometheus restores her hope by providing her with a glimpse into her future, telling her about the eventual end to her suffering after much wandering, the birth of a child whom she will have with Zeus (Epaphus), and the line of Argive kings and ultimately Heracles who shall descend from her child. This glimpse into her future makes her present suffering bearable.

The ability to gain a partial glimpse into the future is what Prometheus offers to humans in order for them to have "blind hopes." Prometheus explains that he provided the basis upon which humans may see into their future through *mantikē* (mantic arts), dreams, voices, and the signs hidden in events and the flight of birds (485–90). These methods to discern the future are not "blind" in the sense that they are *false*. They are, rather, limited. What Io is permitted to know is also limited; she knows that her suffering will end with the "touch" of Zeus, but she does not know that Heracles will also, like her, suffer at the hands of Hera. We are therefore led to understand that such hope consists in the not entirely groundless expectation of a better life, a life less full of pain, if not for oneself then for one's children. Aimless hope is the gift that *natality* brings to human life. This hope is "blind" not because it is illusory, but because it cannot be aware of *how* and *to what extent* one's children will lead a better life. It is in the creation of kinship that humans express their "blind" hope in the future. Natality is nurtured within kinship, but it takes such hope in the future beyond the limits of kinship. Natality, as Arendt argues, is the condition that makes action possible, but action, as the expression of a human plurality, always has unforeseen consequences. Aeschylus seems to suggest that life will in fact become better for humans. His play holds out hope because it shows us that although the rule of Zeus will not end, it will be transformed. That Zeus can change and become gentler is intimated by the name Epaphus, *touch*. The hope that Zeus and the gods may become gentler (no longer acting as a tyrant or slave master would) is all the hope that one needs in order to expect a better life for one's children. It is the hope that action within a human plurality can, for a time, defeat the goddess *Bia* (Force). This ignorant hope — for the struggle with Force is unending — is enough to keep humans above ground, willing to learn new ways to protect themselves through the *tekhnai* that Prometheus's gift of fire makes possible (256). Ironically, it is Prometheus himself who must exercise his pity for the human race one more time in order to bring about the transformation rather than the violent overthrow of Zeus's tyrannical rule. From what we know of the child of Thetis who was fated to overthrow Zeus (if Zeus was his father), this new sovereign would not have been gentler than Zeus. His rule would have been a rule of *mēnis*, "wrath." Prometheus must relent and yield his secret to Zeus if his gifts to humanity are to have any chance at unfolding in a less violent world, a world where human birth and human plurality have a future.

In giving humans ignorant hopes and fire, Prometheus gave mortals the *newness of the day*. In their caves, the ephemeral ones lived every day as the day of their death. Indeed, they had no ability to understand what "day" meant since their caves were "sunless." Their day was, in effect, one long night. Each day for them, when they finally learned the meaning of the day, was no longer measured as a temporal period in relation to the day of death, but in relation to the possibility of creating new life (the life of one's offspring) whose suffering under the tyranny of Zeus may be touched by a measure of grace. With the hope that new life brings comes also the possibility of creating something new through artifice, through *tekhnē*. *Prometheus Bound* comes very close to saying that ephemerality can only be "cured" through natality, that is, through birth, *tekhnē* ("work"), and action within the free (non-tyrannical) *polis*. Given its depiction of heroic defiance of tyranny, it should not come as a surprise that the play has resonated with modern revolutionaries, poets and thinkers.[13] But I would also suggest that *Prometheus Bound*, perhaps uniquely in Greek antiquity, reflects a focus

---

13 Two major works that have been devoted to the appropriation of the Prometheus myth in modernity are Blumenberg (1985) and Hickman (2017).

not on death as the horizon of ephemerality but rather *birth*. The "ephemeral ones" are led into the sun and given faith in the self-transformative activities of humanifying (labor, work, action) within a future that has been freed from a divine decree of collective death, Zeus's earliest decision as a ruler in relation to humans, and also from the fear of tyrannical violence such as Zeus inflicted upon Io. There is reason to have faith in a new day.

Except that now, today, this new day and the natality that makes it possible is threatened precisely by a *tekhnē* that would use natality in order to master the future. Humanity today asserts itself as an *unbound* Prometheus. In these final pages I want to reflect, first, upon what may have been a contributory factor, if not *the* contributory factor, in the Greek world's tendency to understand ephemerality not in relation to birth but rather in relation to death. Second, and very much related to this factor, I will offer some final thoughts about how modernity's turn toward birth and natality might be protected against the temptation to overcome the limits of ephemerality, making the day into an endless *process* of *making life* rather than making life *worth living*. For the temptation to make *more life* the object of *tekhnē,* as Arendt and Foucault teach us, has as its underside the endless violence of the process of *letting die*.

First, the Greek understanding of ephemerality in its relation to death needs to be viewed in relation to the Greek deprecation of birth, that is, of birth from the womb of a mortal woman. Nicole Loraux (2000) has provided us with extensive evidence of the way that Greek myth and ritual, especially as they come to expression in the context of democratic Athens, reduce the woman to an indistinguishable part of a *genos* (race) whose role is to provide the raw material in which the man can fashion an image of himself in a fleshly form (the son) that can survive his death and inherit his *ousia* (being). Apart from the male's controlling power, the female "race" is imagined to pose a grave threat, that it might reproduce itself without men. As Loraux explains: "Naturally, it was necessary that they [women] bear sons that were like their fathers: such is the definition of good social order in all cities. But at the level of mythical thought,

Greek males, with a *frisson* of terrified delight, preferred to imprison women in a *genos* always prepared to secede, perhaps even to reproduce in closed circuit. A fruitful operation of the masculine imaginary, liberating the field for the inverted fantasy—surely the true one—of a reproduction which, in the end, would have no need of women" (2000, 24). How can there be a recognition of *birth* when sexual reproduction itself was denied in a fantasy of motherless self-cloning?

Has this exploration of Greek ephemerality brought us any closer to understanding how to counter the threat that is posed when birth, in the modern era, replaces death as the focus of the problem that ephemerality poses, the problem of how to make life worth living? As we noted in the opening discussion of Arendt and Foucault, the threat posed in modernity to natality is that *making more life* may, in itself, be viewed as what makes life worth living. This is what Arendt feared when she described the distanced technician-engineer looking down at earthly human existence as if it were a process of life mutating into different forms, growing a steel casing, for example. From that de-terrestrialized vantage point, as Arendt tells us in uncanny anticipation of our current crisis, human life is seen as an impersonal process such as that of a bacterial species or virus that mutates to defeat our inoculation defenses. This bioengineering-Archimedian perspective on human life as a process is what Foucault describes as the panoptic perspective of the sovereign state in response to the emergence of biopower in the nineteenth century. Asserting its dominion in the realm of biopower, sovereign power takes responsibility for *making (more) life*. But the logic of sovereign decisive power requires that making live must have a corollary: *letting die*. The discovery that birth, natality's powers of newness and plurality, rather than death constitutes the authentic horizon of ephemerality in the era of biopolitics seems to expose human birth to a graver danger than it confronted in antiquity. The price of freeing ourselves from the tragic sense that, to revisit the words from *Oedipus at Colonus*, "not *to be born* prevails over all other meanings uttered in words" is that to be born is to be subject either to bioengineered enhancement (more life) or social death.[14] By social death I mean to refer to the state's abandonment of certain lives to the play of environmental catastrophes that largely spring from the same (biofuel) technologies that undergird the lives of those who are *born to more life*.

Or is this really the case? Does the sovereign regime of biopolitics really alter the logic of the polis in such a way that natality is more endangered than ever before? Or is the modern biopolitical threat to natality just a variation on the older logic? Can we perhaps speculate that the mythic fantasy of motherless self-cloning that Loraux draws our attention to is also at work in the biotechnologies of gene manipulation? Could we not describe the fantasy of Athenian men who tried to persuade themselves that they were "born of the earth" as a forerunner fantasy of our bioengineering fantasies? We noted that in *Prometheus Bound* Prometheus is portrayed as providing "blind hopes" and the arts as a way to overcome the subterranean ephemerality of human life. But in Hesiod it is Pandora who *lowers* men from commensality with the gods to the level of the "the race of women," *gasteres* (bellies) that drain men of their strength because they demand constant feeding, but who, if they can be domesticated, can provide the blood that can be reworked into a son in the image of his father. If we read *Prometheus Bound* together with Hesiod, we may conclude that men must apply all the power of their new-found *tekhnai* to subjugate the race of women. Put in the terms of my question about the difference between ancient and modern fantasies of motherless self-cloning, the myth of Prometheus makes men the bioengineers of their birth from the "race of women," attempting as far as possible to draw out from their bellies the bodies in which their own image is most visible. In bioengineering the race of women, men imagine themselves to be restoring the purity of autochthonous birth. If they were to hope for a full overcoming of their ephemerality, it would require the bioengineered replacement of the race of women.

---

14 On social death, see Patterson (1985).

Indeed, why should this not seem possible, given that Pandora herself is merely the product of an advanced technology?

If there is something new under the sun of modernity, perhaps it is that the bioengineering of birth from the female "belly" no longer functions within the fantasy of autochthony. Loraux demonstrates that autochthony serves as the ideal origin of the ideal social order, the polis, where, as Aristotle explains about the best *politeia,* most of the citizens should "share the same life as far as possible" (*Politics* 1295a29–30).[15] To be as alike as possible, citizens need to be born from a male template and a single mother. Autochthony assures that the democratic city is the best way to organize human life. At the opposite end of the spectrum is tyranny, where most men are enslaved to one man (*Politics* 1295a24). Loraux quotes these passages from Aristotle's *Politics* in order to demonstrate that the Athenian myth of autochthony provides the perfect rationale for the Athenians' pride in their city as the ideal city, because of its "beautiful homogeneity of the Same from the start" (1993, 53).

In the modern era, the myth of autochthony and its associated notion of the "race of women" as having a different origin than that of men no longer define the ideal social order. We are "made from the earth" by Yahweh, who creates us initially as one being, both male and female (Genesis 1:27) or, less egalitarian but still far from the Hesiodic account of Pandora's creation, Yahweh constructs the woman from the flesh and bone of the man (Gen. 2). Misogyny certainly underlies the West's patriarchal order, but women are no longer regarded as a potentially self-reproducing *genos* ("race"). What, then, in the modern era is driving the bioengineering fantasy of motherless self-cloning, if it is the case that ideal sociality is no longer defined as excluding, as much as possible, the participation of the "race of women"? The answer is that the fear of a dangerous, self-reproducing race that needs to be mastered by the free citizens who make up the "beautiful homogeneity of the Same" within the sovereign state has not gone away. The fear of such a "race" is manifested as the

---

15 I follow the text of Ross (1957); my translation.

fear of Blackness, an "ontological terror" (C. Warren 2018) that threatens to consume white Being and drag it into the horror of pre-technological ephemerality. The enslaved peoples from sub-Saharan Africa were brought to the New World by men whose sense of life's worth came to depend entirely upon the white purity of their birth and their race; the most vulnerable point of attack against racial purity, of course, remains the sexually threatening body of the woman. The enslaved Black people, both women and men, took the space previously occupied by women and enslaved people in the Greek city. As Orlando Patterson (1985) argues, the enslaved was "broken in" to the new condition by first being uprooted from her kinship ties. Slavery turned birth into a process of breeding a labor force. Natality was foreclosed for the slave. Arendt admits as much when she places the slave in the realm of labor and excludes the slave from the action of the *polis*. It is not surprising, then, that it is precisely in relation to the body of the enslaved Black woman that modernity's bioengineering project — a project for the reproduction of a purportedly homogeneous race as nearly free from the constraints of ephemerality as their mortal bodies will allow — has taken its most violent turn. The "belly" of the enslaved Black woman, unlike the belly of the "race of women" in ancient Greece, reproduced *partus sequitur ventrem* (only the form of its mother). This was no disadvantage, however. The Black female was the source of wealth. Chattel slavery allowed patriarchy to capitalize on the Black mother's flesh. The Greek world's mythic fantasy of motherless self-cloning, of the father reproducing his faithful copy in his son, finds its culmination in a regime where the father masters the threat of the mother's alterity by owning both her and her offspring. This has always been the logic behind the West's "white mythology," as Derrida taught us a half century ago (1974): humanifying congealed into property.

In a strange twist of fate, the Promethean power of modern technology has returned humanity to a condition of ephemerality. Achille Mbembe has described this as *"the Becoming Black of the world"* (2017, 6). In terms that eerily parody the language of Ingold with which this essay began, Mbembe describes the "new man" as "capable of absorbing any content […] lacking an essence of his own to protect or safeguard." Mbembe continues (2017, 4):

> There are no longer any limits placed on the modification of his genetic, biological structure. […] He is a neuroeconomic subject absorbed by a double concern stemming from his animal nature (as subject to the biological reproduction of life) and his thingness (as subject to others' enjoyment of the things of this world). As a human-thing, human-machine, human-code, and human-in-flux, he seeks above all to regulate his behavior according to the norms of the market. He eagerly instrumentalizes himself and others to optimize his own pleasure. Condemned to lifelong apprenticeship, to flexibility, to the reign of the short term, he must embrace his condition as a soluble, fungible subject to be able to respond to what is constantly demanded of him: to become another.

I cannot imagine a better description of what modern ephemerality looks like. This is not the ephemerality of the shortness of life, but the ephemerality of the "short term," the never-ending sloughing off of the old in order to be reborn in some new, more pleasureable, bio-technical form. Natality has mutated, under the pressure of racio-capitalist Prometheanism, exactly in the way that Arendt feared.

This is not the note on which I want to end. I would like to offer some *hope for a new day*. I therefore end with a passage near the conclusion of Hortense Spillers's "Mama's Baby, Papa's Maybe: An American Grammar Book" (1987). Spillers imagines a new day that will emerge from the Black mother's power to create kinship as a refusal of the political regime that consigns her to kinlessness. Spillers's essay can profitably be read in tandem with Loraux's numerous essays on the myth of autochthony. Loraux speaks about the deep contradiction within Athenian kinship: because the actual reproduction of kinship depends upon the threatening and alien "race of women" for its continuity, the reality of kinship is reimagined as that of *brothers born of the earth*. The denigration of the reality of human kinship consigns women and enslaved people to unredeemable ephemerality. For both groups, kinship, and the natality which kinship shelters, is placed under erasure; they are judged to live a life that is *not worth living*. Both Spillers and Loraux are trying to parse the "grammar" in which gender difference is declined through a paradigm in which white, free maleness is the nominative case (the Name of the Father) and femaleness is always oblique. Spillers, however, offers hope for a resurrection of kinship and a new embrace of birth rather than death or social death as the horizon of Black existence. Spillers argues that there is one community of men who can know the woman as a subject who stands upright, who affirms her right to name herself, and claim herself as the mother of her child even in the midst of an order that names her a mere *venter* (belly) and her child a "piece" of property. Here is Spillers (1987, 80):

> Therefore, the [enslaved] female, in this order of things, breaks in upon the imagination [of white, free maleness] with a forcefulness that marks both a denial and an "illegitimacy." Because of this peculiar American denial, the black American male embodies the *only* American community of males which has the specific occasion to learn *who* the female is, the infant child who bears the life against the could-be fateful gamble, against the odds of pulverization and murder, including her own. It is the heritage of the *mother* that the African-American male must regain as an aspect of his own personhood — the power of "yes" to the "female" within.

The Black mother's "fateful gamble" of bringing a new life into the world reveals all the powers of natality, newness, and plurality. Spillers affirms birth and natality when she calls upon the Black male to regain "the power of 'yes' to the 'female' within." Only the powers of natality can "break in upon" the bioengineering imagination of a patriarchal order that has never ceased to hope for a birthday like that of the sun, when a man can spring to life in ever-renewable glory, in "the beautiful homogeneity of the Same." Death does not have the power to free us from this *blinding* hope to overcome ephemerality, for death is what drives this hope forward. Only birth can save us.

8

Mourning Mourning: Sophocles, Derrida, and Delay

Sarah Nooter

Delay is surely one of our most human ideas: that one moment is the displacement of another, that importance resides just over the next hill.[1] In *Oedipus at Colonus,* Sophocles portrays the delayed death, or the last delay of death, of Oedipus.[2] The play begins with the arrival of the blind Oedipus and his daughter Antigone in Colonus, a sort of suburb of Athens. Oedipus unwittingly wanders into the grove of the Furies, a trespass that greatly upsets the locals of Colonus, but that pleases him inasmuch as he realizes he has come to his final resting place. After a series of tense events, Oedipus is given refuge by Theseus, king of Athens, and promises in return that his death will provide blessings and protection to the city so long as his place of death within the grove of the Furies remains unknown to all but Theseus and his direct descendants (1760–63). After Oedipus, his

---

1 I warmly thank Sean Gurd and Mario Telò for bringing together this volume and organizing the American Comparative Literature Association (ACLA) panel that preceded it, which gave me a chance to think through my experience in the presence of such wonderfully stimulating interlocutors. I am grateful too to one of the readers for incisive and rich suggestions on this piece.
2 I follow the edition of Lloyd-Jones and Wilson 1990.

daughters, Theseus, and attendants enter the grove, he sends the others away and leads Theseus, and only Theseus, deep into this grove, where he then disappears for good. The play ends with the mourning of the daughters, which focuses both on the loss of their father and their inability to see his resting place. In what follows, I examine Jacques Derrida's take on Sophocles's portrait of Oedipus's death, and also attempt to answer some of the anxieties presented by Derrida in *Of Hospitality* and *Archive Fever* about technology and media, particularly as it all relates to this strange, seemingly everlasting present of the COVID-19 pandemic. What ties these concerns to one another are persistent questions about how — through what rituals and tricks of time — we mediate delay, disruption, and loss.

Sophocles and Derrida: The Delay of Life

In his interpretation of Oedipus's death, Derrida focuses on the multiple privations of Oedipus and his daughters: even as Oedipus lacks a homeland, his daughters lack his body. One absence answers the other. As Derrida (Derrida and Dufourmantelle 2000, 93) comments in *Of Hospitality*:

> Antigone endures and names that dreadful thing: being deprived of her father's tomb, deprived above all, like her sister Ismene, of the *knowledge* as to the father's last resting place. […] [Oedipus] is going to deprive them of their mourning, thereby obliging them to go through their mourning of mourning […] in doing so he offers them a limitless respite, a sort of infinite time.

Let us pause on his notion, all too prescient, of "limitless respite, a sort of infinite time." As I write, this sense of temporality rings too true. It is the summer of 2021, and we who live through this season might also be said to be suspended in an infinite present — not going anywhere, yet not at home in our lives, not free to mourn our losses nor to leave behind our mourning. Indeed, one would have hoped that this state of suspension would be behind us by the time I finished this chapter, but one of the hallmarks of our current crisis is its seemingly endless protraction, and thus Derrida's notions of "limitless respite" and "infinite time" are even more apt now than they were when I first encroached upon this project. So the predicament that we face — or at least one of them — is all the more one of infinite regress, a being on-the-verge of, or in the middle of delay, a pause in life-size parentheses with meaningful events seemingly held suspended, just beyond — a problem, in other words, of affective time. Moreover, this problem of temporality is wrapped up in an amorphous awareness of loss, and this awareness is funneled through large-scale disturbances in our daily ritualistic habits, our modes of sociality, and our uses of technology to connect and simultaneously disconnect from one another. One might not think that Sophocles's late fifth-century play would shed much light on this web of disruptions and delays, but Derrida shows precisely how it can.

The text *Of Hospitality* is the record of two seminars that Derrida delivered in January of 1996. This, of course, is long before the COVID-19 pandemic and also prior to the encroachment of much contemporary technology into our lives, including the ubiquity of "smart" phones, the omnipresence of what is now known as "social media" (let us strain to imagine Derrida on the topic of Twitter and TikTok), and the relocation of many of the world's events to the quasi-unreal space of Zoom. Derrida is terribly apprehensive about the implications of technological advancements, as we see in *Of Hospitality* and also in *Archive Fever* (Derrida 1996c). At first glance, the objects of Derrida's concerns seem almost quaint now: electronic mail, the activities of CompuServe, the implications of facsimiles, the exploding access to pornography on the Internet, and the heavy-footed attempts by some states to control its dissemination. He writes (Derrida and Dufourmantelle 2000, 47):

> Among the innumerable signs of mutation that accompany the development of e-mail and the Internet — I mean every-

thing that these names stand for — let us first privilege those that completely transform the structure of so-called public space.

So, here at least, Derrida structures his concern about technology around *space,* and particularly the breaching, or deformation, of the "frontier between the public and the non-public" (Derrida and Dufourmantelle 2000, 49). Derrida writes of the growing power of the state and the ability of rogue operations to intercept, disrupt, and generally threaten the "interiority of the home," adding parenthetically and in quotation marks "we are no longer at home!" (Derrida and Dufourmantelle 2000, 53). Indeed, Derrida sees not only the boundaries of the home being threatened but also, thereby, "the very integrity of the self, of ipseity" (Derrida and Dufourmantelle 2000, 53). So from space, to home, to our very selfhood.

Not to overstate the matter, then, in this year-plus of pandemic, the existential issues on the table that are abundantly foreseen by Derrida's rather unassuming text *Of Hospitality,* and even (as we will see) by Sophocles's posthumously performed play *Oedipus at Colonus,* concern no less than the parameters of time and the boundaries of the space that constitute and indeed afford the integrity of the self. Ours is not just the pedestrian problem of not being able to make, or keep, plans.[3] It is not only the loss of loved ones and the inability to mourn them safely in the company of family. It is not only that we can hardly leave our own spaces, our homes, while at the same time these same spaces and homes have been made porous and exposed to public notice via the electric eye of Zoom — including our books, cats, and children; our decorating choices and compromises; our flushing toilets and running showers; and the messes in our bedrooms and the voices of our spouses. At stake here, if we

---

3   Pre-pandemic, this state of affairs was known to me affectively only through the heartache of my aunt, who lived with stage-four cancer for eight years and spoke of exactly this anguish — the inability to make plans, this dispossession of futurity.

follow Derrida and Sophocles as our guides, is the very constitution of the self, face to face with its own mortality, constructed as it is through the politics and civilities of time and space. What path is there for us whose borders have suddenly been stamped out? Sophocles gives us Antigone plunged into unquenchable grief and eventually, in *Antigone,* flaming out over the proclamation of the non-burial of her brother: it is one unburied body too many. By burying him, she obtains that her own body, still living, is buried too. Let us see what options may exist for us.

Sophocles: The Delay of Death

So, back to Sophocles. Derrida (Derrida and Dufourmantelle 2000, 101) notes several times the theme of delay and hesitance in the play and puts this theme into conversation with occurrences and urgings of *haste:*

> Oedipus then pushes on toward this place that he keeps secret. He wants to avoid being late for this sort of rendezvous with the gods. It would be worth following the motif of *delay* and haste, the time and the rhythm of this journey, the halting and *hastening* that mark the beat of this tragedy.

Derrida reads Oedipus's haste as a symptom of his foreignness, and then as in line with the reversal of his position from guest to host even as Oedipus suddenly becomes a guide for others, having been guided for so long. As he puts it (Derrida and Dufourmantelle 2000, 109), "Perhaps it even harbors the theme of an organizing *contretemps,* the true master of the house throughout this scene of final hospitality." But my impression is that Oedipus's haste — though it has effects on his relation to, his farewells with, and his separation from his children — is much more intrinsically a sign of his burgeoning relationship to, and even identification with, the divine, as we explore below. If so, then what does it mean to suggest that Oedipus's other relationships have been voided by his alignment with the divine, that his prior identities are supplemented or perhaps even replaced by it, that his previous markers of embodiment are shed too as he enters into this identification? Furthermore, what is the force of suggesting that this newly divine-adjacent identity is the source of a temporal pull, the very notion of haste, and thence the lateness, urgency, delay that Derrida discovers there? Rather than leaning simply on the notion of divinity as an end in itself, one might ask whether divinity that is as abstracted as we find it here is not really an acute configuration of human importance — a way of making meaning, directionality, out of wandering. How, again, do we find paths, we whose borders have been blurred out of existence? We invent new directions, and we rush toward them.

Thus, in counterpoint to Derrida's close attentiveness to the absences left by Oedipus's death, I would like to draw attention to several important presences in *Oedipus at Colonus*. One is just the protracted presence of the play itself: at 1,779 lines, it is by far the longest of Sophocles's extant plays,[4] suggesting that early audiences might have also experienced a sense of delay as the ending seemed to loom ahead but remain at an unexpected distance. Over the course of this exceptional length, there are several large-scale and pervasive transformations of relations: Oedipus, once led, now leads; once cursed, now he blesses. These changes are reflected even on a sensory and elemental level, as light itself is addressed and reconfigured. For in Oedipus's new state, it becomes a form of touch rather than visuality: "O light without light, before you were once mine, but now my body [*demas*] touches [*haptetai*] you for the last time!" (1550–51). The body of Oedipus is the nominal subject here: through it, his perspective, unseeing and unseeable, is brought into focus. As Derrida (Derrida and Dufourmantelle 2000, 103–5) comments,

> the blind man weeps for the *tangible* light, a light caressed, a caressing sun. The day touched him, he was in contact with

---

4   The next longest extant Sophoclean play is *Oedipus Tyrannus* at 1,530 lines, unless the final choral statement is spurious, in which case it is 1,522 lines long. Of course, our extant plays represent only a small fraction of the plays actually produced by Sophocles, so the observation of exceptionality is necessarily speculative.

it, this light both tangible and touching. A warmth touched him invisibly. What he is going to be deprived of in secrecy, at the moment of this encrypting, of this encrypting of encrypting, at the moment when he is going to be hidden away buried in a hideaway, is the extraordinary contact of a light.

While Derrida's focus quickly turns to the deprivation of light — the secret, the crypt, the burial (if indeed there is to be a burial) — we should also take note of what is gained by Oedipus's particular, unique experience and expression thereof. Through Oedipus's apostrophe at a moment of imminent separation, light is reconfigured not as a spectacle of which he has been deprived, but rather as a source of warmth which he has grasped. What other hidden presences — outwardly imperceptible but known by the body — are uncovered by Oedipus? Derrida's reading of Oedipus's death focuses largely on his last speech and on the brief scene of mourning (mourning mourning) between Antigone and Ismene that closes the play. But in between these two scenes comes a lengthy, fascinating speech by a messenger who has witnessed the final moments of Oedipus's life before his departure to disappearance. As the messenger himself asserts at the beginning and at the end of his speech (1586 and 1665), this departure has been a most wondrous occurrence, fitting to the most wondrous of men. The messenger's description of this event is an invitation to consider a range of embodied experiences that are triggered by delay itself, by a pause in the moment *before* the instance of significance. This kind of delay, this pause, deserves a place in the narrative that Derrida weaves too.

In the messenger's speech, we find that Oedipus's path to death is carefully laid through a "wealth of ritual detail" (Kowalzig 2006, 82). The passage that describes this scene is too long to cover entirely here, but suffice it to say that the specifics are framed as important — the particular places where Oedipus positions himself ("the way leading downward, rooted by bronze steps to the earth […] midway between it and the Leaping Rock, by the hollow pear shrub, apart from the tomb of marble, he sat down,"⁵ 1590–91 and 1595–97), the particular physical state he is in, and the request he makes (1596–99):

> next he loosened his filthy clothes
> and then, calling to his children, bid them to bring
> from flowing water enough for washing and drink-offerings

He is dressed in squalid clothing but now at last he *eluse* (frees) himself of them, much as a "word" (he later says, though without identifying the word) *luei* (frees) his children of their burdens (1616). He asks for flowing water (i.e., water from a flowing source), meaning water that is clean, cleansing, kinetic, in a state of change, and thus capable of effecting change. When Oedipus has used this water to make a drink-offering to the gods, and has been washed and dressed in clean clothing, the messenger states that "he had the pleasure of doing everything and there was nothing undone of what he desired" (1604–5). What follows then is a divine summons via a thunderbolt from Zeus, which spurs the weeping of Oedipus's daughters, his embracing them, and his announcement of his approaching demise (1592–615). The moments, then, leading to the death of Oedipus are spent in an extravagance of ritual and intimate exchange. Moreover, the passage is deeply concerned with Oedipus's embodied and affective experiences (cf. Telò 2020, 47). We see here transformations and even synesthetic conversions, as though this moment just before death, this final, significant delay, is itself a time-space of open possibilities.

In *Archive Feelings: A Theory of Greek Tragedy*, Mario Telò shows the centrality of the body of Oedipus in the play, not just as a sign or symbol but also "as a repository of affective experiences" (2020, 47). These experiences encompass his *pathai* (feelings) as well as the seeming imprint of time upon his flesh, by way of filth that has settled into his skin and clothes. As Telò (2020, 48) writes:

---

5   The translations from the Greek are my own.

Materializing time that has "accompanied" Oedipus, the grime sedimented on his clothing has supplied him with a coeval, symbiotic friend and a home, a compensation for his social exclusion. […] The accreted filth, which embodies what remains of the experiences heaped on Oedipus's body, is itself — like the tattered clothing it coats and the body the clothing imperfectly shelters — an archive of *pathai* that disseminates live, albeit repellent, sensations. […] These dispersed sensations are the traces of the archive on Oedipus's skin.

If the "filth" on Oedipus's body are the traces of time and experience, indeed of his "archive," what then is the significance of the washing away of this dirt that has signified time and experience, which in this case (in every case?) constitutes an irreplaceable passage through life? Telò views Theseus's desire to purify Oedipus as the ambition to make of him a talisman, to strip him of human properties and archive him for the future protection of Athens.[6] It is surely true that such a trade-off is represented as central to the dilemmas of the play — the reciprocal gestures between Oedipus and Theseus and, thus, Thebes and Athens, as well as between the realms of mortality and immortality.

But it is also the case that Oedipus himself invites the stripping down of body and selfhood that precedes his death, and that even his oddly disembodied (or disembodying) death is represented as spurred by his own desire, which Telò insightfully reads as his drive to return to the instant of infancy before language, before the formation of self through a painful break from wholeness (2020, 50): a dream of a stage maybe best represented here by Oedipus's feeling of his body caressing the light, as quoted above. Perhaps it is in this completeness that we may contextualize the messenger's summation of what he observes,

---

6 See Telò (2020, 45, 48, and 63) and his evocative description of the dirt itself: "Both human and non-human, living and non-living, the dirt impressed on Oedipus's skin, the bodily surface that, in *OC*, constitutes its own contagious archive, figures the traces of his (and tragedy's) never-fully-dormant experiences" (45).

that "there was nothing undone of what he desired." This sense of fulfillment is true to such an extent that even Antigone later pronounces that Oedipus died in "precisely the way one could most hold in desire" (1679) and again (1705–9):

> He died in the foreign land
> he wanted; he has his well-shaded bed
> below forever;
> and he did not leave behind unlamented grief.

This is surely a privileged state of affairs, though Antigone still mourns (quite reasonably) for her own pain and loss. Her own view of her father's perspective, however, acknowledges *his* triumph — the sense of completion he has achieved even in the face of a moment that is framed as yet another delay.

Let us return, then, to the event, which includes also Oedipus's words to Theseus and his conjoining of Theseus's hands with those of his children. When the thunder of Zeus is heard, Oedipus pronounces himself soon-to-be dead, and he and his children weep together. They continue in this vein (1620–27):

> Embracing each other in this way,
> they all lamented with sobs. But when they came
> to the end of their weeping, and their cries no longer arose,
> there was silence; and suddenly the voice of someone
> called to him, so that everyone's hair stood
> suddenly on end, fearing dreadfully,
> for the god called him over and over:
> "Oh, you, you, Oedipus, why are we delaying
> our departure? For a long time there has been delay from
>   you."

Oedipus is beckoned to his death by a disembodied voice that invites him into the suspended state of hero cult — a not-quite death. As I have argued elsewhere, the voice that calls Oedipus is both strange and singular, as far as divine voices go.[7] For one thing, the voice identifies itself as no particular god, only as part of a "we" and an action alongside Oedipus himself—in Greek the words are *ti mellomen / khōrein* ("why are we in the state of being about to, and yet not, going?") On this point, Karl Reinhardt (1979, 233) has written the following:

> The "we" (which implies the joint nature of what is happening) with its terrifying yet tender kind of intimacy, partly involving Oedipus yet somehow at the same time mysteriously outside him, has no parallel in the entire range of divine voices of all ages and all religions which those who have been favoured by the gods have heard descending from heaven at the moment of their death.

What is the effect of this divinity's interpellation of Oedipus—a heavy-handed *ō houtos houtos, Oidipous* ("hey you"), followed by a pointed direct address, and then an oddly inclusive "we"? Oedipus is interpellated and identified, but only in the moments before he is to be subsumed into the strangely encompassing existence of the forthcoming "we," an absorption that Oedipus is simultaneously accused of delaying, as though he has been struggling to hold onto the singular selfhood that will soon be lost. In linguistic terms, this is a first-person plural inclusive pronoun, which turns Oedipus into a "self-ascriber" alongside the divinity (see Wechsler 2010, 333). Oedipus, against or at least beyond his will, is being identified, or sucked into an identity, in partnership with this force: it pulls him both into death and past it, since his fate in fact rests in the hazy, liminal space of hero cult, a future gestured at consistently by the play as an "institution [...] in the making" (Henrich 1993, 165).

---

[7] See Nooter (2012, 173–77) on this scene and on the divine voice as performing a "reverse apostrophe, addressing an identified presence from an undefined absence" (176).

Derrida (1995b, 41–42) writes also of the imposition of such "we"s in the form of addresses, particularly when applied to infants or to the dead, who cannot truly reply or refuse to reply:

> The violence of this *communal* dissymmetry remains at once extraordinary and, precisely, most *common.* It is the origin of the *common,* happening each time we address someone, each time we call them while *supposing,* that is to say while *imposing* a "we," and thus while inscribing the other person into this situation of an at once spectral and patriarchic nursling.

The idea of using "we" not as a first-person subject but as sublimating a second-person address, and thus as an imposition as Derrida suggests, or an interpellation as Louis Althusser might call it, can be thought of as the dark side of this linguistic set-up. Forces beyond Oedipus's control tell him what he is becoming.

Yet one cannot help but notice the overall, rather warmhearted "we-ness" of the whole enterprise: the sisters and their father mourn tenderly together just before his death; Oedipus and Theseus make sacred covenants; and Oedipus joins the hands of Theseus, now a surrogate son, with those of his daughters. Even the voice of the god that initiates the final steps to Oedipus's death may be slightly aggravated but nonetheless strikes a respectful note and allows Oedipus a last chat with his companions before he voluntarily sends his daughters away to complete his death in the apotheotic manner that is appropriate to him. When death comes at last, the messenger who is reporting this scene adds with some awe that "no fiery thunderbolt / of the god achieved it and no / hurricane stirred up from the sea" (1658–60), but rather that the way of his death was swift and silent, and unknown to anyone except Theseus.[8] Indeed, so unimpinging has this death been that it seems almost as though

---

8   In a similar vein, Antigone approvingly observes thereafter that her father died not by Ares (that is, war) or by the sea, but by some invisible doom (1679–82).

a kindly chaperone has come for Oedipus, or as if the earth itself has generously opened to receive him (1661–62).

Long goodbyes before death are not otherwise unknown in Greek tragedy — we see much the same sort of scene in Euripides's *Alcestis,* for example. But the thematization of the delay before death through the verb *mellomen* — a deferral, hesitation, or lingering *as such* — is unique.[9] One of the qualities of the divine voice that names this delay and also brings it to an end is that it is unidentified — a part of Oedipus, yet not him; or, to turn it around: not him, yet not anyone else. This ground-zero quality of the voice lends its presence a sense of abstraction, as if it is less a personality newly introduced (an impatient Hermes, say) and more an adverbial aspect of the whole scene, the entire situation itself of being on the verge of mortality — being right there, all ready to go, and yet not going; all ready to act, and yet not acting; all ready to change, and yet not changing; *all ready and yet not.* I have written elsewhere about this verb *mellō,* a word of several usages that all accrue around the denoting of existence in the time-space before something else (Nooter 2023). This time-space can be but a hairsbreadth, and *mellō* can often just as well be considered a periphrastic part of a greater verbal phrase, like the English phrase "going to," in, for example, "I'm going to eat breakfast on the couch." Yet at other times, the verb outpaces its periphrastic function and becomes a deferral, or even an impediment toward the action of the infinitive verb. (We have this too in English: "have you called your mother?" "I'm *going* to.") This particular use of the verb, *mellō* as delay, is intrinsically linked to tragedy, wherein action itself often becomes a problem, a cause for handwringing or concern.[10] Tragic heroes from Orestes to Hamlet dally in the void that gapes in the *before.*

---

9 For a different perspective on *mellō,* see Telò's chapter in this volume.
10 Liddell, Scott, and Jones (1996), s.v. μέλλω: "III. *to be always going to do* without ever doing: hence, *delay, put off,* freq. in Trag. […] in this signif. usu. folld. by pres. infin."

Derrida: Dallying in Delay

But the delay, the *mellomen,* the *à venir* opened up by Oedipus's temporal margin before death should, I think, be theorized differently — an attempt that brings me back to Derrida. For what happens to Oedipus in these moments is a very active form of life, a ritualization of it even, a standardization, a laying down of custom, a clasping of bodies and hands, an impressing of codes that takes us from the concerns of Derrida's *Of Hospitality* to the worries and ambitions of his *Archive Fever.* Here, Derrida frequently insists that archives are not about the past (1995b, 36):

> The question of the archive is not, we repeat, a question of the past. It is not the question of a concept dealing with the past that might *already* be at our disposal, *an archivable concept of the archive.* It is a question of the future, the question of the future itself, the question of a response, of a promise and of a responsibility for tomorrow.

Here, Derrida insists that it is always the future at stake in acts of archiving, since to archive is to consign, define, command, and institutionalize. And yet an animating anxiety of Derrida's *Archive Fever* is his uncertainty about what his own technologies of impression make of his own presence, his own archiving of his own future. Witness his account of the standard self-archivization he has performed even to construct the sentences of this lecture (Derrida 1995b, 25–26):

> Without waiting, I have spoken to you of my computer, of the little portable Macintosh on which I have begun to write. For it has not only been the first substrate to support all of these words. On a beautiful morning in California a few weeks ago, I asked myself a certain question, among so many others. […] Was it not at this very instant that, having written something or other on the screen, the letters remaining as if suspended and floating yet at the surface of a liquid element, I pushed a certain key to "save" a text undamaged, in a hard and last-

ing way, to protect marks from being erased, so as to ensure in this way salvation and *indemnity,* to stock, to accumulate, and, in what is at once the same thing and something else, to make the sentence available in this way for printing and for reprinting, for reproduction? Does it change anything that Freud did not know about the computer? And where should the moment of suppression or of repression be situated in these new models of recording and impression, or printing?

We find Derrida in a state of contradicting affects and impulses. It is morning in California and beautiful, exactly the right time and space for a crush of paradoxes to rise up from Derrida's haptic encounter with the world.

His words, these precious thoughts that we ourselves are reading, "float" in a "liquid element," insubstantial to him as ghosts or shadows on a screen. Yet with just the impression of a fingertip or two, he finds that he can bring them into hard, lasting permanence: they will be saved, printed, and then printed again and again, dispassionately and endlessly reproduced, like the multiplying, terrifying brooms of the Sorcerer's Apprentice/ Mickey Mouse in Disney's *Fantasia* (a brilliant figure for the sort of mass production and reproduction of culture that Disney has so forcefully maneuvered).[11] Of course, many of us can "click save," as we might say, without the overweening danger of our words being endlessly reprinted and reproduced, but Derrida's fame — and thus his understanding of the likelihood of his words' lasting futurity — allows him access to a concern that is truly located in mortality, a mortality beyond the supposed rescue of *kleos,* or glory, that the Greeks dreamed up: his words can be easily stored up for the future, but this very ease dislocates them (and him) from his own presence and past. When we "click" save, or "send" emails, or "enter" a Zoom meeting,

---

11 Algar, Armstrong, and Beebe (2000; first published in 1940). The multiplying brooms resonate with states of mass production despite the fact that *The Sorcerer's Apprentice* was based on a 1797 poem "Der Zauberlehrling" by Johann Wolfgang von Goethe, who was presumably not concerned with this topic.

when all our verbs are now pale versions of their prior embodied selves, are we still our same selves, the ones we were before all this disembodying began? What future is there without our connection to the pasts we have constructed from the simpler techniques and technologies we knew before — the rituals we made and that made us in turn?

As you have seen, my interest lies not just in presenting Derrida's reading of Oedipus's death and his daughters' mourning in *Oedipus at Colonus,* but in supplementing it, in the hope of not only offering an interpretation that takes greater account of the actual scenes around Oedipus's death, but also tracing a richer set of implications for how we experience and construct mourning, selfhood, and our own future. The particular passages from two late books of Derrida that I have examined handle changes in technology, specifically ones that seem to the author to provoke shifts in his, or our, idea of space, time, and selfhood. As we have seen, Derrida is afraid that email transforms private into public space, thus evacuating possibilities of hospitality and a certain mode of ethical existence; he is afraid of endless archiving and thus a kind of accumulation and calcification of the self that distorts and separates us from past modes of the archiving unconscious. He insists, over and over again, that our future is at stake and he specifies that this is not *le futur* — a separate, distant kind of future — but *l'avenir,* "so as to point toward the coming of an event" (Derrida 1995b, 68). The future as a state of *it's coming* is, of course, nothing more than the present tense; to dally in the state of tragic *mellō* or delay, Hamlet-like, is to continue to inhabit the present and all its potentials, with almost excruciating attentiveness.

If we look into more recent history, a nearer sense of *it's coming* and the delay/dally before death, we find a stunning set of configurations in the performance of Bill T. Jones called "The Process of Becoming Infinite," which he performed as part of a TED production in 2016 (Jones 2017). Jones's nearly twenty-four-minute long performance revisits his past through an exploration of word, gesture, culture, and cliché, and considers the experience of aging and mortality, as he also commemorates his own ascendance to the age of sixty-four (with reference to the Beatles song, "When I'm Sixty-Four"). Jones ends the piece, his eyes closed, intoning in his signature deep, intense style of vocalization. He recounts a memory of himself as a small child performing one of his assigned tasks, namely the tossing of the corpses of small animals that showed up in the yard over an embankment. I quote here from 21:25 to the end of the performance:

> I am said to have said in the family lore: *that poll cat done paid off. He went spinning into infinity.*
>
> He went spinning into infinity.
>
> Betty, sweet Betty, are you spinning into infinity, girl? Arnie? Estella? Gus? Are you spinning into infinity?
>
> The movement is now going to stop. The names continue. Trisha Brown. Ralph Lemon. Bjorn Amelan. David Thomson. Janet Wong. Talli Jackson.
>
> The right hand is saying goodbye to you, ladies and gentlemen. The back of the neck is sweating. My time is out. My time is out. I'm spinning. I'm spinning, everybody. I'm spinning into infinity. We're all going to spin. We're all going to spin.
>
> And now the feet are still and the scapula slides down the back like the sweat on the bridge of my nose and no, mister sound man, the mic did not come off tonight. I'm spinning, spinning into infinity.
>
> I think, I think — *will you still feed me?* [singing] — I'm spinning. My feet are spreading out. I am the ocean. A man, a woman coughed. Goodbye, binary. Hello, future. I'm dreaming, Chris. I'm dreaming.

These final minutes bring together a number of threads: references to loved ones discussed in this performance (Betty, Arnie, his parents Estella and Gus), the convergence of the abstract (infinity, the future), and the grit of performative process (the back of the neck is sweating, the mic did not come off). He invites his audience to understand an analogy between the end of the performance and the end of life, the movements of the body as it stops performing *this* dance and the movements of our own bodies through time as they slow their own performances of life.

Of the two lists of names Jones offers, the first (which includes Betty and Arnie) are of people deceased, and the second (Trisha Brown, Ralph Lemon, and others) combine the dead and living; the first are called by their first names only and are known to us through Jones's present performance; the second list is pronounced more formally by their full names and consists of public figures from the world of choreography. Inasmuch as "spinning into infinity" is immediately marked out as meaning something like "heading toward the endlessness of death," Jones shows that both the dead and the living share this state, and further identifies this ongoing state with his current, embodied, tired, sweaty state onstage. He is standing right there, becoming ever more still, not literally spinning as it happens, but running out of time: spinning, spinning, saying goodbye and hello, creating of his audience a community to his living and his dying, his teetering at the precipice of that and this, the past of life and the future of death. He marks out this moment of his own mortality at an advanced age, and also reminds his audience that they, we, are all "spinning into infinity," all dallying before death. Our consciousness of this dally, this delay, is what allows us to create a commonality from the techniques we have available, while the dreaming lasts.

In closing, I want to suggest that what *Oedipus at Colonus* offers as exemplar is not merely the despair that Derrida reads there through his singular focus on the moment of the lost body, no more so than Jones offers only a reminder that death will come and nothing else. This loss of life as it has been known actually only preoccupies Sophocles's characters very briefly. In the play, death comes to be understood as the introduction of Oedipus into hero cult, and thus as a different, if somewhat disorienting, kind of death — a new technology of loss and mourning. We have seen that there is substantial focus in *Oedipus at Colonus* on the ritualization of Oedipus's death, his control over its parameters, his communality with his children, and his getting the death he has wanted — a death of dallying. As a latter-day audience to the play, we are invited to wonder whether these are the particular affordances of hero cult: the death-as-life, the afterlife not as an unknowable future (*le futur*), but rather as a still-unknowable extension of the lingering present (*l'avenir*) — this limitless respite.[12]

Well, fine, one might say, but does the direction in which their dead father has gone make a difference to the mourning children? As far as they are concerned, isn't dead dead, and isn't it still unknowable? To this, I would answer, yes, absolutely — except that Sophocles shows us something else, something more, not only here but also in *Ajax,* his other play that seems to offer its tragic hero up for hero cult. In that play too, a plot of deep division and recrimination unexpectedly resolves itself into one of commonality, of we-ness. In that case, we see the surprising turnabout of Odysseus from enemy (to the living Ajax) to friend (in his death):

And now I make it known to Teucer that, from this point,
whereas I was an enemy, so much shall he be a friend,
and that I wish to help bury this man in death
and to help bear the burden and leave nothing undone
of those deeds that mortals must perform for the best of
men.[13]

---

12 See Telò's introduction to this volume.
13 Sophocles, *Ajax* 1376–80. See Burian (1972) and Easterling (1988), on the use of "ritual words and actions" to bring the community together through shared values, and March (1991–1993, 30–32), on how the burial of Ajax rehabilitates him. Cf. Henrichs (1993) on the "ritual anomaly" presented by

Is it death itself that brings about this change? Or is it a new kind of death, an escape from the binary of now/then, mortal/immortal, into a "click save," where the body remains on the page invented by the dictates of hero cult? Ajax has been archived, and the result of his rescue in memory is a different kind of death and honor, a new community and commonality among his mourners, new paths for previously separate factions to cross to one another. Thus, while Derrida's focus on the future tends to concern fears about what is lost in selfhood, much as his discussion of "we"s looks to examples in which the "we" imposes itself and sublimates "you"s, I suggest that we (you?) concentrate also on what novel forms of commonality are gained, what new possibilities for the "we" are unleashed in and through our ongoing separation, even as we Zoom.

---

the play, and Kowalzig (2006, 85–91), on Sophocles's presentation of Ajax's hero cult vis-à-vis the Athenian context.

9

Steps in Time: Derrida's Impossible Hospitality and the Apocalyptic Future of Cormac McCarthy's *The Road*

Carol Dougherty

Pas d'hospitalité: no hospitality, step of hospitality. We are going. We are moving around: from transgression to transgression but also from digression to digression. What does that mean, this *step too many* and transgression, if, for the invited guest as much as for the visitor, the crossing of the threshold always remains a transgressive step? If it even has to remain so? And what is meant by this *step to one side*, digression? Where do these strange processes of hospitality lead? These interminable, uncrossable thresholds, and these aporias? It is as though we were going from one difficulty to another. Better or worse, and more seriously, from impossibility to impossibility. It is as though hospitality were the impossible: as though the law of hospitality defined this very impossibility.
— Jacques Derrida (Derrida and Dufourmantelle 2000, 75)

In many ways, the aporia that structures Jacques Derrida's meditation on the phrase *pas d'hospitalité* — its absence, its transgressions, its digressions — perfectly describes the narrative landscape of Cormac McCarthy's 2006 novel *The Road*. Forced on the road by an unnamed apocalyptic event, a man and his son must keep going, moving around; their prolonged attempt to survive harsh winter and roving cannibalistic gangs necessitates their repeated movement across uncrossable thresholds, crossings that are figured both as "a step too many," transgressions against the homes of former inhabitants, and a "step to one side," digressions from their destination, their march to the sea. Exhausted by the pair's determination to persevere, even as they move from difficulty to difficulty, indeed, and "more seriously, from impossibility to impossibility," the reader asks herself, "where do these strange processes of hospitality lead?" I propose to follow Derrida along McCarthy's post-apocalyptic road to explore the impossible hospitality of a world without the comfort and safety of houses—only their "interminable, uncrossable thresholds." Rather than attend to the ways that an absence of hospitality describes a post-apocalyptic world, however, I suggest that we notice how the novel also explores the opposite—revealing the experience of homelessness as the precondition, both ethical and imaginative, for defining hospitality, that is, our way of relating to others as others. The novel's aporetic conclusion—what are we to make of the boy's choice to join another family after the death of his father?—reduces the novel's protracted engagement with hospitality and its absence to the simple gesture of accepting *à venir* (what comes), a gesture that will, in the end, provide *l'avenir* (a future).

Pas d'Hospitalité: No Hospitality, Step of Hospitality

> "To offer hospitality" […] is it necessary to start from the certain existence of a dwelling, or is it rather only starting from the dislocation of the shelterless, the homeless, that the authenticity of hospitality can open up? Perhaps only the one who endures the experience of being deprived of a home can offer hospitality.
> —Anne Dufourmantelle (Derrida and Dufourmantelle 2000, 56)

The Road takes place in the desolate remains of a "barren, silent, godless" landscape scorched by some vague yet utterly devastating disaster, described only as a "long sheer of light and then a series of low concussions" (McCarthy 2006, 52). Stopping the clocks at 1:17, this apocalyptic event shattered all traces of human civilization along with the natural world; any remnants of a functioning social system have crumbled along with its physical infrastructure. All that remains are bands of marauding gangs roaming through the "wreckage of buildings strewn over the landscape and skeins of wire from the roadside poles garbled like knitting" (274). Amidst this desolation, a man and his boy, anonymous and shelterless, follow a burned, smoking road, across the "cauterized terrain" heading south in search of the sea and warmer temperatures. This is the only world the boy has known, born shortly after the disaster; his mother killed herself rather than try to live in this cold, cruel world, and so the boy travels with his father, "shuffling through the ash, each the other's world entire" (6).[1]

Like so many protagonists of Cormac McCarthy's novels, the man and his boy have no home.[2] And yet, the charred landscape of the novel is littered with the remains of domestic life: "a burned house in a clearing" (8), "aluminum houses" (14), "tall clapboard houses" (21), an "abandoned house" (28), an "old frame house" (68), a "solitary house in a field" (132), and "farmhouses in the field scoured of their paint and the clapboards spooned and sprung from the wallstuds" (177). Not fully erased from the landscape, these multiple iterations of a domesticated past form a powerful absent presence like "the shape of a carpet beneath the silty ash. Furniture shrouded in sheeting. Pale squares on the walls where paintings once had hung" (206). These houses no longer offer shelter to their occupants; rather,

---

[1] The wife explains her decision to kill herself: "Sooner or later they will catch us and they will kill us. They will rape me. They're raping him. They are going to rape us and kill us and eat us and you won't face it. You'd rather wait for it to happen. But I cant. I cant" (McCarthy 2006, 56).

[2] Witek (1994, 1): "Nearly all the protagonists in Cormac McCarthy novels flee from or lose their homes."

like other material objects littered across the bleak wasteland of the novel, they are, as Randall Wilhelm notes, mere "remnants shorn of their previous functions in a post-apocalyptic world" (2008, 129).

Indeed, McCarthy lingers over the physical structures of these houses, carefully describing their tall, palladian windows, brick loggias, or columned porticos, juxtaposing the protective promise of shelter offered by a house's physical architecture to the decay to be found inside, brought on by the force of nature and the absence of human occupation. For the man, these abandoned houses trigger frequent nostalgic digressions, allowing him to step aside in place and time — into a comfortable parlor where family members gather around the antique pump organ or into time spent by a young child sitting with his stuffed dog in a window seat overlooking the garden. Indeed, early on in the novel, they stop in front of the house in which the man grew up — "an old frame house with chimneys and gables and a stone wall" (McCarthy 2006, 25). Once they go inside, the man recalls memories of his life there with his family, memories that, as Gaston Bachelard has suggested,[3] are physically embodied by the house: "He felt with his thumb in the painted wood of the mantle the pinholes from tacks that had held stockings forty years ago" (26). As they walk through the house, the man lets himself be diverted by memories of his childhood, experiences that are linked to particular rooms of the house:

> This is where we used to have Christmas when I was a boy. [...] On cold winter nights when the electricity was out in a storm we would sit at the fire here me and my sisters, doing our homework. The boy watched him. Watched shapes claiming him he could not see. (26)[4]

---

[3] Bachelard (1992, 8): "Of course, thanks to the house, a great many of our memories are housed, and if the house is a bit elaborate, if it has a cellar and a garret, nooks and corridors, our memories have refuges that are all the more clearly delineated."

[4] Compare Bachelard (1992, 15): "But we are very surprised, when we return to the old house, after an odyssey of many years, to find that the

The boy, however, has never pinned Christmas stockings to a mantle and has no siblings to help with homework; he has never lived in any kind of domestic structure — stone walls or no — and for him the house holds no such memories of cozy family life; these are shapes he cannot see, and he is eager to leave: "We should go, Papa. Can we go?" (27). In fact, he only reluctantly crosses the thresholds of these abandoned, decrepit houses in the first place, concerned that their occupants might return, "really scared" of what they may find within.

For the boy, the wide-open doors of these abandoned dwellings offer neither a familiar sign of welcome nor an opportunity for a nostalgic digression, a step back in time. In his eyes, they represent a transgression — this is not their house, someone might come — a step too many and too far across "interminable, uncrossable thresholds." What represents a welcome invitation for the man signals an ominous trap for his boy (205):

> Why is the door open, Papa?
> It just is. It's probably been open for years. Maybe the last people propped it open to carry their things out.

Janus-like in function — facilitating both easy exits and inviting entrances — the doors that enable their movement in and out of the domestic landscape of the novel stand as a physical manifestation of the simultaneously digressive and transgressive mobilities that structure its interrogation of the absence of hospitality.

Indeed the boy's worst fears about what lies on the other side of the door are materialized in the "once grand house" on the outskirts of a small town in which the man and his boy stumble upon a horrific tableau of people waiting to be slaughtered and eaten: "naked people, huddled against the back wall, shielding

---

most delicate gestures, the earliest gestures suddenly come alive, are still faultless. In short, the house we were born in has engraved within us the hierarchy of the various functions of inhabiting that particular house, and all the other houses are but variations on a fundamental theme. The word habit is too worn a word to express this passionate liaison of our bodies, which do not forget, with an unforgettable house."

their faces with their hands, and a man with his legs gone to the hip and the stumps of them blackened and burnt" (110).[5] In defiance of the hunger that had led them to open the basement door ("We've got to find something to eat," 106), the man and his boy scream in sheer terror at the sight, frantically scrambling back across that threshold both literal and ethical ("We wouldnt ever eat anybody, would we?," 128). What started out as a search for food and, perhaps, a welcome detour from their desperate travels into a genteel hospitable past, rapidly turns into the most horrific transgression imaginable — a line they repeatedly refuse to cross.

And so, a bit later in their journey, when the boy and his father stumble upon another door leading into another basement of sorts, the boy again resists ("'Dont open it, Papa,' he whispered" 134), and the man again insists, attempting to reassure a terrified boy (137):

> This door looks like the other door, he said. But it's not. I know you're scared. That's okay. I think there may be things in there and we have to take a look. There's no place else to go. This is it.

Here, however, the anticipated transgression turns into a welcome digression — not death at the hands of man-eating outlaws, but a temporary respite from their travels, a bunker filled with enough food to keep them alive for a long time.

> Crate upon crate of canned goods. Tomatoes, peaches, beans, apricots. Canned hams. Corned beef. Hundreds of gallons of water in ten gallon plastic jerry jugs. Paper towels, toilet

---

[5] Snyder (2008, 80): "This plantation house represents the antithesis of hospitality with its perverse welcome-to-the-larder orientation, complete with a lookout system which warns its decidedly inhospitable inhabitants of the approach of visitors and with a basement full of captives waiting to be slaughtered and eaten." On pages 74–75, Snyder reviews the different encounters in the novel within the framework of hospitality.

paper, paper plates. Plastic trashbags stuffed with blankets. (138)

By contrast to the extreme inversion of hospitality that the cannibal basement represents, this plentiful, undefended bunker might be an expression of Derrida's concept of unconditional hospitality — not just because it offers the man and his boy plentiful food and comfort, no strings attached, but also because of the danger that constrains their experience of it.[6] They run the very real risk that others will come and find their refuge, and if so, these new arrivals will not be guests to be hosted in turn, but hostile invaders eager to destroy the place, stealing everything or killing everyone. This is a bunker after all, not a real home; it is a structure designed as a temporary refuge, a strategic defense against the potential violence and destruction that both enables and constrains Derrida's vision of absolute hospitality, the hostility contained within hospitality.

And so, what initially appears as a "tiny paradise" (150) quickly threatens to become a tomb, the ultimate digression, and the man finally recognizes the bunker as the death-trap that the boy feared it to be from the beginning: "The faintly lit hatchway lay in the dark of the yard like a grave yawning at judgment day in some old apocalyptic painting" (155).[7] Not their ultimate destination, functioning as both transgression and digression, the bunker embodies "those strange processes of hospitality" (150) to which the novel has been leading us along. It is not until they reach this mid-century American fantasy of home — ironically, a confirmation of the unconditional hospitality that the man has

---

[6] Derrida (1998a, 71): "For unconditional hospitality to take place you have to accept the risk of the other coming and destroying the place, initiating a revolution, stealing everything, or killing everyone. That is the risk of pure hospitality."

[7] Derrida and Dufourmantelle (2000, 85–125). The novel lays the groundwork here for framing the man's own death within the discourse of hospitality — naturalizing this ultimate transition as a return to the earth, a return to his family, in ways that resonate with Derrida's meditation on hospitality, death, and mourning in Sophocles's *Oedipus at Colonus* and *Antigone*.

been insisting that house and home can provide and a place that the boy grudgingly comes to recognize as home when he notes "I wish we could live here" (151) — that the man finally comes to terms with the conditionality of his former domestic life and wishes they had never found the bunker in the first place.

As we accompany the man and his boy through the novel, moving through its post-apocalyptic landscape, staggering from digression to transgression, from transgression to digression, we come to see it as a world devoid of traditional, domesticated hospitality, *pas d'hospitalité*. By taking both a step back in time and a step too far in ethics, we begin to wonder, along with Derrida, "where do these strange processes of hospitality lead? These interminable, uncrossable thresholds, and these aporias?" (Derrida and Dufourmantelle 2000, 75). Can there be hospitality without a house? From a position of homelessness — without shelter, without hosts to welcome us? Rather than offer the reader the absence of house and home as an expression of apocalyptic decline, the novel suggests, as does Anne Dufourmantelle, that it is only through the impossibility of shelter that the "authenticity of hospitality can be opened up" (in Derrida and Dufourmantelle 2000, 56).

The man responds to these impossibilities by obsessively trying to recreate for his boy what he once had, camping, squatting in abandoned buildings, scavenging a facsimile of a domestic and social world that no longer exists.[8] The boy, on the other hand, born into an unaccommodated world, looks for another way to connect with others, "as though hospitality were the impossible: as though the law of hospitality defined this very impossibility" (Derrida and Dufourmantelle 2000, 75). And so, the man and the boy continue their journey, their slow walk to the sea, and the novel embraces this challenge as the precondition for articulating an authentic, peripatetic (rather than domesticated) experience of hospitality, for, as Derrida suggests,

---

8   He is an inveterate homemaker. When there are no abandoned houses in which to squat, they camp. He improvises, finding or making shelter, scavenging for food, making tools, and building fires.

"if there was no aporia we wouldn't walk, we wouldn't find our way; path-breaking implies aporia. This impossibility to find one's way is the condition of ethics" (Derrida 1998, 73).

"Let Us Say Yes": Gestures of Hospitality

> Let us say yes *to who or what turns up*, before any determination, before any anticipation, before any *identification* whether or not it has to do with a foreigner, an immigrant, an invited guest, or an unexpected visitor, whether or not the new arrival is the citizen of another country, a human, animal, or divine creature, a living or dead thing, male or female.
> — Jacques Derrida (Derrida and Dufourmantelle 2000, 77)

It is their fear that someone else, one of the bad guys, might come across their fantastic refuge that makes staying in the well-stocked bunker too dangerous for the man and his boy. And yet, as they prepare to set out once again along the road, the boy does not want to leave (McCarthy 2006, 151):

> I wish we could live here.
> I know.
> We could be on the lookout.
> We are on the lookout.
> What if some good guys came?
> Well, I dont think we're likely to meet any good guys on the road.
> We're on the road.
> I know.

For the man, "to be on the lookout" means to be scared, watchful, cautious about the people they meet or the circumstances they encounter. As they march determinedly on down the road, he perpetually "glasses" the horizon before them, trying valiantly to be prepared for unexpected trouble, all the while keeping an eye on the rear-view mirror attached to their grocery cart for those threats that might come from behind. It is a survival strategy developed for the current circumstances — one that has kept them alive so far, and one that he tries to teach his son to embrace, "Maybe you should always be on the lookout. If trouble comes when you least expect it then maybe the thing to do is to always expect it." But when the boy asks, "Do you always expect it, Papa?," the man acknowledges the limits of this approach and wearily replies, "I do. But sometimes I might forget to be on the lookout" (151).

The boy, on the other hand, is on the lookout for something else, for someone else — not in fearful anticipation of the dangers posed to him and his father, not just in case they encounter one of "the good guys," but also for how they might help others. Whether it is a man struck by lightning, "as burntlooking as the country, his clothing scorched and black" (49), or "a boy about his age, wrapped in an out-sized wool coat, with the sleeves turned back" (84), the man's son wants to embrace this fellow traveler ("Cant we help him? Papa?," 50). And as the novel progresses, we find that the boy is not content to offer a handout of food or clothes, he wants to extend hospitality to their fellow travelers in the true sense — to spend time together.

Not long after they leave the bunker, the man and his boy encounter someone else along the road, "an old man, small and bent" (161), filthy, foul-smelling, carrying an old army rucksack on his back and tapping his way with a stick. Again, his father tries to avoid contact with the man; he wants to keep moving, but the boy wants to help: "Maybe we could give him something to eat" (163). Reluctantly, the man digs out a can of fruit cocktail, opens it and hands it to the boy to give to the old man, limiting even this most minimal act of generosity ("He's not getting a spoon," 163), which the man greedily consumes. But the boy wants to do more than give him food and he cautiously suggests, "We could cook something on the stove. He could eat with us" (165). "You're talking about stopping. For the night," the man counters, objecting to this escalation of hospitality, but he reluctantly agrees that the man, who says his name is Ely, can eat with them and stay the night. Ely is as suspicious of accepting the invitation as the man is about extending it, but in the end the three of them share food, conversation, and the next morning, they go their separate ways.

Where the man sees these unexpected encounters with strangers as a source of danger and competition for their scarce resources, the boy greets them as an opportunity. With Derrida, he embraces the opportunity to "say yes to who or what turns up," and we might productively read the novel's juxtaposition of the tension between man and boy over how to treat others in light of Derrida's assertion that the willingness to be open to the unknown other represents hospitality in its truest sense, one that stands in an inextricably impossible relationship to the rules and conditions that we attach to everyday social interactions.[9] Just so, in *The Road,* in the absence of the who and where of hospitality (safe houses occupied by generous hosts), the boy's willingness to say yes highlights the essence of hospitality in Derrida's absolute terms, as a pure gesture of welcome. The novel distinguishes the boy's instinctive decision to welcome the other, no matter who or what it is, from the physical and social conditions (scarce food, absence of shelter, no family obligations) with which the notion of hospitality is encumbered by his father.[10] In a post-apocalyptic world, from the position of peripatetic homelessness, the boy replaces the conditions (place,

---

9   Derrida and Dufourmantelle (2000, 25): "Absolute hospitality requires that I open up my home and that I give not only to the foreigner (provided with a family name, with the social status of being a foreigner, etc.), but to the absolute, unknown, anonymous other, and that I *give place* to them, that I let them come, that I let them arrive, and take place in the place I offer them, without asking of them either reciprocity (entering into a pact) or even their names. The law of absolute hospitality commands a break with hospitality by right with law or justice as rights." For Derrida, these two forms of hospitality belong to two radically discontinuous orders that coexist in paradoxical or aporetic relations that are at once heterogeneous and indissociable.

10 It is interesting to note how the novel engages with what Derrida sees as the indissociable tensions between unconditional and conditional hospitality by offering two scenes in which a key element of the hospitable relationship is suppressed. In the bunker scene, the act of hospitality is defined by the place: the boy and his father experience food, a place to stay, but without hosts; in the scene with Ely (and also at the novel's end), on

prior relationships) of hospitality with pure action: as though, to follow Dufourmantelle, "the place in question in hospitality were a place originally belonging to neither host nor guest, but to the gesture by which one of them welcomes the other — even and above all if he is himself without a dwelling from which this welcome could be conceived" (Derrida and Dufourmantelle 2000, 60–62).

The novel ends when the man can go no further, he cannot take another step — neither a step too far, nor to the side. Recognizing this as the place where he will die, he tells his boy to go on without him: "You need to keep going. You dont know what might be down the road." (McCarthy 2006, 278). After staying with his father's corpse for three days, the boy walks out to the road to see who or what's coming, and once again, the boy chooses to say yes — this time to a family who welcomes him, who helps him. All the work that the novel has been doing exploring the impossibilities of hospitality on the road, elaborating both its transgressions and its digressions, has been leading us to this single gesture of welcoming the unexpected, of being welcomed by the other.

Standing in the middle of the road rather than on the threshold of an abandoned house, the boy has found a way to say yes, to keep the metaphorical if not literal door open to hospitality, to a life with others. And yet, I do not mean to suggest a utopian reading of the novel's conclusion, nor do I agree with those who emphasize the novel's messianic force.[11] There is no reason to think things will suddenly go well for the boy and his new family; the world is still uninhabitable. Rather, with the boy and Derrida (2000, 6),

Now we are beginning or pretending to open the door <that impossible door, sublime or not>. We are on the threshold.

---

the other hand, there is no physical structure of hospitality, only (a small amount of) food and social contact provided by the hosts.

11 Elmore and Elmore (2018, 146n2) collect the bibliography on utopian readings of the novel's conclusion as well as those who find a sense of redemptive hope for humanity at the novel's end.

We do not know what Hospitality is. Not yet.[12]

It is precisely the absence of and transgression against what traditionally defines hospitality — a physical house, plentiful food, family and friends — that pushes us, as readers, to engage with the problem of hospitality alongside the man and his boy, attending to their struggles as they keep moving from impossibility to impossibility down the road.[13] For, as Derrida contends, when the path is clear, nothing is to be learned, nothing new is to be imagined. Instead, he calls for a "certain experience and experiment of the possibility of the impossible, the testing of the aporia from which one may invent the only possible invention, the impossible invention" (Derrida 1992b, 41).[14] The end of *The Road* offers the reader just such an impossible invention: an act of pure hospitality, the unconditional welcome of the boy into a new family upon the death of his father — but one without a home, in a world and time defined by the experience of walking, a perpetual state of undecidability, ever on the precipice of new dangers, or a recovered experience of home, or just good luck somewhere down the road, but never quite there yet.

"Making Time": Steps in Time

> If "making time" is equivalent in Hebrew to "inviting," what is this strange understanding of language which demonstrates that in order to produce time there have to be two of you, or rather there has to be some otherness, a breaking in on the

---

12 The translator notes that angular brackets indicate comments made by Derrida during the symposium and added to the text by its original editors.
13 See Derrida and Dufourmantelle 2000, 149–51: "The problem of hospitality is coextensive with the ethical problem. It is always about answering for a dwelling place, for one's identity, one's space, one's limits, for the ethos as abode, habitation, house, hearth, family, home."
14 See also Derrida (2000a, 5): This aporia is the principle "of both the constitution and the implosion of the concept of hospitality."

original other? The future is given as being what comes to us
from the other, from what is absolutely surprising.
— Anne Dufourmantelle (Derrida and Dufourmantelle 2000, 76)

An act of hospitality can only be poetic.
— Jacques Derrida (Derrida and Duformantelle 2000, 2)

Saying yes to whoever comes, to that which is *à venir* (to come), is to say yes to *l'avenir* (the future). Scholarly attention to the end of *The Road* and its representation of the end of the world has focused on the "peculiar temporality of the novel's post-apocalyptic vision" — namely, its inability to imagine a future.[15] For these scholars, McCarthy's apocalyptic imaginary represents a world that has been exhausted, one that has taken the powers of utopian figuration away with everything else.[16] Others see the messianic gesture of hope embodied in the boy's encounter with a new family at the novel's conclusion not as the articulation of true hope for new world but rather as some kind of literary compensation for the bleakness of its failure to imagine such a future.[17]

I want to argue that *The Road* does in fact represent an act of imagination — not a vision of what the future will look like in a post-apocalyptic world, but rather the possibility that there can

---

15 See, e.g., Schleusener (2017, 2), who discusses "the peculiar temporality (and seeming 'worldlessness') of the novel's post-apocalyptic setting, which is expressed, among other things, in the inability to think and imagine a genuine future." See also Fisher (2009, 2), who contends that while once dystopian novels and films "were exercises in such acts of imagination — the disasters they depicted acting as a narrative pretext for the emergence of different ways of living," today, the world that is projected in such works "seems more like an extrapolation or exacerbation of ours than an alternative to it."

16 Schleusener (2017, 22) reads the novel's absence of futurity in the context of neoliberalism and what he, following Fredric Jameson, calls "late-capitalism's anti-utopian tendencies." See also Radcliffe's chapter in this volume.

17 E.g., Dorson (2016, 184–85). Skrimshire (2011), on the other hand, discusses the destabilizing sense of time expressed by the novel's engagement with the notion of the messianic.

be one. In this respect, I take Derrida's insistence that "an act of hospitality can only be poetic" to mean not only that these acts are fictive, discursive rather than empirical, but also that they are creative, productive. As Dufourmantelle elaborates on Derrida's reading of hospitality and temporality, "The future is given as being what comes to us from the other, from what is absolutely surprising." Along these lines, the novel conjures a sense of futurity out of a notion of hospitality that has been forged from absence, transgression, and digression, one that comes instead from pure gesture, from saying yes to who or what turns up. The novel explores the impossibilities of hospitality to suggest that the solution to the problem of hospitality is not spatial but temporal — or rather poetic and temporal: the solution to the problem that the steps of hospitality pose is one of "making time."

Indeed a peculiar sense of temporality does infuse the novel. It revels in a sense of pastness or obsolescence — not just its abandoned houses but at every level of human existence: rusted tools, disappeared birds and fish, the man's dead wife. And although a concept of time — at least as the man has always engaged with it — has disappeared with the world (stopped clocks, no lists of things to be done, a dead baby), the man and his boy continue to walk together, down the road, toward the sea, improvising one day at a time. Days are measured by the amount of food remaining, the ability to wake up in the morning, and the strength and breath to put one foot in front of the other. This is time made possible because there are two of them. If he cannot promise or create a future for his boy, the man is determined to extend the present, to make sure there is time for the boy, whatever that looks like at the end of the world.[18]

* * *

---

[18] See Skrimshire (2011, 5–6) on the novel's juxtaposition of competing experiences of temporality by the man and his boy.

If the man is trying to stretch time for his boy, Ely is a man whose lack of family or home, his perpetual itinerancy has led him to step outside of time. He is not interested in the past nor does he worry about the future. As Ely tells the boy and his father, "People were always getting ready for tomorrow. I didnt believe in that. Tomorrow wasnt getting ready for them. It didnt even know they were there" (168). When the man asks Ely if he wishes he would die, the old man replies, "No. But I might wish I had died. When you're alive you've always got that ahead of you" (169). It is not just his perpetual mobility or the obsolescence of the world that he once knew, but also his social isolation that leads Ely to erase the future along with the past. And yet the sight of a child, the boy, does appear to have thrown him temporarily, temporally (172):

> I've not seen a fire in a long time, that's all. I live like an animal. You dont want to know the things I've eaten. When I saw that boy I thought that I had died. […] I didnt know what he was. I never thought to see a child again. I didnt know that would happen.

Alone on the road, without the civilizing force of fire, and all that it symbolizes in the novel about being the "good guys" (129), Ely no longer has to answer for anything or to anyone — there is no reciprocity to his encounter with the man and boy, no offer or expectation of future hospitality. He takes their food without offering anything in return; he gives no straight answers to the man's questions, not even his real name. When the man asks Ely why he does not thank the boy for giving him food, the beggar replies, "I wouldnt have given him mine" (173). Conversely, Ely's rejection of temporality, his disinterest in the past and suspicions about the future, are reflected in his refusal of company: "It's better to be alone" (172).

It turns out that what has kept the man and boy going is not just the man's ability to scavenge and improvise, but also that there are two of them, something the man's wife knew from the beginning. About to kill herself, she predicts that her husband will not survive for himself (57), but if he does, it will be for the boy, because of the boy. But *The Road* is no heartwarming tale of an estranged father and son who eventually come to appreciate each other, bonded in recognition of their common experiences on the road and able to survive the challenges of the journey thanks to this rekindled paternal connection. Here the opposite is true. Time and again, the boy struggles to make sense of his father's strange references: Where's the neighborhood? (95) How does a crow fly? (156) What is a telephone? (7). When they discover the bounty of the bunker, the man must introduce his son to the once familiar signs of his world, such as canned peaches, hot buttered biscuits, and a toilet.

Moreover, the gap reflecting their different experiences of the world gradually increases rather than diminishes as a result of their travels together. Finally, as they prepare to leave, the man turns to look at the boy, fully recognizing the insurmountability of their difference (153–54):

> Maybe he understood for the first time that to the boy he was himself an alien. A being from a planet that no longer existed. The tales of which were suspect. He could not construct for the child's pleasure the world he'd lost without constructing the loss as well and he thought perhaps the child had known this better than he.[19]

And it is not just that the boy fails to recognize his father or the world from which he came, but the man grows equally unable to comprehend his son's worldview, especially his repeated gestures of hospitality—actions that the father interprets as dangerous at worst, such as when he runs out to find the boy and futile at best because he is going to die anyway. In response to Ely's question about why the boy agreed to share their food with him, the man replies "you wouldnt understand. […] I'm not sure I do" (173). Finally, the man recognizes that "Some new

---

19 Earlier he had seen "the look of an alien" in the "all but translucent skin" of his boy with his "great staring eyes" (129).

distance between them" (190) is not merely a gap of experience but also one of time: "He'd stop and lean on the cart and the boy would go on and then stop and look back and he would raise his weeping eyes and see him standing there in the road looking back at him from some unimaginable future, glowing in that waste like a tabernacle" (273).

But if, as Dufourmantelle suggests in the epigraph to this section, "the future is given as being what comes to us from the other, from what is absolutely surprising," the gradual estrangement of the man and his boy over the course of the novel signals not just the heartbreaking consequences of a world lost to the past but also the conditions for its renewal by making time with the other. In this respect, Derrida's work on hospitality reorients our attention to issues of temporality in the novel. Hospitality, imagined as a practice defined by gesture rather than place, gesture that embraces the surprise encounter with the other, offers the future to a novel that begins at the end of time. Ely has stepped away from others and out of time; the man, hindered by both bittersweet memories of the past and terrifying fears of the future, has run out of time. But the boy has learned how to "make time," and the novel acknowledges the futurity that emerges from pure acts of hospitality, forged from its absence, from gestures of welcome, from saying yes to whatever comes down the road.

The apocalyptic force of the novel thus offers neither redemptive hope for humanity nor an elegiac tribute to a lost world. Instead, it leaves us to sit with the ultimately aporetic uncertainty of living after the end of the world.[20] And yet, Derrida

---

[20] Scholars have, indeed, called our attention to the novel's aporetic conclusion, its refusal to offer the reader a clear choice between redemption or despair. Rambo (2008, 115) links the aporetic nature of the novel's conclusion to the imperative to witness what remains after the collapse of the world: "In the face of these impossibilities, the impulse to impose redemption is replaced, instead, by an imperative to witness what remains." Skrimshire (2011) reads the undecidability of the novel's conclusion in light of work by Derrida and Blanchot on disaster and apocalypse in ways that are compatible with my reading here although

helps us read this aporetic uncertainty as productive rather than dystopian, as poetic rather than disconsolate. We, as readers, move alongside the man and his boy, from impossibility to impossibility, from the absence of shelter to acts of unspeakable horror, and across interminable, uncrossable thresholds of the imagination. By acting "as though hospitality were the impossible" (Derrida and Dufourmantelle 2000, 75), the novel addresses the ethical problem of hospitality: how do we account for the other? How do we live with ourselves as others? The novel ends by saying yes to whatever, whoever turns up — both the boy and his new family — suggesting that we re-place our sense that the essence of hospitality belongs to the "certain existence of the dwelling"(56) in which guest and host meet, that we consider in its place "the gesture by which one of them welcomes the other (62)."[21] It is not a happy ending — it is an "impossible invention" and yet from the impossible, we can imagine hospitality, and from hospitality, we can construct a future. Even at the end of time. Especially at the end of time.

Postscript: Oedipus, Antigone, and the Impossible Chronology of Hospitality

Woven through Derrida's essay with which we began this contemplation of hospitality and time in *The Road* are the figures of Oedipus and his daughter Antigone, especially as figured in Sophocles's three Theban plays.[22] And I would like to conclude with a few thoughts about what we might learn from reading these three texts together: how Derrida's insights into Oedipus's

---

    less attentive to how the discourse of hospitality structures the aporetic experience. On Derrida and Blanchot, see Telò's chapter in this volume.

21 Elmore and Elmore (2018) make a compatible argument about the distinction the novel makes between the ways that the man and his son engage with others in the novel, suggesting that the novel thus offers an ethical critique of late industrial, patriarchal, capitalist individualism represented by the father.

22 For the text of Sophocles, I follow the edition of Lloyd-Jones and Wilson (1990)

death as a final, transgressive act of hospitality might spark new insights into the man's death in *The Road* as well as how a Derridean reading of the impossible poetics of hospitality in *The Road* prompts a similarly productive engagement with time in Sophocles's *Oedipus at Colonus*.

Not unlike the father and son in McCarthy's *The Road,* Sophocles's Antigone and her father appear in *Oedipus at Colonus* as homeless, itinerant refugees, fleeing not an ecological disaster but a familial catastrophe of equally devasting proportions. And just as McCarthy's heroes stagger endlessly through the unwelcoming, post apocalyptic landscape of the novel, forced to cross unspeakable boundaries in their search for somewhere to call home, some people to claim as family, so too have Oedipus and his daughter long been on the road in search of a place to live. Oedipus opens the play by asking (1–4),

> Antigone, child of a blind old man, to what
> lands, to the city of what men have we come?
> Who now on this day will welcome the wandering Oedipus
> with the smallest gifts?

When he learns that they have arrived at the grove of the all-seeing Eumenides on the outskirts of Athens, Oedipus announces — to the horror of the local inhabitants — that he will take up residence as a suppliant within their sacred shrine, never again to leave this spot (44–45). Oedipus's insistence that he violate this sacred boundary, that the local inhabitants make space for him in their city, echoes the transgressive actions that initially sent him into exile, figuring him once again as a man outside the law, and it is for this reason that Derrida reads Oedipus as the embodiment of the contradictory nature of hospitality. His story is the "tragedy of destiny," one that perfectly represents the antagonistic yet necessary relationship between the law of absolute hospitality and those individual laws that both enable and constrain it.[23]

Indeed we see this tension enacted over the course of the play when Theseus, playing the role of the generous host, offers Oedipus absolute hospitality, the home in death that he was repeatedly denied in life. It is, Derrida suggests, as everything is with Oedipus, both an act of ultimate generosity by giving unending power to Athens, and one that constrains his host indefinitely, for permanently buried in Athenian soil Oedipus is the guest who will never leave, effectively holding Theseus his host as hostage.[24] And so the play puts an end to Oedipus's digressions, his wanderings, with one final act of transgression, one step too far.

This act — Oedipus's death and Theseus's hospitality — derails Antigone. Her father has found his resting place, and yet his embrace of an alien tomb as home — one that can never be shared with family — has deprived his daughters of what little family or home they had with him. Unsure of where she can now turn, Antigone cries out, "Where shall I flee?" (1737). Above all, a longing seizes her to see his grave, to grieve for her father, to grieve with her sister, and yet this, too, will be taken from her. Theseus tells Antigone and her sister, "Stop your lament, girls. One should not mourn for those to whom the chthonic night is a gift of grace; for there will be revenge" (1751–53).

---

23 Derrida in Derrida and Dufourmantelle (2000, 79) refers to the inherently contradictory nature of the law of hospitality as a "tragedy of destiny": "*The* law is above the laws. It is thus illegal, transgressive, outside the law, like a lawless law, *nomos anomos,* law above the laws and law outside the law (*anomos,* we remember, that's for instance how Oedipus, the father-son, the son as father, father and brother of his daughters is characterized)." Indeed, the latter are the laws, Derrida continues, that "Antigone will have to transgress to offer her brothers the hospitality of the land and of burial" (85).

24 In Derrida and Dufourmantelle (2000, 107), Derrida characterizes Theseus's position thus: "the *xenos,* the dearest foreigner or host, the host as friend but a host who is friend and ally who thereby becomes a sort of hostage, the hostage of a dead man, the possible prisoner of a potential absent person."

Antigone has lost not just her father, but also the possibility of mourning him. And yet it is this final transgression that Derrida reads as Oedipus's ultimate act of generosity:

> Oedipus doesn't even give his daughters the time of mourning, he refuses them that; but in doing so he also offers them, simultaneously, a limitless respite, a sort of infinite time. (Derrida and Dufourmantelle 2000, 93)

In this respect, Derrida argues, although Oedipus's unmournable death deprives his children of their responsibilities, duties, and connections to their father, to their family, this final act of hospitality (in all its transgressive contradictions) offers them — at the same time — the gift of infinite time.

Derrida's reading of Oedipus's death as an act of hospitality, one that endows the gift of infinite time, encourages us to revisit McCarthy's novel, to linger a bit longer — even as the novel's narrative trajectory pushes us to keep moving along with the boy — on the experience of the man, a father also buried in an alien land, never to be mourned by his son, as itself another expression of the novel's engagement with the temporal possibilities of transgressive hospitality. In this respect, it is not just the boy's willingness to say yes, to embrace the new family he has found on the road, that creates a sense of future for the boy, but also — at the same time — his father's death and the refusal of mourning, the ultimate contradiction of hospitality, that offers the boy, and the reader, "a sort of infinite time."

This reading also takes us back to Antigone to whom we now see an impossible future is given, as to the boy in *The Road*, from her willingness to leave her father unmourned in a foreign land. In this his final play Sophocles embraces what Derrida has called "the impossible chronology of hospitality" (Derrida and Dufourmantelle 2000, 127) to enable Antigone and her audience to revisit the mythic or dramatic past, to imagine a new future for her family and her city on the Athenian stage.

Having first engaged with the Oedipus's "tragedy of destiny" in the play *Antigone,* produced in 440 BCE, the playwright returns to the myth ten years later in *Oedipus the King,* moving the story back in time in a prequel of sorts to reconstruct the backstory of Antigone's dilemma: the hero's unthinkable yet unavoidable acts of violence and love that ultimately led to the civic crisis at the heart of *Antigone*. In the play *Oedipus at Colonus,* then, composed nearly a quarter century after *Oedipus the King,* Sophocles returns to the tragedy of Oedipus for the third time, at the end of his life and of Oedipus's life, once again bending time. As this play ends, Antigone rushes off stage, heading to Thebes in a desperate attempt to turn back time, to create a different future for her family and her city. She begs Theseus, "Send us to ancient Thebes, in the hope that we may somehow prevent the slaughter that is coming to our brothers" (1769–72). Deprived of her duties as daughter to mourn her father's death, Antigone is free to embrace an impossible future, while Sophocles stretches the dramatic time between the end of Oedipus's life and the beginning of Antigone's own play. He gives Antigone this gift of infinite time, time for her to return to Thebes before the play begins, time to create a new story out of an impossible future in which her brothers do not kill each other and her city is not brought down by civil war.

For Sophocles, then, engaging with the tragic destiny of Oedipus and his family is not just about place—about finding a place to belong—but also, as we have seen in *The Road,* about making time, and Sophocles's final play, like McCarthy's novel, conjures a sense of futurity, "a sort of infinite time" out of a notion of hospitality that has been forged from absence, transgression, and digression. Such is "the impossible chronology of hospitality."

10

Blanchot, Derrida, and the Gimmick: Writing Disaster in Euripides's *Bacchae*

Mario Telò

In the introduction to the collection *Derrida and Queer Theory*,[1] published by punctum books in 2017, Christian Hite begins by queering the Derridean *à venir*:

> The "future" — what lies ahead — is already "behind" (*derrière*). But a "future" that is already "behind" is perhaps less a "no future" than a *"catastrophic* future" […], precisely in the etymological sense of an "overturning" […] a future, then, as if turned to its "back" (*dos*) — or even backside up (who can tell?) (Hite 2017, 11)

What is "queer" here — besides the playful innuendo suggested by Derrida's own name, its evocation of *derrière-ness* — is the concern with the politics of futurity, which has characterized queer theory since Lee Edelman's *No Future* (2004).[2] While alluding to Edelman's position — a rejection of the future as

---
1 Thanks, as always, to Alex Press.
2 On Derrida's onomastic puns on *derrière,* see Hite (2017, 16), and Hayes (2017, 167–68).

reprofuturity, with its malignant aspiration to reproduce the status quo — Hite resorts to Derrida to propose a future that is past, that is, *behind* us: one that is not lacking, self-annihilating, impossible but, rather, turned upside down, that is, literally *cata-strophic*. In this chapter, I develop a model of chronopolitical resistance in which the impossible *after* — the lack or denial of a future — is an opening, rather than a closure, of possibility. I consider Derrida's *à venir* together with Maurice Blanchot's *disaster*, employing them to reread Euripides's *Bacchae* and, in particular, to retrieve elements of a temporal resistance against the totalizing regime of Dionysian *mania* (madness). Building upon the dialogue between Derrida's *Demeure* and Blanchot's *The Writing of Disaster* (Blanchot and Derrida 2000), which generated a kind of queer bond, I use the scene of Tiresias and Cadmus's Dionysian transing, long before the disaster of Pentheus's sparagmatic murder, to re-parse the initial "a" in the Derridean *à venir* not as a directional preposition but as an alpha privative.[3] In my rereading of *à venir*, one looks not to a future that will never be realized but, rather, to the temporal lack inherent in a continuous present and to the possibilities that emerge from this stasis, from the negativity of the lack.[4] Never to experience the dismemberment, the separation to come, Tiresias and Cadmus at the beginning of *Bacchae* embody a certain undecidability in their gimmicky performance. In this static scene, there is an overdetermined presentness or no-futurity, a productive lack of *de-cision* (also in the etymological sense of "cutting" or "splitting"), the poten-

---

3   As far as I know, Derrida never explictly interprets *à venir* in this way. Nancy (2020, 97) says that the Derridean *à venir* "*is not, and in not-being it exposes us to an absence or a void.*"

4   As Caputo (2021, 41–42) most recently put it, "Deconstruction affirms what is to come, *à venir* [… which] is not to be construed in terms of presence, viz., as the 'future present' […] but rather as something that is structurally and necessarily to come, always still outstanding, never present." Derrida (1994a, 81) remarks that "the to-come" is "awaiting without horizon of the wait, awaiting what one does not expect yet or *any longer*" (my italics). In a sense, the lack that I am focusing on is a possible interpretation of this "any longer."

tiality of undecidability visualized in their interwoven bodies.⁵ I will first explore the intermingling of Derridean *à venir* and Blanchotian *disaster* in the two thinkers' textual corpora.⁶ I will then illustrate how in imminence (central to the Derridean *à venir*) one can find the immanence of Blanchot's disaster — that is, a fundamental inexperience of the catastrophic event. The early gimmicky scene of *Bacchae* and, late in the play, Agave's arrival both show an imminence morphing into a "remaining in." My goal is to illuminate the chronopolitical potentialities of a Derridean/Blanchotian slippage of *mania* into *monia,* a non-experience, and into unde-cidability ("un-cutting") through a re-reading of *à venir* as a present lack, or the present's lack. This lack manifests itself as waiting. Since waiting is at once an unwelcome intrusion in the COVID era and the perennial condition of migrants and refugees denied coevalness⁷ as they are subjected to racialized dispossession, the challenge arises of how to turn waiting upside down, to open up spaces of resistance and paradoxical mobility within its apparent immobility.⁸ In my reading of *Bacchae,* I will emphasize the potentiality of immanence and *monia* ("un-experience") in the counterfactual scenario of indecision spectrally, or anti-representationally, emerging in the account of Dionysian *mania* and its aftermath. Through and in

---

5   For the connection between *de-cision* and various violent acts of "cutting," see what Derrida says in *Clang,* in the Genet column: "Must we decide [*y a-t-il à décider*] between the two effects of this so-called literature of theft, betrayal, denunciation? Expropriation or reappropriation? Decapitation or recapitation? Dissemination or recapitulation, recapitalization? Which way to slice it?" (Derrida 2021, 19b). See also Derrida (2007, 237): "A decision should tear — that's what the word decision means; it should disrupt the fabric of the possible."
6   On the intertextual relationship between Derrida and Blanchot, see esp. L. Hill (2016).
7   Prevented from sharing time with other people (coevalness), refugees experience waiting as a condition of protracted displacement, a perennially, cruelly deferred recognition of basic rights. On the deprivation of coevalness, see Ramsay (2019, 20).
8   Khosravi (2021, 206) observes that "navigation through the spatio-temporal contexts of waiting might create openings for new political orientations."

waiting, the present's immobility, materializing in this counterfactual as in-decision, is the *venir* (arrival) of an *a* (lack), which has the potential to forestall the totalizing, deceptively liberatory future of ecstatic, Dionysian time with a form of extended chronicity that is Dionysian in a different sense, as I will explain.

A line-by-line commentary on Blanchot's *The Instant of My Death,* Derrida's *Demeure* can also be read as a commentary on *The Writing of Disaster,* which in turn closely engages with Derrida through forms of coded citationality.[9] *The Instant of My Death* imagines a young man about to be executed by Nazis who experiences death as an impossibility, as something that has already passed him by. The essay's conclusion, "The instant of my death [… is] always in abeyance" (Blanchot and Derrida 2000, 11), picks up on Blanchot's observation in *The Writing of Disaster* that "there is no reaching the disaster," for when disaster "comes upon us, it does not come" (Blanchot 1986, 1).[10] Disaster, according to Blanchot, is a matter of "imminence" or "the advent of what doesn't happen, of what would come without arriving […] and as though by drifting away" (Blanchot 1986, 1 and 5).[11] Using language that could be applied to the SARS-CoV-2 virus, Blanchot says that "the disaster […] has no regard for us" (Blanchot 1986, 2). When he remarks that the temporal marker of disaster is an evanescent *déjà* ("already"), or an "always already,"[12] he alludes to a specific passage from Derrida's

---

9 See Langlois (2015) and Hill (2016). *The Writing of Disaster (L'écriture du désastre)* and *The Instant of My Death (L'instant de ma mort)* were originally published in 1980 and 1994 respectively, and *Demeure* in 1986.
10 Bident (2018, 408) observes that all the books of Blanchot are "nothing but detached fragments" of *The Writing of Disaster.*
11 In *Specters of Marx* (1994a, 45), Derrida famously describes "the future-to-come" as an "always imminently eschatological coming." On the idea of imminence integral to the Derridean *à venir,* see Cheah and Guerlac (2009b, 14): "It is an advent or coming that is structurally *imminent* to every present reality insofar as it is the pure event that interrupts present reality but without which reality could not maintain or renew itself as a presence" (my italics).
12 See Blanchot (1986, 1–2): "The disaster is its imminence, but since the future […] belongs to the disaster, the disaster has *always already* withdrawn," (4): "The disaster has *already* passed," and (40): "'Already'

Glas (*Clang*). In that work, an experimental juxtaposition of Georg W.F. Hegel and Jean Genet, Derrida refers to "I am" and "I am dead" as "two indistinguishable statements sensewise," adding that "the *déjà* that I am," that is, as a being that has already come into existence, "clangs its own knell" (its own *glas*), "signs its own death warrant" (Derrida 2021, 92). When Blanchot identifies dying with "the imminence of what has always already (*déjà*) come to pass," his *déjà* brings to mind "Derrida, Jacques" as an inverted signature reduced to its edges — the after and the before, the death after but also before life (Blanchot 1986, 41).[13] Similarly, for Derrida, Blanchot's oracular writing — even Blanchot himself — instantiates the *à venir*. As he put it in 1976, "Never as much as today have I imagined him so far ahead of us. *Waiting for us, still to come,* still to be read and reread" (Derrida 2010).[14] The very name of Blanchot evokes the "still to come" of the *page blanc,* of words still hidden in the abyss of virtuality, withholding themselves; it evokes the overdetermined sense of lateness inherent in writing as such. From the alignment that Blanchot arguably makes of "alreadyness" with Derrida himself, and from Derrida's assimilation of *à venir* with Blanchot, emerges a conceptual and even affective bond, a cathectic cross-identification.

In *Demeure,* discussing a section of *The Writing of Disaster* entitled "A Primal Scene," Derrida theorizes the affect of lateness — the feeling generated by the un-experience of the event — as "elation." For Derrida, the initial words of "A Primal

---

or 'always already' marks the disaster, which is outside history." See Hill (2016, 191).

13 This passage is discussed by Derrida in *Demeure* (Blanchot and Derrida 2000, 49–50), where he comments: "Death will come. […] What will come, what is coming at me, this is what will already have taken place: death has already taken place. I can testify to it, because it has already taken place. Yet this past, to which I testify, namely, my death itself, has never been present." In the introduction to *Clang* (2021, xviii), Geoffrey Bennington and David Wills say that *déjà* is "used repeatedly by Derrida as a signet or signature through play on, and inversion of, his own initials."

14 Derrida (1993c, 162) declares that he first stumbled upon the notion of *à venir* in Blanchot.

Scene" — "You who live *later*" — "addres[s] themselves to the future, later, of those — the readers, the addressees — who will then live or believe they live and remember in the present" (in Blanchot and Derrida 2000, 97). In particular, the adverb "later" singles out "an anachronistic simultaneity [...] between the present of the one who speaks and says 'later' and the present of those who, one day, later, will read it, who are already reading it" (in Blanchot and Derrida 2000, 97–98). "Disjointed present," the phrase used in this passage by Derrida, captures the lateness of Blanchot's disaster, that is, his notion of "passivity" in relation to the disaster conventionally understood as an event (in Blanchot and Derrida 2000, 97).[15] As the experience of something that has passed and consequently is "in the past, out of date,"[16] passivity can be thought of as the experience of the arrival of a lack, of an alpha privative — that is, a non-experience, or what Derrida calls, in reference to death, "an encounter between what is going to arrive and what has already arrived, between what is on the point of arriving and what has just arrived, between what is going to come and what has just finished coming, between what goes and comes" (in Blanchot and Derrida 2000, 64). In such an encounter, Derrida says, "lightness, elation, beatitude remain the only affects that can take the measure of th[e] event as 'an unexperienced experience'" (in Blanchot and Derrida 2000, 65).[17] While Blanchotian disaster, like the Derridean *à venir*, counters the idea of the future present (a future made present), it also unsettles our perception of the Derridean future-to-come — inviting us to view it not as a perennial non-arrival, an always postponed materialization, but rather as the materialization of a non-arrival, experienced, in Blanchot's terms,

---

15 See Blanchot (1986, 33): "The passive is the torment of the time which has always already passed and which comes [...] as a return without any present."

16 Blanchot (1986, 3): "We are passive with respect to the disaster, but the disaster is perhaps passivity, and thus past, even in the past, out of date."

17 Compare Blanchot (1986, 7): "The disaster, unexperienced. It is what escapes the very possibility of experience."

as a gratifying immanence, the elation of "remaining in."[18] As Derrida and Blanchot position themselves in relation to disaster and *à venir,* each appropriating the other, a mutual towardness entails both a lack, a desire even, and elation — not unlike the affects that arise in *Glas,* Derrida's queerest text, where a wayward, quasi-(homo)-erotic encounter graphically unfolds between Hegel's and Genet's textualities through their continuous, wild juxtapositions, in an assemblage that starts and ends mid-sentence, with no recognizable beginning or ending.[19]

In an early scene of Euripides's *Bacchae,* Dionysian disaster arrives in the mode of Blanchotian disaster through the movements and words of two old men interwoven like Derrida and Blanchot themselves. Coming just *after* the prologue, where Dionysus the foreigner ominously announces his arrival, and well before the play's climactic bloodbath, the scene, which features the trans preparation of Cadmus and Tiresias (with implications for Dionysus's transgender birth), has been regarded as a tragicomic aesthetic problem.[20] But before I focus on the scene, I will consider another expression of Blanchotian disaster, alluded to in the parodos, when the Chorus describes Dionysus's queer or wild gestation after his rescue from the catastrophe visited upon his mother, Semele.

Transferring Dionysus from Semele's womb into his own thigh, Zeus distances him from the *astēr* ("star") that is his thunderbolt; he detaches his son from the event, subjecting him

---

18 Blanchot (1986, 11): "The disaster is what one cannot welcome except as the imminence that gratifies."
19 There is an erotic energy in this text — produced by "a *love* of language" (my italics) and "oblique interconnections," as Hartman (2007, 127) puts it. On the multiple sexual innuendoes that enhance the queer atmosphere of *Glas,* see Hayes (2017).
20 Rather than defining Tiresias and Cadmus's preparation as transvestitism, I prefer to think in terms of the all-compassing notion of *trans, about which see Halberstam (2018); on Tireisas's transgenderism, see Corfman (2020). For the various takes on this problem, see most recently Seidensticker (2016, 276nn5–6). Taplin (1996, 190–91) detects "a strange uncertainty of tone." "Strangeness," "uncertainty," and "tone": these words are key to the queer aesthetics of the scene.

to the unexperiential experience of a lack. In this passage, the Chorus describes Dionysus's double gestation and double birth (88–99):

> Once, Dionysus's mother had him *in the parturient necessities of pangs* [*en ōdinōn lokhiais anankaisi*], and when the thunder of Zeus flew she gave birth to him, thrown out of her womb prematurely, leaving her *life* [*aiōna*] to the stroke of the thunderbolt; and Zeus, Cronus's son, immediately received him in *the parturient chambers* [*lokhiois thalamois*], and covering him in his thigh he closes him in with *golden brooches* [*khruseaisin... peronais*], keeping him *hidden* [*krupton*] from Hera. And then he *gave birth* [*eteken*].[21]

Rescued from the thunderbolt, Dionysus experiences a Blanchotian disaster, the gap of lateness, which is captured by Blanchot's hyphenation of *dis-aster*.[22] Zeus's "delivery," the *lokhos* in *lokhiais/lokhiois,* punningly overlaps with the word for "ambush" or "lying-in-wait," the before of a catastrophe, the not-yet-eventful dimension of Blanchotian disaster. While the word *aiōn* in this context is used simply as a synonym for "life," for the life that Semele has been forced to leave, it evokes the time beyond the event and beyond history, which flows from the disastrous non-experience of Dionysus when he was *krupton* ("hidden") in Zeus's thigh. Zeus's imposition of dis-aster — a salvation and separation from the catastrophe — is an act of violence, similar to Laius's symbolic castration of Oedipus, as indicated by the phrase *khruseaisin* [...] *peronais* ("golden brooches," 97–98), an unmistakable evocation of Jocasta's brooches — the instrument

---

21 On the polyvalence of *thalamos* in this passage, see Segal (1997, 84–85). For a range of rationalistic interpretations of lines 94–95, see Seaford (1996, 160). For the text of *Bacchae,* I follow the edition of Seaford (1996); transations are mine.
22 See Hill (2016, 193): "Not for nothing did Blanchot on occasion detach the word from itself and neutralize it by the addition of a silent, almost invisible hyphen."

of Oedipus's maternal re-enactment of the paternal wounding.[23] While apparently used to protect the child and bring him to birth, these objects become the agents of an oppressive closing-in, which we can call hyper-parentality—an Oedipality both paternal and maternal enacted in Zeus's transgender gestation.[24] Yet in this queer reproduction, in Dionysus's waiting in Zeus's thigh, there is a sense of "uncanny futurity" or of a "negative future,"[25] that is anti-hierarchical, the alreadyness of a prolonged present, an excess apart from the impending, ecstatic yet hierarchical Dionysian chaos. The un-experience caused by Dionysus's prenatal rescue returns in the Messenger's account of the rituals on Cithaeron—in the *ellokhizomen* ("lying-in-ambush") of Pentheus's men (722), their *krupsantes* ("hiding," 723) and waiting, as in Wole Soyinka's adaptation: "We hid / Among the undergrowth covered in leaves. We waited" (Soyinka 1974, 60). In the second strophe of the parodos, the Maenads who *menei* (wait) on the mountain for victims are described as an *okhlos* (crowd), an anagram of *lokhos* (114–20):

> The whole land will immediately dance whenever Bromius leads the thiasoi *to the mountain, to the mountain* [*eis oros eis oros*], where the female *crowd* [*okhlos*], stung by Dionysus, away from looms and shuttles, is *waiting* [*menei*].

Constituting another Blanchotian disaster, this waiting for and before the event (the sparagmatic dissolution of bodies), underscored by the repetition "to the mountain, to the mountain," overlaps with the waiting for and after the event (the dissolution of Semele's body) implicated with Dionysus's birth.

---

23 See Sophocles, *Oedipus the King* 1268–69; for Euripides's play with the confusion between Laius's goad and Jocasta's brooches, see Telò (2020, 75–76) on *Phoenician Women* 805. On the elements of anti-Oedipal sexuality in *Bacchae,* see Wohl (2005).
24 On Zeus's gestation in a contemporary perspective, see Telò (2024, 73–88).
25 Thus Davidson (2012, 126 and 128) on the figure of the pregnant male in modernism.

The sense of undifferentiated time at the heart of Blanchotian disaster extends from Dionysus's gestation to the moment when Tiresias and Cadmus slog onto the stage, casting themselves, with a polyptotic or quasi-polyptotic insistence, as a couple of aged bodies — or, more abstractly, a pair of temporal expanses — leaning into each other. In the last line of the parodos the Chorus envisions a bacchant "joyously [*ēdomena*] [...] mov[ing] her legs, *swift-footed in her leapings* [*takhu-poun skirtēmasi*]" (166). However, in contrast with bacchic swiftness, the long, conjoined words *takhu-poun* and *skirtēmasi* decelerate the syntactic flow, anticipating the slow entrance of the would-be-bacchants Cadmus and Tiresias. When the latter, speaking of himself and his companion, says, "I, *an old man, agreed with the old man* [*xun-ethemēn presbus... geraiterōi*] to weave [*anaptein*] thyrsoi and to *have* [*ekhein*] fawns' skins and to *crown* [*stephanoun*] the head with ivy shoots" (174–76), the dative of accompaniment (*geraiterōi*) is a marker not just of the queer attachments enacted in the scene but also of the temporal accumulation of old age. In a perverse *aiōn*, infinite and finite at the same time and reflected in the polysyndetic list of present infinitives (*anaptein, ekhein,* and *stephanoun*), actions delay the Dionysian event while they ostensibly set it up with its distinctive prostheses. A polyptoton (*gerōn geronti*) occurs in Cadmus's exhortation, "Be a guide, you for me, *an old man for an old man* [*gerōn geronti*]" (185–86), which is accompanied by a declaration of futile tenacity, a claim to *jouissance:* "I would never tire of shaking the earth with the thyrsus day and night; *with joy, we have forgotten that we are old* [*epi-lelēsmeth' hēdeōs / gerontes ontes*]" (187–88). The adverb *hēdeōs* (with joy) encapsulates the elation of what Derrida calls the "encounter between what is going to arrive" and "what has already arrived," respectively, in this case, the Dionysian slaughter and the initial epiphany of Dionysus himself, disguised as a foreigner.[26] The tirelessness of the Dionysian movements that Cadmus speaks of is conducive

---

26 Dionysus exemplifies the Derridean foreigner/guest, who ought to be received unconditionally, the absolute Other, both a promise and a threat:

to a perpetual alreadyness, a Blanchotian immanence, while the self-forgetting (*epi-lelēsmeth'*), the self-annihilation, the arrival of the disastrous event—all promised by the Dionysian ritual—are held off by the temporality, the continuous present, of the thyrsus-shaking. Two lines later in the same position, parallel to *gerōn geronti,* we read *gerontes ontes* ("being old men"), a rhyming phrase in which the malignant perseverance of *ontes* (being) delays oblivion, offering, instead of the event, the advent of a lack.

The continuous alreadyness of disaster emerges from a third instance of polyptotic intimacy, a gathering of *gerōn geronta* ("old age"), in which the hierarchy of subject/object seems to give way to a sprawling horizontality as two weary bodies burden each other (193–98):

> CADMUS I *an old man, you an old man* [*gerōn geronta*], I will lead you like a child.
> TIRESIAS The god will lead us there without toil.
> CADMUS Will we be *the only ones* [*monoi*] in the city for Dionysus?
> TIRESIAS Yes, we are *the only ones* [*monoi*] to have a sane mind; the others don't.
> CADMUS *Delaying is long* [*makron to mellein*]. But cling to my arm.
> TIRESIAS Here we go, clasp my hand and make a pair.

Both lines 195 and 196 begin with the word *monoi* (the only ones), in the same location as *gerōn* (old man), creating a sequence of horizontal and vertical repetitions—*gerōn geronta* and *monoi monoi. Monoi* evokes *monē* and *monia*—or *moniē,* as we find it in Empedocles—derivatives from *menō* (to wait), meaning some kind of "stillness" or "persistence."[27] While they

---

see Derrida and Dufourmantelle (2000, esp. 25). See also Nooter in this volume.
27 Fragments 27.4 and 28.2 (Diels and Kranz 1958). For the connection of *moniē* with *menō,* see O'Brien (2010).

aspire to rush toward the experience of disaster, the two old men, bodies joined, transing together, express prolonged "stillness," prolonged "waiting," through the expansive *m* sounds (*monoi monoi, makron,* and *mellein*), reconfiguring the longed-for experience as a kind of post-eventual imminence or anterior alreadyness. This stillness brings us back to the parodos's image of an *okhlos,* anagrammatically a *lokhos,* of Maenads who *menei* ("wait"), worshippers of Dionysus who, even immersed in the ritualistic madness of Cithaeron, experience the sparagmatic "event" as past-ness, as they will again and again. We might locate the wildness of the play in *monia* as much as its quasi-homonym — *mania*. At the end of the scene, when Tiresias warns Pentheus that he has already been subjugated by the god he stubbornly rejects — *memēnas ēdē* ("you are already mad," 359) — the paronomastic resonance of the verbal form *memēnas* (you are mad) with *menō* (to wait) subliminally yields "you are already waiting." The temporality of the dissonant statement "you are already mad" is thus further confounded or queered, as with Dionysus's interrupted and doubled gestation, in which, removed from his mother, he could be said to have experienced a Blanchotian/Derridean "waiting for an already" — or the arrival of a lack.

Cadmus and Tiresias's relationship to the play's catastrophic event, like Dionysus's with his gestation, is informed not just by separation and inexperience but by transing. Involving flesh cut and resewn, Dionysus's birth, discussed in the old men's dialogue with Pentheus (243–44, 286–87), is a process of transing, a somatotechnical procedure, which, in this case, breaks one body and transplants another even before it is fully formed, rupturing time by confusing the before and the after, the beginning and the ending.[28] The biological ontology of birth becomes a haun-

---

28 In her analysis of "kinship trouble," Butler (2017) observes that "Dionysus has two mothers," and Zeus is more a mother than a father; he can be called "a pregnant father" and, in that sense, almost resembles a trans man. On the *Bacchae* and transsexuality, see Gabriel (2018) and Ruffell (2022). On somatotechnics and the notion of the transgender body as "flesh torn apart and sewn together again," see esp. Stryker (1994, 238, and

tology, or a para-ontology — a term that I borrow from trans studies and critical race theory to locate the inexperience of the event *beside* the event, in the same position as the *a* in relation to *venir* in *à venir*.[29] "Far from referring to a given catastrophic event," Blanchotian disaster is located *para* ("beside") that event; as Leslie Hill has observed, it "belongs to history only in so far as it exceeds" history, that is, history understood as a meaningful sequence of events. The scene of Cadmus and Tiresias — "an experience without experience" — exceeds the play's story, introducing what Leslie Hill calls "an absence of action […] a hiatus" (L. Hill 2016, 193).

In this scene, the sense of Blanchotian disaster recalls the temporality of the "gimmick," which, as Sianne Ngai has observed, "strikes us as technologically backward or just as problematically advanced" (Ngai 2020, 2). For Ngai, "there is […] a sense in which the gimmick confronts us with a mode of bad contemporaneity akin to the 'elongated present,' 'endless present,' or 'perpetual present'" (2020, 64). This aesthetic temporality corresponds to what Frederic Jameson calls, in reference to action films as well as several high-cultural products, a "singularity," which he defines as a "pure present without a past or a future" characteristic of products of late capitalism meant to be thrown away once the trick — the "singularity" (like the "gimmick") — has been performed (Jameson 2015, 113). The *Bacchae* scene is unexpected and novel, with no consequences beyond the moment. All the same, the gimmick is a conceit that can be mechanically repeated ad libitum. It is, as Ngai remarks, "at once dynamic (like an action) and also inert (like a thing), […] like a cause but also its effect […] both a singular event and the pro-

---

2015). In the *Bacchae* on lines 243–44 and 286–87, the verbs *rhaptō* (sew) and *en-rhaptō* (to sew in) describe the conditions of the birth of Dionysus, "sewn" in Zeus's thigh.

29 See esp. Bey (2017, 276 and 284): "*Trans** and *black* […] denote paraontological forces. […] They move in and through the abyss underlying ontology, rubbing up alongside it and causing it to fissure"; see Telò (2023a, ch. 4). On hauntology, see Martelli in this volume and Radcliffe in this volume.

verbial old saw" (Ngai 2020, 68). In Ngai's view, as a "paradoxical unity of discrepant temporalities — instantaneity and duration, disruption and continuity, singularity and repetition — the gimmick embodies one of the most significant contradictions of capitalism: the way in which the movement of time is continually converted into present time" (2020, 68). The scene with Tiresias and Cadmus feels both like a one-off and a worn-out gag: both dynamic and inert, it is set in a gimmicky present that impedes the flow of time as well as the future to come. In such a gimmicky present, the *venir* is experienced as an alpha privative — the equivalent non-arrivals of a one-off and an iterable materialization bring about this lack. Like the sense, circulated by the pandemic, of a present with no arrival — both a one-off state of emergency and an a-chronic duration — the gimmicky present inhabited by Cadmus and Tiresias is an anti-vitalistic, anti-manic waywardness, a *monia,* which may be regarded as a possible response to crisis itself: as a break from the *mania* of the crisis, an evasion of the symbolic's anxious call for solutions and decisions, and of the frantically proliferating states of emergency.[30]

In both Messengers' speeches, dismemberment, the *de-cision* erupting from Dionysian *mania,* follows a decision — the outcome of collective deliberation or of Pentheus's ostensible volition. In the first Messenger's account, after deliberations[31] of the cowherds and shepherds conclude with the unanimously approved decision to "hunt Pentheus's mother, Agave, from the bacchanals" (719–20), we are told, the Messenger and his group decided to lie in wait, their *lokhos* (*ellokhizomen,* 722) verbally recalling, again, Dionysus's time in Zeus's thigh (*en ōdi- / nōn lokhiais anankaisi,* 88–89). In quasi-official language, the Messenger reports that the proponent of this action *eu d' hēmin*

---

30 Butler (2020, 688) speaks of "the sometimes manic effort to restart the market economy" during the COVID pandemic. Bratton (2021) warns against the "facile 'solutionism'" prompted by the pandemic. See Toscano (2020) on the militarization of the pandemic in some European countries.
31 "We, cowherds and shepherds, gathered [*xun-ēlthomen*] to offer each other a contest [*erin*] of shared speech [*koinōn logōn*]" (714–15).

legein / edoxe ("seemed to us to have spoken well," 721–22) — a phrase split into two parts by an enjambment, which iconically links this decision with the impending *de-cision*, the act captured by the verb *dia-phoreō* ("to bring apart," 739, 746) and by the image of "bodily parts thrown up and down" (741).[32] The decision to separate Agave from Dionysus — in effect, to re-enact the separation, the *de-cision*, of Semele from her son — engenders multiple, visceral *de-cisions*. We can say that in making themselves visible by leaving the bushes — a self-disclosure comparable to Dionysus's exit from his second prenatal *lokhos* — the Messenger and his cohort cause the vocalic opening of *monia* into *mania*. In the second Messenger's speech, which details the mechanics of Pentheus's death, we find another lying-in-wait: Pentheus, the disguised Dionysus, and the Messenger initially *hizomen* ("sit," 1048) in an isolated, silent space where they can see without being seen, while the Maenads are similarly depicted as *kathēntai* ("seated," 1053), "keeping their hands busy *in delightful occupations* [*en terpnois ponois*]," not differently from the cows peacefully grazing (735) before being attacked by them, as reported in the previous speech. Pentheus's declared decision to climb a tree for a better view is not just escalating hubris and mania before the eruption of Maenadic mania, but a *de-cision* from the group prior to his own *de-cision*. Both *de-cisions* are visualized in the vertiginous lines detailing Dionysus's sadistic bending of a branch to accommodate Pentheus's decision and facilitate his downfall: *kat-ēgen ēgen, ēgen es melan pedon* ("he brought it down, brought it, brought it to the black ground," 1065).[33] The shift from the compound

---

32 In making the case for the identification of "decision/*de-cision*" with *mania*, I am reacting against the structuralist reading that sees "a striking contrast between [...] bacchantic hunting [...] and the men's 'strife of words'" (Segal 1997, 284).

33 Seaford (1996, 235) says that "the threefold repetition [...] reflects the slow pulling down of the branch." The following lines give an overdetermined sense of Pentheus's death-driven circling around: *kuklouto d' hōste toxon ē kurtos trokhos / tornōi graphomenos peri-phoran helkedromon* ("like a bow or a curved wheel, he circled around, tracing a course-dragging perimeter with a compass," 1066–67).

kat-ēgen to the simple *ēgen* — a beheaded *kat-ēgen* — captures Pentheus's separation from the group while anticipating his decapitation. My emphasis here is not the moralistic notion of punishment for wanting to see too much, for making a *bad* decision, but rather the connection between *mania* and decision as such — understood as an individuation, an exit from the pack and from unindifferentiated (or *un-decided*) time, a plunge into the event. Following Søren Kierkegaard, Derrida repeatedly enunciates in his writings an assimilation of "the instant of decision" to "madness."[34] In the Messengers' speeches, we can locate the counterfactual of in-decision, of temporal de-individuation, a prolonging of the wait, a delaying of the birth of the event, as it were.

The *monia* that can be located in *Bacchae* subsists in a space of un-decidability or in-decision that is at the same time a space of possibility. In-decision and un-decidability play a major role in Derrida's theorization of *différance* and deconstruction in general in his early writings as well as in later ones.[35] If decision can be conceptualized, etymologically, as a cutting, an instant, like each sparagmatic separation of Pentheus's limbs, the gimmicky *monia*, the Blanchotian disaster, of Cadmus and Tiresias's scene bespeaks non-instantaneity. For Derrida, because free, genuine decision can emerge only from a space of radical, unrealized possibility, undecidability is not to be thought of as a state of inability to act but as the very condition of possibility for political action (see esp. Sokoloff 2005). Massimo Cacciari has observed that in the context of the European Union, where decision-making frequently serves to confirm the hegemonic position of some states over others, the stasis of undecidabil-

---

34 See, e.g., Derrida (1978, 31; 1992a, 26; and 1995b, 59). See esp. Bennington (2011, 110–11).

35 As Derrida (2002a, 231) puts it, "the undecidable is not merely the oscillation between two significations or two contradictory and very determinate rules. [...] A decision that would not go through the test and ordeal of the undecidable would not be a free decision; it would only be the programmable application or the continuous unfolding of a calculable process."

ity — we could say, *monia* — can become political resistance.³⁶ Drawing out the etymological force of *decision,* Derrida refers to the death penalty as a *"cutting* decision" (Derrida 2014, 259, emphasis added). As he puts it, "what we rebel against when we rebel against the death penalty is not death" but "rather the interruption of the principle of indetermination [...] of the incalculable chance." Such an interruption disavows a living being's imponderable "relation to what comes, to the to-come and thus to some other," whether that other appears "as event, as guest, as *arrivant"* (Derrida 2014, 256–57). The death penalty is thus a disavowal, on the part of the one who inflicts it, of the finitude of one's agency in the face of the uncertainty defining life — it is a disavowal of the inability to control time. This disavowal is also a rejection of the "undecidability" that comports with this finitude (Derrida 2014, 256). While Tiresias and Cadmus have made a decision of sorts, to follow Dionysus, their gimmicky present introduces an element of worn-out duration, of non-evental elation that generates the alternative or counterfactual possibility of the plot's deviation from its movement forward, from its decided course, which here coincides with the destructive decision of Pentheus. We can say that this deviation from the decided course is an element of undecidability unsettling the plot. More than the Dionysian decision of Pentheus and the Maenads, which operates in the tight interval between free will and coercion, it is indecision that refuses interpellation and the "logic that stages refusal as inactivity, as the absence of a plan and as a mode of stalling real politics."³⁷ As Stefano Harney and Fred Moten put it in *The Undercommons:*

> We're more than politics, more than settled, more than democratic. We surround democracy's false image in order

---

36 Cacciari (2009a and 2009b); see Lampert (2018, 240–41). See also Esposito (2022, 159–61), on the dangerous decisionism that has been customary since the beginning of the pandemic.
37 Here I cite Jack Halberstam's introduction to Harney and Moten (2013, 7 and 9). On "the idea of a possibility that exceeds every attempt at final realization," see Butler (2000, 162).

to unsettle it. Every time it tries to enclose us in a decision, we're undecided. (Harney and Moten 2013, 19)

In their queer kinship, the two old, heavy bodies, accumulations of time, constitute the alpha privative (the *a* in *à venir*), obstructing time, the arrival of the event. Like the "wild" ontology of Dionysus's birth, but unlike the regime of his ritualized worship, this obstruction hinders decision, that is, the emergence of a political determination out of the shapeless, undifferentiated realm of aesthetic, existential, and political possibility. The explosion of Dionysian intoxication has been seen, à la Friedrich Nietzsche, as a kind of ecstatic liberation, a re-emergence of the primordial joy of being. Bonnie Honig has reoriented this thesis in political terms, seeing the Theban women's abandonment of their homes to follow the Dionysian cult as an act of feminist refusal or even a gynocratic enterprise (see Honig 2021). Not altogether different from Pentheus's repressive binding, his intoxicated, rushed, autocratic decision making, Dionysian intoxication is its own form of "enclosing" decision, a biopolitical subjugation to and assimilation into an all-encompassing power, as well as the most brutal expression of a future present.[38]

The "enclosure" of decision marks the end of *Bacchae*, when Cadmus brings Agave back into consciousness — a restoration of cognition and of the distinction between a before and an after that severs her from her state of *remaining in,* from her

---

38 In this respect, the emancipatory Agambian "inoperativity" that Honig reads into the life of leisure offered to the Theban women by Dionysus on the mountains may be complicated a priori by their incorporation into the Dionysian world. Butler (2017, 11) observes that *Bacchae* "is not a story about women's liberation" and "women are not really liberated but submit deliriously to another man's command"; see also Morales (2022, 29), who observes that "maddened by Dionysus," the women of Thebes "have no, or far less, agency." Honig (2022, 41) responds that, in her reading, "Dionysus cannot force people to do things they do not desire. He can only [...] uninhibit them, and free them to do what they desire." While the murder of Pentheus may be seen as a dismantling of patriarchy, the women's violence against animals makes them enforcers of what has been called "inanimal" biopolitics, on which see Pugliese (2020, 36).

queer absorption in undifferentiated time. When Agave arrives onstage carrying Pentheus's head, she refers to it with a deictic ("this [*tade*] prize," 1238) and mentions hands or arms three times: "having left the distaff by the loom, I have moved on to bigger things, hunting animals with my hands [*kheroin*]" (1236–37); "as you see, I carry this prize in my arms [*en ōlenaisin*]" (1238–39); "father, please take this in your hands [*kheroin*]" (1240). How shall we translate this verbal insistence into haptic persistence, into theatrical effect and affect? Among the various staging possibilities afforded by the wording, we can imagine Agave caressing her son's head, fondling his hair as if it were a leonine mane. The verbal repetition can be read as gestural repetition, continuously touching and being touched in return, a form of *immanence,* affective and temporal, that we can regard not only as fetishistic but also queer.[39] Agave's tactile attachment to what she takes to be an animal trophy, a non-living companion, results in a care relation between human and non-human, a connectivity "across normative categorizations" (Hohti and Osgood 2020, 10).[40] The queer *animacy* engendered by this bond — in a scene as campy as the one with Tiresias and Cadmus — also crosses (and queers) temporal bounds, confusing the before and the after, opening up a capsule of temporal stasis within the linear mobility of the dialogue.[41] Petting the head of a dead child/animal shelters Agave in a queer dimension where time is dilated and the event, the dividing line between before and after, is removed from perception, turned into an alpha privative. Pentheus's head becomes a "feral child" anchoring Agave within a pre- or post-symbolic realm whose temporality

---

39 On fetishism as immanence and imminence, see Deleuze and von Sacher-Masoch (1991).

40 Honig (2021, 22–23) focuses on the Maenads' breastfeeding of animals as a form of non-heteronormative reproduction. Dell'Aversano (2010, 103) sees the inherent queerness of the animal as the embodiment of "no future": "Unlike the parent-child bond, which is defined by teleology, the human-animal bond […] does not sagely postpone gratification, it does not project anything into, or onto, the future."

41 On the idea of animacy, see Chen (2012).

is at odds with the eruptive ecstasy of the Dionysiac rituals.[42] Agave's *mania* has slipped into a *monia* comparable to the gimmicky Dionysian preparations of Tiresias and Cadmus. In both of these scenes, which are *para*-ontological in the sense of being *beside* or almost outside the plot, a queer bond blocks the plot's de-cisive rhythm, its structural distinction between a before and an after. In forcing Agave to disconnect from a continuous present and acquire awareness of her dead son, Cadmus's command to "look and learn more clearly" (1281) — a version of the Aeschylean *pathei mathos* — works as the voice of the law.[43] Cadmus commits another sparagmatic act, a repetition of Dionysian de-*cision:* he breaks Agave's bond, her queer fondling of the lion's/child's head and, consequently, her idyll in *unbroken, undifferentiated, un-decided* time. The apparent return to sanity converges, paradoxically, with the loss of it orchestrated by Cadmus's grandson, an enforcer of his own form of symbolic constriction.[44] *Monia* in *Bacchae* is a rejection of the event as the dividing marker between a before and an after; as such, it amounts to a "wild" or deeply un-decided or in-decisive *mania,* a convergence and synchrony of apparently incompatible conditions — a Blanchotian non-experience of ecstatic, anarchical Dionysian hierarchy and a clinging to its consequences when one is pushed to move on.

With his arrival in Thebes, disguised as an emissary, Dionysus, the absolute foreigner, promises or threatens a messianic arrival — an idea that haunts the Derridean future to come[45] — but the gimmicky aesthetics, the non-experience at

---

42 On the "feral child," see Halberstam (2020a, 145), who observes that "in the implicit ties between the unscripted nature of the infant/wild child's desires, we can begin to understand the wildness of the child and the queerness of the animal."

43 On the "closure" of *Bacchae* as *pathei mathos,* see Segal (1999–2000). For other aspects of the play's finale, see Telò (2020, 261–74).

44 See Honig (2021, 79): "Cadmus [...] reinterpellates [Agave] into the world. [...] Cadmus carefully shifts Agave from a proud revolutionary to a mourning mother."

45 See my introduction to this volume.

the beginning of *Bacchae* suggests the arrival of a lack, of a disjointed present. In his recent re-evaluation of "negation" for the purposes of what he calls "an affirmative philosophy," Roberto Esposito observes that "the negative is […] the forewarning of a lack […] the empty point that […] pushes the present beyond itself, towards the eternally eluded promise of the origin […] the inactual that continues to disrupt our actuality" (Esposito 2019, 207). This notion of the "negative" converges with Judith Butler's critique of "realizability," a critique that is not "a cynical or defeatist attenuation of struggle" but rather "an unceasing engagement with a desire for the political, sustained by its ultimate unattainability" (see Butler and Athanasiou 2013, 156). The gimmick of Tiresias and Cadmus fecklessly adorned as Maenads models the infinite possibility that is undecidability — a resistance to re-solution embodied in the very yoking of the old men's bodies, in Agave's tactile attachment to (in)animate kin, or in the bond of Derrida and Blanchot, which makes it impossible to separate out their respective textual bodies. The Derridean *à venir,* which Jacques Rancière critiques for its ethical messianicity, for being too theological and not political enough, could be seen as a kind of political bond of before and after against the cutting decisions of the state.[46] The Dionysian *à venir,* the arrival of a lack, at the margins of the Euripidean plot invites us to shift our attention from *mania* to *monia* as the stilling wherein "the potential to be otherwise" is contained (Bissell 2007, 279). For Rebekah Sheldon, "the future is […] in dynamic torsion with the present as a series of feedback loops […] the give and take of a future neither wholly determined by the present nor mystically sealed by the carapace of chance" (Sheldon 2019, 127). In the encounter of tragic bodies, human and no-longer human, filling the interval between before and after, con-

---

46 See Rancière (2009). The theological framing that Rancière attributes to Derrida's political messianicity (distinct from messianism) means, for Rancière, "a democracy without demos, with no possibility that a subject performs the *kratos* of the *demos.*" Derrida (1994a, 82) speaks of messianicity as "messianism without content," that is, a "messianic without messianism."

torting decision through the anti-kinetic agency of slowness and repetition, we see the materialization of an affirmative negative. By curtailing the ostensibly liberating and ecstatic but totalizing cutting of Dionysian *mania,* the gimmicky *à venir,* the arrival of an alpha privative, creates an un-de-cided space of possibility as we bond together — waiting.

11

The Future of the Past: Pericles, History, and Athenian Democracy

Ahuvia Kahane

Ethics is an integral part of diffraction. […] Responsibility is not an obligation that the subject chooses but rather an incarnate relation that precedes the intentionality of consciousness.

— Karen Barad (2010, 265)

Modernity's *l'avenir*, as Jacques Derrida's famous critique describes it — or, in Jean-Luc Nancy's paraphrase, "the present-future that is projected, represented, given in advance as an aim and as a possible occurence" (in Fabbri 2007, 431)[1] — would have been there forever, long before modernity. This kind of "ancient" time and its trajectory — to the degree that it is concomitant with linear causes and effects, "classical" modern science, transcendental subjects, and sovereign theologies — is eternity itself. It is a time in which there is no past and no future, no *krisis*, no "taking into account" of responsibility, no history. Such time is strictly, and famously, opposed to Derrida's *à-venir*, the

---

1 Paraphrasis (Greek *para*, "beyond, beside, before, etc." + *phrazō*, "show, tell," med. "indicate to one's self," etc.) is, of course, of importance here.

future-to-come that "designates the proper nature of what is essentially and always in the coming, of what has never come or come about, come down and made itself available," a future which — if we consider its relation to politics — is inseparable from what we mean when we speak the name of democracy.[2]

Democracy in this sense is not a "regime," a system, or a given, and it is not already *is*. It must alway be "to come" since, as Nancy puts it, "if democracy is given, if it is there, made, confected [*faite*], established, then one will no longer be able to say that democracy is to be improved" (in Fabbri 2007, 431).

The ethical and ontological force of this position is, in the first instance, a matter of common sense. If democracy were confected, *faite,* without change, it would be cloning itself as a fixed object or set of relations. It would have no historical exceptionality *by which* to separate one moment from another, *from which* to take account of and attend to suffering, inequality, or injustice or, indeed, to justice, equality, and happiness. It would have no promise, no future *for which* to hope and *in which* to acknowledge responsibility, and no sense of risk or loss by which to motivate change.

The point can perhaps be framed even more clearly by looking at some prominent formal argument for the completeness of time. Consider briefly, for example, Pierre-Simone Laplace (1749–1827) and his Demon, as it later came to be known. In *A Philosophical Essay on Probabilities* (1951), the great physicist, mathematician, and polymath states that all events, even those of seeming minimal significance, of necessity follow the laws of nature of which they are part. Thus (Laplace 1951, 4, my emphasis):

---

[2] See Nancy (2012). See also Derrida (2005a, 108): "I tried to persuade you [in Derrida 1997b] that the democratic injunction does not consist in putting off until later or in letting itself be governed, reassured, pacified, or consoled by some ideal or regulative Idea. It is signalled in the urgency and imminence of an *à-venir,* a to-come, the *à* of the à-venir, the *to* of the to-come, inflecting or turning into an injunction as well as into messianic waiting the a of *a différance* in disjunction."

Given for one instant an intelligence which could comprehend all the forces by which nature is animated and the respective situation of the beings who compose it — an intelligence sufficiently vast to submit these data to analysis — it would embrace *in the same formula the movements of the greatest bodies of the universe and those of the lightest atom; for it, nothing would be uncertain and the future, as the past, would be present to its eyes.*

Indeed, Laplace stresses that "the curve described by a simple molecule of air or vapor is regulated in a manner just as certain as the planetary orbits" (6) .

According to this principle, of necessity and by the laws of nature, Athenian *democracy,* for example, as it is characterized by Pericles in Thucydides's *History,* will have produced its futures precisely as they are attested in Western sovereign nation-states since, say, the eighteenth century. The meaning of the modern word *democracy* will have been knowable to the Demon by algorithmic "etymological" laws. This *faite* future of the past in which "nothing would be uncertain" would clearly, by the terms of its own definition, be identical with eternity and will thus be no future at all.[3] We, and Thucydides's ancient readers, already know that this is not the case. Indeed, the moment Pericles's oration transitions from voiced performance to text (regardless of the "fictionality" of Thucydidean speechs) is the ontic moment forcing the recognition and thus an ontology of change. Pericles fell victim to the plague. Athenian democracy did not survive the War. It is in our retrospective knowledge of these fragile historical moments, of the absence of deterministic continuity, that hope and the *care* for the future-to-come inextricably reside.

---

3   See Barad (2010, 249) on Derrida, continuity, and justice: "All time is calculable, laid out, the entirety of the past, of all that lays behind us, and the entirety of the future, of all that is before us, starting with but one moment, any moment, all moments made equal. […] All time in no time at all."

Algorithmic, "empty" time[4] is the substrate of instrumental, clockwork calculation of synchronized train timetables, weather predictions, stock markets, and forecasts of gain (see, e.g., Galison 2003). And yet we know that train schedules, the weather, stock markets, indeed, political institutions and language, do not quite follow such algorithmic trajectories.[5] One might illustrate this point in relation, not to the whole Laplacian world but, more narrowly and thus more clearly, to the movement of just three observable bodies: say, the Earth, the Moon, and the Sun. We might take such movement as a metaphor, or perhaps even as a literal instance of the incalculable component of multi-variable systems.[6]

Students of the heavens, both ancient and modern, have often sought to give a full account of the trajectories of these celestial bodies. In this world, we work from a state of ignorance — as already argued by Laplace (1951, 4), writing on what probability allows. Yet in classical mechanics, an intelligence capable of mathematical analysis should in principle — assuming gravity as a constant, as well as mass, position, and momentum — have been able to determine all past positions of the Earth, Moon, and Sun and to predict their future trajectories.[7] Such predictive

---

4 Famously, Benjamin (1969, 261) opposed "empty time" to "messianic time."
5 The bibliography, and the questions themselves, relating to dynamic systems, complexity, "chaos," non-linear processes, etc., lie well beyond the scope of this essay and do not constitute a unified "theory." Broadly, see, e.g., Nicolis and Prigogine (1989); Prigogine and Stengers (1984); and, for weather, Lorenz (1972).
6 The question of whether such exempla are methodological metaphors or to be taken more literally — discussed, e.g., by Barad (2010), by exponents of, mutatis mutandis, "applied metaphysics," "new materialism," etc., and also by earlier critics such as Gaston Bachelard (1992) and others — belongs elsewhere.
7 Galison 2003, 59: "The motion of a single body is given by Newton's injunction that a body in motion tends to stay in motion. The motion of two bodies, attracted to one another by Newtonian gravity, could also be solved. With the simplifying assumption that the planets were only attracted by the sun (and not by each other), it was a straightforward exercise for Newton and his successors to calculate the precise trajectory of these bodies around the sun. But for a system of three or more mutually

calculations might be useful if, for example, we wanted to assure ourselves that Earth will not at some time in the future fly out of orbit, ending all life as we know it.[8]

A modern problem of such composite movement can be more generally described as the "three body" problem. As Henrí Poincaré put it at the end of the nineteenth century:[9]

> Could one not ask whether one of the bodies will always remain in a certain region of the heavens, or if it could just as well travel further and further away forever?

In 1899, Poincaré won the King Oscar of Sweden Prize for his mathematical work on dynamic systems.[10] Practically speaking, we can, of course, develop excellent general approximations of an answer to his question. Using Newtonian calculations, or even (though with lesser precision and greater difficulty) Ptolemaic algebra, we can set out the movements of the Earth, Moon, and Sun with good accuracy. Reducing the motion of three bodies to a fixed plane in space, for example, provides some significant but limited modern solutions. Yet, as already Poincaré himself proved in 1889 and as is still accepted today, the three-

---

attracting objects, such as the sun, the moon, and the earth, the situation was far more difficult. Eighteen interrelated equations had to be satisfied to solve the problem. If space is measured by three axes x, y, and z, then a full description of the motion of the orbs would require the positions x, y, z at each moment in time for each of the three heavenly bodies (that makes nine equations), along with the momentum of each in each direction (another nine). By choosing the right coordinates, these eighteen equations could be reduced to twelve."

8   This "planetary" model of the relations between bodies was, broadly speaking, also the model, associated with Earnest Rutherford, of the atom. See, e.g., Bailey (2013).

9   Daniel Goroff in Poincaré 1993, 19, and Poincaré 1881, 376–77 (see Galison 2003, 61 and n20). As Poincaré says (1928, 90, quoted in Galison 2003, 61): "One simply cannot read […] parts of this memoir without being struck by the resemblance between the various questions which are treated there and the great astronomical problem of the stability of the solar system."

10 See Poincaré (2017) and Barrow-Green (1997). For Poincaré's error, see also Barrow-Green (1994).

body problem (and, *a fortiori,* the *n*-body problem, where the number of bodies and hence the complexity of the system is increased from three to "n") provides no general deterministic solution.[11]

The scientific argument surrounding motion and dynamic systems is hardly so simple, nor, of course, is it my objective to consider it here. The three-body problem nevertheless points, in a more formal manner, away from the principles of deterministic algorithms and towards the idea of stochastic movement, and hence to the future-to-come.[12] What should we say, then, of the movement of history, of the history of democracy and of democracy "in-itself," which cannot truthfully be described as a determinate calculus of interactions among *faite* objects nor itself as a *faite* object? Indeed, to speak of "objects," whether material, conceptual, or historical, in this context is a misnomer.[13] While we often formulate the instrumental practice of

---

[11] "H. Poincaré (1889) […] proved that the equations of motion of the three-body problem do not have transcendental integrals expressible in terms of single-valued analytic functions." See Musielak and Quarles (2014). Poincaré's work led to the study of chaos in complex dynamic systems; see, e.g., Rajeev (2013) and Diacu and Holmes (1996). At issue are mathematics, astronomy, classical mechanics, Newtonian physics, quantum mechanics (in relation to the Helium atom, for example), and more. For quantum mechanics, see Yamamoto and Kaneko (1993).

[12] For Poincaré and Derrida see, e.g., Bates (2005) and Tasić (2001 and 2012). It is tempting to draw in other notions of temporality, for example, Benjamin's famous notion of time as a "catastrophe" (Benjamin 1969, 261) and "messianic time." Benjamin does not cite Poincaré in "Theses on the Philosophy of History" (1969, 253–64), but was certainly aware of his mathematical work (discussed, e.g., with Gershom Scholem, July 24, 1915). See Scholem (1995–2000, 1.134).

[13] Barad (2010, 260), to whom we shall return in the concluding sections of this essay, with reference to Derrida, speaks of "the mistaken assumptions of a classical ontology based on the belief that individual determinately bounded and propertied objects are the actors on this stage, and the stage itself is the givenness of a container called space and a linear sequence of moments called time. But the evidence indicates that the world does not operate according to any such classical ontology, an ontology exorcised of ghosts. On the contrary, *this is empirical evidence for a hauntology!*" As Barad continues, "It's not that (in erasing the information after the fact) the experimenter changes a past that had already been present.

everyday life in such terms, we cannot, strictly speaking, use a finite definition of such objects to determine their position relative to each other over time.[14] We cannot determine present futures as occurences "given in advance" nor, for precisely the same reason, calculate the movement of history or the past.[15]

Clearly, movement and history, or rather change and time, do exist—in scientific narratives, in critical reflection, and in everyday cognition. "In a certain manner," as Derrida says, "nothing appears that does not require or take time" (1992a, 6).[16] Futures have pasts and pasts have futures which, if they are of substance rather than fantasy, must be futures-to-come. Athenian democracy did not survive. Something happened in history. We might therefore ask, generally but also in a pointed manner, what are the pasts of such futures of the past, and what, historically and ethically are the pasts, for example, of democracy, if it is a democracy-to-come? What, if we are to admit historical exceptionality into our question, is, for example, the past that was Athenian democracy? These are the questions I would like to consider in the discussion to follow.

Democracy-to-come, like the word democracy itself, does have a time and thus, by definition, a *history*. As Derrida, for example, stresses, it is an *inheritance,* a future of the past (2005a, 10):

Rather, the point is that the past was never simply there to begin with and the future is not simply what will unfold; the 'past' and the 'future' are iteratively reworked and enfolded through the iterative practices of spacetimemattering—including the which-slit measurement and the subsequent erasure of which-slit information—all are one phenomenon." From a different perspective, see, e.g., Daston (2000) and her notion of "applied metaphysics" and the "orthogonal" relation between the reality and historicity of scientific objects.

14 For Einstein's definition of reality, see Einstein, Podolski, and Rosen (1935). Contra Bohr (1935), Einstein believed that a complete theory and thus a description of reality as he defined it was in principle possible.

15 As one might be able to in classical Newtonian science, where reversibility is a prominent quality.

16 Cf., e.g., Grosz (1999, 1).

I don't imagine it was ever possible to think and say, even if only in Greek, "democracy," before the rotation of some *wheel*. When I say "wheel," I am not yet or not necessarily referring to the technical possibility of the *wheel* but, rather, rather earlier, to the roundness of a rotating movement, the rondure of a return to self before any distinction between *physis* and *tekhne*, *physis* and *nomos*, *physis* and *thesis*, and so on.

And he adds (2005a, 18):

Even though we know so little about what "democracy" should mean, it is still necessary, through a kind of precomprehension, to know something about it. And so the hermeneutic circle turns yet again. We must already anticipate, even if only by a bit; we must move toward the horizon that limits the meaning of the word, in order to come to know better what "democracy" will have been *able* to signify, what it *ought*, in truth, to have meant. We already have some "idea" of what democracy should mean, what it will *have already meant* — and the idea, the ideal, the Greek *eidos* or the *idea* also designates the turn of a contour, the limit surrounding a visible form. Did we not have some idea of democracy, we would never worry about its indetermination. We would never seek to elucidate its meaning or, indeed, call for its advent.

"Democracy" is an *inheritance*, a *heritage*, which nevertheless,

did not [...] exclude the possibility, even the right, of perhaps one day abandoning the inheritance or heritage of the name, of changing names. But always in the name of the name, thereby betraying the heritage in the name of the heritage. (Derrida 2005a, 89–90)

Famously invoking his own (*auto-*)inheritance and *The Politics of Friendship* (1997b, 109), indeed, remarking on his past — here in the text in square brackets within a footnote — Derrida (2005a, 90) says,

> one keeps this indefinite right to the question, to criticism, to deconstruction (guaranteed rights, in principle, in any democracy: no deconstruction without democracy, no democracy without deconstruction). One keeps this right strategically to mark what is no longer a strategic affair: the limit between the conditional (the edges of the context and of the concept enclosing the effective practice of democracy and nourishing it in land and blood) and the unconditional which, from the outset, will have inscribed a self-deconstructive force [I could have in fact said "autoimmune" force] in the very motif of democracy, the possibility and the duty for democracy itself to de-limit itself. Democracy is the *autos* [I would today say the *ipse* or ipseity] of deconstructive self-delimitation. Delimitation not only in the name of a regulative idea and an indefinite perfectibility, but every time in the singular urgency of a *here and now.*

This regulative idea of indefinite perfectability, we should remind ourselves, "does not await an indefinitely remote future assigned by some regulative Idea" (Derrida 2005a, 90). It is a future-to-come that "actually announces nothing" and it is thus also a past that has, in fact, announced nothing. Yet precisely as such — I want to trace some of the horizons of these "autoimmune" symptoms — democracy can be read into history and, taking our cue from Derrida, into the singular urgency of a *here and now* of Greek democracy and some of the ways it was written and read.

Perhaps the most famous moment of what democracy "will have been *able* to signify, what it *ought,* in truth, to have meant" is inscribed in Thucydides's *History of the Peloponesian War,* in Pericles's funeral oration.[17] As Pericles says (2.37.1–3):[18]

> We live under a form of government that does not emulate the institutions of our neighbors; on the contrary, we are ourselves a model which some follow, rather than the imitators of other peoples. On the one hand, by name, it is true that our government is called a democracy, because its administration is in the hands, not of the few, but of the many; yet while as regards the law all men are on an equality for the settlement of their private disputes, as regards the value set on them it is as each man is in any way distinguished that he is preferred to public honors, not because he belongs to a particular class, but because of personal merits; nor, again, on the ground of poverty is a man barred from a public career by obscurity of rank if he but has it in him to do the state a service. And not only in our public life are we liberal, but also as regards our freedom from suspicion of one another in the pursuits of every-day life; for we do not feel resentment at our neighbor if he does as he likes, nor yet do we put on sour looks which, though harmless, are painful to behold. But while we thus avoid giving offence in our private interactions, in our public life we are restrained from lawlessness chiefly through reverent fear, for we render obedience to those in authority and to the laws, and especially to those laws which are ordained for the succor of the oppressed and those which, though unwritten, bring upon the transgressor a disgrace that all men recognize.

What *ought* these famous words to have meant? The passage is not actually cited by Derrida (2005a, chapter 10), though clearly

---

17 Ober (1993, 26), with a view to Pericles's description in the funeral oration, suggests that "no systematic defence of democracy — no democratic theory — survives from an Athenian pen." But this verdict is, let us suggest, pre-determined by his method and perhaps, at least in part, by his politics.

18 All quotations refer to the translation by C.F. Smith (2015), with small adjustments. Smith follows the text of Hude (1901).

he often keeps the oration and its readings (by Nicole Loraux, for example) in mind in *The Politics of Friendship* and elsewhere. In Athenian democracy, he famously sees something that is, on the one hand, a portrayal of the Law and, on the other hand, always in excess of the laws, as necessarily the Law must be, an Institution always in excess of its institutions.[19] Among other texts, Derrida (1997b, 95, and 2005a, 88) cites Plato's paraphrase of Pericles's oration (*Menexenus* 238c–d):[20]

> Then as now, and indeed always, from that time to this, speaking generally, our government was an aristocracy — a form of government that receives various names, according to the fancies of men, and is sometimes called democracy, but is really an aristocracy or government of the best which has the approval of the many.

Here, for Derrida, is the "suspended use of the word *democracy*" wherein lies the question of the manner by which the word "allies itself or competes with that of aristocracy" and with the "number, the reference to the required approbation of the greatest number." This is "the arithmetical dimension that will mark the entire history of the concept of friendship" (Derrida 1997b, 99–101).

What, then, *ought* democracy to have meant? Half a century before Derrida, Arnold W. Gomme (1886–1959), the preeminent reader of Thucydides of his day and author of a classic historical commentary on the *Histories* (1945), projects his analysis (a paraphrase) of democracy in Pericles's oration onto the formalities of grammar and its contrasting clause structure, "On the one hand, by name (*onoma men*) our government is called a

---

19 On the one hand, if democracy were not by nature oriented towards its formalization into a system of laws, Derrida writes, "[i]t would risk being abstract, utopian, illusory, and so turning over into its opposite". On the other hand, democracy is always in excess of its institutions which, "deny it, or at any rate threaten it, sometimes corrupt or pervert it. And must always be able to do this" (Derrida and Dufourmantelle 2000, 79).
20 Cf. Rancière (2007, 84). See also Monoson (1998).

democracy" and "on the other hand (*metesti de*), [...] as regards the law." (1968, 107). Herein is the Law of Grammar superimposed on Thucydides's words. Gomme's analysis itself is somewhat technical, but its gist is straightforward. As he says:[21]

> The main *de*-clause [the *metesti de*... clause] must either qualify or more closely define the *men*-clause [the *onoma men*... clause]. Such qualification or definition being necessary because of the inevitable ambiguity of the word *dēmokratia*. (Gomme 1968, 107)

Here, it seems, the name of democracy sets the regulative rule, and not, it seems, the other way around.[22] For Gomme, formal grammar here exposes an essential underlying element that is not subject to regulative idea. The ambiguity, as he puts it (1968, 107–8),

> arises from the two common meanings of *dēmos,* the whole people, the state, the populous, and the masses, in effect, the poor, populares (as in 65.2); so that *demokratia* can mean either simply majority rule in a state where all citizens have the vote (cf. Athenagoras' statement at vi. 39. 1, *egō de phēmi prōta men dēmon xumpan ōnomasthai, oligarchian de meros;* and Alcibiades at v. 89. 6, *hēmeis de tou xympantos proestēmen*) or the consistent domination of the state by the

---

21 For a summary of later classical scholarship on the oration see Hornblower (1991, 292–316).
22 From a more technical perspective, see work influenced by contemporary cognitive-functional linguists, e.g., Larsen-Freeman (1997) and Ellis and Larsen-Freeman (2009) and, applied to ancient Greek, Kahane (2018a) and Kahane (2018b). Such work, partly inflected through arguments about complexity in the sciences, fundamentally opposes rule-based approaches to grammar (e.g., *mutatis mutandis*, paradigmatic grammars of Greek and Latin, Saussurean notions of *langue,* Chomskyan and other structural and generative grammars, etc.) in favor of stochastic, non-deterministic historical "constructions" and historically mutable patterns. Grammatical "laws" are generally epiphenomenal within such approaches.

masses — the vulgar and ill-educated, as, for example, the Old Oligarch understood democracy.

We are dealing, then, with an "arithmetical dimension" again, which is a mark of the "inevitable," as Gomme puts it, or, as we might say, of the suspended distance within the name of democracy *itself* between the Law and the laws. This suspended distance unites the excluded "poor" and those who possess *axiōsis* (privilege), but it also unites, in their separateness, two regimes (indeed, those that are part of formal taxonomies of political orders in Thucydides, as well as in Plato, Aristotle, and beyond): the one reducing democracy to a fundamental principle, legislated by those who are deemed qualified to guide the state, the other following the law of the whole people.[23]

Writing half a century later, in Derrida's chronological era yet representing very different, largely Anglo-American traditions of politics and the Law, historian Josiah Ober (1993 and 2015) too comments on Thucydides's words.[24] He has read Gomme, and, like Gomme and others, must allow for the grammatical tension within Pericles's speech. "The [...] two clauses of the passage ['on the one hand' and 'on the other']," Ober says, "which should explain and clarify the referent *politeia,* are spectacularly antithetical" (Ober 1998, 87; see further Kahane 2020). The count here does not tally. Ober proceeds to consider another passage slightly later in the funeral oration (2.40.2–3):

---

23 There is first, "the general democratic principle of equality before the law of all citizens as individuals", and then, as Gomme saw (1968, 108) it, an important modification stating that, *kata tēn axiōsin,* (broadly, "in accordance with their distinction"), "for public affairs there is not complete equality since in fact everyone is not as good as his neighbour, but *axiōsis, aretē* determines election to office."

24 Ober is a prominent exponent of American liberalism within the study of classics and politics in antiquity, writing in a scholarly tradition that, by and large, ignores Derrida and the critical engagement of French and "continental" phenomenology with classical antiquity (see Leonard 2000). In a recent review of Ober (2015), Peter Rose suggests that Ober's work "ultimately tells us more about the ideology of the Stanford classics department than it does about ancient Greece" (2017, 149).

> We ourselves can [collectively] judge rightly regarding affairs, even if [each of us] does not [individually] originate the arguments; we do not consider words [*logous*] an impediment to action [*ergois*], but rather [regard it] essential to be previously instructed [*prodidakhthēnai*] by speech [*logōi*] before embarking on necessary action [*ergōi*]. We are peculiar also in that we hold that we are simultaneously persons who are daring and who debate what they will put their hands to. Among other men ignorance [*amathia*] leads to rashness while seasoned debate [*logismos*] just bogs them down.

"This passage," Ober (1993, 93) states, "is virtually a definition of democratic knowledge and its relation to enactment and action." Here, in his view, the Athenians claim to "reject the existence of a hierarchy between *logoi* (words, speeches) and *erga* (actions, deeds)." Thus, by necessity, differences of opinion in an open, equal debate (the democratic principle of *isēgoria*) lead, as Ober sees it, to ineffective action. Ober (1993, 97) finds Athens' "exceptional" principle of democracy and "democratic knowledge"[25] politically and, we ourselves might say, numerically (that is, in terms of both action and ontology) in need of resolution. Yet it is precisely in Ober's scholarly *Unbehagen*, as we might perhaps describe it, that we ourselves can find the political symptom of a future that is not *faite*.

In an attempt to foreclose his discontent with ineffective democratic action and to re-establish the principle of epistemic hierarchy and political sovereignty, Ober (1993, 96) suggests that Pericles's role as a statesman, here and in the *Histories*, mimics that of Thucydides the historian as an authoritative interpreter of the history of democracy:

---

25 Ober does here draw on the Foucauldian idea of "regimes of truth" (Foucault 1980, 78–133, hence "regimes of knowledge"), but, crucially, without internalizing the ethical or ontological foundations of the use of the term in Foucault. As Ober puts it: "Once again I adopt the term without necessarily accepting the negative connotations" (1993, 82n2). Leonard (2000) is fundamentally correct in her critique of Ober's position.

> Thucydides considers untested and competing *logoi* to be a very dubious basis for understanding reality, and he elevates *erga* above *logoi* in his hierarchy of explanatory values. [... T]he hard work of fact-sifting and interpretation (at all levels, we might again suggest) is done in advance by the expert [like Thucydides], rather than being left to the assemblyman or reader.

Here, in Ober's corrective attempt to re-impose the Law on democratic surplus, is the explicit symptom, the *non-dit* of democracy-to-come. Thucydides's actions, his *erga,* the basis of his understanding of reality, are, needless to say, technically, irreducibly *logoi,* that is to say, not action (as Ober would have it) but, precisely, speech.

Writing at about the same time as Derrida's *The Politics of Friendship* within a closely related, but not identical tradition of contemporary French discussions of democracy, Jacques Rancière too turns to Pericles's oration, which he describes as a "founding text of democracy's reflection on itself" (1995, 40). Like Derrida, he considers the radical character of Pericles's words:

> This speech immediately proposes a concept of freedom which treats it as the unity of two ideas: a particular idea of the *public* and a particular idea of the *private*. In the words that Thucydides puts in his mouth, Pericles says something like this: in public we conduct the affairs of the city; as for the private, as for the affairs of the individual, we leave those things to be handled as each person sees fit. (Rancière 1995, 40)

Rancière's double paraphrase, "in the words that Thucydides puts in his mouth, Pericles says something like this," takes us, by a different route, to the number again. But it is worth briefly looking back again to Thucydides's exact words to see what Rancière makes of them (2.37.2):

And not only in our public life are we conducting our life in the polis freely [*eleutherōs politeuomen*], but also as regards our freedom from suspicion [*es tēn... hupopsian*] of one another in the pursuits of every-day life; for we do not feel resentment at our neighbour if he does as he likes, nor yet do we put on sour looks which, though harmless, are painful to behold.

Rancière (1995, 41, my emphasis) explains:

The concept of freedom unifies the private and the public, then, but *it unifies them in their very separateness* [...] the democratic political subject has a shared domain in the very separateness of a way of life characterized by two great features: the absence of constraints and the absence of suspicion.[26]

We need to emphasize the *philological* precision and distinctness of Rancière's observation. Ober (1993) resolves the indeterminacy concomitant to multiple vectors of action (or constituencies, or democratic words, or the number, etc.) by separating "the people" from the people, and thus providing a symptom that defines the principle. Yet Thucydides's explicit use of number — that is to say his use of the first person plural present-tense of the main verb *politeuomen*, his use of a grammatical form that formally marks *the many* — confirms that, *contra* Ober, the par-

---

26 The key phrase here is "the absence of constraints and the absence of suspicion." To understand Rancière, we must look at his paraphrase, at his practice of paraphrase and avoidance of direct quotation, and at Thucydides's own "paraphrastic" formulation. Like the paraphrase, Thucydides's precise language is as clear as it is free and is thus, let us suggest, an isomorphic grammatical illustration of the inherent unity-in-separateness of the concept of democracy. On the one hand, the structure of Thucydides's sentences tends to be clear to many readers of Greek yet, on the other hand, it is almost always (and certainly in the passsages discussed) not reducible to the formalized laws of Greek grammar and can be difficult to translate verbatim. Herein, let us suggest, we can see Thucydides's genius as a historian, political thinker, and writer of prose.

ties involved, that is, a) Thucydes's Pericles, the foremost man of action in Athens' democracy who, had he lived, might perhaps have saved democracy from itself; b) Thucydides "himself," the preeminent narrator of the history of Athenian democracy; and c) the "poor," the *demos*,[27] are included, in their separateness, precisely as Rancière argues, within the unity of the *demos* in the singularity of a here and now.

Paradoxically, the meaning of this main verb, *politeuomen* (what this word "will have been *able* to signify, what it *ought* to have meant," to borrow Derrida's expression) is absolutely clear. Yet its reference is, just as plainly, an open-ended number of activities that, in their separateness, comprise the unity of the actions of all *politai* (citizens) in the *polis,* including Pericles and Thucydides, as plurals within the singularity of the *politeia* (the commonwealth). *Politeuomen* means *"we* conduct our business in the *polis,"* *"we* live our lives as citizens," and "we do so *within the polis and the collective of the demos."*

Thucydides's words, Rancière stresses, point to the essential "sporadic character" of democracy, which, as we have just seen, is also recognized in the identity of disparate readings of Thucydides by Derrida and, no less, *mutatis mutandis,* by Gomme (1968) and Ober (1993). Rancière (1995, 94, my emphasis) concludes:[28]

> There can be no *arche* corresponding to the *demos* as subject, no way of ruling according to some *inaugural* [what we might scientifically call "deterministic"] principle; there is only a *-cracy,* a manner of prevailing. Prevailing because one is the best, say Pericles' admirers Thucydides and Callicles; prevailing because one prevails, retorts his detractor Plato. The -cracy of the best — of the *kreitton* — is no quality, no definable expertise, but rather the sheer extra weight

---

27 The terms "poor" and the *dēmos* are of fundamental importance to Rancière's conception of democracy. See, e.g., Rockhill in the glossary to Rancière (2004, 84) with further references.

28 See further Kahane (2020).

borne by the one best able to submit to the dictates of his own desire, who prevails among the people; for he who gives the people the greatest number of arsenals, the greatest number of colonies and the greatest sense of their own importance, is the one who receives the most power from them in return. *The "one too many" of democracy here allows itself to be reduced to the "more, always more" of unsatisfied desire, of the economic imperialism that turns democracy into the child of oligarchy and the mother of tyranny.*

Democracy, Rancière points out, is a regime that is the unity of the *"one too many"* and *"the 'more, always more'* of unsatisfied desire", a regime, he says, "governed by the judicious use of its own un-governability" (1995, 95). Which in Rancière's political philosophy is, of course, precisely the arithmetical purpose of politics itself: "leading the community harmoniously through discord itself, through the impossibility of the people being equal to themselves" (1995, 95).[29]

The question, which has often been directed at Derrida, which emerges in Gomme's analysis, which is "resolved" symptomatically by Ober's assertion of Pericles's and Thucydides's authority over the poor and un-educated and which has also been raised by Rancière himself in at least two essays discussing Derrida's democracy[30] — the question which we can, *mutatis mutandis,* also direct towards Rancière (and his view of judicious government by the use of un-governability) — is how, within the political freedom of democracy and the ontological and ethical freedom of a future-to-come, can we account for political agency? How, in other words, can there be a force that strives towards a *"justice*-to-come"? How can we *responsibly* relate, say, Periclean

---

29 Though I cannot here discuss them here in detail, there are, of course, important differences between Derrida and Rancière that correspond to basic methodological distinctions and to the place of these thinkers in the history of contemporary "continental" and "post-continental" thought. In essence, where Derrida stresses radical difference, Rancière relies on radical equality. See Rancière (2007 and 2009); see also Hoa (2020).
30 See various responses in Rancière (2007 and 2009).

democracy to action in a democratic future? Or, more simply, if the future and the future of responsible action are not *faite* but free, how *does* ungovernable democracy govern and act? These are as much questions of ethics and ontology as they are questions of history.

Responses to these questions have, and will have, occupied many long discussions (see, e.g., Cheah and Guerlac 2009a). Here, turning again to the formalities of the material world and its relation to political agency and to history, I want to briefly consider just one form of response. Whatever the ontological state of matter, the broad implication of the assumption of the inherent complexity of dynamic systems is that, though there is certainly action in the history of the world and though we can relate to action by functional approximations (for example, though probabilities), we cannot, strictly speaking, act upon the world in such a way as to affect an ontologically determinate projection — such as when we act through the principle of democracy or study the history of its inheritance.

Consider briefly another, famous and more-recent thought experiment invoked in the sciences: imagine a box containing radioactive material, some poison, and a cat. Inside the box, an atom decays. By some mechanism or another this action releases the poison, which kills the cat (Schrödinger 1935). Now, fundamentally, at least according to proponents of the widely-held Copenhagen Interpretation of quantum mechanics, prominently Niels Bohr, I cannot know in advance the state of the atom in the future. The atom state is in "a superposition of having decayed and having not decayed" (Barad 2010, 250).[31] What, then, is the state of the cat? Erwin Schrödinger's macabre illustration (1935) was designed to project one of quantum physics' basic paradoxes, the state of superposition, onto the world

---

31 A quantum superposition is "a non-classical" relation between different possibilities" (Schrödinger 1935.); thus, the atom is both "decayed" and "non-decayed." See also Crockett (2018), with further comments on Barad and on Derrida.

at large and to problematize it within a wider frame of human discourse.

The point for us here, of course, is the implication of this strange thought experiment on our understanding of agency and future action. The prospects of Schrödinger's cat inside the box may worry me. But if Schrödinger's claim is correct, I, as an agent, cannot act with a determinate view of how things (the state of the atom or of the cat) are and thus to a future that, as Nancy, paraphrasing Derrida, puts it, is "projected, represented, given in advance as an aim" (in Fabbri 2007, 431). This, for Derrida, as, *mutatis mutandis*, in quantum physics, is not a matter of my state of ignorance or the imperfect condition of my instruments or, in the realm of history, my historical grasp of Pericles and Thucydides. It is a matter of fundamental states. As Karen Barad (2010, 251) explains,[32]

> it is not the case that the cat is either alive or dead and that we simply do not know which; nor that the cat is both alive and dead simultaneously (this possibility is logically excluded since "alive" and "dead" are understood to be mutually exclusive states); nor that the cat is partly alive and partly dead (presumably "dead" and "alive" are understood to be all or nothing states of affair); nor that the cat is in a definitive state of being not alive and not dead (in which case it presumably wouldn't qualify as a (once) living being).

The point, she adds, is that:

> Quantum superpositions radically undo classical notions of identity and being (which ground the various incorrect interpretative options just considered). Quantum superpositions (at least on Bohr's account) tell us that being/becoming

---

32 Barad (2010) considers quantum entanglements, hauntological relations and justice-to-come (though not, perhaps surprisingly, their relation to democracy-to-come); see also Barad's influential *Meeting the Universe Halfway* (2007).

is an indeterminate matter: there simply *is not a determinate fact of the matter* concerning the cat's state of being alive or dead. (250–51, emphasis original)

The future of the atom, and the cat (a troubling example, that nevertheless stresses the urgency of the fundamental issue), and my future as a democratic agent, is, let us thus say, a future-to-come, which is a future that will have come, but only through the indeterminate agency of my participation in the material world.

When I speak here of a participation in the "material" world, I have no wish to brush aside acts of will or the mind in a manner that is implied, for example, by Laplace's assumptions. In the absence of a certain type of calculable determinism — available, in principle, to the superior intelligence of the Demon — the world and all its atoms, its cats, its boxes, and its wills *will be* — even as it will not be pre-determined or knowable to the Demon — through my participation in the world. My will is not null, but I as an agent and my will are entangled in the material world. While Pericles lives, before the Sicilian Expedition, the fate of Athens' democracy is a "fate-to-come."

To stress, I *can* act upon the world through my will. I can take such-and-such actions, which, in my best ethical earnest, I may believe to be "good." To *not* think, for example, about how to act to save the cat or how to resist injustice or save the state would be to relinquish my ethical responsibility. The stakes in taking action may be higher or lower. But I cannot look to *the act that matters,* that *really* matters, and calculate its effect. I act knowing that I cannot calculate that effect with determinate force, yet knowing that my actions are inseparable from the world. In that action, as Derrida effectively says, lies responsibility and the ethics of a justice to come.

To stress: as Schrödinger himself would agree, I can observe the world in retrospect to see for myself, for example, if the cat is dead or alive by opening the box, or indeed in Thucydides's *History*, to see what happened to Pericles, to Athens, and to Athenian democracy. That, however, does not tell me anything about the world, about the atom "itself," about the entangled order of things or about how to act in relation to this order. Here, the world of material behavior, the world of material objects and states, and the world of ethics seem to align. As Barad (2010, 251), for example, says:

> *Quantum entanglements* are not the intertwining of two (or more) states/ entities/events, but *a calling into question of the very nature of two-ness, and ultimately of one-ness as well. Duality, unity, multiplicity, being, are undone.* "Between" will never be the same. *One is too few, two is too many.*

Barad adds:

> *Entanglements are not intertwinings of separate entities, but rather irreducible relations of responsibility.* There is no fixed dividing line between "self" and "other," "past" and "present" and "future," "here" and "now," "cause" and "effect." (2010, 265, my emphasis.)

We are back, then, to an arithmetical dimension of time and the world, and — it seems almost obvious to say so — of democracy too.[33]

As with the atom and the cat, so with action in history and with Athenian democracy: I know that Pericles, struck by the plague, died in 429 BCE. From that year his advice was no longer available to the Athenians. I know that the Sicilian Expedition (415–413 BCE) did not end well, that Athens lost the war, and that Athenian democracy eventually came to an end.

In conclusion, then, my first point is simply to suggest that disputes about the nature of democracy offer symptomatic

---

33 Aristotle (in *Physics* 4.220a24–26, ed. Ross 1950) famously says "time, then, is the dimension of movement in its before-and-afterness, and is continuous (because movement is so)." In Derrida too, albeit in a fundamentally different sense, time is *indeed,* the number of change.

proof that the trajectory of democracy, already of Athenian democracy, is distinct but incalculable. It is incalculable, not because there have not been determined attempts to calculate it or because of our incomplete knowledge of the facts. Rather, it is so simply because the "arithmetic" nature of democracy and of any and all attempts to close-off its meaning require a supplement. Pericles's words are not an incomplete description of democracy. They are, rather, a complete description of democracy's entangled state; they are always more than one pronouncement and always less than two. Any attempt to argue to the contrary will itself confirm this dual state, of course — it does not obliterate the history of our reading of Thucydides, but constitutes a part of that one "history."

My second point is that the diverse history of the readings of the funeral oration describes a relation between the past of the future and the future of the past that is precisely "to-come." We can certainly name this relation — a relation, say, between Athenian democracy and modern democracy. But any such naming would not be reducible to an algorithmic trajectory that can be expressed in terms of formal descriptions. More importantly, any such naming, though it clearly occurs, would not simply characterize the past, or the future, but would actively re-configure, in the *here and now,* the trajectories of the future-to-come. Thus, regardless of the specific positions that readings of the oration offer, where such readings attempt to "disentangle" the entanged state of Pericles's statement, they would, in fact, be re-affirming its entanglement.

My third point is that any interpretation of Pericles's statement maneuvers fundamentally between radical inclusiveness and exclusion — of individuals and groups, in one form or another, between what is "public" and what is "private" — and does so, as we have seen above, undecidably. Again, where interpreters attempt to remove the terms of the supplementary character of democracy, their attempts may be seen precisely as proof of the supplement.

What constitutes the essence of a democratic action and an ethics-to-come then, is, not a willful foreclosure on the part of an independent agent nor meaningless resignation to an unknowable future but a recognition, both absolute and entirely possible (thus absolutely true to "the facts"), by actors, of the ontological status of democracy and of the entangled nature of any action within it. That recognition, because it is itself entangled, is true to the world and true to *itself.*

12

Before and after Greece and Egypt in the Eighteenth Century

Daniel Orrells

Ordering history into a narrative of "before and after" is always an ideological process, which means making political judgements about the relationship between the past and the present, between cause and effect, between tradition and reception. The construction of a narrative of before and after so often involves the question of origins: what made that event happen? What happened before it? What produced us? And crucially, where do we come from? A grand narrative of modern European intellectual history has structured the story about its before and after around the binary opposition of ancient/modern, looking back in particular to ancient Greece in search of origins. Indeed, from the late eighteenth century onwards, western scholars and intellectuals became increasingly invested in arguing that Europe's origins could be found in ancient Greece and that the achievements of the ancient Greeks were autochthonous and independent of other eastern Mediterranean cultures. The compartmentalization of academic disciplines encouraged this paradigm of thought. Classical studies, theology, Egyptology, and Assyriology went their separate ways (see Marchand 1996, and Conybeare and Goldhill 2020). Egyptology is an interesting case in point. The decipherment of the hieroglyphs in the second decade of the nineteenth century put to bed the idea that ancient Egyptian hieroglyphs recorded timeless, erudite wisdom handed down by God to Adam, a belief that had attracted many Renaissance humanists and early modern intellectuals.

And yet, the older story about Egypt being an archive and preserver of Christian doctrine — that Egypt was a crucial link in the transmission of Christianity from the east to the west — persisted precisely when a different narrative about the Greek origins of European culture was emerging. Indeed, biblical archaeology in the nineteenth century continued to be captivated by the potential of Egyptological excavations for the demonstration of the accuracy of Sacred History.[1] Despite the institutionalization and professionalization of academic knowledge into discrete disciplinary formations, the place of Egypt in the modern European imagination shows how this process was, in fact, much messier. While Egyptology emerged into a university discipline at the end of the nineteenth century, ancient Egypt also retained its allure as the key to the secrets of the origins of modern civilization. Even if academic posts and curatorial positions in Egyptology reflected the rising importance of "nationalizing" academic specialization, the relationship of Egypt to the rest of the ancient Mediterranean and therefore to Europe itself continued to be the subject of much debate both inside universities and museums and way beyond.[2] The first volume of Martin Bernal's *Black Athena: The Afroasiatic Roots of Classical Civilization* (1987) argued that the European admiration for Egypt was eclipsed by the veneration of Greece around 1785. As a result of Bernal's important intellectual history, others have honed his account to show how much nineteenth-century philhellenism framed the endeavors of classical scholarship, which became increasingly embedded in a racialized under-

---

1   On ancient Egypt in Renaissance and early modern culture and scholarship, see Curran (2007) and Stolzenberg (2013) with further references. On biblical archaeology, see Goldhill (2021).
2   On the complex position of Egypt in the western nineteenth- and early twentieth-century cultural imaginations, see Irwin (1980) and Schotter (2018).

standing of the ancient world (see Bernal 1987, and further discussion in Marchand 1996). European and American empires all too often turned back to biblical, Egyptian, and Greco-Roman antiquity to justify their ideologies of racial superiority. At the same time, the cultures of the modern Black Atlantic turned colonialist or imperialist narratives on their head. The ancient Mediterranean basin became a potent and complex resource for many Black writers, artists, and intellectuals from the eighteenth century onwards (see Gilroy 1993; Rankine 2006; Greenwood 2010; Orrells, Bhambra, and Roynon 2011; and Moyer, Lecznar, and Morse 2020).

This chapter explores the question of the historical relationship — the before and the after — of ancient Greece and Egypt in the eighteenth century, to further nuance and complicate the narratives of the rise of philhellenism. While the eighteenth-century antiquarian turn to material culture has indeed been seen as foundational — the "before" — for the development and institutionalization of the discipline of classics, we will see that the emerging narrative about Europe's ancient Greek origins was constructed in dialogue with eighteenth-century debates about the Egyptian hieroglyph, the history of writing, and the relationship between image and text. Indeed, the look back to Greek origins was famously made through a contrast between the material and the textual by Johann Joachim Winckelmann, a key figure in the emergence of classical studies as a discrete, academic discipline. His 1764 *History of the Art of Antiquity* told a story about the "origin, growth, change, and fall of art" (Winckelmann 2006a, 71) and encouraged his readers to see ancient Greek sculpture — as opposed to Egypt and the east — as the point of origin for the European Renaissance and in turn the rebirth of classicism in the eighteenth century.[3] But in the conclusion of his book, Winckelmann lamented the impossibility of writing the history of ancient art. He compared himself to a "beloved stand[ing] on the seashore, as she follows with tearful eyes her departing sweetheart, with no hope of seeing him

---

3 See Harloe (2013).

again, and believes she can glimpse even in the distant sail the image of her lover." "So we," Winckelmann continued, "like the lover, have as it were only a shadowy outline of the subject of our desires remaining." And he summed up, "[h]ad the ancients been poorer, they would have written better about art: compared to them, we are like badly portioned heirs" (Winckelmann 2006a, 351). The historian could only desire the outline of her lover in the canvas of his boat as he sails away. The modern historian is doomed to write, whereas the ancients, who produced the art, did not have to. Winckelmann contrasted ancient and modern as an opposition between ancient visual and material culture and modern textual historiography. Katherine Harloe has shown, however, that Johann Gottfried van Herder was highly critical of Winckelmann's discussion of Egyptian art and the argument that the origins of European art should be traced back to Greece instead of further east (Harloe 2013). Indeed, Winckelmann made his contrast between ancient art and modern historiography at a time when there was much discussion about the Egyptian hieroglyph which seemed to be neither image nor text in the eighteenth-century imagination. In this chapter, then, we will see that the emerging philhellenism, that posited a Greek "before" to the European "after," developed in response to images of and ideas about ancient Egypt. The Horatian dictum *ut pictura poesis* was a central maxim of aesthetic theory and practice in the eighteenth century (see Braider 1999 and Marshall 1997). While Winckelmann lamented the melancholic distance between modern scholarly narrative and the ancient world, the antiquarian desire to blur the divide between modern historiographical text and ancient visual and material culture would be fuelled by eighteenth-century fantasies about the Egyptian hieroglyph.

This chapter begins by exploring the Egyptian hieroglyph in the eighteenth-century imagination as a frame for our discussion with the help of Jacques Derrida. We will then move on to examine the centrality of Homer's *Iliad* and the description of Achilles's Shield to the Quarrel of the Ancients and Moderns which was so important to the emergence of eighteenth-century debates about the relationship between antiquity and modernity. Homer resisted periodization because of the perceived sublime visuality of his language. Both visual and verbal, the Iliadic shield of Achilles engaged antiquarians to think about the historical relationship between Homeric epic and ancient art, and in turn the relationship between ancient visuality and modern, scholarly textuality. As we shall see, these debates coincided with attempts to historicize language and writing and to insert the Egyptian hieroglyph into those historical narratives. But like Homer, the hieroglyph was hard to put in its historical place because it appeared to behave like a primitive pictographic mode of representation and a more modern semiotic sign system. Giambattista Vico's *New Science* was one of the most important responses to these debates. As we will see, the hieroglyph was a crucial device for Vico to explore the relationship between the ancient world and modern scholarship in thinking about Homer's place in history. The second half of this chapter will then turn to two of the most important mid-century antiquarians, Winckelmann and Pierre-François Hugues, the self-styled "Baron d'Hancarville," to examine how their scholarly attempts to visualize ancient Greek culture were haunted by the hieroglyphic fantasy of bridging the divide between modern text and ancient art.

Greece and Egypt in the History of Language and Writing

In Renaissance and early modern culture, many scholars had argued that Egyptian hieroglyphs were vessels of *prisca theologia* or Adamic wisdom — which nevertheless required decipherment and translation. Egyptian hieroglyphs seemed to envision the possibility of non-discursive communication, bypassing the opacity of language, and yet their meaning was veiled in obscurity and frustratingly resistant to comprehension (see Stolzenberg 2013). By the eighteenth century, scholars had become interested in the history of language and writing and in inserting hieroglyphs into their narratives. Jacques Derrida's *Of Grammatology* (1976) provides us with an important overview for understanding this moment in intellectual history. For Derrida, the history of the conceptualization of language seems to begin with the ancient Greeks. Aristotle's *On Interpretation* is positioned as a foundational text in the history of the understanding of the sign. As Derrida explains, Aristotle instituted the distinction between the "signifier" (the given sound or mark) and the "signified" (the idea or concept). Furthermore, Aristotle distinguished between two types of signifier, the spoken and the written. Derrida cites Aristotle: "Just as all men do not have the same writing, so all men do not have the same speech sounds, but mental experiences, of which these are the *primary symbols,* are the same for all" (1976, 1).[4] Speech directly signifies the ideas or intention of the speaker, whereas writing is merely the sign of the spoken sign. What we think is universal, but how we write is conventional and culturally specific, entailing for Aristotle that speech was chronologically prior to writing. The next important moment in the history of the sign for Derrida is the "epoch of Christian creationism and infinitism when these appropriate the resources of Greek conceptuality." In other words, Christianity's appropriation of Aristotle erected a theological distinction between the sensible and the intelligible worlds, between the language of mortal humans and the truthful language of God. And it is this Greek-Christian heritage that underpins modern conceptualizations of the sign. Derrida quotes the twentieth-century linguist Roman Jakobson who pointed out in 1949 that "the mediaeval [Christian] definition of sign — 'aliquid stat pro aliquo' [*something stands for something else*] — has been resurrected and put forward as still valid and productive" (1976, 13, additions in original) by modern linguistic science. And if speech seemed closer to the presence of the signified than writing, then this was also reflected in how the history of writing was understood. The image was deemed as chronologically prior to writing systems that used conventional signs. The visual seemed closer to speech and to the "language

---

4 Derrida cites Aristotle, *On Interpretation* 1, 16a (edition of Cooke-Tredennick 1938); translation modified.

of nature" than writing, which was condemned to being a mere sign of a sign. The idea that speech has conceptual and historical priority over writing is, then, an idea which finds its origins for Derrida with the ancient Greeks and their Christian successors.

At the same time, however, Derrida also shows that at the heart of this tradition on the history of language and writing the Egyptian hieroglyphs emerged as a troublesome question. Rather than simply turning back to Greek-Christian origins, Derrida deploys the Egyptians as underpinninng an alternative vision of the history of language and writing. And for Derrida, the moment when modern intellectuals became interested in a "general history of writing" is the moment when the Egyptians were already troubling the Greek-Christian understanding of the sign. As Derrida shows in *Of Grammatology,* the first modern scholar to use the expression "general history of writing" was the English churchman William Warburton in 1742 (1977, 75). And hieroglyphs were central to Warburton's understanding of the history of writing. At the Enlightenment origins of scholarship on the history of language and writing, then, the Egyptians were vying for attention, just as for Plato at the origins of philosophy, the Egyptian invention of writing so concerned Socrates in the *Phaedrus,* as Derrida would explore in his 1972 essay "Plato's Pharmacy" (published as part of Derrida 1981). In 1977, Warburton's essay on the hieroglyphs, which had originally appeared as part of his larger work *The Divine Legation of Moses* (1738–41), was reprinted in French and introduced by a commentary by Derrida called "Scribble (writing-power)" (Derrida 1979). As Derrida would show, Warburton's history of language, which began with signs of "natural" origins and then moved onto "arbitrary" semiotic systems, would not be quite so straightforward.

For Warburton, the hieroglyph exemplified an early stage in the history of writing, when pictographic representation used "natural," transparent images to signify what was being referred to. But as Derrida demonstrates, for Warburton, the "natural" process of the development of writing meant that man can represent the world around us with increasing economy, with more abridgement, with more time and space of the archive saved. Each modification of representing the world was a step towards the situation where one "sign" — or alphabetical letter or word — can be used to mean several different things. This "natural" process continues "quite naturally" one step further so that a sign can refer to any signified whatsoever. And yet, as Warburton worried, this entirely "natural" development allowed for the possibility of cryptography and the corruption of the hieroglyph that led it to be used by priestly classes to conceal their wisdom behind enigmatic symbols (in Derrida 1979, 137).

As Derrida shows, paradoxically, the difference between clear writing and cryptography must be blurred for there to be a distinction between clear writing and cryptography. It is writing (be it hieroglyphic or pictographic or alphabetic) as iterable, borrowable and usable by others in different contexts, that conditions the very possibility of cryptography. This repeatability, however, both ensures and denies the success of a truly cryptic sign that could conceal a secret; as Warburton notes, as soon as a cryptic system is invented, one has to know that it is a cryptic system (see Derrida 1979, 145–47). This additional secret has to be conveyed to those who are meant to be in the know, so that distinguishing between simple and secret signage is possible. Yet the very iterability of written signs always brings with it the risk that the secret can be discovered owing to the very fact that what makes these signs secret is precisely the fact that more than one person to the exclusion of certain others must know that they are secret. This then means another new system must be invented and so on *ad infinitum*. The arbitrary relationship between signifier and signified ensures the success of cryptography, but at the same time this arbitrariness means that a signifier can be used in any context so that the cryptic secret can never be completely secret and is always liable to discovery. As Derrida writes, quoting Warburton:

> Always more veil, "continual revolution" (*incessant revolutions of things*) since the crypt is uncovered regularly and another must be invented which in turn […] etc. At each

turn, more veil: "But as a result of the continual revolution of things, these same figures that had at first been invented for clarity and then converted into mystery, at length resumed their initial use." (1979, 139)

The hieroglyph in Warburton's account, then, occupied a complex historical position, both primitive and more modern, between image and text, between natural clarity and political obfuscation, becoming a symbol of the "incessant revolution" of the history of writing itself. The hieroglyph was literally positioned at the center of Warburton's general history of writing between the pictographic and the alphabetic, a positioning of significance for Derrida: "The hieroglyph is thus clearly the exemplary center of writing, its medium, an element, a species and the genus, a part and the whole, general writing" (1979, 128). Various eighteenth-century intellectuals would rehearse arguments that hieroglyphs were used both to communicate messages to the public and to symbolically conceal priestly secrets about divine or political truths deemed too dangerous for public consumption. As both pictorial and textual, the hieroglyph seemed to blur the historical rupture between natural and conventional semiotics. The hieroglyph complicated the historical narrative of "before" and "after." The paradoxical nature of the hieroglyph — it was a natural picture that anyone could understand as well as a symbolic text read only by the initiated — would captivate the eighteenth-century imagination.[5] We have heard Winckelmann lament the chasm between ancient art and modern historiography. As we shall shortly see, while antiquarians explored the relationship between ancient Greek art and their own modern textual discourse, they would repeatedly turn back to the hieroglyph, as they dreamed of making their writing visual.

---

5 On hieroglyphs in the seventeenth and eighteenth centuries more generally, see Assmann (2014) and Graczyk (2015).

Achilles's Shield: Visualizing History and Inspiring Artists

Pliny's history of art in his *Natural History* was a foundational text from the Renaissance onwards for modern accounts of ancient art. The *Natural History* was full of stories that, in Leonard Barkan's words, praised "an artistic image by declaring that it is absolutely indistinguishable from the thing it was meant to represent. [...] Pliny expressed a fervent nostalgia for a time when art objects and the things they represented could be measured against one another in clear and simple ways" (Barkan 1999, 81).[6] But if Pliny looked back in celebration to the naturalistic marvels of ancient Greek art, creating a Renaissance longing to unearth the marvellous images and objects that Pliny had described, then the eighteenth-century cultural imagination sought to go even further back than Pliny to disinter the very origins of art. Eighteenth-century antiquarians became fascinated with the idea of uncovering not what Pliny longingly looked back to but what he was not even aware of existing in the past. The antiquarian turn to material and visual culture in the early eighteenth century sought to go beyond and outdo the reports on ancient art in Pliny. Indeed, this desire for origins was part of a much larger intellectual culture where the search for origins was a crucial and ubiquitous question among Enlightenment thinkers, whose multifarious interests reflected a profound interest in the possibilities and challenges of excavating the beginnings and subsequent progress of human society.[7] The antiquarian quest for the origins of art meant turning from Roman Pliny's text to another text, Homer's *Iliad*, supposedly the earliest poem of the Greco-Roman tradition, in order to disinter the history of art at the time of the Trojan War, a time when, according to Pliny, painting was completely undeveloped.

---

6 On Pliny's art history, see Barkan (1999, 65–117); Carey (2006); Doody (2010); Isager (1991); and McHam (2013).
7 On the Enlightenment interest in the "primitive" and narratives of origins and beginnings, see Grell and Michel (1989) and Novak (1997).

This fascination with the "before" of the "after" of European culture took place precisely at a time when a new discourse on Greek primacy focusing on Homeric originality was emerging. The debate about Homeric epic was a central issue in the Quarrel of the Ancients and the Moderns. As Anthony Grafton, Glenn Most, and James Zetzel have put it, "Homer had served as a sort of litmus test; views about the sort of poetry he wrote and the sort of society he wrote for tended to define a critic's stance on a much wider and deeper range of intellectual issues" (1985, 251). Homer was central and crucial to the disputes that constructed the very notion of a historical relationship between antiquity and modernity in the European Enlightenment imagination (see Simonsuuri 1979, and Porter 2004 and 2021). The debate over whether Homeric epic was a later written version of an earlier oral performance emerged out of the Quarrel about Homer's antiquity and modernity.[8] As Derrida has shown us, the relationship between the oral and the written sign was highly contested in the eighteenth century. In the Quarrel, the Moderns' argument that Homer's lack of knowledge of numerous areas of scientific and technological expertise was so powerful that the Ancients took it on in their defence of the ancient poet. For the Ancients, Homer was a sublime poet, whose talent was instinctive and natural and could not have been taught. While the Moderns often looked back to Plato and philosophy as the beginning of modernity, continuing with the Augustan age which was seen as a model and precursor of the reign of Louis XIV, the Ancients emphasized Homer's remoteness in an older past. The Quarrel over Homer was decisive for the emergence of the idea of the historical distinctiveness of Greece as original and Rome as secondary and derivative (see Norman 2011, and Edelstein 2010, 37–43).

At the same time, his natural sublimity made Homer seem alive and real for the present day, allowing the Ancients to highlight the emotional impact of Homer's poetry on modern read-

---

8 For a recent, succinct discussion of the so-called "Homeric Question," see Dué and Marks (2020).

ers. And the raw and primitive naturalness of Homer's language permitted his admirers to compare his poetry to the visual arts. The emphasis on the sublime visuality of Homer's poetry reflected Enlightenment theories about the history of signs as a historical development from the visual and natural to the scriptural and arbitrary. The Ancients would argue that Homeric epic did not appeal to reason but appealed — and continued to appeal — to the senses. His sublime words led you beyond his words. One Ancient voice, Jean Boivin, Professor of Greek at the Royal College, keeper of the King's Library, and member of the Académie des inscriptions in Paris, argued in 1715 that Homer's poetry was "full of natural images that are perfectly painted" (Boivin 1715, 33 and 31). Or as François Fénelon put it in his *Lettre à l'Académie* in the same year, "He painted with lifelike directness."[9] In other words, "Homer's unadorned naturalism" was able "to transport readers to his own times, customs, and beliefs" (Norman 2011, 187). The painterly sublimity of Homer's poetry was a product of the raw and realistic naturalism of his language and positioned the epic poet both at the dawn of artistic expression and simultaneously accessible to modern eighteenth-century feelings and sensibilities (see also Norman 2011, 208–11).

The issue of the antiquity or the modernity of Homer would become central in the discussions about Achilles's shield in the *Iliad* (18.478–608). Homer's description had been a source of critique by the Moderns: it proved their argument about the rudimentary standard of Homer's poetry, as no shield, it was contended, could have borne as many scenes on its face as represented by Homer. The epic poet clearly knew nothing about military warfare. How could an ancient shield have represented so many details? *Apologie d'Homère et Bouclier d'Achille* is the title of the short book published in 1715 by Boivin, who had employed the French painter Nicholas Vleughels to design an image of what the shield could have looked like and then had it engraved by Charles-Nicholas Cochin (fig. 1). Boivin's analysis

---

9   Quoted, translated, and discussed in Norman (2011, 187).

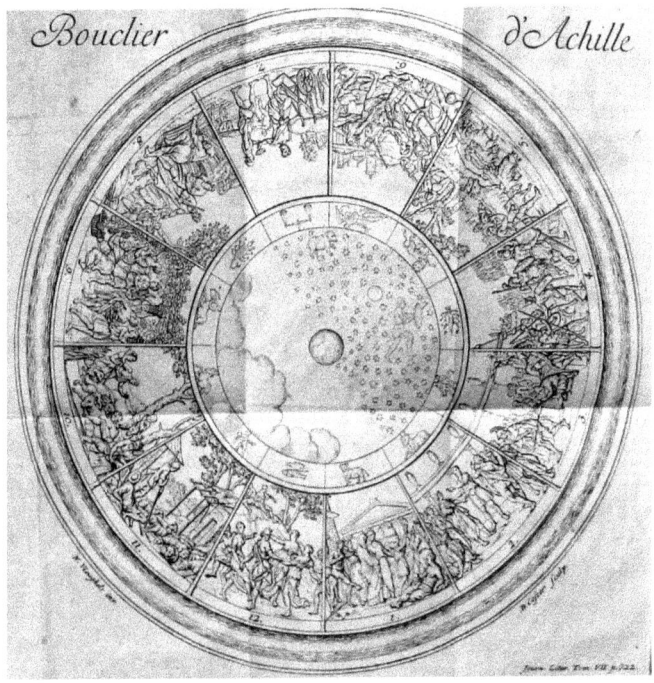

Fig. 1. J. Boivin, *Apologie d'Homère et Bouclier d'Achille* (1715).

of this design formed the culmination of his book. Vleughels came up with an ingenious solution for how everything that Homer describes could be encapsulated on a single surface. He divided the shield into concentric circles: the central circle symbolized the earth and the sea; the next ring depicted the sky, the sun, the moon and the stars; then, the twelve signs of the Zodiac; then, the next ring after that was divided up into twelve panels representing scenes from Homer's description; and then the outermost ring represented the Ocean (see Lecoq 2010, 118–23). In his commentary, Boivin argued that if an engraving could hold what Homer had described, then it must have been possible for a shield that covered most of the body to have done so as well: Homer's shield could indeed have been based on an already-existing example of ancient artistry. But Boivin's ingenious image did not settle the matter about Homer's poetic expertise and Achilles's shield. Instead, it provoked the question further; did the antiquarian print provide a window into a hitherto-unknown early history of art or was it an admirable feat of modern technology to compress the entirety of Achilles's shield into an engraving of a diameter of twenty centimetres? At a time when numerous scientific publications of natural history were opening new vistas of the remote historical past going back further than the Bible, awakening the Enlightenment search for origins, had modern printing expertise managed to open up and visualize another more distant period at the dawn of art history? Or was this a modern production of the past?

Various commentators assumed different positions. For the eminent French antiquarian Bernard de Montfaucon, Boivin's engraving was compelling proof that it was possible to have represented all of Homer's description on a shield. The abbé Claude François Fraguier (1736) had already argued in his "De l'ancienneté de la Peinture" that the *Iliad* makes numerous references to the visual arts, especially Achilles's shield, leading him to conclude that the art of painting was more ancient than most thought and Pliny had believed. Such a possibility was profoundly exciting, for until the mid-eighteenth-century, ancient painting had been a lacuna in the antiquarian archive. With the publication of Boivin's defence of Homer, Achilles's shield appeared to corroborate the well-known stories about the remarkable feats of painterly ancient masters like Zeuxis and Parrhasius, but pushed the art of painting even further back in time than Pliny had ever imagined, as if to the very origins of art history in the classical tradition. The idea captivated Alexander Pope who discussed it in his notes to his translation of Homer's *Iliad*. Some thirty years later, the leading French art connoisseur, the Comte de Caylus, published a series of essays on ancient painting and reprinted Boivin's image. In one essay, Caylus suggested that the shield of Achilles testified to Homer himself having travelled to Egypt where he learnt about the arts. As Anne-Marie Lecoq puts it, "It is only a short step from there, which Caylus takes, to imagine the Greek painter-poet on a Grand Tour on the Nile" (2010, 139).

And yet, antiquarians also questioned whether the engraving really did provide an image of very ancient painting. The original image by Vleugels reflected his admiration of Raphael's paintings. Hadn't Boivin's *Apologie d'Homère,* a work of modern scholarship, in fact inspired the production of other modern works of art such as that by Vleugels? It was easy, then, to see Homer not as a historian of an earlier period of art but as a connoisseur who had provided an aesthetic program for subsequent artists. Indeed, in a 1757 book called *Tableaux tirés de l'Iliade, de l'Odyssée d'Homère et de l'Énéide de Virgile,* Caylus himself suggested scenes from the epics of Homer and Virgil that might form heroic and noble and therefore more suitable subjects for modern painting.[10] Boivin's image did not convince everyone: instead of providing a history of art, Homeric epic might have offered inspiration for later Greek painters and sculptors. Pope himself also thought that Homer might have "designed to give a scheme of what might be performed, [rather] than a description of what really was so" (1996, 897). Winckelmann similarly would write: "Homer's imagination had painted for us on the shield of Achilles what he believed possible but not what one could execute at that point" (1760, 408). In his lavish catalogue of William Hamilton's vases, the Baron d'Hancarville called Homer "a sublime genius" who has allowed us to peer into the earliest periods of Greek art (*Antiquités* 3:162). In a later volume, however, he changes his position. Even if Homer is still "guided by the sublimity of his genius," now he is the poet who "saw into the obscurity of the future and prophesied, as it were, the great feats to be accomplished by the arts" (Winckelmann 1760, 408). If d'Hancarville cannot make up his mind, seeing Homer as both historian and prophet, this equivocation nevertheless reflects a bigger debate about the historical relationship between the visual arts and the Homeric text: which comes before and after? Which is the cause, and which is the development and

---

10   On Caylus's *Tableaux,* see Lavezzi (1999).

elaboration? Which explains and frames the other? Did Homer do a Grand Tour of Egypt, or was he the progenitor of European art?

If Homer's description of Achilles's shield was an important issue in the debates about the relationship between ancient and modern, then, in asking whether the printed engraving of the shield was an image into or of the past or a triumph of modern publishing technology, we see that the question of the relationship between Homeric text and Achillean shield was also a question about the relationship between modern scholarship and ancient art. Just as the question of whether a work of art had instigated the Homeric description or the Homeric description had instigated the subsequent production of art, so the following questions pressed: how far did ancient art condition the nature of modern historical scholarship? Or was modern scholarship actually constructing the ancient past and producing new artistic compositions? As we shall now see, the eighteenth-century conception of the hieroglyph would frame the debate about the historicity of Homer.

Vico's Hieroglyphic Homer

The debate about the historicity of Homer and the visualization of Achilles's shield emerged precisely at a time when antiquarians were attempting to bolster the scholarly respectability of their endeavors in response to the critiques of ancient textual authority made in the latter part of the seventeenth and in the earlier part of the eighteenth centuries. Giambattista Vico's *New Science* was one of the most thoughtful responses to these discussions about the visualization of Homer and its ramifications for the authority of ancient texts in the face of the assaults from modern science and philosophy (see Levine 1991). Vico argued that there never had been a single individual called "Homer." In Vico's history of the emergence of civil society, the ancients were unable to formulate and comprehend abstract concepts and processes. Instead, the ancients envisioned what Vico called "poetic characters" or "imaginative universals," as

Fig. 2. Giambattisa Vico, *New Science,* frontispiece (1744).

metonyms which condensed long material historical processes into a single figure. The ancient Greeks had invented the very idea of "Homer," a single man who supposedly composed the two poems about Achilles and Odysseus. Other ancient peoples similarly invented "poetic characters," to poetically imagine historical developments of the human mind and society. In this manner, then "the Egyptians attributed to Hermes Trismegistus all the inventions that were useful to human life. [. . .] Solon may well be a poetic archetype of the Athenian plebeians in their call for equality" (Vico 1999, 412–14). Furthermore, Vico argued, "In the same way, the Romans attributed to Romulus all their laws about social orders" (1999, 417). This was what Vico called the "master key of my New Science" (1999, 34): his discovery that early man saw inanimate objects, abstract concepts, and historical processes as concrete individuals.

Vico introduced the *New Science* with a remarkable frontispiece, which sought to visually encapsulate his historical account of the invention of Homer (fig. 2). On first glance, the image looks like other early modern prints introducing a learned text. It appears to be an allegory of scholarship, emanating from God, symbolized by the sun emitting its rays to an allegorical figure which might be Philosophy, who in turn passes knowledge down to the scholar who is surrounded by various objects, signifying the different domains of expertise and knowledge. As Vico explains in his introduction, the frontispiece was designed to summarize his text. Indeed, frontispieces and aide-memoires were common features in early-modern book culture. As Francis Bacon — one of Vico's favorite authors — wrote, "an emblem reduces intellectual conceptions to sensible images; for an object of sense always strikes the memory more forcibly and is more easily impressed upon it than an object of intellect" (1870, 4.436–37).[11] But as we learn in Vico's introduction, the statue of the old, bearded man is no symbol of an "intellectual conception," no allegory of timeless wisdom handed down from God. Rather the statue "standing on a broken pedestal signifies my discovery of the true Homer," that is, how "our previous ignorance of the true Homer kept hidden from us the true origins and institutions of the nations" (Vico 1999, 6). The image signifies how the true Homer was no great sage after all — rather "Homer" was an invention or a fantasy made up by the ancient Greeks. Indeed, he was nothing more than an engraved frontispiece of a statue. The image of Homer's statue, then, does not signify the transmission of ancient esoteric wisdom from God into the human realm. Rather, just as Vico asks us to look behind the ancient idea of "Homer" to see the historical processes that produced the tales of Achilles and Odysseus, so we should see the "idea" — the thing to be seen, the image — of Homer in the

---

11 On Vico's frontispiece within its early modern context, see Gilbhard (2012); Mazzotta (2014, 113–39); and Verene (2015).

frontispiece as an allegorical image not of a timeless truth, but of a historical narrative about the development of early man's invention of their primeval past.

On the one hand, then, Vico's frontispiece reflected early modern book culture that was building on significant developments in print technology to allow for seemingly ever more accurate and detailed visual representation across a range of scientific areas such as astronomy and natural history. And yet, Vico's two-dimensional depiction of Homer's statue was designed to be a pointedly self-conscious vision of the complexity of the relationship between original and copy, precisely because the statue is a representation of an original that had never actually existed — of an individual who was supposed to be nothing but a later invention. Vico's frontispiece is, then, a profoundly self-reflexive commentary on the relationship between the ancient world and later, more modern print scholarship: the frontispiece visualizes how the "poetic characters" of the ancient world such as Homer, Hermes Trismegistus, Solon, and Romulus are nothing but more modern constructed images of historical processes. Vico's frontispiece accurately envisions the development of early man by visualizing that no ancient past can be envisioned without being composed and constructed from the perspective of the modern. "Thus for Vico," as Joseph Levine has put it, "Homer was neither ancient nor modern in the terms of contemporary parlance but a voice from a wholly different age that could only be understood or retrieved with the aid of a wholly new science" (1991, 78–79). The true history of the ancient world is a new story, a new science. The debate about the visualization of Homer allowed Vico to re-think the relationship between the before and the after.

It is fascinating, then, that in his introduction, Vico writes that in the bottom half of the image various "hieroglyphs lay out the history of the development of civil society" (1999, 25). As we have already seen, Egyptian hieroglyphs captivated and puzzled the Enlightenment imagination. On the one hand, Egyptian hieroglyphs seemed to envision the possibility of non-discursive communication, bypassing the opacity of language, and yet their meaning was veiled in obscurity and frustratingly resistant to comprehension (see Stolzenberg 2013). The eighteenth-century conceptualization of the hieroglyph as looking like both primeval, natural sign and a later deceptive symbol which did not mean what it claimed is crucial for understanding Vico's "hieroglyphic" frontispiece. Vico used what he called "hieroglyphs" to visualize his narrative of historical rupture between antiquity and modernity and, as such, his frontispiece was designed to be a natural and clear image of or into the past, reflecting its place in early modern technologies of print culture. And yet, the statue of Homer is a visual representation of the later invention of the individual named "Homer" which summed up a long series of historical processes. Vico's statue of Homer was a representation for which there was no real-life, true original. Vico's hieroglyphs, then, were *both* like ancient, "natural" signs, designed to provide his reader with a memorable visualization of the past, *and* a modern technological device to summarize its historical narrative. The statue of Homer in the center left of the frontispiece was a symbol both of a previously unknown period of early man's primitive history and of the fact that Homer himself was a more modern invention. The characterization of natural, raw, instinctual sublimity had positioned Homeric epic in a remote, distant past *and* had underlined his continuing, living purchase on the present. Homer was an anachronism who did not fit into historical time as envisaged by the Enlightenment metanarrative of progress. Vico's frontispiece comprised hieroglyphs as ancient, primitive signs *and* modern techniques of communication: it *both* offered the possibility of a view into a hitherto unknown ancient past *and* emphasized the notion that the past was actually the invention of a more modern vision. Vico's hieroglyphization of Homer — his turning Homer into a visual-textual symbol — represented the desire for the possibility of a visual historiography. On the other hand, however, that Homer's statue represented for Vico the fact that there was no original behind it also betrayed the anxiety that a picture of a historical narrative is nothing but a modern fabrication — that there is nothing behind it, that it is just a modern creation. The

Fig. 3. Johann Joachim Winckelmann, *History of the Art of Antiquity*, Preface (1764).

messy temporality of the hieroglyph provided for Vico a visual frame for the debates about how to think about Homer as a historical figure.

Winckelmann's Egyptianizing Greeks

If we now turn back to Winckelmann's 1764 *History*, which sought to emphasize the primacy of Greek sculpture in the story of the emergence of European art, we will see that the vignette that heads his preface nevertheless visualizes these questions about the historical relationship between Greece and Egypt (fig. 3). It is an image of a Roman relief probably in commemoration of Augustus's victory in Actium. Apollo appears with long hair in the costume of a citharode, accompanied by Artemis and Leto; he is making a libation with Nike/Victory in front of a wall of a holy precinct, in which rising above the partition can be seen a temple with Corinthian columns.[12] Winckelmann, on the other hand, saw "four draped female deities in a procession," correctly recognizing Artemis (or "Diana" as he calls her) and Victory. What interested Winckelmann was the contrast between the deities' archaic-looking costumes and the architecture in the background: "At first glance, the work could seem to be in an Etruscan style, but the architecture of the temple challenges this. It thus seems that this work is a product of a later Greek master who wanted to imitate the style of the more ancient period" (Winckelmann 2006a, 239). Despite the archaic, Etruscan look of the clothing of the goddesses, Winckelmann realized that the Corinthian columns would have appeared only later (at the end of the fifth century BCE). The relief provided Winckelmann with a way of imaging the deterioration of ancient art after its highpoint in the classical Greek period. "The decline of art," Winckelmann wrote on the relief, "must inevitably have become noticeable when comparisons were drawn with the works of the highest and most beautiful period, and it is likely that a few artists sought to return to the grand manner of their predecessors." He continued: "In this way, it may have happened that, just as things in the world often move in a circle and return to where they started, artists strove to imitate the earlier style, which with its only slightly curved contours approximated Egyptian work. [...] I believe that what we have here is one of the distinguishing features or characteristics of the Egyptian style"(2006a, 239). The relief, as Winckelmann saw it, is an example of a later piece trying to imitate styles of earlier periods. In correctly registering

---

12 See Zanker (1987, 70–72, and figure 50); Bol and Allroggen-Bedel (1989–1998, 1.380–88, and plates 218–21), with further bibliography; and Winckelmann (2006b, 365–66, nos. 846–46a). On Winckelmann on this vignette, see also Osterkamp (1989).

the archaizing nature of the relief, Winckelmann demonstrates his antiquarian abilities to differentiate between ancient artistic traditions.

And yet, Winckelmann also presents in front of his reader's eyes how ancient art was a complicated series of imitation and impersonation. Indeed, an image of the work of a Greek artist under imperial Rome might also be seen to visualize Winckelmann's own position when he was writing his *History* in the 1750s and 1760s, as he imagined himself a Hellene toiling under the patronage of powerful masters in Rome. Winckelmann's relief visualized an important contemporary issue for his eighteenth-century readers, when painters and sculptors were turning back to the ancient world for artistic inspiration in an attempt to revivify the artistic tradition of the ancient Greeks. Underpinned by an intense interest specifically in ancient Greek material and visual culture, what art historians now call "Neoclassicism" was evolving precisely in the 1750s and 1760s.[13] Winckelmann's vignette powerfully envisions a later Greek's attempt to look back to an earlier, better period of Greek art — an attempt that at the same time, nevertheless, takes place in a complicated, cluttered cultural environment. Just as Winckelmann's text sought to distinguish the Greek artistic form from its Egyptian and Etruscan predecessors and its Roman successors, so his relief at the beginning of his text also visualized how the work of the Greek artist was part of a larger Mediterranean history. The image showcases, for Winckelmann, the work of a Greek artist living in the Roman Empire using an archaizing, Egyptianizing style, which blurs Etruscan and Greek forms. The relief, then, visualizes the complexities of situating ancient Greek culture in relation to the rest of the Mediterranean for the eighteenth-century viewer. Even if Winckelmann uses this image to put his antiquarian skills on display, he also ends up showing how ancient Greek art looked back to the achieve-

---

13 For accounts of eighteenth-century European neoclassical art, see Rosenblum (1967) and Bückling and Mongi-Vollmer (2013).

ments of the Etruscans and the Egyptians just as it was also made possible by the patronage of Rome.

Just as we saw with the debate about the visualization of Achilles's Shield and Vico's response, so the question of an ancient object being turned into the bearer of modern meaning was precisely the issue that opens Winckelmann's *History:* the vignette at the head of his Preface was not only an engraving of a historical artifact to be placed within a specific period of time, but also a modern portrait of the 1760s artist struggling to revivify the beauty of ancient Greek art via an Egyptian style. And this image was programmatic for the visual organization of the *History*. Twenty-four engravings — vignettes and cul-de-lampes — adorn the beginnings and ends of chapters. In the text, Winckelmann places these ancient objects into separate historical periods, thereby offering a demonstration of his skill as an antiquarian scholar. The images seem designed to visualize the different "national" styles of ancient artistic traditions: Egyptian, Etruscan, Greek, and Roman. But, fascinatingly, these images that top and tail his chapters on the different periods of the history of ancient art are mostly examples of artists who imitated earlier styles or anticipated later developments. The images in Winckelmann's *History* dramatize the relationships between historical periods. Winckelmann's narrative, which celebrated Greek sculpture and encouraged modern European artists to see their ancestry in ancient Greek forms, is nevertheless introduced by an image that, for Winckelmann, envisions a Greek artist in Rome using Egyptian-style aesthetics, to revivify the artistic examples of the past for the present. Winckelmann's philhellenic narrative about the "before" of the "after" of modern European culture could not ignore ancient Egypt.

D'Hancarville and Hieroglyphizing Greek Art

Despite his admiration of the Apollo Belvedere and the Hercules Torso, Winckelmann did not include any engravings of his favorite examples of classical Greek sculpture. The visualization of ancient Greek art was most spectacularly on display in the eighteenth century in the catalog of the vase collection of Sir William Hamilton, the British Envoy Extraordinary in Naples. Over more than a decade, from 1768 to the late 1770s, and costing Hamilton tens of thousands of pounds, four sumptuous elephantine folios were made containing over five hundred plates of vase paintings in terracotta and black enhanced with other colors. Hamilton employed a scholar, the previously mentioned Baron D'Hancarville, to produce the publication, *Antiquités Étrusques, Grecques et Romaines, Tirées du Cabinet de M. Hamilton, Envoyé Extraordinaire de S.M. Britannique en cour de Naples* (1766–1767). It was one of the most extravagant works of eighteenth-century antiquarianism, the first ever color-plate book on the history of art in a standard edition of several hundred copies. It introduced many modern eyes to the exquisite beauty of ancient Greek vase painting and was crucial to the development of European discourse of philhellenism.[14]

D'Hancarville's essays on ancient art and his visualizations of Hamilton's collection were, however, a direct response to Winckelmann's *History,* and built on the debates about the early history of art examined above. While Winckelmann was fascinated with historically locating the apogee of classical Greek sculpture as a model to modern European art, d'Hancarville used the paintings on Hamilton's vases to push back the history of art centuries before Winckelmann would have dared. As we have already seen, Homer's description of Achilles's Shield suggested to antiquarians that the art of painting existed in the earliest periods of Greek history, thereby filling in a lacuna in modern accounts of ancient art. For d'Hancarville, the vase paintings came from those early periods of the Greek artistic tradition. D'Hancarville also responded to Winckelmann's interest in the relationship between ancient art and modern forms. We saw above how Winckelmann set up a mournful contrast between ancient art and modern historiography in the conclu-

---

14 On d'Hancarville, Hamilton, and their publication, see Jenkins and Sloane (1996); Lissarrague and Reed (1997); J. Moore (2008); Heringman (2013); and Hönes (2014).

sion of his book, which looked back at the marvellous achievements of classical Greek sculpture, encouraging contemporary, eighteenth-century artists to do the same. D'Hancarville had a very different sense of the relationship between (ancient) image and (modern) text, which again involved him thinking about the relationship between ancient Greece and Egypt — something hardly surprising, as he sought to push back in time the history of Greek art.

While, in the four volumes of the *Antiquités,* d'Hancarville's historical account changed, he consistently argued that ancient objects and images depicted evidence about the origins of art. In the first two volumes, he proposed that art referenced its natural origins: statues look back to tree trunks, candelabra to stripped vines, and vases to shells. In the latter two volumes, d'Hancarville avoided postulating a natural, founding moment for the history of representation and contended that early peoples set up arbitrary "signs" of commemoration for various reasons — whether it was out of a need to convey a message or to memorialize a specific event — and that classical art recorded those original meanings. Early art, in this latter account, might have been visual images or scriptural representations. But whichever the precise narrative d'Hancarville offered, he argued that ancient art recorded its own origins, so that the ancient image or object might be said to resemble a modern historiographical text composed of signs. Or as d'Hancarville put it himself, "their history written by themselves [*leur histoire écrite par eux mêmes*] can be read [*se lit*] on these monuments" (*Antiquités* 4:9). D'Hancarville's vision of the comparability of (ancient) image and (modern) text was envisioned, for example, in a pair of vignettes in volume two (fig. 4), whose inscriptions mirror each other: "just like a picture, so poetry will be"; "similar to poetry may a picture be." The first is, of course, a quotation from Horace's *Ars Poetica,* while the second is the opening line from Charles Alphonse Dufresnoy's 1668 poem *De Arte Graphica,* which was an important and highly influential aesthetic document arguing that painting should imitate poetry. Of course, the dictum *ut pictura poesis* would become a central maxim

Fig. 4. William Hamilton/Baron D'Hancarville, *Antiquités étrusques, grecques et romaines,* vol. 2, headpiece (1767).

of art theory in the eighteenth century (see Braider 1999, and Marshall 1997). Crucially for us, the hieroglyphic frieze framing the Horatian dictum reflects the eighteenth-century vision of ancient Egyptian hieroglyphs as comprising a combination of image and text as picture-writing. The mirroring of Horace and Dufresnoy visualizes d'Hancarville's argument about the mirroring between ancient image and modern historiographical text.

D'Hancarville's response to Winckelmann's historical narrative is sumptuously pictured in the frontispiece in the same volume (fig. 5), where d'Hancarville envisioned his mourning of the death of Winckelmann. An inscription again dominates the center of the image, lamenting over Winckelmann's death "far from home" (ORCO PEREGRINO).[15] The tomb in this frontispiece, then, is a cenotaph. The emptiness of the tomb is echoed by the unpopulated columbarium niches, originally used by ancient

---

15 On this inscription, see Orrells (2011).

Fig. 5. William Hamilton/Baron D'Hancarville, *Antiquités étrusques, grecques et romaines*, vol. 2, frontispiece (1767).

Romans for the safekeeping of cinerary urns, and the two missing paving stones at the bottom of the image. The engraving presents a sign bereft of a signified, a text without a body. As such, d'Hancarville heralds the text as the work of art, the work of art as a text. The fantasy of the Egyptian hieroglyph in the eighteenth-century imagination, which blurred the contrast between image and text, underpinned d'Hancarville's construction of the history of ancient Greek art, which itself becomes a hieroglyph, both visual and textual sign.

In the third volume, it is even clearer that d'Hancarville was responding to such debates about the relationship between ancient art and modern scholarship, between ancient visual and material culture and modern textual historiography. As mentioned above, in the second two volumes, d'Hancarville changed his mind about the origins of ancient art, to argue that

Fig. 6. William Hamilton/Baron D'Hancarville, *Antiquités étrusques, grecques et romaines,* vol. 3 (1776).

man's original representations were not "natural" signs, but that original signs might have either been visual gestures or written letters, and that the earliest works of art were not "natural" but "arbitrary" signifiers of what they were representing. In the frontispiece to the third volume (fig. 6), d'Hancarville erected a fictional tomb to himself, announcing to his readers his new narrative for art history. And again, it is the text that dominates the image:

> To the departed spirits
> Pierre Victor d'Hancarville
> Around the age of 44
> Made [this monument] for himself
> Having died abroad
> He lived in Naples now Florence holds [his body]
> If there is any amusement among you
> Spirits repair [his] sorrowful soul
> You who read this I salute you and goodbye

The closing line is, of course, a nod to the last line of Catullus's famous elegiac poem 101, written for his brother, who had also died far from home. D'Hancarville, on the other hand, remembered his own alter ego imprisoned in debt in Florence far from his previous home in Naples. Catullus's poem mournfully addresses the "mute ashes" the brother has now become, silent signifiers of a long-gone speaking body. D'Hancarville's engraving is another cenotaph. And the pedestal in the engraving supports no body: there is no statue, just three vultures circling in the sky. As Hans-Christian Hönes has already argued, the engraving looks back to Vico's hieroglyphic Homer (Hönes 2014, 70–71). We saw how the statue of Homer allowed Vico to make a visual comment about the relationship between ancient culture and modern scholarship. D'Hancarville recycles Vico's pedestal but this time without the statue to visualize his own image of that relationship.

The engraving marks the death of one d'Hancarville and the birth of another, who argued that the earliest works of art were comprised of arbitrary signs, produced by ancient geniuses who were not constrained by the limits of "natural" representation. Just as the engraving celebrates the arbitrary creativity of earliest man, so it revels in d'Hancarville's own attempt to recommence the history of art arbitrarily just where he wishes: in this account, d'Hancarville avoids trying to uncover a single origins-point for the history of ancient art. Just as ancient art bears signs of its most primitive origins into the modern present, now d'Hancarville erases any original, single founding moment for the history of art. Both the beginnings and the ends of art's history are effaced, as d'Hancarville's modern text of arbitrary signs paradoxically visualizes the most ancient stages of artistic development. D'Hancarville's desire to merge modern historiographical text and ancient art reflects the persistence of the eighteenth-century fantasy of the Egyptian hieroglyphic blurring of the visual and the verbal.

The Before and After of Classics

D'Hancarville's interpretation of Hamilton's Greek vases did not stand the test of time: classical archaeologists would not end up adopting his semiotic theories. Rather, it was Winckelmann's historical narrative that would prove to be the catalyst of almost two hundred years of classical scholarship. Writing the history of the discipline of classics has indeed involved telling the story about the material turn in the eighteenth century that allowed Winckelmann to construct his foundational, master narrative. Another founding debate for classical studies was the question of the orality of Homeric epic: the search for the original oral stratum of Homer's poems reflected the promise and the glamour of the burgeoning science of classical archaeology. But as we have been seeing, the antiquarian fascination with materiality was not simply a turning away from the textual, but a product of the Quarrel over the historicity of the Homeric poems, which posed a question about the relationships between the visual and the textual and between the ancient and the modern, which in turn reflected the importance of eighteenth-century debates about the Egyptian hieroglyph for the possibilities of visualizing ancient Greek art. How could ancient images and objects become the proofs of a historical narrative? How could and should ancient images and objects become like the texts of modern historiography? The question of the extent to which the Homeric text could evoke and make visible the history of ancient art was also a question about the extent to which modern antiquarian scholarship and its technologies of print could visualize that history. Did antiquarian scholarship really make the ancient past visible or were those visualizations just modern constructions? Visual-verbal Homeric epic became very good to think with for eighteenth-century antiquarians interested in the idea of the visualization of historical narrative. Indeed, the question of the possibility that the verbal could become the visual — the possibility that the textual narratives of antiquarian scholarship could be made into visible signs with the help of printed engravings of ancient images and objects — would profoundly interest the leading antiquarians of the mid-eighteenth century, such as Winckelmann. But these debates about the visualization of ancient Greek culture were intimately bound up with eighteenth-century discussions of the relationship between image and text and the Egyptian hieroglyph. D'Hancarville is not now seen as the founding father of *Altertumswissenschaft,* and yet his extravagant attempts to marry ancient image and modern text sumptuously envision the importance of the eighteenth-century fantasy of the Egyptian hieroglyph at the origins of the emergence of modern western Hellenism.

This chapter offers, then, a different narrative of the "before" and "after" of classics, a different story about the origins of the foundational scholarly narrative of classical studies. In writing about the concealed importance of ancient Egypt in modern European intellectual history, Peter Sloterdijk has argued that "the history of ideas takes the form of a massive game of displacement in which motifs from Egyptian universalism are acted out by non-Egyptian protagonists" (2009, 16). Derrida's insertion of Egypt at the Hellenic origins of Europe's vision of its past has helped us see that the reception of ancient Egypt in the Enlightenment was fundamental to the emergence of the European narrative about its Hellenic origins. But what might we achieve by rethinking the history of the discipline of classics? Registering Enlightenment Orientalism at the origins of modern European Hellenism is so crucial because it forces us to recognize the foundational debates, contests, and schisms that have gone on to frame and structure professional classical scholarship until today. The scholarly politics of positioning and relating ancient Greece to other ancient cultures has been a defining debate especially in the last thirty years since the publication of *Black Athena.* For classics to respond progressively to its dangerous weaponization by the numerous and proliferating rightist discourses and ideologies of the twenty-first century, which look back to Greece to bolster neo-nationalist, neo-fascist, racializing myths of western origins, then the discipline would do well to think about the historical narratives it tells about its "before" and "after."

13

After (News That Stays News)

Sean Gurd

In the last volume of Marcel Proust's *In Search of Lost Time,* the narrator catches his foot on a flagstone—and the concept of the past as a submerged stratum of archaic experience, a pure region separated from the present, dies, as involuntary memory brings the past rushing into the present.[1] Proust's last volume, and with it the whole novel, seeks to articulate in narrative form the uncanny effect produced by what in photography would be called double exposure: old faces juxtaposed with their younger instantiations, past passions illuminating present coolness. The condition this heralded, as Walter Benjamin saw with particular clarity, marked a radical reformulation of the experience of time. "Linear, empty" time (as Benjamin called it in the "Theses on the Philosophy of History," 1969) was replaced with dialectical images, fraught with tension, in which the past flashed up in

---

1   I cite *In Search of Lost Time* from memory; my last reading was in the winter of 2007, when I read Kilmartin's revision of the Moncrief translation (Proust 1982); the first time I read it was in the summer of (I think) 1992, when I read a disintegrating copy of Moncrief's unedited translation (first published between 1922 and 1932), in what edition I couldn't now say. I was working as a counselor at a summer camp on Beausoleil Island in Georgian Bay. The light was luminous, especially at dawn if you went out on your own in a canoe. In between I have read or consulted portions of the Pleiade edition (Proust 1987).

the present, transforming all around it as an electric lightbulb transforms a darkened room. This was the end, too, of the first phase of Freudianism, in which the past resided concealed in the breast, influencing consciousness only through symptom and dream. Now, and again it was Benjamin who saw this with unusual clarity, a more seamless integration of past and present, dream world and waking world, began to appear. French surrealism, though indelibly marked by Freud's writings, brings dream and the archaic into the light without resolving them, effectively transforming dream symbol from symptom into tautegoric statement. Even Freud, in his theory of the instincts and his explorations of history and art, would become interested in a more fluid juxtaposition of past and present than what was suggested by his earliest writings on psychoanalysis.

The phenomenon Proust named involuntary memory remains the keynote of our reality. There is no pure here and now: no pure there and then, either. There is only before and after, an inescapable entanglement of anachronisms. Surrealism is no longer a cultural option: it is the light by which we see. Consider the massive and largely involuntary inversion of temporal relations brought about in 2006, when Facebook, previously a kind of private club for in-the-know collegiates, opened its doors to general membership and rapidly expanded its user base across North America and the world. When I joined in 2007, I found myself suddenly in daily contact with people I had neither seen nor spoken to in many years. Faces I loved but had long left, thanks to the inevitable social and geographical dislocations of aging, university, graduate school, and the peripatetic life of a professional academic, were now habitual presences again. For me — and I suspect I am far from alone — Facebook represented a massive and very sudden collapse of the division between past and present, with consequences at every level of my existence. It was, to put it simply, a technologically-induced involuntary memory, a re-establishment of the haunted present that had been a cultural fact, one way or another, at least since Proust. Marshall McLuhan (1994) predicted that electronic media would become extensions of our nervous system, and anticipated that this would collapse space in unforeseen ways. He did not anticipate that they would become a vector for the circulation of memory as well, that they would play such a central role in the maintenance of our surreal form of time.

As digital addiction became more severe and widespread, everyone seemed to be in two places at once, and there were times when the only empty place seemed to be the place where everyone was, their phones and laptops drawing them away from mutual presence in space. I suspect that the divided attention that became the norm in that era was as temporal as it was spatial: suddenly everyone was occupied by the past, which haunted them more vividly than, for many, it had ever done.

All that came to a sudden end in late 2019, when physical co-presence became dangerous for most and fatal for some. In a fashion that has been normal in Euro-American societies for millennia, the public forum was replaced by the private interior, as we retreated to our apartments to avoid the new pandemic. This repeated gestures to be found throughout the long expanse of the classical tradition, in which seclusion and retreat, initially acts of self-preservation, became the platform for self-creation and self-reflection. But unlike the many instances of retreat from disease to be found in history, this one was distinguished by two historically unprecedented characteristics. First, the public agora which we physically abandoned had been psychically abandoned for almost a decade, as our electronic media had extended us outwards in space and backwards in time: it was, as a result, only half an abandonment. Those of us who teach large university classes know that the pandemic-era anxiety displayed by many administrators over the need to preserve "face-to-face" teaching was, essentially, anachronistic: there has been no pure face-to-face teaching on campus since wifi routers were installed in classrooms and lecture halls. The attention of all but the most unusual students and teachers has been more or less permanently split between the space they are in and the alternative temporality of digitalia since that moment. Second, our "seclusion" was no such thing, as our homes have been totally penetrated by the digital agora. Being-with did not end, did not enter into temporary suspense, as we waited for those early waves to recede. It was, rather, accelerated and intensified, no longer juxtaposed or counterpointed with physical sociality. We discovered that participating in a Zoom call while texting or scanning the latest COVID data on the *New York Times* webpage was a different state than the distraction typical of coffeeshop conversations with phone in hand. That was a splitting, a haunting: this was an intensification, a single stream packed with multiple types of data. Perhaps we overloaded our screens to compensate for the fact that all these sources were so information-poor in comparison with "real life," as though conversing over Zoom, checking email, reading the news, and shopping for power tools together added up to about the same level of stimulation as looking at a dear friend's face over dinner. But the result was the categorical end of the divided temporalities of the Facebook age, for digital and physical spaces had now become strictly separate. There is one rule that is never violated on Zoom. You may display your cat or your bathroom; your spouse may wander by in the background; but you must *only* talk to the screen. Any intrusion of social interaction in the physical realm must be muted by turning off the screen and microphone. The digital has become pure and isolating.

When the computers were off, what was revealed to us — for the first time, perhaps, in almost fifteen years — was a space illuminated from above rather than behind; space which was stable and did not transform suddenly and to the soundtrack of odd artificial sounds; space that actually receded into depth before us, into and through which we could move constrained only by the laws of physics. And in those spaces we found people with whom we had chosen to live long before the phone intruded, people who finally again returned our gaze with the same undivided attention. As readers, we discovered that our books were qualitatively different in terms of their content than the thousands of pages on our screens: they were difficult, intransigent, but also curiously slow. If our screens gave us a million changes a minute, here in our books was news that stays news, as Ezra

Pound once put it to define poetry. And when the books were put down, that taste for news that stays news did not recede but was amplified and extended: the slow growth of the oak, the arrogant step of the cat seemed as vital and urgent and contemporary as the pages of Proust or H.D. or Hermann Broch.

Not that this new predicament is any less anachronistic than the last one. In the digital sphere the selective amplification of the past has, if anything, accelerated; and new ways of disrupting simple presence have continued to emerge. University workers might think, in this context, of the notion of "asynchronicity," which became a preferred mode of course-delivery in the first year of the pandemic. In the new mode, teaching was not directed at short bursts of intense content delivery and student engagement, but was instead cast into a potentially endless and recursive process in which each lesson could be written and re-written, each video the consequence of potentially endless takes and retakes. This is a time which loops, in which each new moment contains within it a refraction or a resonance of all previous similar moments. And once our courses are uploaded, the regime of asynchronicity means that student engagement is similarly dispersed, attention popping in and out according to the dictates of individual work schedules and diurnal rhythms. Times, here, are not so much out of joint as completely dismembered, recast as an infinity of individuated patterns.

As for the "real world": analogue presence-to-the-world is already inherently anachronistic, the sudden and largely unwelcome return of a mode of existence obsolete since 2006. The real world has become the old world, an archaism forced upon us by the intensification of the digital onslaught and the inherent danger of the physical agora. Not that the old real world would have been any kind of simple present: "news that stays news" connotes, in its very name, a mode of perdurance that outlives the smaller enclosure of any particular "now." Indeed, what we learn from the most committed acts of poetic presence is that the present isn't really there. For Matsuo Bashō, whose attentive eye set the paradigm for generations of serial poets in the twentieth century, attention reveals passing, not presence.

the old pond —
a frog jumps in,
water's sound (Ueda 1970, 53)

For serialist poets working in the wake of Ezra Pound's *Cantos,* the dedicated transcription of experience in time reveals endless variations, as the evolving self modulates the evolving world, and past, present, and future mutually entangle.

Consider Robert Kroetsch's *Delphi: Commentary* (included in the collection of long poems *Advice to My Friends,* 1985; I cite from a copy I bought around 1990 at "The Word," a second-hand bookstore on Milton Avenue in Montreal, a few blocks from where I was living at the time). The core of this long poem is a text in which the first-person narrator visits Delphi as a tourist with his nearly grown daughters. There are unguarded descriptions of breakfast at the hotel, of the bus ride to the base of the Sacred Way, the walk to Apollo's temple and contemplation of the *omphalos,* the climb to the stadium, and the return to the bus. The prose is simple, the details recognizable, even clichéd. But the text is set in blocks juxtaposed with smaller blocks of text containing Pausanias's description of the site and, at the top of each page, a fragment from an unfinished sequence of poems called "the eggplant poems."

"The eggplant poems," I said, "is a poem for which we have no reliable text. In fact, I haven't quite, you might say, wrapped it up. […] Is there a difference between a Greek poem which is lost and a poem of mine which I haven't been able to, for whatever reasons, complete?" (Kroetsch 1985, 107)

The assemblage of materials (future poem, past text, present journey) destroy any hope that we will find uncomplicated immediacy here, any kind of straightforward here-and-now. Kroetsch walks with his daughters, and also with those who have walked the same way before him. Indeed, he walks with ghosts: in the whistling of the wind, at the temple to Apollo, he hears the voice of his father (Kroetsch 1985, 111). But he doesn't actually *hear* his father's voice. Rather, it is on the climb to the stadium that "the voice reminded me that it had spoken" (109). It isn't a sudden emanation of the past into the present: it is a memory of such an emanation, an after-echo of an after-echo, its reality as fragile and frail as a voice carried on the wind or buried beneath the din of cicadas — "a smaller sound, in the wind itself, under pulsing rhythm of the cicadas," he calls it (108). What does anyone do when they visit *a lieu de mémoire* but try to remember the details of what transpired there, long before we were born? For Kroetsch that impossible act of remembering is carried within the involuntary signal of his father's voice, patiently asking why he made the trip in the first place.

I love this poem for the artlessness achieved by a writer I know to be capable of extreme technical virtuosity as both novelist and poet. These notes seem like my memories — or they do until I remember that I have never been to Delphi; the site, for me, is a series of color slides, projected on the wall of my parents' dining room, depicting in Kodachrome tints the photographic traces of a camping trip to Greece half a decade before I was born. And there's nothing simple, after all, about Kroetsch's text. Indeed, it proclaims itself a commentary and reinforces that assertion with its layout, reminiscent of the way commentary surrounds scripture, or the way scholia surround the *Iliad* in its most famous manuscript copy. But what's commenting on what here? At times Kroetsch's first-person narrative surrounds Pausanias, as though his visit were a scholion on Pausanias's, but at other times it is Pausanias's text which surrounds Kroetsch's, as though the earlier traveler uncannily surrounded or even contained the later experience. And both of the texts unfold beneath the fragments of the incomplete "eggplant poems," as though somehow they were both commenting on that text-to-come, that *livre à venir,* as Maurice Blanchot has it.

None of this makes *Delphi: Commentary* any less an example of "news that stays news." Rather, Kroetsch reminds us that before/after is the ineluctable situation we are always and inevitably in. There is no escaping it: we must move to its ever-shifting polyrhythms.

Bibliography

Adams, James N. 1982. *The Latin Sexual Vocabulary.* Baltimore: Johns Hopkins University Press.
Adorno, Theodor W. 1973. *Negative Dialectics.* Translated by E.B. Ashton. New York: Continuum.
———. 1998. *Aesthetic Theory.* Translated by Robert Hullot-Kentor. Minneapolis: University of Minnesota Press.
———. 2002. "Late Style in Beethoven (1937)." In *Essays on Music,* edited by Richard Leppert, 564–67. Berkeley: University of California Press.
Agamben, Giorgio. 2019. *Creation and Anarchy: The Work of Art and the Religion of Capitalism.* Translated by Adam Kotsko. Stanford: Stanford University Press.
———. 2021. *Where Are We Now? The Epidemic as Politics.* Translated by Valeria Dani. Lanham: Rowman & Littlefield.
Aiello, Lucia. 2016. "'Postscript.'" *Journal of Literature and Trauma Studies* 5, no. 2: 127–34. DOI: 10.1353/jlt.2016.0025.
Algar, James, Samuel Armstrong, and Ford Beebe Jr., dirs. 2000. *Fantasia.* Burbank: Walt Disney Enterprises.
Allen, Danielle S. 2000. *The World of Prometheus: The Politics of Punishing in Democratic Athens.* Princeton: Princeton University Press.

Allinson, Jamie, China Miéville, Richard Seymour, and Rosie Warren. 2021. *The Tragedy of the Worker: Towards the Proletarocene.* London: Verso.

Althusser, Louis. 1971. "Ideology and Ideological State Apparatuses (Notes Towards an Investigation)." In *Lenin and Philosophy and Other Essays,* translated by Ben Brewster, 85–126. New York: Monthly Review Press.

Anderson, Perry. 1992. "The Ends of History." In *A Zone of Engagement,* 279–376. London: Verso.

Andre-Driussi, Michael. 1994. *Lexicon Urthus: A Dictionary for the Urth Cycle.* San Francisco: Sirius Fiction.

Andrew, Edward. 1989. "Equality of Opportunity as the Noble Lie." *History of Political Thought* 10, no. 4: 577–95. http://www.jstor.org/stable/44797160.

Arendt, Hannah. 1990. *On Revolution.* London: Penguin.

———. 1998. *The Human Condition.* Chicago: University of Chicago Press.

Armstrong, David, and Michael McOsker, eds. and trans. 2020. *Philodemus, On Anger.* Atlanta: SBL Press.

Armstrong, Richard H. 2005. "Contrapuntal Affiliations: Edward Said and Freud's *Moses*." *American Imago* 62, no. 2: 235–57. DOI: 10.1353/aim.2005.0020.

———. 2006. *A Compulsion for Antiquity: Freud and the Ancient World.* Ithaca: Cornell University Press.

Arnim, Hans von, ed., 1986. *Stoicorum Veterum Fragmenta.* New York: Irvington Publishers .

Assmann, Jan. 2014. *Religio Duplex: How the Enlightenment Reinvented Egyptian Religion.* Translated by Robert Savage. Cambridge: Polity Press.

Bachelard, Gaston. 1992. *The Poetics of Space.* Translated by Maria Jolas. Boston: Beacon Press.

Bacon, Francis. 1870. *The Works of Francis Bacon.* Edited by James Spedding, Robert L. Ellis, and Douglas Denon Heath. London: Longmans.

Bailey, Charles. 2013. "Early Atomic Models — From Mechanical to Quantum (1904–1913)." *European Physical Journal H.* 38: 1–38. DOI: 10.1140/epjh/e2012-30009-7.

Barad, Karen. 2007. *Meeting the Universe Halfway: Quantum Physics and the Entanglement of Matter and Meaning.* Durham: Duke University Press.

———. 2010. "Quantum Entanglements and Hauntological Relations of Inheritance: Dis/continuities, SpaceTime Enfoldings, and Justice-to-Come." *Derrida Today* 3, no. 2: 240–68. DOI: 10.3366/DRT.2010.0206.

Barkan, Leonard. 1999. *Unearthing the Past: Archaeology and Aesthetics in the Making of Renaissance Culture.* New Haven: Yale University Press.

Barrow-Green, June. 1994. "Oscar II's Prize Competition and the Error in Poincaré's Memoir on the Three Body Problem." *Archive for History of Exact Sciences* 48: 107–31. DOI: 10.1007/BF00374436.

———. 1997. *Poincaré and the Three Body Problem.* Providence: American Mathematical Society.

Bataille, Georges. 1991. *The Accursed Share: An Essay on General Economy.* Translated by Robert Hurley. New York: Zone.

Bates, David. 2005. "Crisis Between the Wars: Derrida and the Origins of Undecidability." *Representations* 90, no. 1: 1–27. DOI: 10.1525/rep.2005.90.1.1.

Baudrillard, Jean. 1989. "Anorexic Ruins." In *Looking Back on the End of World,* edited by Dietmar Kamper and Christoph Wulf, translated by David Antal, 29–48. New York: Semiotext(e).

Benjamin, Walter. 1969. *Illuminations: Essays and Reflections.* Edited by Hannah Arendt. Translated by Harry Zohn. New York: Harcourt, Brace and World.

Bennington, Geoffrey. 2011. "A Moment of Madness: Derrida's Kierkegaard." *Oxford Literary Review* 33, no. 1: 103–27. https://www.jstor.org/stable/44030838.

Benveniste, Émile. 1969. *Le vocabulaire des institutions indo-européennes.* Paris: Minuit.

Berlant, Lauren. 2007. "Slow Death (Sovereignty, Obesity, Lateral Agency)." *Critical Inquiry* 33, no. 4: 754–80. DOI: 10.1086/521568.

———. 2011. *Cruel Optimism*. Durham: Duke University Press.

———. 2020. "In the Morning I Yell." *Los Angeles Review of Books,* April 14. https://lareviewofbooks.org/article/quarantine-files-thinkers-self-isolation/.

Bernal, Martin. 1987. *Black Athena: The Afroasiatic Roots of Classical Civilization,* Vol. 1: *The Fabrication of Ancient Greece, 1785–1985.* New Brunswick: Rutgers University Press.

Bettini, Maurizio. 2011. *The Ears of Hermes: Communication, Images, and Identity in the Classical World.* Translated by William Michael Short. Columbus: Ohio State University Press.

Bey, Marquis. 2017. "The Trans*-Ness of Blackness, the Blackness of Trans*-Ness." *Transgender Studies Quarterly* 4, no. 2: 275–95. DOI: 10.1215/23289252-3815069.

Bident, Christophe. 2018. *Maurice Blanchot: A Critical Biography.* Translated by John McKeane. New York: Fordham University Press.

Bissell, David. 2007. "Animating Suspension: Waiting for Mobilities." *Mobilities* 2, no. 2: 277–98. DOI: 10.1080/17450100701381581.

Blanchot, Maurice. 1971. *L'Amitié.* Paris: Gallimard.

———. 1986. *The Writing of Disaster.* Translated by Ann Smock. Lincoln: University of Nebraska Press.

———. 1995. *The Work of Fire.* Translated by Charlotte Mandell. Stanford: Stanford University Press.

Blanchot, Maurice, and Jacques Derrida. 2000. *The Instant of My Death / Demeure: Fiction and Testimony.* Translated by Elizabeth Rottenberg. Stanford: Stanford University Press.

Blumenberg, Hans. 1985. *Work on Myth.* Translated by Robert M. Wallace. Cambridge: MIT Press.

Bohr, Niels. 1935. "Can Quantum-Mechanical Description of Physical Reality Be Considered Complete?" *Physical Review* 48, no. 8: 696–702. DOI: 10.1103/PhysRev.48.696.

Boisseron, Bénédicte. 2015. "After Jacques Derrida (More to Follow): From A-cat-emic to Caliban." *Yale French Studies* 127: 95–109. https://www.jstor.org/stable/44512263.

Boivin, Jean. 1715. *Apologie d'Homère et Bouclier d'Achille.* Paris: François Jouenne.

Bol, Peter C., and Agnes Allroggen-Bedel, eds. 1989–1998. *Forschungen zur Villa Albani: Katalog der antiken Bildwerke.* Berlin: Mann.

Bouffartigue, Jean, and Michel Patillon, eds. 1979. *Porphyre: De l'abstinence.* Vol 2. Paris: Les Belles Lettres.

Boxall, Peter. 2020. *The Prosthetic Imagination: A History of the Novel as Artificial Life.* Cambridge: Cambridge University Press.

Braider, Christopher. 1999. "The Paradoxical Sisterhood: 'ut pictura poesis.'" In *The Cambridge History of Literary Criticism,* Vol. 3: *The Renaissance,* edited by Glyn P. Norton, 168–75. Cambridge: Cambridge University Press.

Bratton, Benjamin. 2021. *The Revenge of the Real: Politics for a Post-pandemic World.* London: Verso.

Braunstein, Néstor. 2021. "The Return of Antigone: Burial Rites in Pandemic Times." In *Coronavirus, Psychoanalysis, and Philosophy: Conversations on Pandemics, Politics, and Society,* edited by Fernando Castrillón and Thomas Marchevsky, 66–75. Abingdon: Routledge.

Brink, C.O. 1956. "Οἰκείωσις and Οἰκειότης: Theophrastus and Zeno on Nature in Moral Theory." *Phronesis* 1, no. 2: 123–45. https://www.jstor.org/stable/4181603.

Brittain, Charles. 2016. "Cicero's Sceptical Methods: The Example of the *De Finibus.*" In *Cicero's* De Finibus: *Philosophical Approaches,* edited by Julia Annas and Gábor Betegh, 12–40. Cambridge: Cambridge University Press.

Brown, Peter. 1971. *The World of Late Antiquity: AD 150–750.* New York: W.W. Norton.

Brown, Wendy. 2020. "From Exposure to Manifestation." *Los Angeles Review of Books,* April 14. https://lareviewofbooks.org/article/quarantine-files-thinkers-self-isolation/#_ftn4.

Bruns, Gerald. 2008. "Derrida's Cat (Who Am I?)." *Research in Phenomenology* 38, no. 3: 404–23. DOI: 10.1163/156916408X336765.

Brunschwig, Jacques. 1986. "The Cradle Argument in Epicureanism and Stoicism." In *The Norms of Nature: Studies in Hellenistic Ethics,* edited by Malcolm Schofield and Gisela Striker, 113–44. Cambridge: Cambridge University Press.

Bückling, Marieke, and Eva Mongi-Vollmer, eds. 2013. *Schönheit und Revolution: Klassizismus 1770–1820.* Munich: Hirmer.

Burian, Peter. 1972. "Supplication and Hero Cult in Sophocles' *Ajax*." *Greek, Roman, and Byzantine Studies* 13, no. 2: 151–56. https://grbs.library.duke.edu/index.php/grbs/article/view/9561.

Burnet, John. 1901–1907. *Platonis Opera.* 5 Vols. Oxford: Oxford University Press.

Butler, Judith. 2000. *Antigone's Claim: Kinship Between Life and Death.* New York: Columbia University Press.

———. 2009. "Finishing, Starting." In *Derrida and the Time of the Political,* edited by Pheng Cheah and Suzanne Guerlac, 291–306. Durham: Duke University Press.

———. 2017. "Breaks in the Bond: Reflections on Kinship Trouble." UCL Housman Lecture, University College London, February 8. https://www.ucl.ac.uk/classics/sites/classics/files/housman_butler_2017.pdf.

———. 2020. "Companion Thinking: A Response." *New Literary History* 51, no. 4: 687–94. DOI: 10.1353/nlh.2020.0042.

———. 2022. *What World Is This? A Pandemic Phenomenology.* New York: Columbia University Press.

Butler, Judith, and Athena Athanasiou. 2013. *Dispossession: The Performative in the Political.* Cambridge: Polity.

Cacciari, Massimo. 2009a. *Hamletica.* Milan: Adelphi.

———. 2009b. *The Unpolitical: On the Radical Critique of Political Reason.* Translated by Massimo Verdicchio. New York: Fordham University Press.

Calarco, Matthew. 2004. "Deconstruction Is Not Vegetarianism: Humanism, Subjectivity, and Animal Ethics." *Continental Philosophy Review* 37: 175–201. DOI: 10.1007/s11007-005-3925-4.

Caputo, John D. 2021. *Deconstruction in a Nutshell: A Conversation with Jacques Derrida*. New York: Fordham University Press.

Carey, Sorcha. 2006. *Pliny's Catalogue of Culture: Art and Empire in the* Natural History. Oxford: Oxford University Press.

Castrillón, Fernando, and Thomas Marchevsky. 2021. "Introduction: Of Pestilence, Chaos, and Time." In *Coronavirus, Psychoanalysis, and Philosophy: Conversations on Pandemics, Politics, and Society*, edited by Fernando Castrillón and Thomas Marchevsky, 1–19. London: Routledge.

Cheah, Pheng. 2009. "The Untimely Secret of Democracy." In *Derrida and the Time of the Political*, edited by Pheng Cheah and Suzanne Guerlac, 74–96. Durham: Duke University Press.

———. 2016. *What Is a World? On Postcolonial Literature as World Literature*. Durham: Duke University Press.

Cheah, Pheng, and Suzanne Guerlac, eds. 2009a. *Derrida and the Time of the Political*. Durham: Duke University Press.

———. 2009b. "Introduction: Derrida and the Time of the Political." In *Derrida and the Time of the Political*, edited by Pheng Cheah and Suzanne Guerlac, 1–37. Durham: Duke University Press.

Chen, Mel Y. 2012. *Animacies: Biopolitics, Racial Mattering, and Queer Affect*. Durham: Duke University Press.

Clausen, W.V., ed. 1992. *A. Persi Flacci et D. Iuni Iuuenalis Saturae*. Oxford: Oxford University Press.

Colebrook, Claire. 2002. *Irony in the Work of Philosophy*. Lincoln: University of Nebraska Press.

———. 2020. "Fire, Flood and Pestilence as the Condition for the Possibility of the Human." *Derrida Today* 13, no. 2: 135–41. DOI: 10.3366/drt.2020.0229.

Conybeare, Catherine, and Simon Goldhill, eds. 2020. *Classical Philology and Theology: Entanglement, Disavowal, and the Godlike Scholar.* Cambridge: Cambridge University Press.

Cooke, H.P., and Hugh Tredennick, trans. 1938. *Aristotle: Categories; On Interpretation; Prior Analytics.* Cambridge: Harvard University Press.

Corbeill, Anthony. 1997. "Thumbs in Ancient Rome: Pollex as Index." *Memoirs of the American Academy in Rome* 42: 1–21. DOI: 10.2307/4238745.

Corfman, S. Brook. 2020. "Melting Muscles: Cassils's *Tiresias* at the Intersection of Affect and Gendered Embodiment." *TSQ: Transgender Studies Quarterly* 7, no. 1: 5–19. DOI: 10.1215/23289252-7914472.

Cornell, Drucilla, and Stephen D. Seely. 2014. "There Is Nothing Revolutionary about a Blowjob." *Social Text* 32, no. 2: 1–23. DOI: 10.1215/01642472-2419540.

Crépon, Marc. 2008. "Déconstruction et traduction: le passage à la philosophie." In *Derrida, la tradition de la philosophie*, edited by Marc Crépon and Frédéric Worms, 27–44. Paris: Galilée.

Crockett, Clayton. 2018. *Derrida after the End of Writing: Political Theology and New Materialism.* New York: Fordham University Press.

Crowley, Timothy. 2008. "Aristotle's 'So-Called Elements.'" *Phronesis* 53, no. 3: 223–42. DOI: 10.1163/156852808X307061.

Csapo, Eric. 1993. "Deep Ambivalence: Notes on a Greek Cockfight (Part I)." *Phoenix* 47, no. 1: 1–28. DOI: 10.2307/1088916.

Curran, Brian A. 2007. *The Egyptian Renaissance: The Afterlife of Ancient Egypt in Early Modern Italy.* Chicago: University of Chicago Press.

Damasio, Antonio. 2019. *The Strange Order of Things: Life, Feeling, and the Making of Cultures.* New York: Vintage.

Daston, Lorraine. 2000. *Biographies of Scientific Objects.* Chicago: University of Chicago Press.

Davidson, Michael. 2012. "Pregnant Men: Modernism, Disability, and Biofuturity." In *Sex and Disability,* edited by

Robert McRuer and Anna Mollow, 123–44. Durham: Duke University Press.

Deleuze, Gilles. 2004. "How Do We Recognize Structuralism?" In *Desert Islands and Other Texts: 1953–1974*, edited by David Lapoujade, translated by Michael Taormina, 170–92. New York: Semiotext(e).

Deleuze, Gilles, and Félix Guattari. 2005. *Qu'est-ce que la philosophie?* Paris: Minuit.

Deleuze, Gilles, and Leopold von Sacher-Masoch. 1991. *Masochism: Coldness and Cruelty / Venus in Furs.* Translated by Jean McNeil. New York: Zone Books.

Dell'Aversano, Carmen. 2010. "The Love Whose Name Cannot Be Spoken: Queering the Human-Animal Bond." *Journal for Critical Animal Studies* 8, nos. 1–2. https://www.criticalanimalstudies.org/volume-viii-issue-iii-2010/.

De Man, Paul. 1983. "The Rhetoric of Temporality." In *Blindness and Insight: Essays in the Rhetoric of Contemporary Criticism*, 187–228. Minneapolis: University of Minnesota Press.

Derrida, Jacques. 1973. "Differance." In *Speech and Phenomena, and Other Essays on Husserl's Theory of Signs*, translated by David B. Allison, 129–60. Evanston: Northwestern University Press.

———. 1974. "White Mythology: Metaphor in the Text of Philosophy." *New Literary History* 6, no. 1: 5–74. DOI: 10.2307/468341.

———. 1976. *Of Grammatology.* Translated by Gayatri Chakravorty Spivak. Baltimore: Johns Hopkins University Press.

———. 1978. *Writing and Difference.* Translated by Alan Bass. Chicago: University of Chicago Press.

———. 1979. "Scribble (Writing-Power)." *Yale French Studies* 58: 117–47. DOI: 10.2307/2929975.

———. 1980. *The Archeology of the Frivolous: Reading Condillac.* Translated by John P. Leavey Jr. Pittsburgh: Duquesne University Press.

———. 1981. *Dissemination*. Translated by Barbara Johnson. Chicago: University of Chicago Press.

———. 1984a. "Of an Apocalyptic Tone Recently Adopted in Philosophy." *Oxford Literary Review* 6, no. 2: 3–37. http://www.jstor.org/stable/43973661.

———. 1984b. "No Apocalypse, Not Now." *Diacritics* 14: 20–31. https://doi.org/10.2307/464756.

———. 1986. *Memoires for Paul de Man*. Translated by Cecile Lindsay, Jonathan Culler, and Eduardo Cadava. New York: Columbia University Press.

———. 1987. *The Post Card: From Socrates to Freud and Beyond*. Translated by Alan Bass. Chicago: University of Chicago Press.

———. 1992a. "Force of Law: The 'Mystical Foundation of Authority.'" In *Deconstruction and the Possibility of Justice*, edited by Drucilla Cornell, Michel Rosenfeld, and David Gray Carlson, 3–67. New York: Routledge.

———. 1992b. *The Other Heading: Reflections on Today's Europe*. Translated by Pascale-Anne Brault and Michael B. Naas. Bloomington: Indiana University Press.

———. 1993a. *Spectres de Marx: l'état de la dette, le travail du deuil et la nouvelle Internationale*. Paris: Galilée.

———. 1993b. *Khōra*. Paris: Galilée.

———. 1993c. "On a Newly Arisen Apocalyptic Tone in Philosophy." In *Raising the Tone of Philosophy: Late Essays by Immanuel Kant, Transformative Critique by Jacques Derrida*, edited by Peter D. Fenves, 117–71. Baltimore: Johns Hopkins University Press.

———. 1993d. *Memoirs of the Blind: The Self-Portrait and Other Ruins*. Translated by Pascale-Anne Brault and Michael Naas. Chicago: University of Chicago Press.

———. 1994a. *Specters of Marx: The State of Debt, the Work of Mourning, and the New International*. Translated by Peggy Kamuf. London: Routledge.

———. 1994b. *Politiques de l'amitié. Suivi de L'oreille de Heidegger*. Paris: Galilée.

———. 1994c. "The Spatial Arts: An Interview with Jacques Derrida." In *Deconstruction and the Visual Arts: Art, Media, Architecture,* edited by Peter Brunette and David Wills, 9–32. Cambridge: Cambridge University Press.

———. 1995a. *Mal d'archive: une impression freudienne.* Paris: Galilée.

———. 1995b. "Archive Fever: A Freudian Impression." *Diacritics* 25, no. 2: 9–63. DOI: 10.2307/465144.

———. 1996a. *Apories: mourir — s'attendre aux 'limites de la vérité.'* Paris: Galilée.

———. 1996b. "A Silkworm of One's Own (Points of View Stitched on the Other Veil)." *Oxford Literary Review* 18, no. 1/2: 3–65. http://www.jstor.org/stable/44244481.

———. 1996c. *Archive Fever: A Freudian Impression.* Translated by Eric Prenowitz. Chicago: University of Chicago Press.

———. 1997a. *Adieu: À Emmanuel Lévinas.* Paris: Galilée.

———. 1997b. *The Politics of Friendship.* Translated by George Collins. London: Verso.

———. 1998a. "Hospitality, Justice and Responsibility: A Dialogue with Jacques Derrida." In *Questioning Ethics: Contemporary Debates in Continental Philosophy,* edited by Richard Kearney and Mark Dooley, 65–83. London: Routledge.

———. 1998b. *Resistances of Psychoanalysis.* Translated by Peggy Kamuf, Pascale-Anne Brault, and Michael Naas. Stanford: Stanford University Press.

———. 2000. "Hostipitality." Translated by Barry Stocker with Forbes Morlock. *Angelaki* 5, no. 3: 3–18. DOI: 10.1080/09697250020034706.

———. 2002a. *Acts of Religion.* Translated by Gil Anidjar. New York: Routledge.

———. 2002b. *Marx & Sons.* Paris: Galilée.

———. 2003. "Autoimmunity: Real and Symbolic Suicides: A Dialogue with Jacques Derrida" and "Deconstructing Terrorism." In *Philosophy in a Time of Terror: Dialogues with*

Jürgen Habermas and Jacques Derrida, edited by Giovanna Borradori, 85–136. Chicago: University of Chicago Press.

———. 2005a. *Rogues: Two Essays on Reason.* Translated by Pascale-Anne Brault and Michael Naas. Stanford: Stanford University Press.

———. 2005b. *Sovereignties in Question: The Poetics of Paul Celan.* Edited by Thomas Dutoit and Outi Pasanen. New York: Fordham University Press.

———. 2007. "A Certain Impossible Possibility of Saying the Event." In *The Late Derrida,* edited by W.J.T. Mitchell and Arnold I. Davidson, 223–44. Chicago: University of Chicago Press.

———. 2008. *The Animal That Therefore I Am.* Edited by Marie-Louise Mallet. Translated by David Wills. New York: Fordham University Press.

———. 2010. *Parages.* Edited by John P. Leaver. Translated by Tom Conley, James Hulbert, John P. Leavey, and Avital Ronell. Stanford: Stanford University Press.

———. 2011. *The Beast and the Sovereign.* Vol. 2. Translated by Geoffrey Bennington. Chicago: University of Chicago Press.

———. 2014. *Death Penalty.* Vol. 1. Translated by Peggy Kamuf. Chicago: University of Chicago Press.

———. 2020. *Life Death.* Edited by Pascale-Anne Brault and Peggy Kamuf. Translated by Pascale-Anne Brault and Michael Naas. Chicago: University of Chicago Press.

———. 2021. *Clang.* Translated by Geoffrey Bennington and David Wills. Minneapolis: University of Minnesota Press.

Derrida, Jacques, and Anne Dufourmantelle. 2000. *Of Hospitality.* Translated by Rachel Bowlby. Stanford: Stanford University Press.

Derrida, Jacques, and Élisabeth Roudinesco. 2001. *De quoi demain…: Dialogue.* Paris: Galilée.

Diacu, Florin, and Philip Holmes. 1996. *Celestial Encounters: The Origins of Chaos and Stability.* Princeton: Princeton University Press.

Diels, Hermann, and Walther Kranz, eds. 1958. *Die Fragmente der Vorsokratiker.* 3 Vols. Berlin: Weidmann.

Dodds, E.R., ed. 1959. *Plato: Gorgias.* Oxford: Clarendon Press.
Doody, Aude. 2010. *Pliny's Encyclopedia: The Reception of the Natural History.* Cambridge: Cambridge University Press.
Doody, Margaret Anne. 1996. *The True Story of the Novel.* New Brunswick: Rutgers University Press.
Dorson, James. 2016. *Counternarrative Possibilities: Virgin Land, Homeland, and Cormac McCarthy's Westerns.* Frankfurt: Campus Verlag.
Dué, Casey, and Jim Marks. 2020. "The Homeric Question." In *The Cambridge Guide to Homer,* edited by Corinne Ondine Pache, 585–89. Cambridge: Cambridge University Press.
Duke, E.A., W.F. Hicken, W.S.M. Nicoll, D.B. Robinson, and Christopher Strachan, eds. 1995. *Platonis Opera.* Vol. 1. Oxford: Oxford University Press.
Eagleton, Terry. 1999. "Marxism without Marxism." In *Ghostly Demarcations: A Symposium on Jacques Derrida's Spectres of Marx,* edited by Michael Sprinker, 83–87. London: Verso.
Easterling, Patricia E. 1988. "Tragedy and Ritual." *Mètis* 3, nos. 1–2: 87–109. https://www.persee.fr/doc/metis_1105-2201_1988_num_3_1_907.
Edelman, Lee. 2004. *No Future: Queer Theory and the Death Drive.* Durham: Duke University Press.
———. 2011. "Against Survival: Queerness in a Time That's Out of Joint." *Shakespeare Quarterly* 62, no. 2: 148–69. DOI: 10.1353/shq.2011.0015.
———. 2017. "Learning Nothing: *Bad Education.*" *differences* 28, no. 1: 124–73. DOI: 10.1215/10407391-3821724.
Edelstein, Dan. 2010. *The Enlightenment: A Genealogy.* Chicago: University of Chicago Press.
Eden, Kathy. 2012. *The Renaissance Rediscovery of Intimacy.* Chicago: University of Chicago Press.
Einarson, Benedict, and George Link, eds. 1976. *Theophrastus: On the Causes of Plants.* Cambridge: Harvard University Press.
Einstein, Albert, Boris Podolsky, and Nathan Rosen. 1935. "Can Quantum-Mechanical Description of Physical Reality Be

Considered Complete?" *Physical Review* 47: 777–80. DOI: 10.1103/PhysRev.47.777.

Ellis, Nick C., and Diane Larsen-Freeman, eds. 2009. *Language as a Complex Adaptive System*. Malden: Blackwell Publishing.

Elmore, Rick, and Jonathan Elmore. 2018. "'You Can Stay Here With Your Papa and Die or You Can Go With Me': The Ethical Imperative of *The Road*." *The Cormac McCarthy Journal* 16, no. 2: 133–48. DOI: 10.5325/cormmccaj.16.2.0133.

Esposito, Roberto. 2019. *Politics and Negation: Towards an Affirmative Philosophy*. Translated by Zakiya Hanafi. Cambridge: Polity.

———. 2021. "Vitam Instituere." In *Coronavirus, Psychoanalysis, and Philosophy: Conversations on Pandemics, Politics, and Society*, edited by Fernando Castrillón and Thomas Marchevsky, 87–88. London: Routledge.

———. 2022. *Immunità comune: Biopolitica all'epoca della pandemia*. Turin: Einaudi.

Evans, Fred. 2016. "'Murmurs' and 'Calls': The Significance of Voice in the Political Reason of Foucault and Derrida." In *Between Foucault and Derrida*, edited by Yubraj Aryal, Vernon W. Cisney, Nicolae Morar, and Christopher Penfield, 153–68. Edinburgh: Edinburgh University Press.

Fabbri, Lorenzo. 2007. "Philosophy as Chance: An Interview with Jean-Luc Nancy." *Critical Inquiry* 33, no. 2: 427–40. DOI: 10.2307/4497729.

Falconer, William Armistead, ed. 1923. *Cicero: On Old Age, On Friendship, On Divination*. Cambridge: Harvard University Press.

Felman, Shoshana. 2014. "Fire in the Archive: The Alignment of Witnesses." In *The Future of Testimony: Interdisciplinary Perspectives on Witnessing*, edited by Jane Kilby and Antony Rowland, 48–67. London: Routledge.

Ferradou, Carine. 2003. "Le banquet de Byrrhène dans les *Métamorphoses* d'Apulée (II, 19-31): la mise en scène de la parole et du rire." *Pallas* 61: 349–59. http://www.jstor.org/stable/43605565.

Finch, Bill. 2015. "The True Story of Kudzu, the Vine That Never Truly Ate the South." *Smithsonian Magazine,* September 2015. https://www.smithsonianmag.com/science-nature/true-story-kudzu-vine-ate-south-180956325/.

Finkelpearl, Ellen D. 2014. "Gender in the Ancient Novel." In *A Companion to the Ancient Novel,* edited by Edmund P. Cueva and Shannon N. Byrne, 456–72. Chichester: Blackwell.

Fisher, Mark. 2009. *Capitalist Realism: Is There No Alternative?* Winchester: Zero Books.

Formisano, Marco, and Therese Fuhrer, eds. 2014. *Décadence: "Decline and Fall" or "Other Antiquity"?* Heidelberg: Winter.

Forster, Edward, and Edward Heffner, eds. and trans. 1968. *Columella, On Trees.* Cambridge: Harvard University Press.

Foucault, Michael. 1977. *Discipline and Punish: The Birth of the Prison.* Translated by Alan Sheridan. New York: Pantheon.

———. 1980. *Power/Knowledge: Selected Interviews and Other Writings, 1972–1977.* Edited by Colin Gordon. Translated by Colin Gordon, Leo Marshall, John Mepham, and Kate Soper. New York: Vintage.

———. 1984. *L'Usage de plaisirs.* Vol. 2: *L'Histoire de la sexualité.* Paris: Gallimard.

———. 2001. *L'herméneutique du sujet. Cours au Collège de France, 1981–1982.* Paris: Seuil.

———. 2008. *Le gouvernement de soi et des autres. Cours au Collège de France, 1982–83.* Paris: Gallimard.

Fraguier, Claude François. 1736. "De l'ancienneté de la Peinture." *Histoire de l'Académie royale des inscriptions et belles-lettres; avec les Mémoires de littérature tirez des registres de cette académie* 1: 75–89.

Frangoulidis, Stavros. 2002. "Mutilation as Emasculation in Apuleius's Tale of Thelyphron (*Met.* 2.21–30)." In *Hommages à Carl Deroux,* Vol. 2: *Prose et linguistique, médecine,* edited by Pol Defosse, 164–72. Brussels: Latomus.

———. 2008. "Rewriting *Metamorphoses* 1–10: The Isis Book." In *Witches, Isis and Narrative: Approaches to Magic in Apuleius's* Metamorphoses, 175–203. Berlin: De Gruyter.

Fränkel, Hermann. 1946. "Man's 'Ephemeros' Nature According to Pindar and Others." *Transactions and Proceedings of the American Philological Association* 77: 131–45. DOI: 10.2307/283450.

Freud, Sigmund. 1955a. "Beyond the Pleasure Principle." In *The Standard Edition of the Complete Psychological Works of Sigmund Freud*, Vol. 18: *Beyond the Pleasure Principle, Group Psychology and Other Works (1920–1922)*, edited and translated by James Strachey with Anna Freud, 1–64. London: Hogarth Press.

———. 1955b. "Civilization and Its Discontents." In *The Standard Edition of the Complete Psychological Works of Sigmund Freud*, Vol. 21: *The Future of an Illusion, Civilization and Its Discontents and Other Works (1927–1931)*, edited and translated by James Strachey with Anna Freud, 64–145. London: Hogarth Press.

———. 1955c. *Moses and Monotheism*. In *The Standard Edition of the Complete Psychological Works of Sigmund Freud*, Vol. 23: *Moses and Monotheism, An Outline of Psycho-analysis and Other Works (1937–1939)*, edited and translated by James Strachey and Anna Freud, 7–137. London: Hogarth Press.

———. 2014. *Delusion and Dream in Jensen's Gradiva*. Translated by Helen M. Downey. Echo: Echo Library.

Fritsch, Matthias. 2020. "Virology and Biopolitics." *Derrida Today* 13, no. 2: 142–48. DOI: 10.3366/DRT.2020.0230.

Froment-Meurice, Marc. 2007. "From (Within) Without: The Ends of Politics." In *The Politics of Deconstruction: Jacques Derrida and the Other of Philosophy*, edited by Martin McQuillan, 157–72. London: Pluto Press.

Gabriel, Kay. 2018. "Specters of Dying Empire: The Case of Carson's *Bacchae*." *Tripwire* 14: 315–23. https://tripwirejournal.files.wordpress.com/2018/06/tw14gabrieloncarson.pdf.

Galison, Peter L. 2003. *Einstein's Clocks, Poincaré's Maps: Empires of Time*. New York: W.W. Norton.

Gasché, Rodolphe. 2002. "L'expérience aporétique aux origines de la pensée: Platon, Heidegger, Derrida." *Études françaises* 38, no. 1–2: 103–21. DOI: 10.7202/008394ar.

Gay, Peter. 1988. *Freud: A Life for Our Time.* New York: Norton.

Gering, Eben, Darren Incorvaia, Rie Henriksen, Jeffrey Conner, Thomas Getty, and Dominic Wright. 2019. "Getting Back to Nature: Feralization in Animals and Plants." *Trends in Ecology & Evolution* 34, no. 12: 1137–51. DOI: 10.1016/j.tree.2019.07.018.

Gilbhard, Thomas. 2012. *Vicos Denkbild: Studien zur 'Dipintura' der Scienza Nuova und der Lehre vom Ingenium.* Berlin: De Gruyter.

Gildenhard, Ingo. 2007. *Paideia Romana: Cicero's* Tusculan Disputations. Cambridge: Cambridge University Press.

Gill, Christopher. 2016. "Antiochus' Theory of *Oikeiōsis*." In *Cicero's* De Finibus: *Philosophical Approaches,* edited by Julia Annas and Gábor Betegh, 221–47. Cambridge: Cambridge University Press.

Gilroy, Paul. 1993. *The Black Atlantic: Modernity and Double Consciousness.* Cambridge: Harvard University Press.

Glazier, Jacob W. 2017. "Derrida and Messianic Subjectivity: A Hauntology of Revealability." *Journal for Cultural Research* 21, no. 3: 241–56. DOI: 10.1080/14797585.2017.1338600.

Gleason, Maud. 1990. "The Semiotics of Gender: Physiognomy and Self-Fashioning in the Second Century C.E." In *Before Sexuality: The Construction of Erotic Experience in the Ancient Greek World,* edited by David M. Halperin, John J. Winkler, and Froma I. Zeitlin, 389–415. Princeton: Princeton University Press.

Goetz, Georg, ed. 1929. *Terenti Varronis Rerum Rusticarum Libri Tres.* Leipzig: Teubner.

Goldhill, Simon. 2021. "Freud, Archaeology and Egypt: Religion, Materiality and the Cultural Critique of Origins." *Arion* 28, no. 3: 75–104. DOI: 10.1353/arn.2020.0010.

Gomme, Arnold W. 1968. *A Historical Commentary on Thucydides.* Vol. 2. Oxford: Oxford University Press.

Gowers, Emily. 2011. "Trees and Family Trees in the *Aeneid.*" *Classical Antiquity* 30, no. 1: 87–118. DOI: 10.1525/CA.2011.30.1.87.

Graczyk, Annette. 2015. *Die Hieroglyphe im 18. Jahrhundert: Theorien zwischen Aufklärung und Esoterik.* Berlin: De Gruyter.

Grafton, Anthony, Glenn W. Most, and James E.G. Zetzel, eds. 1985. *F.A. Wolf: Prolegomena to Homer, 1795.* Princeton: Princeton University Press.

Greenwood, Emily. 2010. *Afro-Greeks: Dialogues Between Anglophone Caribbean Literature and Classics in the Twentieth Century.* Oxford: Oxford University Press.

Grell, Chantal, and Christian Michel, eds. 1989. *Primitivisme et mythes des origines dans la France des Lumières.* Paris: Presses de l'Université de Paris-Sorbonne.

Grosz, Elizabeth. 1999. *Becomings: Explorations in Time, Memory, and Futures.* Ithaca: Cornell University Press.

Groves, Joseph. 2017. "Polybius' Vocabulary of World Domination: τῶν ὅλων and ἡ οἰκουμένη." *Greece & Rome* 64, no. 1: 1–13. DOI: 10.1017/S0017383516000206.

Guenther, Lisa. 2009. "Who Follows Whom? Derrida, Animals and Women." *Derrida Today* 2, no. 2: 151–65. DOI: 10.3366/E1754850009000499.

Guerlac, Suzanne. 2012. "Derrida and His Cat: The Most Important Question." *Contemporary French and Francophone Studies* 16, no. 5: 695–702. DOI: 10.1080/17409292.2012.739442.

Güthenke, Constanze. 2020. *Feeling and Classical Philology: Knowing Antiquity in German Scholarship, 1770–1920.* Cambridge: Cambridge University Press.

Guthrie, W.K.C., ed. 1939. *Aristotle: On the Heavens.* Cambridge: Harvard University Press.

Habinek, Thomas N. 1990. "Towards a History of Friendly Advice: The Politics of Candor in Cicero's *de Amicitia.*" *Apeiron: Journal for Ancient Philosophy and Science* 23, no. 4: 165–85. http://www.jstor.org/stable/40913647.

———. 2000. "Seneca's Renown: *Gloria, Claritudo,* and the Replication of the Roman Elite." *Classical Antiquity* 19, no. 2: 264–303. DOI: 10.2307/25011122.
Hadot, Pierre. 2002. *Exercices spirituels et philosophie antique.* Paris: Albin Michel.
Hägglund, Martin. 2008. *Radical Atheism: Derrida and the Time of Life.* Stanford: Stanford University Press.
Halberstam, Jack. 2018. *Trans*: A Quick and Quirky Account of Gender Variability.* Oakland: University of California Press.
———. 2020a. *Wild Things: The Disorder of Desire.* Durham: Duke University Press.
———. 2020b. "'Frantic.'" *Los Angeles Review of Books,* April 14. https://www.lareviewofbooks.org/article/quarantine-files-thinkers-self-isolation/.
Hall, Robert W. 1967. "On the Myth of the Metals in the *Republic.*" *Apeiron: A Journal for Ancient Philosophy and Science* 1, no. 2: 28–32. http://www.jstor.org/stable/40891403.
Hamilton, William, and Pierre d'[François Hugues] Hancarville. 1766–67. *Collection of Etruscan, Greek, and Roman Antiquities from the Cabinet of the Hon.ble W.m Hamilton His Britannick Maiesty's Envoy Extraordinary at the Court of Naples / Antiquités Étrusques, Grecques et Romaines, Tirées du Cabinet de M. Hamilton, Envoyé Extraordinaire de S.M. Britannique en cour de Naples.* Naples.
Hanson, J. Arthur, ed. 1996. *Apuleius: Metamorphoses (The Golden Ass),* Vol. 1: *Books 1–6.* Cambridge: Harvard University Press.
Haraway, Donna. 2015. "Anthropocene, Capitolocene, Plantationocene, Chthulucene: Making Kin." *Environmental Humanities* 6, no. 1: 159–65. DOI: 10.1215/22011919-3615934.
Harloe, Katherine. 2013. *Winckelmann and the Invention of Antiquity: History and Aesthetics in the Age of Altertumswissenschaft.* Oxford: Oxford University Press.
Harney, Stefano, and Fred Moten. 2013. *The Undercommons: Fugitive Planning & Black Study.* Wivenhoe: Minor

Compositions. https://www.minorcompositions.info/wp-content/uploads/2013/04/undercommons-web.pdf.

Harrison, Stephen J. 1990. "The Speaking Book: The Prologue to Apuleius' *Metamorphoses*." *Classical Quarterly* 40, no. 2: 507–13. DOI: 10.1017/S000983880004307X.

Hartman, Geoffrey. 2007. "Homage to *Glas*." In *The Late Derrida*, edited by W.J.T. Mitchell and Arnold I. Davidson, 126–43. Chicago: University of Chicago Press.

Hatley, James. 2012. "The Virtue of Temporal Discernment: Rethinking the Extent and Coherence of the Good in a Time of Mass Species Extinction." *Environmental Philosophy* 9, no. 1: 1–22. http://www.jstor.org/stable/26169393.

Hayes, Jarrod. 2017. "Derrida's Queer Roots(s)." In *Derrida and Queer Theory*, edited by Christian Hite, 164–82. Earth: punctum books. DOI: 10.21983/P3.0172.1.00.

Hegel, Georg Wilhelm Friedrich. 1971. *Leçons sur l'histoire de la philosophie*. Paris: Vrin.

Heidegger, Martin. 1992. *Parmenides*. Translated by André Schuwer and Richard Rojcewicz. Bloomington: Indiana University Press.

Henderson, Jeffrey, ed. 1998. *Aristophanes: Clouds; Wasps; Peace*. Cambridge: Harvard University Press.

Henrichs, Albert. 1993. "The Tomb of Aias and the Prospect of Hero Cult in Sophokles." *Classical Antiquity* 12, no. 2: 165–80. DOI: 10.2307/25010992.

Heringman, Noah. 2013. *Sciences of Antiquity: Romantic Antiquarianism, Natural History, and Knowledge Work*. Oxford: Oxford University Press.

Herodotus. 2015. *Histories: Books 5–9*. Edited by N.G. Wilson. Oxford: Oxford University Press.

Heyes, Cressida J. 2020. *Anaesthetics of Existence: Essays on Experience at the Edge*. Durham: Duke University Press.

Hickman, Jared. 2017. *Black Prometheus: Race and Radicalism in the Age of Atlantic Slavery*. Oxford: Oxford University Press.

Hill, Leslie. 2016. "From Deconstruction to Disaster (Derrida, Blanchot, Hegel)." *Paragraph* 39, no. 2: 187–201. http://www.jstor.org/stable/44016413.

Hill, Rebecca. 2019. "Immanent Maternal: Figures of Time in Aristotle, Bergson, and Irigaray." In *Antiquities Beyond Humanism,* edited by Emanuela Bianchi, Sara Brill, and Brooke Holmes, 271–86. Oxford: Oxford University Press.

Hinds, Stephen. 2005. "Defamiliarizing Latin Literature, from Petrarch to Pulp Fiction." *Transactions of the American Philological Association* 135, no. 1: 49–81. http://www.jstor.org/stable/20054120.

Hite, Christian. 2017. "The Gift from (of the) 'Behind' (*Derrière*): Intro-extro-duction." In *Derrida and Queer Theory,* edited by Christian Hite, 10–23. Earth: punctum books. DOI: 10.21983/P3.0172.1.00.

Hoa, Jen Hui Bon. 2020. "The Law or the Demos? Derrida and Rancière on the Paradox of Democracy." *Paragraph* 43, no. 2: 179–96. DOI: 10.3366/para.2020.0331.

Hodge, Joanna. 2007. *Derrida on Time.* London: Routledge.

Hohti, Riikka, and Jayne Osgood. 2020. "Pets that Have 'Something Inside': The Material Politics of In/Animacy and Queer Kin within the Childhood Menagerie." *Genealogy* 4, no. 2: 1–15. DOI: 10.3390/genealogy4020038.

Hollinger, Veronica. 1987. "Deconstructing the Time Machine." *Science Fiction Studies* 14, no. 2: 201–21. http://www.jstor.org/stable/4239816.

Hönes, Hans Christian. 2014. *Kunst am Ursprung: Das Nachleben der Bilder und die Souveränität des Antiquars.* Bielefeld: Transcript.

Honig, Bonnie. 2021. *A Feminist Theory of Refusal.* Cambridge: Harvard University Press.

———. 2022. "A Method in the Madness: After *AFTR,* in Grateful Reply." *Classical Antiquity* 41, no. 2: 34–49. DOI: 10.1525/ca.2022.41.2.34.

Hooke, Roger LeB., José F. Martín-Duque, and Javier Pedraza. 2012. "Land Transformations by Humans: A Review." *GSA Today* 22, no. 12: 4–10. DOI: 10.1130/GSAT151A.1.

Hornblower, Simon, ed. 1991. *A Commentary on Thucydides.* Vol. 1. Oxford: Oxford University Press.

Hort, Arthur, ed. 1916. *Theophrastus: Enquiry into Plants.* Cambridge: Harvard University Press.

Hude, Karl, ed. 1901. *Thucydidis Historiae.* Leipzig: Teubner.

Hunter, Virginia. 1992. "Constructing the Body of the Citizen: Corporal Punishment in Classical Athens." *Echos du Monde Classique* 36: 271–91. https://www.muse.jhu.edu/article/653747.

Hyvönen, Ari-Elmeri. 2020. "Labor as Action: The Human Condition in the Anthropocene." *Research in Phenomenology* 50, no. 2: 240–60. DOI: 10.1163/15691640-12341449.

Ingenkamp, Heinz Gerd. 1972. "Thelyphron: Zu Apuleius, *Metamorphosen* II 20ff." *Rheinisches Museum für Philologie* 115: 337–42. http://www.jstor.org/stable/41244707.

Ingold, Tim. 2015. *The Life of Lines.* London: Routledge.

Inwood, Brad. 2016. "The Voice of Nature." In *Cicero's De Finibus: Philosophical Approaches,* edited by Julia Annas and Gábor Betegh, 147–66. Cambridge: Cambridge University Press.

Irwin, John T. 1980. *American Hieroglyphics: The Symbol of the Egyptian Hieroglyphics in the American Renaissance.* Baltimore: Johns Hopkins University Press.

Isager, Jacob. 1991. *Pliny on Art and Society: The Elder Pliny's Chapters on the History of Art.* Translated by Henrik Rosenmeier. London: Routledge.

Jameson, Fredric. 1981. *The Political Unconscious: Narrative as Socially Symbolic Act.* Ithaca: Cornell University Press.

———. 1984. "Postmodernism, Or The Cultural Logic of Late Capitalism." *New Left Review* 146: 53–92. https://newleftreview.org/issues/i146/articles/fredric-jameson-postmodernism-or-the-cultural-logic-of-late-capitalism.

———. 1992. *The Geopolitical Aesthetic: Cinema and Space in the World System.* Bloomington: Indiana University Press.

———. 2005. "World Reduction in Le Guin." In *Archaeologies of the Future: The Desire Called Utopia and Other Science Fictions,* 267–80. London: Verso.

———. 2015. "The Aesthetics of Singularity." *New Left Review* 92: 102–32. https://newleftreview.org/II/92/fredric-jameson-the-aesthetics-of-singularity.

Jenkins, Ian, and Kim Sloane, eds. 1996. *Vases and Volcanoes: Sir William Hamilton and His Collection.* London: British Museum Press.

Johnson, Barbara. 1986. "Apostrophe, Animation, and Abortion." *Diacritics* 16, no. 1: 28–47. DOI: 10.2307/464649.

Johnson, Keith Leslie. 2016. "The Extinction Romance." *Modernism/modernity* 23, no. 3: 539–53. DOI: 10.1353/mod.2016.0050.

Jones, Bill T. 2017. "The Process of Becoming Infinite." *YouTube,* July 17. https://www.youtube.com/watch?v=QBWe05FK0OA.

Jones, Ernst. 1957. *The Life and Work of Sigmund Freud,* Vol. 3: *The Last Phase,* 1919–1939. New York: Basic Books.

Jones, William, ed. 1963. *Pliny: Natural History, Vol. VIII (Books 28–32).* Cambridge: Harvard University Press.

Kahane, Ahuvia. 2018a. "Cognitive Functional Grammar and the Complexity of Early Greek Epic Diction." In *The Routledge Handbook of Classics and Cognitive Theory,* edited by Peter Meineck, William Michael Short, and Jennifer Devereaux, 21–38. London: Routledge.

———. 2018b. "The Complexity of Epic Diction." *Yearbook of Ancient Greek Epic Online* 2, no. 1: 78–117. DOI: 10.1163/24688487-00201003.

———. 2020. "Demos, Democracy and Method: Political Trust and the Science of Suspicion." In *Reconciling Ancient and Modern Philosophies of History,* edited by Aaron Turner, 231–60. Berlin: De Gruyter.

Kahane, Ahuvia, and Andrew Laird, eds. 2001. *A Companion to the Prologue of Apuleius' Metamorphoses.* Oxford: Oxford University Press.

Kamuf, Peggy. 2020. "Visitation." *Derrida Today* 13, no. 2: 171–77. DOI: 10.3366/drt.2020.0234.

Kassel, Rudolf, ed. 1976. *Aristotelis Ars Rhetorica*. Berlin: De Gruyter.

Kaufman, Eleanor. 2013. "The Mineralogy of Being." In *Architecture in the Anthropocene: Encounters Among Design, Deep Time, Science and Philosophy*, edited by Etienne Turpin, 153–66. Ann Arbor: University of Michigan Press.

Kenaan, Vered Lev. 2019. *The Ancient Unconscious: Psychoanalysis and the Ancient Text*. Oxford: Oxford University Press.

Khosravi, Shahram. 2021. "Afterword: Waiting, A State of Consciousness." In *Waiting and the Temporalities of Irregular Migration*, edited by Christine M. Jacobsen, Marry-Anne Karlsen, and Shahram Khosravi, 202–7. London: Routledge.

Kofman, Sarah. 1989. *Socrate(s)*. Paris: Galilée.

Kortetmäki, Teea. 2017. "Applying the Capabilities Approach to Ecosystems: Resilience as Ecosystem Capability." *Environmental Ethics* 39, no. 1: 39–56. DOI: 10.5840/enviroethics20179263.

Kowalzig, Barbara. 2006. "The Aetiology of Empire? Hero-Cult and Athenian Tragedy." *Bulletin of the Institute of Classical Studies, Supplement* 87: 79–98. http://www.jstor.org/stable/43768111.

Kroetsch, Robert. 1985. *Advice to My Friends: A Continuing Poem*. Toronto: Stoddart.

Kurke, Leslie V. 1995. "Herodotus and the Language of Metals." *Helios* 22: 36–64.

Lacan, Jacques. 1977. *Écrits: A Selection*. Translated by Alan Sheridan. New York: W.W. Norton.

Lai, Chung-Hsiung. 2016. "On (Im)Patient Messianism: Marx, Levinas, and Derrida." *Levinas Studies* 11: 59–94. https://www.jstor.org/stable/26942985.

Lampert, Jay. 2018. *The Many Futures of a Decision*. London: Bloomsbury.

Langlois, Christopher. 2015. "Temporal Exile in the Time of Fiction: Reading Derrida Reading Blanchot's *The Instant of*

My Death." *Mosaic: An Interdisciplinary Critical Journal* 48, no. 4: 17–32. http://www.jstor.org/stable/44030404.

Laplace, Pierre-Simon. 1951. *A Philosophical Essay on Probabilities.* New York: Dover.

Laplanche, Jean. 1976. *Life and Death in Psychoanalysis.* Translated by Jeffrey Mehlman. Baltimore: Johns Hopkins University Press.

Larsen-Freeman, Diane. 1997. "Chaos/Complexity Science and Second Language Acquisition." *Applied Linguistics* 18, no. 2: 141–65. DOI: 10.1093/applin/18.2.141.

Lateiner, Donald. 2001. "Humiliation and Immobility in Apuleius' *Metamorphoses*." *Transactions of the American Philological Association* 131: 217–55. http://www.jstor.org/stable/20140970.

Lavezzi, Élisabeth. 1999. "Homère en peinture: À propos des tableaux tirés de *L'Iliade* de Caylus." In *Homère en France après la Querelle (1715–1900),* edited by Françoise Létoublon and Catherine Volpilhac-Auger, 265–76. Paris: Honoré Champion.

Leach, Eleanor Winsor. 1993. "Absence and Desire in Cicero's *De Amicitia.*" *The Classical World* 87, no. 2: 3–20. DOI: 10.2307/4351452.

Lecoq, Anne-Marie. 2010. *Le Bouclier d'Achille: Un Tableau qui bouge.* Paris: Gallimard.

Lee, H.D.P., ed. 1952. *Aristotle Meteorologica.* Cambridge: Harvard University Press.

Leonard, Miriam. 2000. "The *Politiques de l'amitié:* Derrida's Greeks and a National Politics of Classical Scholarship." *Proceedings of the Cambridge Philological Society* 46: 45–78. http://www.jstor.org/stable/44696758.

Levinas, Emmanuel. 1976. *Noms Propres.* Montpellier: Fata Morgana.

———. 1979. *Totality and Infinity: An Essay on Exteriority.* Translated by Alphonso Lingis. Pittsburgh: Duquesne University Press.

Levine, Joseph M. 1991. "Giambattista Vico and the Quarrel between the Ancients and the Moderns." *Journal of the History of Ideas* 52, no. 1: 55–79. DOI: 10.2307/2709582.

Lewis, Michael. 2008. *Derrida and Lacan: Another Writing.* Edinburgh: Edinburgh University Press.

Liddell, Henry George, Robert Scott, and Henry Stuart Jones, eds. 1996. *A Greek–English Lexicon.* Oxford: Oxford University Press.

Lin, Yael. 2013. *The Intersubjectivity of Time: Levinas and Infinite Responsibility.* Pittsburgh: Duquesne University Press.

Lindsay, W.M., ed. 1905. *T. Macci Plauti: Comoediae.* Oxford: Oxford University Press.

———, ed. 1985. *Isidori Hispalensis Episcopi: Etymologiarum Sive Originum, Libri XX: Tomus I, Libros I–X.* Oxford: Clarendon Press.

Lissarrague, François, and Marcia Reed. 1997. "The Collector's Books." *Journal of the History of Collections* 9, no. 2: 275–94. DOI: 10.1093/jhc/9.2.275.

Lloyd, Genevieve. 2018. *Reclaiming Wonder: After the Sublime.* Edinburgh: Edinburgh University Press.

Lloyd-Jones, Hugh, and Nigel G. Wilson, eds. 1990. *Sophoclis Fabulae.* Oxford: Oxford University Press.

Loney, Alexander C. 2021. "The Medicine of Blindness and Human Time in the *Prometheus Bound*." *Classical World* 114, no. 3: 251–80. DOI: 10.1353/clw.2021.0011.

Loraux, Nicole. 1993. *The Children of Athena: Athenian Ideas about Citizenship and the Division between the Sexes.* Translated by Caroline Levine. Princeton: Princeton University Press.

———. 2000. *Born of the Earth: Myth and Politics in Athens.* Translated by Selina Stewart. Ithaca: Cornell University Press.

Lorenzini, Daniele. 2021. "Biopolitics in the Time of Coronavirus." *Critical Inquiry* 47, S2: S40–S45. DOI: 10.1086/711432.

Louis, Pierre, ed. 1956. *Aristote: Les parties des animaux.* Paris: Les Belles Lettres.

Lowe, Dunstan. 2010. "The Symbolic Value of Grafting in Ancient Rome." *Transactions of the American Philological Association* 140, no. 2: 461–88. http://www.jstor.org/stable/40890986.

Lucas, D.W., ed. 1968. *Aristotle: Poetics.* Oxford: Oxford University Press.

Lundström, Vilhelm, ed. 1897. *L. Iuni Moderati Columellae Opera Quae Extant: Fasc. 1 (De Arboribus).* Uppsala: Eranos.

Macherey, Pierre. 2008. "Le Marx intempestif de Derrida." In *Derrida, la tradition de la philosophie,* edited by Marc Crépon and Frédéric Worms, 135–54. Paris: Galilée.

Madvig, Nicolaus, ed. 1876. *M. Tullii Ciceronis de Finibus Bonorum et Malorum Libri Quinque.* Copenhagen: Gyldendal.

Mal-Maeder, Danielle van, ed. 2001. *Groningen Commentaries on Apuleius: Apuleius Madaurensis,* Metamorphoses, *Livre II.* Leiden: Brill.

March, Jennifer R. 1991–1993. "Sophocles' *Ajax:* The Death and Burial of a Hero." *Bulletin of the Institute of Classical Studies* 38: 1–36. http://www.jstor.org/stable/43646729.

Marchand, Suzanne L. 1996. *Down from Olympus: Archaeology and Philhellenism in Germany, 1750–1970.* Princeton: Princeton University Press.

Marder, Michael. 2018. "Ecology as Event." In *Eco-Deconstruction: Derrida and Environmental Philosophy,* edited by Matthias Fritsch, Philippe Lynes, and David Wood, 141–64. New York: Fordham University Press.

Mars, Messaoud, M. Trad, and Badii Gaaliche. 2017. "The Unique Fig Caprification System and its Effects on Productivity and Fruit Characteristics." *ISHS Acta Horticulturae* 1173: 127–36. DOI: 10.17660/ActaHortic.2017.1173.22.

Marshall, David. 1997. "Literature and the Other Arts: (ii) The Picturesque." In *The Cambridge History of Literary Criticism,* Vol. 4: *The Eighteenth Century,* edited by Hugh Barr Nisbet and Claude Julien Rawson, 700–18. Cambridge: Cambridge University Press.

Martelli, Francesca. 2024. *Souvenirs of Cicero: Shaping Memory in the* Epistulae Ad Familiares. Oxford: Oxford University Press.

Martinon, Jean-Paul. 2007. *On Futurity: Malabou, Nancy, and Derrida.* New York: Palgrave Macmillan.

Marx, Karl. 1978. "Theses on Feuerbach." In *The Marx-Engels Reader,* edited by Robert C. Tucker, 143–45. New York: Norton.

Matlock, Andres. 2020. "Time and Experience in Cicero's Ethical Dialogues." PhD Diss., University of California, Los Angeles.

———. 2021. "The Solitude of a Lifetime in Cicero's *De Finibus* 5." In *Being Alone in Antiquity: Ancient Ideas and Experiences of Misanthropy, Isolation, and Solitude,* edited by Rafał Matuszewki, 245–63. Berlin: De Gruyter.

Matzner, Sebastian. 2016. "Queer Unhistoricism: Scholars, Metalepsis, and Interventions of the Unruly Past." In *Deep Classics: Rethinking Classical Reception,* edited by Shane Butler, 179–201. London: Bloomsbury.

Mayrhofer, Colin M. 1975. "On Two Stories in Apuleius." *Antichthon* 9: 68–80. DOI: 10.1017/S0066477400004469.

Mazzotta, Giuseppe. 2014. *The New Map of the World: The Poetic Philosophy of Giambattista Vico.* Princeton: Princeton University Press.

Mbembe, Achille. 2017. *Critique of Black Reason.* Durham: Duke University Press.

McCarthy, Cormac. 2006. *The Road.* New York: Vintage Books.

McLuhan, Marshall. 1994. *Understanding Media: The Extensions of Man.* Cambridge: MIT Press.

McHam, Sarah Blake. 2013. *Pliny and the Artistic Culture of the Italian Renaissance: The Legacy of the* Natural History. New Haven: Yale University Press.

McNulty, Tracy. 2017. "Unbound: The Speculative Mythology of the Death Drive." *differences: A Journal of Feminist Cultural Studies* 28, no. 2: 86–115. DOI: 10.1215/10407391-4151785.

Meillassoux, Quentin. 2008. *After Finitude: An Essay on the Necessity of Contingency.* Translated by Ray Brassier. London: Continuum.

Michelini, Ann. 1978. "Ὕβρις and Plants." *Harvard Studies of Classical Philology* 82: 35–44. DOI: 10.2307/311019.

Miller, David A. 2021. *Second Time Around: From Art House to DVD.* New York: Columbia University Press.

Miller, Paul Allen. 2015. "Cicero Reads Derrida Reading Cicero: A Politics and a Friendship to Come." In *Brill's Companion to the Reception of Cicero,* edited by William H.F. Altman, 173–97. Leiden: Brill.

———. 2016. "Ghosts in the *Politics of Friendship*." In *Dead Theory: Derrida, Death, and the Afterlife of Theory,* edited by Jeffrey R. Di Leo, 111–32. London: Bloomsbury.

———. 2021a. *Foucault's Seminars on Antiquity: Learning to Speak the Truth.* London: Bloomsbury.

———. 2021b. "Plato's *Seventh Letter* or How to Fashion a Subject of Resistance." In *The Politics of Form in Greek Literature,* edited by Phiroze Vasunia, 125–44. London: Bloomsbury.

Mitchell, W.J.T., and Arnold I. Davidson, eds. 2007. *The Late Derrida.* Chicago: University of Chicago Press.

Monoson, S. Sara. 1998. "Remembering Pericles: The Political and Theoretical Import of Plato's *Menexenus*." *Political Theory* 26, no. 4: 489–513. http://www.jstor.org/stable/192201.

Moore, James. 2008. "History as Theoretical Reconstruction? Baron D'Hancarville and the Exploration of Ancient Mythology in the Eighteenth Century." In *Reinventing History: The Enlightenment Origins of Ancient History,* edited by James Moore, Ian Macgregor Morris, and Andrew J. Bayless, 137–67. London: University of London.

Moore, Jason W. 2015. *Capitalism in the Web of Life: Ecology and the Accumulation of Capital.* London: Verso.

Morales, Helen. 2022. "Bonnie Honig's *A Feminist Theory of Refusal* with Kehinde Wiley's *After John Raphael Smith's 'A*

Bacchante (after Sir Joshua Reynolds).'" *Classical Antiquity* 41, no. 2: 25–33. DOI: 10.1525/ca.2022.41.2.25.

Morley, Neville. 2004. "Decadence as a Theory of History." *New Literary History* 35, no. 4 : 573–85. http://www.jstor.org/stable/20057861.

Morton, Timothy. 2012. "The Oedipal Logic of Ecological Awareness." *Environmental Humanities* 1, no. 1: 7–21. DOI: 10.1215/22011919-3609949.

Most, Glenn W. 1997. "Hesiod's Myth of the Five (or Three or Four) Races." *Proceedings of the Cambridge Philological Society* 43: 104–27. http://www.jstor.org/stable/44696741.

Moyer, Ian S., Adam Lecznar, and Heidi Morse, eds. 2020. *Classicisms in the Black Atlantic.* Oxford: Oxford University Press.

Murgatroyd, Paul. 2004. "Thelyphron's Story (Apul. *Met.* 2.21-30)." *Mnemosyne* 57, no. 4: 493–97. http://www.jstor.org/stable/4433583.

Musielak, Zdzislaw E., and Billy Quarles. 2014. "The Three-Body Problem." *Reports on Progress in Physics* 77: 065901. DOI: 10.1088/0034-4885/77/6/065901.

Mynors, R.A.B., ed. 1958. *C. Valerii Catulli carmina.* Oxford: Oxford University Press.

———, ed. 1969 *P. Vergili Maronis Opera.* Oxford: Clarendon Press.

Nagy, Gregory. 1979. *The Best of the Achaeans: Concepts of the Hero in Archaic Greek Poetry.* Baltimore: Johns Hopkins University Press.

———. 2000. "'Dream of a Shade': Refractions of Epic Vision in Pindar's *Pythian* 8 and Aeschylus' *Seven against Thebes.*" *Harvard Studies in Classical Philology* 100: 97–118. DOI: 10.2307/3185211.

Nancy, Jean-Luc. 1997. *The Sense of the World.* Translated by Jeffrey S. Librett. Minneapolis: University of Minnesota Press.

———. 2012. *The Inoperative Community.* Translated by Peter Connor, Lisa Garbus, Michael Holland, and Simona Sawhney. Minneapolis: University of Minnesota Press.

———. 2020. *Doing.* Translated by Charlotte Mandell. London: Seagull Books.

———. 2021. *The Fragile Skin of the World.* Translated by Cory Stockwell. Cambridge: Polity.

Ngai, Sianne. 2020. *Theory of the Gimmick: Aesthetic Judgment and Capitalist Form.* Cambridge: Harvard University Press.

Nicolis, Grégoire, and Ilya Prigogine. 1989. *Exploring Complexity: An Introduction.* New York: Freeman.

Nooter, Sarah. 2012. *When Heroes Sing: Sophocles and the Shifting Soundscape of Tragedy.* Cambridge: Cambridge Universiy Press.

———. 2023. *Greek Poetry in the Age of Ephemerality.* Cambridge: Cambridge University Press.

Norman, Larry F. 2011. *The Shock of the Ancient: Literature & History in Early Modern France.* Chicago: University of Chicago Press.

Novak, Maximillian E. 1997. "Primitivism." In *The Cambridge History of Literary Criticism,* Vol. 4: *The Eighteenth Century,* edited by Hugh Barr Nisbet and Claude Julien Rawson, 456–69. Cambridge: Cambridge University Press.

Noys, Benjamin. 2010. "On the Edge of Affirmation: Derrida." In *The Persistence of the Negative: A Critique of Contemporary Continental Theory,* 23–50. Edinburgh: Edinburgh University Press.

Nussbaum, Martha C. 2011. *Creating Capabilities: The Human Development Approach.* Cambridge: Harvard University Press.

Ober, Josiah. 1993. "Thucydides' Criticism of Democratic Knowledge." In *Nomodeiktes: Greek Studies in Honor of Martin Ostwald,* edited by Ralph M. Rosen and Joseph Farrell, 81–98. Ann Arbor: University of Michigan Press.

———. 1998. *Political Dissent in Democratic Athens: Intellectual Critics of Popular Rule.* Princeton: Princeton University Press.

———. 2015. *The Rise and Fall of Classical Greece.* Princeton: Princeton University Press.

O'Brien, Denis. 2010. "Movίη in Empedocles: Slings' 'Iron Rule.'" *Mnemosyne* 63, no. 2: 268–71. http://www.jstor.org/stable/40649049.

Oliver, Kelly. 2001. "Paternal Election and the Absent Father." In *Feminist Interpretations of Emmanuel Levinas,* edited by Tina Chanter, 224–40. University Park: Pennsylvania State University Press.

Orrells, Daniel. 2010. "Derrida's Impression of Gradiva: Archive Fever and Antiquity." In *Derrida and Antiquity,* edited by Miriam Leonard, 159–84. Oxford: Oxford University Press.

———. 2011. "Burying and Excavating Winckelmann's *History of Art.*" *Classical Receptions Journal* 3, no. 2: 166–88. DOI: 10.1093/crj/clr005.

Orrells, Daniel, Gurminder K. Bhambra, and Tessa Roynon, eds. 2011. *African Athena: New Agendas.* Oxford: Oxford University Press.

Osterkamp, Ernst. 1989. "Zierde und Beweis: Über die Illustrationsprinzipien von J.J. Winckelmanns *Geschichte der Kunst des Alterthums.*" *Germanisch-romanische Monatsschrift* 39: 301–25.

Page, Carl. 1991. "The Truth about Lies in Plato's *Republic.*" *Ancient Philosophy* 11, no. 1: 1–33. DOI: 10.5840/ancientphil199111132.

Page, Denys, ed. 1972. *Aeschyli Tragoediae Quae Supersunt.* Oxford: Oxford University Press.

Parr, Adrian. 2020. "Crisis." *Los Angeles Review of Books,* April 14. https://www.lareviewofbooks.org/article/quarantine-files-thinkers-self-isolation/.

Patterson, Orlando. 1985. *Slavery and Social Death: A Comparative Study.* Cambridge: Harvard University Press.

Payne, Mark. 2020. "Post-Apocalyptic Humanism in Hesiod, Mary Shelly, and Olaf Stapledon." *Classical Receptions Journal* 12, no. 1: 91–108. DOI: 10.1093/crj/clz022.

Peck, Arthur, ed. 1970. *Aristotle: History of Animals Vol. II (Books 4–6).* Cambridge: Harvard University Press.

Perry, Ben Edwin. 1929. "The Story of Thelyphron in Apuleius." *Classical Philology* 24, no. 3: 231–38. DOI: 10.1086/361134.

———. 1949. Review of *Ad Apulei Madaurensis Metamorphoseon librum secundum commentarius exegeticus* by B.J. de Jonge. *Classical Philology* 44, no. 1: 38–42. http://www.jstor.org/stable/267082.

Phillips, James. 2005. *Heidegger's Volk: Between National Socialism and Poetry.* Stanford: Stanford University Press.

Pitts, Martin, and Miguel John Versluys. 2014. "Globalization and the Roman World: Perspectives and Opportunities." In *Globalization and the Roman World: World History, Connectivity, and Material Culture,* edited by Martin Pitts and Miguel John Versluys, 3–31. Cambridge: Cambridge University Press.

Poincaré, Henri. 1881. "Mémoire sur les courbes définies par une équation différentielle." *Journal de Mathématiques pures et appliquées* 3, no. 7: 375–422.

———. 1928. "Sur les courbes définies par les équations différentielles." In *Oeuvres,* Vol. 1: 9–161. Paris: Gauthier-Villars.

———. 1993. *New Methods of Celestial Mechanics.* Cham: Springer.

———. 2017. *The Three-Body Problem and the Equations of Dynamics.* Translated by Bruce D. Popp. Cham: Springer.

Pope, Alexander, trans. 1996. *The Iliad of Homer.* London: Penguin.

Porter, James I. 2004. "Homer: The History of an Idea." In *The Cambridge Companion to Homer,* edited by Robert Fowler, 324–43. Cambridge: Cambridge University Press.

———. 2021. *Homer: The Very Idea.* Chicago: University of Chicago Press.

Postclassicisms Collective. 2020. *Postclassicisms.* Chicago: University of Chicago Press.

Povinelli, Elizabeth A. 2021. *Between Gaia and Ground: Four Axioms of Existence and the Ancestral Catastrophe of Late Liberalism.* Durham: Duke University Press.

Powell, J.G.F., ed. 1988. *Cicero: Cato Maior De Senectute*. Cambridge: Cambridge University Press.

———, ed. 1990. *Cicero, On Friendship and The Dream of Scipio*. Liverpool: Liverpool University Press.

Prigogine, Ilya, and Isabelle Stengers. 1984. *Order out of Chaos: Man's New Dialogue with Nature*. Toronto: Bantam Books.

Proust, Marcel. 1982. *Remembrance of Things Past*. Translated by C.K. Scott Moncrief and Terence Kilmartin. New York: Vintage.

———. 1987. *À la recherche du temps perdu*. Edited by Jean-Yves Tadié. Paris: Gallimard.

Pugliese, Joseph. 2020. *Biopolitics of the More-Than-Human: Forensic Ecologies of Violence*. Durham: Duke University Press.

Quintilian. 1920–1922. *The Institutio Oratoria*. 4 Vols. Translated by Harold Edgeworth Butler. Cambridge: Harvard University Press.

Rackham, Harris, trans. 1931. *Cicero: De Finibus Bonorum et Malorum*. Cambridge: Harvard University Press.

———, ed. 1945. *Pliny: Natural History, Vol. IV (Books 12–16)*. Cambridge: Harvard University Press.

Radt, Stefan, ed. 1977. *Tragicorum Graecorum fragmenta*. Vol. 4. Göttingen: Vandenhoeck & Ruprecht.

Rajeev, Sarada G. 2013. *Advanced Mechanics: From Euler's Determinism to Arnold's Chaos*. Oxford: Oxford University Press.

Rambo, Shelly L. 2008. "Beyond Redemption? Reading Cormac McCarthy's *The Road* after the End of the World." *Studies in the Literary Imagination* 41, no. 2: 99–120.

Ramsay, Georgina. 2019. "Humanitarian Exploits: Ordinary Displacement and the Political Economy of the Global Refugee Regime." *Critique of Anthropology* 40, no. 1: 1–25. DOI: 10.1177/0308275X19840417.

Rancière, Jacques. 1995. *On the Shores of Politics*. Translated by Liz Heron. London: Verso.

———. 2004. *The Politics of Aesthetics*. Translated by Gabriel Rockhill. London: Bloomsbury.

———. 2007. "Does Democracy Mean Something?" In *Adieu Derrida,* edited by Costam Douzinas, 84–100. London: Palgrave Macmillan.

———. 2009. "Should Democracy Come? Ethics and Politics in Derrida." In *Derrida and the Time of the Political,* edited by Pheng Cheah and Suzanne Guerlac, 274–90. Durham: Duke University Press.

Rankine, Patrice D. 2006. *Ulysses in Black: Ralph Ellison, Classicism, and African American Literature.* Madison: University of Wisconsin Press.

Reinhardt, Karl. 1979. *Sophocles.* Translated by Hazel Harvey and David Harvey. Oxford: Blackwell.

Reinhart, Eric. 2021. "Pandemicity without Pandemic: Political Responsibility in the Exponential Present." *b20,* January 20. https://www.boundary2.org/2021/01/pandemicity-without-pandemic-political-responsibility-in-the-exponential-present/.

Richards, Arnold D. 2014. "Freud's Jewish Identity and Psychoanalysis as a Science." *Journal of the American Psychoanalytic Association* 62, no. 6: 987–1003. DOI: 10.1177/0003065114559835.

Richardson, John S. 1991. *"Imperium Romanum:* Empire and the Language of Power." *The Journal of Roman Studies* 81: 1–9. DOI: 10.2307/300484.

Richlin, Amy. 1992. *The Garden of Priapus: Sexuality and Aggression in Roman Humor.* Oxford: Oxford University Press.

Rolfe, John C., ed. 1929. *Cornelius Nepos: On Great Generals. On Historians.* Cambridge: Harvard University Press.

Rollins, Brooke. 2020. *The Ethics of Persuasion: Derrida's Rhetorical Legacies.* Columbus: Ohio State University Press.

Rose, Peter. 2017. "Secrets of the Ancients?" *New Left Review* 103: 139–49.

Rosenblum, Robert. 1967. *Transformations in Late Eighteenth-Century Art.* Princeton: Princeton University Press.

Rosenstock, Bruce. 1992. "Fathers and Sons: Irony in the *Cratylus*." *Arethusa* 25, no. 3: 385–417. http://www.jstor.org/stable/26308620.

Rosivach, Vincent J. 1987. "Autochthony and the Athenians." *The Classical Quarterly* 3, no. 2: 294–306. http://www.jstor.org/stable/638830.

Ross, William David, ed. 1950. *Aristotelis Physica*. Oxford: Oxford University Press.

———, ed. 1957. *Aristotelis Politica*. Oxford: Oxford University Press.

Rowe, Christopher, ed. 2023. *Aristotle's Eudemian Ethics*. Oxford: Oxford University Press.

Rouse, William, and Martin Smith, eds. 1992. *Lucretius: On the Nature of Things*. Cambridge: Harvard University Press.

Ruffell, Isabel. 2022. "*Bacchae*: 'An Excessively High Price to Pay for Being Reluctant to Emerge from the Closet'?" In *Queer Euripides: Re-Readings in Greek Tragedy,* edited by Sarah Olson and Mario Telò, 239–48. London: Bloomsbury.

Rush, Fred. 2016. *Irony and Idealism: Rereading Schlegel, Hegel, and Kierkegaard*. Oxford: Oxford University Press.

Said, Edward W. 2006. *On Late Style: Music and Literature Against the Grain*. New York: Pantheon Books.

Samuels, Ellen, and Elizabeth Freeman. 2021. "Introduction: Crip Temporalities." *South Atlantic Quarterly* 120, no. 2: 245–54. DOI: 10.1215/00382876-8915937.

Santner, Eric L. 2022. *Untying Things Together: Philosophy, Literature, and a Life in Theory*. Chicago: University of Chicago Press.

Sartre, Jean-Paul. 1943. *L'être et le néant: Essai d'ontologie phénoménologique*. Paris: Gallimard.

Schleusener, Simon. 2017. "The Dialectics of Mobility: Capitalism and Apocalypse in Cormac McCarthy's *The Road*." *European Journal of American Studies* 12, no. 3: 1–14. DOI: 10.4000/ejas.12296.

Schober, Adolph Karl Ernst. 1904. "De Apulei *Metamorphoseon* compositione numerosa." PhD diss., University of Halle.

Schofield, Malcolm. 2007. "The Noble Lie." In *The Cambridge Companion to Plato's Republic,* edited by Giovanni R.F. Ferrari, 138–64. Cambridge: Cambridge University Press.

Scholem, Gershom. 1995. *Tagebücher nebst Aufsätzen und Entwürfen bis 1923.* Frankfurt am Main: Jüdischer Verlag.

Schotter, Jesse. 2018. *Hieroglyphic Modernisms: Writing and New Media in the Twentieth Century.* Edinburgh: Edinburgh University Press.

Schrödinger, Erwin. 1935. "Die gegenwärtige Situation in der Quantenmechanik." *Naturwissenschaften* 23: 807–12. DOI: 10.1007/BF01491891.

Scott, Joan Wallach. 2018. *Sex and Secularism.* Princeton: Princeton University Press.

Seaford, Richard, ed. 1996. *Euripides: Bacchae.* Warminster: Aris & Phillips.

Segal, Charles. 1997. *Dionysiac Poetics and Euripides' Bacchae.* Princeton: Princeton University Press.

———. 1999–2000. "Lament and Recognition: A Reconsideration of the Ending of the *Bacchae*." *Illinois Classical Studies* 24–25: 273–91. http://www.jstor.org/stable/23065372.

Seidensticker, Bernd. 2016. "The Figure of Teiresias in Euripides' *Bacchae*." In *Wisdom and Folly in Euripides,* edited by Poulheria Kyriakou and Antonios Rengakos, 275–83. Berlin: De Gruyter.

Shackleton Bailey, David R., ed. 1999. *Cicero: Letters to Atticus.* 4 Vols. Cambridge: Harvard University Press.

Sheldon, Rebekah. 2019. "Accelerationism's Queer Occulture." *Angelaki* 24, no. 1: 118–29. DOI: 10.1080/0969725X.2019.1568739.

Shumate, Nancy. 1999. "Apuleius' *Metamorphoses:* The Inserted Tales." In *Latin Fiction: The Latin Novel in Context,* edited by Heinz Hofmann, 113–25. London: Routledge.

Simonsuuri, Kirsti. 1979. *Homer's Original Genius: Eighteenth-Century Notions of the Early Greek Epic.* Cambridge: Cambridge University Press.

Skinner, Marilyn B. 1993. *"Ego mulier:* The Construction of Male Sexuality in Catullus." *Helios* 20: 107–30.

Skrimshire, Stefan. 2011. "'There Is No God and We Are His Prophets': Deconstructing Redemption in Cormac McCarthy's *The Road." Journal for Cultural Research* 15, no. 1: 1–14. DOI: 10.1080/14797585.2011.525099.

Sloterdijk, Peter. 2009. *Derrida, an Egyptian: On the Problem of the Jewish Pyramid.* Cambridge: Polity.

Smith, Charles F., ed. 2015. *History of the Peloponnesian War.* Cambridge: Harvard University Press.

Smith, Warren S. 2001. Review of *The Golden Ass or Metamorphoses. A New Translation* by Apuleius, translated by Edward J. Kenney. *International Journal of the Classical Tradition* 7, no. 3: 435–38. http://www.jstor.org/stable/30222730.

Smith, Zadie. 2020. *Intimations: Six Essays.* London: Penguin Books.

Snyder, Phillip A. 2008. "Hospitality in Cormac McCarthy's *The Road." The Cormac McCarthy Journal* 6: 69–86. http://www.jstor.org/stable/42909384.

Sokoloff, William W. 2005. "Between Justice and Legality: Derrida on Decision." *Political Research Quarterly* 58, no. 2: 341–52. DOI: 10.2307/3595634.

Sommer, Michael. 2014. "ΟΙΚΟΥΜΕΝΗ: *Longue Durée* Perspectives on Ancient Mediterranean 'Globality.'" In *Globalisation and the Roman World: World History, Connectivity, and Material Culture,* edited by Martin Pitts and Miguel John Versluys, 175–97. Cambridge: Cambridge University Press.

Soyinka, Wole. 1974. *The Bacchae of Euripides: A Communion Rite.* New York: W.W. Norton.

Spillers, Hortense J. 1987. "Mama's Baby, Papa's Maybe: An American Grammar Book." *Diacritics* 17, no. 2: 65–81. DOI: 10.2307/464747.

Stolzenberg, Daniel. 2013. *Egyptian Oedipus: Athanasius Kircher and the Secrets of Antiquity.* Chicago: University of Chicago Press.

Stryker, Susan. 1994. "My Words to Victor Frankenstein above the Village of Chamounix: Performing Transgender Rage." *GLQ* 1, no. 3: 237–54. DOI: 10.1215/10642684-1-3-237.
———. 2015. "Transing the Queer (In)Human." *GLQ* 21, nos. 2–3: 227–30. DOI: 10.1215/10642684-2843323.
Szendy, Peter. 2021. "Viral Times." *Critical Inquiry* 47, no. S2: S63–S67. DOI: 10.1086/711438.
Taplin, Oliver. 1996. "Comedy and the Tragic." In *Tragedy and the Tragic: Greek Theatre and Beyond,* edited by Michael S. Silk, 188–202. Oxford: Oxford University Press.
Tasić, Vladimir. 2001. *Mathematics and the Roots of Postmodern Thought.* Oxford: Oxford University Press.
———. 2012. "Poststructuralism and Deconstruction: A Mathematical History." *Cosmos and History: The Journal of Natural and Social Philosophy* 8, no. 1: 177–98. https://cosmosandhistory.org/index.php/journal/article/view/242/441.
Tatum, James. 1969. "The Tales in Apuleius' *Metamorphoses*." *Transactions and Proceedings of the American Philological Association* 100: 487–527. DOI: 10.2307/2935927.
Telò, Mario. 2020. *Archive Feelings: A Theory of Greek Tragedy.* Columbus: Ohio State University Press.
———. 2022. "Foucault, Oedipus, and Virality." *symplokē* 30, nos. 1–2: 383–93. DOI: 10.1353/sym.2022.0025.
———. 2023a. *Resistant Form: Aristophanes and the Comedy of Crisis.* Earth: punctum books. DOI: 10.53288/0445.1.00.
———. 2023b. *Greek Tragedy in a Global Crisis: Reading through Pandemic Times.* London: Bloomsbury.
———. 2024. *Reading Greek Tragedy with Judith Butler.* London: Bloomsbury.
Thanos, Costas A. 1994. "Aristotle and Theophrastus on Plant-Animal Interactions." In *Plant-Animal Interactions in Mediterranean-Type Ecosystems,* edited by Margarita Arianoutsou and R.H. Groves, 3–11. Dordrecht: Kluwer Academic Publishers.
Theophrastus. 1992. *Theophrastus of Eresus: Sources for His Life, Writings Thought and Influence.* Edited and translated

by William W. Fortenbaugh, Pamela M. Huby, Robert W. Sharples, Dimitri Gutas, Andrew D. Barker, John J. Keaney, David C. Mirhady, David Sedley, and Michael G. Sollenberger. Leiden: Brill.

Thomas, Richard F. 1988. "Tree Violation and Ambivalence in Virgil." *Transactions of the American Philological Association* 118: 261–73. DOI: 10.2307/284171.

Tougher, Shaun. 2020. *The Roman Castrati: Eunuchs in the Roman Empire*. London: Bloomsbury.

Tilg, Stefan. 2007. "Lucius on Poetics? The Prologue to Apuleius' *Metamorphoses* Reconsidered." *Studi Italiani di Filologia Classica* 5, no. 2: 156–98. DOI: 10.1400/165276.

Toadvine, Ted. 2018. "Thinking after the World: Deconstruction and Last Things." In *Eco-Deconstruction: Derrida and Environmental Philosophy*, edited by Matthias Fritsch, Philippe Lynes, and David Wood, 50–80. New York: Fordham University Press.

Toscano, Alberto. 2018. "Antiphysis/Antipraxis: Universal Exhaustion and the Tragedy of Materiality." *Mediations* 31, no. 2: 125–44. https://mediationsjournal.org/articles/antiphysis-antipraxis.

———. 2020. "The State of the Pandemic." *Historical Materialism* 28, no. 4: 3–23. DOI: 10.1163/1569206X-12342804.

Toscano, Alberto, and Jeff Kinkle. 2015. *Cartographies of the Absolute*. Winchester: Zero Books.

Tsing, Anna Lowenhaupt. 2015. *The Mushroom at the End of the World: On the Possibility of Life in Capitalist Ruins*. Princeton: Princeton University Press.

Tsing, Anna Lowenhaupt, Jennifer Deger, Alder Keleman Saxena, and Feifei Zhou, eds. 2021. *Feral Atlas: The More-Than-Human Anthropocene*. Stanford: Stanford University Press. http://feralatlas.org.

Ueda, Makoto. 1970. *Matsuo Bashō*. New York: Twayne.

Umachandran, Mathura, and Tim Rood. 2020. "Introduction." *Classical Receptions Journal* 12, no. 1: 1–9. DOI: 10.1093/crj/clz021.

Verene, Donald Phillip. 2015. *Vico's New Science: A Philosophical Commentary.* Ithaca: Cornell University Press.

Vernant, Jean-Pierre. 1990. "The Lame Tyrant: From Oedipus to Periander." In Jean-Pierre Vernant and Pierre Vidal-Naquet, *Myth and Tragedy in Ancient Greece*, translated by Janet Lloyd, 207–36. New York: Zone Books.

Vico, Giambattista. 1999. *New Science: Principles of the New Science concerning the Common Nature of Nations.* Translated by David Marsh. London: Penguin.

Warburton, William. 1977. *Essai sur les hiéroglyphes des Égyptiens: Où l'on voit l'origine et le progrès du langage et de l'écriture, l'antiquité des sciences en Égypte, et l'origine du culte des animaux.* Translated by Léonard des Malpeines. Paris: Aubier.

Walde, Alois, and J.B. Hofmann. 1938. *Lateinisches Etymologisches Wörterbuch.* Heidelberg: Winter.

Warren, Calvin L. 2018. *Ontological Terror: Blackness, Nihilism, and Emancipation.* Durham: Duke University Press.

Warren, James. 2001. "Lucretius, Symmetry Arguments, and Fearing Death." *Phronesis* 46, no. 4: 466–91. http://www.jstor.org/stable/4182682.

Webb, David. 2003. "On Friendship: Derrida, Foucault, and the Practice of Becoming." *Research in Phenomenology* 33: 119–40. http://www.jstor.org/stable/24660612.

Weber, Samuel. 2011. "Sidestepping: 'Freud After Derrida.'" *Mosaic* 44, no. 3: 1–14. http://www.jstor.org/stable/44029581.

Wechsler, Stephen. 2010. "What 'You' and 'I' Mean to Each Other: Person Indexicals, Self-Ascription, and Theory of Mind." *Language* 86, no. 2: 332–65. DOI: 10.1353/lan.0.0220.

West, William N. 1999. "Repeating Staging Meaning Between Aristotle and Freud." *SubStance* 28, no. 2: 138–58. DOI: 10.2307/3685794.

Westoby, Peter, and Verne Harris. 2020. "Community Development 'Yet-To-Come' During and Post the COVID-19 Pandemic: From Derrida to Zuboff." *Community Development Journal* 55, no. 4: 553–69. DOI: 10.1093/cdj/bsaa026.

Wilberding, James. 2014. "The Secret of Sentient Vegetative Life in Galen." *Bulletin of the Institute of Classical Studies*. Supplement 114: 249–68. http://www.jstor.org/stable/44215146.

Wilhelm, Randall S. 2008. "'Golden Chalice, Good to House a God': Still Life in The Road." *The Cormac McCarthy Journal* 6: 129–46. http://www.jstor.org/stable/42909389.

Williams, David Lay. 2013. "Plato's Noble Lie: From Kallipolis to Magnesia." *History of Political Thought* 34, no. 3: 363–92. http://www.jstor.org/stable/26225836.

Wimmer, Friedrich, ed. 1854. *Theophrasti Eresii Opera: Tomus Primus Historiam Plantarum Continens*. Leipzig: Teubner.

Winckelmann, Johann Joachim. 1760. *Description des Pierres Gravées du feu Baron de Stosch*. Florence: André Bonducci.

———. 2006a. *History of the Art of Antiquity*. Translated by Harry Frances Mallgrave. Los Angeles: Getty Research Institute.

———. 2006b. *Geschichte der Kunst des Alterthums: Allgemeiner Kommentar: Erste Auflage Dresden 1764, Zweite Auflage Wien 1776*. Edited by Adolf Heinrich Borbein. Mainz am Rhein: Phillip von Zabern.

Winkler, John J. 1985. *Auctor & Actor: A Narratological Reading of Apuleius's* The Golden Ass. Berkeley: University of California Press.

Witek, Terri. 1994. "Reeds and Hides: Cormac McCarthy's Domestic Spaces." *The Southern Review* 30: 136–42.

Wohl, Victoria. 2005. "Beyond Sexual Difference: Becoming-Woman in Euripides' *Bacchae*." In *The Soul of Tragedy: Essays on Athenian Drama*, edited by Victoria Pedrick and Steven M. Oberhelman, 137–54. Chicago: University of Chicago Press.

Wolfe, Cary. 2010. *What Is Posthumanism?* Minneapolis: University of Minnesota Press.

Wolfe, Gene. 1994a. *Shadow and Claw: The First Half of the Book of the New Sun*. New York: Orb Books.

———. 1994b. *Sword and Citadel: The Second Half of the Book of the New Sun*. New York: Orb Books.

Wyschogrod, Edith. 1990. *Spirit in Ashes: Hegel, Heidegger, and Man-Made Mass Death.* New Haven: Yale University Press.

Yamamoto, Tomoyuki, and Kunihiko Kaneko. 1993. "Helium Atom as a Classical Three-Body Problem." *Physical Review Letters* 70: 1928–31. DOI: 10.1103/PhysRevLett.70.1928.

Yao, Xine. 2021. *Disaffected: The Cultural Politics of Unfeeling in Nineteenth-Century America.* Durham: Duke University Press.

Yerushalmi, Yosef Hayim. 1991. *Freud's Moses: Judaism Terminable and Interminable.* New Haven: Yale University Press.

Yusoff, Kathryn. 2013. "Geologic Life: Prehistory, Climate, Futures in the Anthropocene." *Environment and Planning D: Society and Space* 31, no. 5: 779–95. DOI: 10.1068/d11512.

Zanker, Paul. 1987. *Augustus und die Macht der Bilder.* Munich: C.H. Beck.

Zhuo, Yue. 2018. "Derrida and the Essence of Poetry." In *After Derrida: Literature, Theory, and Criticism in the Twenty-First Century,* edited by Jean-Michel Rabaté, 126–42. Cambridge: Cambridge University Press.

Zimmerman, Maaike, ed. 2012. *Apulei Metamorphoseon Libri XI.* Oxford: Oxford University Press.

Žižek, Slavoj. 2020. "Monitor and Punish? Yes, Please!" *The Philosophical Salon,* March 16. http://thephilosophicalsalon.com/monitor-and-punish-yes-please.

Index

achrony 17, 19–20, 27
anachrony 21, 41, 54, 58, 60, 65, 69, 133, 138, 246, 306, 320–21, 323
animal 28, 30, 105, 137–42, 145–46, 149, 151–52, 160, 163, 165–67, 176–77, 185, 225, 258–59
apocalypse 27, 31, 138, 218–20, 223–24, 227, 230, 234, 236
aporia 34, 38–40, 43, 127, 217, 224, 229
apostrophe 117–18, 120, 129, 132, 135, 203
archaeology 15, 27, 46, 122, 133–34, 288, 317
archive 19–20, 30, 47, 56, 57, 93–96, 98, 104, 111, 113–14, 116, 121–24, 127–28, 130–31, 134–35, 205, 210, 212, 216, 288, 293, 300
arkhē 18–19, 35, 93–94, 123–24, 139–40
asynchrony 71–72, 323
atopia 29, 35, 40, 43, 143
à venir 18–20, 25, 28, 30–31, 36, 42–43, 45–46, 51, 72, 100, 120, 123, 127, 129, 132, 210, 212, 215, 218, 230, 241–47, 253–54, 258, 261, 263–64, 325

biopolitics 166–68, 171, 190–91, 258
birth 15, 27, 118, 152, 169, 170–72, 175–77, 179, 180–81, 183–85, 187–93, 195, 247–49, 252, 256, 258, 289, 316

colonialism 16, 46, 51, 66, 280, 289
concept 29, 33–44, 47, 49, 50–51, 54, 146, 210, 271, 273, 278, 292, 304
crisis 15–20, 29, 30–31, 56, 61, 147, 168, 190, 199, 238, 254

death drive 27, 30, 94–95, 116, 120–23, 125, 126–28, 155, 157, 159
decadence 19, 61, 64
decision 31, 34–35, 40, 49, 126–27, 229, 242–44, 254–58, 260–61
deconstruction 40, 44, 50, 101, 113, 138–40, 148, 256, 271
delay 15, 25, 95, 146, 197–99, 201–4, 206, 209–10, 212, 214, 250–51, 256
democracy 19, 28, 48, 192, 257, 263–65, 268–81, 283–85
disaster 31, 219, 236, 241–48, 250–51, 253, 256

Earth 30, 56, 58, 117–18, 167, 169, 171–72, 184–85, 266–67
ecology 20, 140, 146–47, 152, 160
end of the world 18–19, 22, 24, 64–65, 168, 218, 220, 224, 227, 230, 231, 234
ephemerality 30, 167–68, 170, 172–73, 175, 177–81, 183, 184–85, 188–90, 193, 194
epistemology 23, 94, 116, 122, 129, 276
eschatology 15, 30, 65, 67, 117, 122
event 15–16, 22–23, 26–27, 42, 48, 89, 126, 132, 212, 218–19, 243, 245–47, 249–53, 256–57
extinction 21, 67

ferality 137, 140, 148, 151–55, 157, 160, 163, 259
fertility 118, 153–54, 158–60, 163,
friendship 19, 29, 34, 71–85, 88–91, 273
future 19–20, 24–25, 29, 31, 36, 39, 43, 46, 49, 56, 59, 65, 67, 71, 75, 85, 87–88, 117, 123, 127–28, 131, 140, 148, 160–63, 173, 182, 187, 189, 210, 212, 214, 218, 230–31, 232, 234, 238–39, 241–42, 246, 254, 261–62, 264–65, 269, 271, 280–83, 285
globalization 54–55, 59–60, 68

hauntology 21, 24–25, 27, 29, 31, 36, 43, 47, 51, 88, 126

history 24, 42, 51, 65, 69, 72–73, 119, 131–32, 146, 173, 248, 253, 263, 268–69, 281, 285, 287, 292–93, 295–96, 305, 311, 318
homelessness 53, 218, 224, 227, 236
hospitality 20, 31, 42, 47, 67, 201, 212, 217–18, 221, 222–24, 226–39

immanence 243, 246, 251, 259
imminence 17, 25, 31, 89, 243–45, 252
irony 27, 33, 35–39, 41, 43, 45, 49, 102

kinship 173–75, 187, 194, 195

lateness 17–21, 30, 31, 113, 138, 202, 245, 246, 248
logos 28, 34, 36, 114, 167, 176–77, 179, 184
loss 21, 56, 94, 96, 107, 108, 113–14, 156, 172, 198–99, 206, 214–15, 260

messianic 25, 43, 48, 68, 228, 230, 260–61
mortality 116, 171, 201, 205, 209, 211–12, 214
mourning 22, 31, 71, 75, 81–82, 103, 198, 200, 203, 206, 208, 212, 215, 237–39, 313
natality 169–75, 178–79, 181, 183–84, 187, 189–91, 193–95
new world, 49–50, 55–56, 66, 187, 193, 230, 231

origin 18–19, 25, 31, 49–50, 74, 113, 115, 117, 119, 121–23, 125–26, 129, 132, 134, 138–40, 158, 192, 229, 261, 287–89, 293, 296, 300, 305–6, 312, 315–16, 318

pandemic 15, 16, 17, 21–26, 31, 123, 198–200, 254, 321, 323
performance 212–14. 242, 265, 297
present 17, 19–22, 25–26, 36, 39–41, 43–46, 49–50, 51, 54, 66–67, 69, 72, 88, 91, 118, 166, 182, 198, 212, 214–15, 231, 242–43, 246, 249–51, 253–54, 257–58, 260–61, 263, 278, 284, 287, 310, 316, 319, 320, 323–25

repetition 23, 39, 67, 95, 100–101, 116, 119–22, 125–28, 156–57, 163, 249, 251, 253, 259–61

responsibility 28, 49, 147, 190, 210, 238, 263–64, 280–81, 283–84
return 19, 22–24, 29, 31, 44–45, 88, 91, 99, 111, 121–22, 132, 134, 138, 151, 156, 168, 172, 186, 193, 205, 238, 260, 308
revolution 25, 27, 29–30, 35–36, 39, 47, 49–51, 146, 168, 171, 175, 294–95

spectrality 20, 24, 29–30, 36, 43–46, 49, 53–54, 57, 64, 73, 82, 88–89, 91, 94–95, 101, 105, 111, 132, 153, 208, 243
survival 27, 31, 44, 57, 71–75, 80–81, 85, 117–18, 134, 152, 181, 189, 218, 225, 232

telos 19, 24–25, 34, 38, 50, 56, 114, 141, 144, 155, 160, 181

virus 18, 20, 22, 28, 190, 244

waiting 21–26, 31, 50, 68, 134, 210, 221, 242–43, 248–49, 251–52, 254–56, 264, 271, 322
world picture 54, 58, 61–63, 66–69
world reduction 29, 66, 68

Contributors

Karen Bassi is Research Professor Emerita of Classics and Literature at the University of California, Santa Cruz. She is the author of *Acting Like Men, Drama and Nostalgia in Ancient Greece* (1998) and *Traces of the Past: Classics between History and Archaeology* (2016). She co-edited *When Worlds Elide: Classics, Politics, Culture* with Peter Euben (2010). She is now working on a book titled *Imitating the Dead: Facing Death in Ancient Greek Tragedy and Philosophy*.

Carol Dougherty is Professor of Classical Studies and Director of Comparative Literary Studies at Wellesley College. She is the author of several books and articles on the literature, politics, and history of mobility and settlement in archaic and classical Greece, including *The Raft of Odysseus: The Ethnographic Imagination of Homer's Odyssey* (2011) and, most recently, *Travel and Home in Homer and Contemporary Literature* (2019). Her current research approaches Greek tragedy within the discourse of hospitality, exploring the political and ethical issues raised by narratives about welcoming the foreigner on the Athenian stage.

Sean Gurd is a professor in the Department of Classics at the University of Texas at Austin. He has written four monographs: *Iphigenias at Aulis: Textual Multiplicity, Radical Philol-*

ogy (2006); *Work in Progress: Literary Revision as Social Performance in Ancient Rome* (2012); *Dissonance: Auditory Aesthetics in Ancient Greece* (2016); and *The Origins of Music Theory in the Age of Plato* (2019). He also edited *Philology and Its Histories* (2010), and co-edited *'Pataphilology, an Irreader* (2018) with Vincent W.J. van Gerven Oei. With Pauline LeVen he edited the *Bloomsbury Cultural History of Western Music in Antiquity* (2023). He is an editor of Tangent, an imprint of punctum books dedicated to publishing innovative books and projects that touch on classical antiquity and director of the Ancient Music and Performance Lab at the University of Texas at Austin.

Ahuvia Kahane is a Fellow of Trinity College Dublin, where he is Regius Professor of Greek and A.G. Leventis Professor of Greek Culture. His forthcoming book is titled *Epic, Novel, and the Progress of Antiquity* and *Orality and the Formula: A Political Rethinking*. The co-edited collection *Walking Cities: Layer, Trace, Zone, Vector* came out in 2024. Together with colleagues from the Royal College of Art and the Ruskin School of Art, he is writing a book, provisionally entitled *The Panoramico,* on the politics of geometry.

Francesca Martelli is Associate Professor of Classics at University of California, Los Angeles. She is the author of two books on Ovid: *Ovid's Revisions: The Editor as Author* (2013) and *Ovid: Brill Research Perspectives on Ancient Poetry* (2020), and co-editor (along with Giulia Sissa) of a volume of essays on Ovid's *Metamorphoses* as a seminal work of ecocritique (2023). Her most recent publication is a book on Cicero's letters, *Souvenirs of Cicero: Shaping Memory in the* Epistulae ad Familiares (2024), which maintains a persistent interest in placing Latin texts in dialogue with the work and thought of Jacques Derrida.

Andres Matlock is an assistant professor in Classics at the University of Georgia, Athens. His research ranges widely over ancient philosophy, Roman literature and culture, and critical theory, with a special focus on ideas of time, nature, and change.

Paul Allen Miller is Carolina Distinguished Professor at the University of South Carolina. He is the former editor of *Transactions of the American Philological Association*. He is the author of *Lyric Texts and Lyric Consciousness* (1994), *Latin Erotic Elegy* (2002), *Subjecting Verses* (2004), *Latin Verse Satire* (2005), *Postmodern Spiritual Practices* (2007), *Plato's Apology of Socrates* (2010, with Charles Platter), *A Tibullus Reader* (2013), *Diotima at the Barricades: French Feminists Read Plato* (2015), *Horace* (2019), and *Foucault's Seminars on Antiquity: Learning to Speak the Truth* (2021). He has edited fifteen volumes of essays on literary theory, gender studies, and topics in classics as well as published more than 90 articles on Latin, Greek, French, and English literature, theory, and philosophy. He is currently at work on *Truth and Enjoyment: Cicero Beyond the Pleasure Principle*.

Sarah Nooter is the Edward Olson Professor of Classics and Theater and Performance Studies at the University of Chicago. She is the author of *When Heroes Sing: Sophocles and the Shifting Soundscape of Tragedy* (2012), *The Mortal Voice in the Tragedies of Aeschylus* (2017), and *Greek Poetry in the Age of Ephemerality* (2023). She is co-editor with Shane Butler of *Sound and the Ancient Sense*s (2018) and co-editor with Mario Telò of *Radical Formalisms: Reading, Theory, and the Boundaries of the Classical* (2023). She is the editor and translator of *How to Be Queer: An Ancient Guide to Sexuality* (2024).

Daniel Orrells is Professor of Classics at King's College London. He is author of the monographs *Classical Culture and Modern Masculinity* (2011), *Sex: Antiquity and Its Legacy* (2015), and *Antiquity in Print: Visualizing Greece in the Eighteenth Century* (2024).

Ben Radcliffe is a lecturer in Classics at Loyola Marymount University. His research and teaching focus on Homer, ancient

Greek literature, ancient and modern political thought, utopianism, and aesthetic theory. His work has recently appeared in the *American Journal of Philology, Ramus,* and *Classical Antiquity,* and he co-organized a seminar on paranoia in Greek and Roman literature at the 2022 American Comparative Literature Association conference. He is currently working on a project about the aesthetics of surplus in archaic Greek poetry.

Bruce Rosenstock was Professor of Religion and Hebrew Studies, at the University of Illinois, Urbana-Champaign. He is the author of *Philosophy and the Jewish Question: Mendelssohn, Rosenzweig, and Beyond* (2010) and *Transfinite Life: Oskar Goldberg and the Vitalist Imagination* (2017).

Mario Telò is Professor of Rhetoric, Comparative Literature, and Ancient Greek and Roman Studies at University of California, Berkeley. He is the author of *Aristophanes and the Cloak of Comedy: Affect, Aesthetics and the Canon* (2016); *Archive Feelings: A Theory of Greek Tragedy* (2020); *Greek Tragedy in a Global Crisis: Reading through Pandemic Times* (2023); *Resistant Form: Aristophanes and the Comedy of Crisis* (2023); *Judith Butler and the Ethics of Greek Tragedy* (2024), and the forthcoming *Roman Comedy against the Subject* and *Edward Said and the Late Animal: The Queer Politics of Greco-Roman Style*. He is also the co-editor of *Greek Comedy and the Discourse of Genres* (2013); *The Materialities of Greek Tragedy* (2018); *Queer Euripides* (2022); *Radical Formalisms* (2023); and *Niobes: Antiquity, Modernity, Critical Theory* (2024)

David Youd is a PhD candidate in classics and critical theory at University of California, Berkeley. His published work includes articles and essays on Euripides, Plautus, and Terence. His dissertation, "The Queer Art of Terence," offers a rereading of Terence's comedies through the lens of psychoanalysis and queer theory.

www.ingramcontent.com/pod-product-compliance
Lightning Source LLC
Chambersburg PA
CBHW071733150426
43191CB00010B/1565